FAMILIES
AND
YOUTH

A Resource Manual

FAMILIES AND YOUTH

A Resource Manual

Edited by
Leif Kehrwald
and John Roberto

THE WORLD OF
DON BOSCO
MULTIMEDIA

NEW ROCHELLE, NY

Families and Youth: A Resource Manual is published as part of the Catholic Families Series—resources to promote faith growth in Families.
Materials available for parish and diocesan leaders, parents and families

Available titles:

For leaders and ministers:
Families and Young Adults
Families and Young Adolescents
Growing in Faith: A Catholic Family Sourcebook
Media, Faith, and Families: A Parish Ministry Guide
Rituals for Sharing Faith: A Resource for Parish Ministers
Faith and Families: A Parish Program for Parenting in Faith Growth

For parents and families:

Families Nurturing Faith: A Parents' Guide to the Preschool Years
Families Sharing Faith: A Parents' Guide to the Grade School Years
Families Experiencing Faith: A Parents' Guide to the Young Adolescent Years
Families Exploring Faith: A Parents' Guide to the Older Adolescent Years
Families Encouraging Faith: A Parents' Guide to the Young Adult Years
Media, Faith, and Families: A Parents' Guide to Family Viewing
Family Rituals and Celebrations

The Catholic Families Series is a publishing project of Don Bosco Multimedia and the Center for Youth Ministry Development

Families and Youth: A Resource Manual
©1992 Salesian Society, Inc. / Don Bosco Multimedia
475 North Ave., P.O. Box T, New Rochelle, NY 10802
All rights reserved

Library of Congress Cataloging-in-Publication Data

Families and Youth: A Resource Manual / Leif Kehrwald and John Roberto, Eds.
p. cm. — Catholic Families Series
Includes bibliographical references.
    1. Family 2. Family and Youth Development
        I. Kehrwald, Leif and Roberto, John II. Families and Youth: A Resource Manual
                III. Catholic Families Series

ISBN 0-89944-260-9 $18.95

Design and Typography by Sally Ann Zegarelli, Long Branch, NJ 07740

Printed in the United States of America

9/92   9 8 7 6 5 4 3 2 1

CONTENTS

CREDITS

CATHOLIC FAMILIES PROJECT YOUTH MINISTRY DESIGN TEAM

The activities in *Families and Youth* were designed, piloted, and/or reviewed by a team of specialists in youth ministry who have been involved in the Catholic Families Project since its inception in 1988.

> John Roberto—Project Coordinator
> Carolyn Mary Coll, RSM—Diocese of Charlotte
> Irene Friend—Archdiocese of Chicago
> Leif Kehrwald—Archdiocese of Portland
> Alicia M. Marcos—Archdiocese of Atlanta
> Felipe Salinas—Diocese of Brownsville
> Audrey Taylor—Archdiocese of Chicago
> Cheryl Tholcke—Diocese of Sacramento

ABOUT THE AUTHORS

Thomas Bright is a staff member of the Center for Youth Ministry Development where he serves as coordinator of justice ministries. He has served as editor for *Access Guides to Youth Ministry: Justice, Poverty: Do It Justice!*, and *Human Rights: Do It Justice!*

Gary Chamberlain is Director of SUMORE, a graduate program in ministry and religious education, and Associate Professor of Theology at Seattle University. He is the author of numerous articles and the book, *Fostering Faith—A Minister's Guide to Faith Development.*

Nettie Cook-Dove, Ph.D., a member of Christ the King Catholic Church, has worked as a teacher, school administrator, and manager of several federal programs. She lives in Miami, FL.

Reynolds R. Ekstrom is an associate staff member of the Center for Youth Ministry Development and has edited *Access Guides to Youth Ministry: Media & Culture, TeenMedia, Access Guides to Youth Ministry: Evangelization* and *Access Guides to Youth Ministry: Retreats.*

Angela Erevia, a Missionary Catechist of Divine Providence, is diocesan director of Religious Education and Hispanic Ministry for the Diocese of Victoria, TX and the author of *Quince Anos: Celebrating a Tradition.*

Francis A.J. Ianni is professor of education at Teacher's College, Columbia University, and is the Director of the Institute of Social Analysis. He is a board-certified psychoanalyst and a consultant in medical psychology at St. Luke's Hospital in New York City. He is author of *The Search for Structure—A Report on American Youth Today.*

Michael Galvan, a member of the Ohlone tribe, is a pastor in the Diocese of Oakland, CA and serves as the Director of Clergy Formation for the diocese. He holds a Ph.D. in Christian spirituality. He has published articles on Native American spirituality and catechesis, one of which is included in *Faith and Culture.*

Leif Kehrwald is Director of Family Ministry for the Archdiocese of Portland, OR. He has served on several national projects to enhance the quality of family life, and chaired a task force on Family Perspective Implementation sponsored by the National Association of Catholic Diocesan Family Life Ministers. Leif is the author of *Caring That Enables: A Project for Developing Parish Family Ministry* (Paulist Press).

Joe H. Leonard Jr is a Consultant in Family Life Education, Wayne, PA; the author of *Planning Family Ministry* and co-author of *Ministry with Families in Flux*.

Eva Marie Lumas, SSS is a doctoral student in theology at Catholic University of America and has served as a Christian education consultant for Black communities. She lectures widely and writes on Christian education from a Black perspective. Several of her essays appear in *Families Black and Catholic, Catholic and Black*.

Gelasia Marquez is the Director of Hispanic Family Life Ministry for the Diocese of Brooklyn, NY and holds a doctorate in psychology. She has created a counseling program for Hispanic families in cultural transition.

David Ng is professor of Christian Education at San Francisco Theological Seminary. Dave has been involved with youth ministry for much of his career, doing many workshops on confirmation, multicultural youth ministry, and leadership development. He has written *Youth in the Community of Disciples, Developing Leaders in Youth Ministry*, and many articles.

Richard P. Olson is Senior Minister, Prairie Village Baptist Church, Prairie, KS; and co-author of *Ministry with Families in Flux*.

Nydia Garcia Preto, A.C.S.W. is clinical coordinator at Adolescent Day Hospital of the UMDNJ-Community Medical Mental Health Center in Piscataway, NJ.

Elisa Rodriguez, SC is a specialist in Hispanic ministry and catechesis. She has served as USCC regional coordinator of Hispanic ministry. She is currently on assignment for her religious community.

John Roberto is Director and co-founder of the Center for Youth Ministry Development. He is the managing editor of the Catholic Families Series. John has served as editor for *Growing in Faith: A Catholic Families Sourcebook*; and for *Access Guides to Youth Ministry* on *Evangelization, Liturgy and Worship, Justice*, and *Early Adolescent Ministry*.

Randy Smith is a licensed marriage, family, and child counselor who practices at Kairos Psychological Services in Costa Mesa, CA. He is the co-author of *Divorce Recovery for Teenagers*.

John H. Westerhoff, III is professor of Religion and Education at Duke University Divinity School and former editor of the journal, *Religious Education*. He is a worldwide lecturer and author of more than 15 books, including *Will Our Children Have Faith, Liturgy and Learning*, and *Living the Faith Community*.

ACKNOWLEDGMENTS

"A Family Life Cycle Perspective on Families with Adolescents" by Nydia Garcia Preto first appeared as "The Transformation of the Family System in Adolescence" in *The Family Life Cycle*, edited by Betty Carter, M.S.W. and Monica McGoldrick, M.S.W. (1989) and is reprinted courtesy of Allyn and Bacon.

"Perspectives on the Changing Family" and "A Perspective on Remarried Families" by Richard P. Olson and Joe H. Leonard, Jr. are excerpts from Chapters 1 and 4, respectively, of *Ministry with Families in Flux* by Richard P. Olson and Joe H. Leonard, Jr. (1990). Used with permission of Westminster/John Knox Press.

"A Perspective on Teenagers and Divorce" by Randy Smith first appeared in "What Teenagers Go Through When Their Parents Divorce"in *Divorce Recovery for Teenagers* by Stephen Murray and Randy Smith (1990). Used with permission of Youth Specialties.

"A Faith Development Perspective" by Gary Chamberlain is excerpted from Chapters 2 and 3 in *Fostering Faith—A Minister's Guide to Faith Development* (1988) by Gary Chamberlain. Reprinted courtesy of Paulist Press.

"A Social Perspective" by Francis A.J. Ianni is reprinted from *Phi Delta Kappan*, volume 70, number 9 (May 1989). Used by permission of the author.

"Developing Alternative Rites of Passage for Adolescents" by John H. Westerhoff, III is condensed from "Confirmation: An Episcopal Church Perspective," in *Confirming the Faith of Adolescents: An Alternative Future for Confirmation*, ed. Arthur J. Kubick (1991). Reprinted courtesy of Paulist Press.

"Orita: A Rite of Passage for Youth of African-American Heritage" by Dr. Nettie Cook-Dove is condensed from her article by the same name in *Modern Liturgy*, Volume 17, Number 7. Used with permission.

Typist: Alicia Carey

PREFACE TO THE CATHOLIC FAMILIES SERIES

Welcome to the *Catholic Families Series!* In 1987, the Center for Youth Ministry Development began a five-year, three-phase national project, made possible by a generous grant from a Catholic foundation. Guided by the conviction that the family is the primary context for faith growth and faith sharing, the *Catholic Families Project* was designed to explore the dynamics of faith maturing and faith sharing in Catholic families, and to develop new initiatives for promoting faith maturity in families throughout the entire family life cycle. *Catholic Families: Growing and Sharing Faith* is a unique national effort designed to create new pastoral and educational approaches to fostering faith growth in families. Don Bosco Multimedia is serving as the publisher for these new initiatives by introducing a new line of important resources for *Catholic families*, themselves, and for *Church leaders* involved in ministry with families throughout the life cycle.

The *Catholic Families Project* believes that . . .

- the family is a community of life and love in service to God's kingdom, with a specific identity and mission
- the family is the primary context for faith growth and faith sharing,

profoundly shaping religious identity among its members

- family life is a privileged locale for encountering God in everyday life experiences and in the Christian Tradition/Story
- the Family Life Cycle stages provide a framework for faith growth in the entire family system
- the parish community and its ministries need to be in partnership with the family in nurturing faith growth, in sharing the Catholic Christian faith, and in empowering the family to live the Christian faith both in the family and in the world.

A national effort, the Project has involved over 300 people as authors, critical reflectors, members of design teams and pilot project teams, and as members of the steering committee. These participants represent 70 dioceses and 15 national organizations, as well as the following ministries: higher education; youth ministry; liturgical ministry; lay ministry; rural ministry; special education; ministry with ethnic cultures; and RCIA. This involvement attests to the national and collaborative nature of the *Catholic Families Project*.

The *Catholic Families Project* has been conducted along the following timeline:

1987—RESEARCH

- Identify how families grow in faith
- Study the patterns and dynamics of sharing faith and values in Catholic Christian families

1988—NATIONAL SYMPOSIUM

- Explore and discuss the research base
- Explore and discuss approaches for enriching faith growth and faith sharing in families
- Publish the theoretical-research understandings and pastoral approaches in *Catholic Families: Growing and Sharing Faith*

1988–89—PROJECT DEVELOPMENT AND PILOTING

- Develop strategies for assisting faith growth throughout the entire family life cycle, incorporating family and cultural perspectives
- Creation and testing of project designs by practitioners in the field

1991-92—PUBLICATIONS AND CONFERENCES

- Publish print and audio-visual resources and conduct regional conferences that:
  - + offer a family perspective in faith growth and faith sharing
  - + address the entire family life cycle
  - + forge a partnership between parish and family in promoting faith growth

The Center for Youth Ministry Development and Don Bosco Multimedia are proud to make available the new programs and resources to assist church leaders and families themselves in promoting faith maturing and faith transmission in the family system. These resources fill an important need in the contemporary Church. Included in the *Catholic Families Series* are the following publications:

Growing in Faith: A Catholic Family Sourcebook

Families and Young Adolescents

Families and Youth: A Resource Manual

Families and Young Adults

Parenting for Faith Growth Series
　Families Nurturing Faith: A Parents' Guide to the Preschool Years.
　Families Sharing Faith: A Parents' Guide to the Grade School Years.
　Families Experiencing Faith: A Parents' Guide to the Young Adolescent Years.
　Families Exploring Faith: A Parents' Guide to the Older Adolescent Years.
　Families Encouraging Faith: A Parents' Guide to the Young Adult Years.

Faith and Families: A Parish Program for Parenting in Faith Growth

Rituals for Sharing Faith: A Resource for Parish Ministers

Family Celebrations and Rituals

Media, Faith, and Families—A Parents' Guide to Family Viewing

Media, Faith, and Families—A Parish Ministry Guide

A Partnership Between Family and Parish: A Parish Planning Guide

A Partnership Between Family and Parish: Family and Parish, The Video

A Partnership Between Family and Parish: Family and Parish, Wall Chart

The importance of developing, supporting, and encouraging the Catholic faith life of families has never more urgent. The *Catholic Families Project* is committed to creating and promoting new pastoral and educational approaches for fostering faith growth in families and for building an intentional partnership between families and the parish. The *Catholic Family Series* represents a significant contribution toward realizing these goals.

INTRODUCTION

As a part of the *Catholic Families Project, Families and Youth—A Resource Manual* is concerned with exploring the dynamics of faith maturing and faith sharing in families with youth. *Families and Youth* seeks to help all those involved in ministry with youth (from young adolescents through older adolescents) to begin viewing youth ministry with a family perspective. This means viewing youth ministry in light of the family system and developing a comprehensive ministry from that perspective. *Families and Youth* calls all those involved in youth ministry to become partners with the family in promoting faith growth and healthy adolescent development.

The National Conference of Catholic Bishops describes a family perspective in this way:

1. Viewing individuals in the context of their family relationships and other social relationships.

   As a systems orientation, a family perspective is a lens that focuses on the interaction between individuals, their families, and social institutions.

2. Using family relationships as a criterion to assess the impact of the Church's and society's policies, programs, ministries, and services.

   As a criterion to assess ministry, a family perspective provides a means to examine and adjust systematically policies, program design, and service delivery. Its goal is to incorporate a sensitivity to families and to promote the partnership, strengths, and resources of participating families (*Family Perspective* 8).

A family sensitivity in youth ministry means looking at our ministry and programs through a "family lens," and making appropriate adjustments. It means doing all we can for youth and their families without always creating new programs. Pope John Paul II in his Exhortation on the Family, *Familiaris Consortio*, captured the essence of family perspective when he wrote, "No plan of organized pastoral work at any level must ever fail to take into consideration the pastoral area of the family."

Families and Youth is designed to assist you in the task of develop a family perspective in ministry with young and older adolescents. We hope to help all those in ministry with youth:

- to become more aware of the realities of family life and the distinctive characteristics of families with adolescents from the perspectives of family systems, family life cycle, family diversity, faith development, sexuality, pop culture, sociology, and ethnic cultures.

- to develop the attitudes and approaches for creating a family perspective in your current ministry with youth.

- to sponsor and conduct activities for the whole family, and for parents and youth that incorporate a family perspective.

- to become a partner with families in your community in a common effort to promote the faith growth and healthy development of adolescents and their families.

To accomplish these aims *Families and Youth* is organized into three sections. **Section One** includes essays to help you become more aware of the realities of family life and the distinctive characteristics of families with youth. **Chapter 1**, "A Family Systems Perspective" presents several of the key concepts of family systems theory as applied to ministry with youth. **Chapter 2**, "A Family Life Cycle Perspective on Families with Adolescents" summarizes the particular life tasks of families with adolescents. **Chapter 3**, "A Faith Development Perspective" examines the particular faith stages of adolescents. **Chapters 4, 5, and 6** look at the changes experienced by the family over the past three decades with particular attention to divorce and remarried families. **Chapter 7**, "A Pop Culture Perspective" examines the impact of popular culture on the values, faith, and identity of families with adolescents. **Chapter 8**, "A Social Perspective" reports on a ten-year study of adolescents, their families, and their communities that emphasizes the importance of the family in the socialization of youth. **Chapter 9**, "An Ethnic Cultural Perspective" provides both an understanding of the influence of ethnicity on adolescent development and specific guidelines for cultural sensitivity with African Americans, Hispanics, Native Americans, and Pacific Asian Americans.

Section Two offers essays on developing a family perspective in youth ministry. **Chapter 10** develops the foundational concepts and principles for the entire *Catholic Families Project*, providing an understanding of faith growth, family life cycle, and family systems. **Chapter 11** by Leif Kehrwald examines the attitudes and perspectives needed to develop a family perspective. **Chapter 12** by John Roberto analyzes the structural or programmatic barriers to creating a family perspective and proposes directions for "re-inventing" youth ministry to incorporate a family perspective. **Chapter 13** is a three-hour training designed to assist parish staff and adult leaders in understanding the particular dynamics of families with adolescents and discover ways to develop a family perspective in ministry.

Section Three contains a variety of youth ministry activities developed with a family perspective. The activities included in this section offer practical suggestions on how parishes and families with youth can work together to enhance family growth. The activities are grouped around five tasks central to family life: sharing faith, enriching family relationships, celebrating prayer and ritual, involvement in justice and service, and developing an appreciation for ethnic and cultural diversity. The approaches offered differ considerably in focus and format. The activities for faith sharing, for example, outline six learning sessions that a parish could conduct for parents and/or youth to help them better understand the faith development of adolescent families and apply church teaching to the areas of sexuality and pop culture. The activities suggested for involving families in justice and service, on the other hand, offer practical strategies for at-home use by families. The intent of this section is to be illustrative rather than exhaustive—modeling a variety of ways in which parish and family can work together around a common concern for faith growth, challenging parishes to develop approaches and programs of their own which proclaim an active partnership between families and their community of faith.

It is our hope that *Families and Youth* will initiate or expand efforts toward an intentional and planned partnership between parishes and families in the process of fostering faith growth in adolescents and their families.

SECTION 1

Understanding Families with Adolescents

CHAPTER 1

A Family Systems Perspective

Leif Kehrwald

How can we practically apply a family perspective in ministry with youth and their families? What concrete, practical application does the information on family systems, family change, and family cohesion (togetherness) have for my ministry with adolescents? How can I put on a family lens to evaluate my current ministry? Good questions. The intent of this chapter is to analyze these questions by exploring the interconnecting system of youth, youth ministry, and families with adolescents. These systems are highly interrelated although they may not always appear to be. They all operate according to the rules of systems theory which we will explore in some detail. An adequate understanding of these systems and their interdependent relationships can reveal interesting and valuable insights for working with adolescents and their families.

In Part I we will explore emotional family process and analyze the importance of a systems approach for understanding the family. Part II will examine four ways families deal with change and four ways that they deal with togetherness. In each section, I will present implications and suggestions for ministry with youth. An honest effort to apply family systems and family perspective insights into ministry with youth would make a valuable contribution to the entire field of youth ministry.

PART I: EMOTIONAL FAMILY PROCESS

What is emotional family process? Using a systems approach to view the family, it is the dynamic interplay of relationships within the family as members confront change, maturity, faith growth, and day-to-day life. It is the emotional push and pull within a family that serves as a catalyst for change and growth, but also provides focal point(s) for struggle and pain.

Youth ministers need not become family systems experts, but some knowledge of emotional family process can be greatly beneficial. The information below has implications for both youth ministry programming (how we develop our activities and programs in light of family dynamics), and relational work with young peoples (how we listen and respond to the concerns of teens in with respect to family relationships).

SYSTEMS THINKING

A system is any collection of parts organized in such a way that whatever affects one part affects all other parts (Braun). In a system, all parts are connected and interdependent, meaning the relationships between the parts are more important than the parts themselves. The experts simply say that the basic idea of systems theory is that the whole is greater than the sum of its parts (Power 4).

Family systems are organic, alive, and fluid; making it impossible to have total knowledge of the people (parts) and their interdependence. They are not completely predictable, but they will follow the "rules" of systems theory in a lively, dynamic way. Some systems are static, mechanical, and (given sufficient knowledge of the parts and their interdependence) therefore completely predictable, such as automobiles and computers.

In his book, *Family Matters*, Thomas A. Power states,

> . . . members of a family system . . . function together for two common goals: the emotional well-being of the adults and the growth and development of children. This inter-dependence means that members of a family need each other to get along. . . . Family member are connected by the things they share and the things they do for one another. . . . [T]he most important connections are the feelings they have for each other (Power 5).

These emotional connections are so strong in most family systems that they determine the personalities and pathologies of family members and the family as a whole. These characteristics can last for generations.

There are numerous principles encompassing the whole of systems theory. Stemming from the description above, some basic principles include:

- Parts of the system maintain their own identity, rendering the whole system greater than the sum of its parts.
- Change in one part of the system affects all other parts and the whole.
- All systems strive for equilibrium, and thus resist change.
- Systems relate to their environment with some degree of openness or closeness. Healthy systems are normally more open.
- All systems have boundaries for adaptiveness and cohesiveness which help the system determine its own identity and relationships with other systems.

This essay explores three "rules" or principles of emotional family process: change vs. homeostasis, symptoms, and triangles. While this by no means covers all the dynamics of family systems theory, these three principles provide a helpful introduction for those who work in ministry with teens and their families. We will also explore specific implications of these principles as they apply to youth ministry.

CHANGE VS. HOMEOSTASIS

All families seek a state of relational balance that, when achieved, resists change. All members contribute to this balance determining the health or weakness of the family system. When one person experiences change, the relational balance is upset and all members must adjust to incorporate the change and find a new balance. This has potentially great implications for ministry to/with individuals, particularly adolescents.

Homeostasis refers to the balance of relationships in the family that allow the system to function. It takes on form, personality, and identity (Friedman 23). Like individuals, families have their own personalities. Some are closed and reserved; others open and outgoing. Some are structured and disciplined; others are flexible and easy going.

Homeostasis does not always mean healthy balance. In fact, sometimes the family resistance to change is so strong that family members will survive on adverse symptoms and live with them for many years, sometimes generations, rather than shift the balance of relationships in order to incorporate a new change.

Homeostasis does not imply that family systems cannot change. Families must adapt to their own life cycle development and the changing realities of society (Durka). A healthy family will effectively shift the balance of relationships as it encounters change. Unhealthy families will be more resistant to change and less successful in finding a new homeostasis.

Because we are creatures of habit and familiarity, change is an upsetting experience. Change also tends to set off a chain reaction; one change leading to another and to another (Power 145). The best way to deal with change is to anticipate and be braced for its impact. Easy to say, but difficult to do. Families with adolescents will confront many changes, large and small, and their healthy survival may well depend on how they deal with resistance to change.

Family members resist change not because they are bad, but because change is upsetting. It causes anxiety. When a family establishes its balance of relationships, members are comfortable with each other. Anything new, even if positive, will likely be resisted, and a subtle message of "change back" will be communicated.

Change, according to Power, requires at least three steps: the change itself, the family's reaction to the change, and dealing with the family's reaction to the change (Power 155). Most families deal well with the first two steps, but are often ill-equipped to handle the third. Consequently, the message of "change back" is too strong to resist.

Implications for Youth Ministry

With these concepts of balance and resistance to change in mind, think about the primary goals of youth ministry: to create an atmosphere for a young person to:

- discover God's activity in his/her life, and respond to it;
- grow and mature in his/her faith;
- become an active participant in the life of the faith community.

In a word, the goal of youth ministry is *change*, and, without anyone being fully conscious of it, this change may be resisted on the homefront.

When a family member experiences change—even a positive, faith-growth change—all others must adjust in order for that change to be lasting. The family must seek a new balance to accommodate an individual's change and growth. Even when the change is positive, many families will unconsciously try to change the individual back to the way he or she was, rather than seek a new balance.

Most youth ministry efforts go toward helping individual young people recognize God's activity in their lives and respond to it. This is just as it should be. The challenge, however, is to help families adjust to the changes we encourage in the lives of individual teens. If we cannot help families find a new balance, our best work with teens will not be lasting.

How is this done? Well, the obvious answer is to involve the entire family in the program in which the individual is enrolled. Some gallant efforts are being made here, particularly in the areas of family catechesis. Yet, for most aspects of youth ministry, it's simply not realistic for the whole family to participate, e.g., retreats, regular youth night, confirmation preparation, etc. The alternative then is to create "bridger experiences." By this I mean exercises designed to "bridge" the experience of the parish program with the individual's home life. Family members will adjust to the changes in the individual if they can be kept abreast of the progress of the ministry efforts.

Some examples of *bridger experiences* include:

- A "retreat re-entry" session for parents of youth returning from a retreat experience. This session is designed to sensitize parents and family members to the powerful faith experiences which may occur on the weekend, and give practical advice for nurturing on-going growth.

- Confirmation preparation—students are given a 50 question review of the Catholic faith and told to take it home and ask anyone to help them answer the questions. The goal of this "bridger" exercise is not so much correct answers, but rather spurring dialogue about faith issues in the home.

As systems, families must change and grow to remain healthy. They must continually adjust their balance (homeostasis) according to both the ongoing maturity of its members, and the significant experiences that each encounter. This adjustment process can be particularly challenging for families with adolescents because the level of unpredictability rises for both children and parents.

Healthier families are more capable of adjusting their balance without too much resistance. They realize that adolescence can be turbulent for all family member, and they try to remain flexible. These parents provide healthy doses of unconditional love and flexible discipline, mixed with much praise and encouragement. They maintain high expectations for themselves and their children, and they strive very hard to listen well. As families, they are committed to each other and involved in each others' lives. These families are cohesive. They are more interested in each others' personal attributes than in society's measure of success (Guarendi). These healthy characteristics help families embrace both the predictable and unforeseen changes they encounter in the adolescent years.

Families with adolescents also find it easier to adjust to the change and growth of an individual when they interact with others dealing with similar tasks. They benefit from opportunities to draw support and encouragement from others having like experiences. For this reason, like-to-like support groups are extremely valuable.

SYMPTOMS

When a family system is stressed, the usual balance of relationships and interaction is disturbed and a symptom occurs. The symptom reflects a source of tension infecting the entire system (Friedman 57). The symptom will likely occur in the most vulnerable person in the system, not necessarily the person/relationship responsible for the stress.

Vulnerable does not mean physically weak, but rather, the person who is least capable of dealing with the stress on the family system. For example, our family recently moved to a new city. Contrary to the U-HAUL advertising slogan, "Moving is an Adventure," most would agree that it is indeed a stressful experience. My wife and I had thousands of details to talk about and attend to, which consumed nearly all of our energy for at least several weeks.

Right after the move was completed, we took a short vacation on the coast to reward

ourselves. Our youngest son had never seen the ocean before, and we were excited for his five-year-old enjoyment of the beach, the sand and waves, etc. Yet for four days, he showed no signs of enjoying himself whatsoever. He was grumpy, whiny, and upset the entire time. He literally ruined the vacation for all of us like only a five-year-old can do. Worse yet, his inconsolable behavior continued for several weeks. We were beginning to wonder if he had an emotional problem. But as the anxiety of our move began to lessen, and my wife and I were able to give better attention to our children, our youngest son become a happier child. It is obvious now that he was the symptom bearer of our family's stress over moving to a new city.

Systems theory contends that since the interdependent relationships between the members are more important to the health of the system than the individual parts themselves, the root cause of any problem in the system will be found in the imbalance of relationships, not in the individual exhibiting abnormal behavior. An imbalance of relationships causes stress, and symptoms indicate a difficulty in coping with stress. It is a way of covering up or sidestepping the real problem. If we were to focus only on the symptom or the problem bearer, we would likely miss the real problem altogether. This is no simple task, because usually the problem bearer literally "screams" for attention; to be the center of focus.

This is especially true for adolescents whose identity and belonging needs are peaking. Combine those needs with a family stress that, simply because of their youth, they are ill-equipped to handle, and we end up with a classic problem bearer who becomes the socially acceptable scapegoat for the family problem. Teenagers are supposed to have problems anyway, right? If we focus all our attention on "fixing" the teenager, we'll likely miss the marital, or parental, or even generational family problem.

Likewise, if we concentrate only on fixing the symptom, another one like it will certainly surface when the family confronts a new stress. It is important to understand the purpose of the symptom and what it might be covering up. For example, children are quite sensitive to their parent's problems, but, because they are children, they lack the ability to deal with such things as marital discord, substance abuse, workaholism, etc. Adolescents may "act out" with inappropriate behavior seeking attention from their parents. They may be crying out for love, attention, and boundaries because mom and/or dad are too preoccupied with their own issues. Or, a teen may become the center of attention in order to distract parents from their own marital problems, thus keeping the family intact. If mom and dad did not have to fret about the behavior of their teenager, then their own relational problems would loom causing them to split. In these situations, teens are usually not fully aware of why they behave in this manner.

The person identified as the problem bearer—the one we expect to do all the changing—may be the family member least equipped to change (Power 15). Tunnel vision focused solely on either the symptom or the one person exhibiting the problem will yield the least helpful results.

Implications for Youth Ministry

Not every adolescent misbehavior is rooted in serious family dysfunction. Nearly all teens make poor choices at one time or another. However, when we observe a pattern of "acting out" behavior and/or unhealthy choices, this may signal some kind of serious difficulty. When teens are hurting they scream out in pain in many different ways.

While working with teens, one must keep in mind their individual developmental issues, but avoid tunnel vision that fails to see family connections and significant relationships. Out of a genuine desire to serve and heal, it is tempting to rush in and "fix" their problems. Better to resist that temptation at least long enough to reflect on the problem situation and ask yourself several questions:

- Is it really an individual problem, or is there evidence of a symptom of something deeper?
- What do I know about the young person's family, and does that make a difference in how I hear his/her story?
- Has the young person changed behavior or attitudes recently? Has anything significant happened in his/her life in recent weeks or months?
- How well do I know this young person, and his/her feelings, habits, and attitudes? Is the problem a result of the normal life tasks and behavior of adolescents, or cause for greater concern?

Youth workers must be sensitive to those teens who are symptom bearers, but not overly presumptuous of all adolescent activity. A 15-year-old boy mentioned to me that the counselors at his Catholic high school were always trying to find some problem in the family whenever the slightest thing went wrong.

On the other hand, the young worker may find himself drawn into a family problem that needs intervention. A systems approach will attempt to identify the relational imbalance and gently work for change. Naturally, these relationships are complex and vulnerable. Efforts to intervene must be cautious and neutral. When encountering teens with "problems":

- *Reserve judgment on the rightness or wrongness of the behavior.* Placing blame on the teen or any member of the family has no benefit for resolution and change.
- *Talk with the teen about the significant relationships in his/her life—especially family members.* It is quite likely one or more of these persons plays a part in the distress.
- *Get to know the family member and assess the health of the system.* Who is the vulnerable person in the system? Are there other symptoms of trouble?
- *Know the referral agencies available for help.* Don't be afraid to recommend them. Many families want to seek help but do not know how to take the first step.

■ *Don't try to do family therapy as an amateur.* Your presence will benefit the system simply by establishing positive relationships and remaining neutral. Leave the therapy to professionals.

TRIANGLES

Two persons in relationship with each other will usually communicate and work things out directly. Yet for any significant relationship, this is risky, vulnerable work. When tensions build and disagreements emerge (which is inevitable in all sincere relationships), we are tempted to bring in a third party to diffuse the anxiety or have someone on our side. Triangles decrease the tension between two parties, but they can prevent direct communication and therefore the real issues cannot be addressed. Triangles can avoid a problem rather than face it directly. However, in some cultures triangles are used positively because there is a tradition of using an intermediary (a third party) in easing tensions between people, especially between parents and teens. Where such a cultural tradition exists it is important to observe the action behavior and the way problems or tensions are resolved. The triangle may even be promoting problem-solving rather than avoiding it.

Triangles are basic to human relationships. Two people cannot maintain unresolved conflict or sustained intimacy without bringing in a third party. Triangles are common in all human relationships—family, friends, work. They form most commonly in family life because of greater emotional intensity. When anxiety mounts for whatever reason, a third party will unconsciously be drawn in. Focusing on the third party reduces immediate anxiety and deflects the emotional intensity of the situation. However, the third party can complicate the issues, which makes it more difficult for the original parties to work out their problem. Again if a culture has a functioning tradition of using a third party, the third party can solve the problems.

Many varieties of triangles exist in family life. Youth ministers and pastoral leaders frequently become hooked into these triangles because of a sincere desire to be of significant help in their relationships. Let me point out two common instances of triangles in family life.

Some parents use children to deflect important issues between themselves. They are blinded to the real issues of a troubled marriage by focusing intense scrutiny on a teenage son or daughter. This in turn results in acting out behavior by the teen, who will unconsciously continue that questionable behavior as long as it garners so much attention. Before long, the whole family is stuck in crisis and doesn't know how to get out.

Alternatively, some families use church or school or teachers to deflect important family issues or relational problems. Parents of teens may complain bitterly about the quality of the parish youth programs as a way of not facing issues and problems between themselves and an adolescent child:

> "If the youth program accomplished what it's suppose to, my son wouldn't be so disrespectful at home."

> "If the youth group spent more time reading the Bible and memorizing prayers, our family wouldn't fight every Sunday morning about going to Mass."

Issues in one relationship can fuel fires in others (Lerner 155). As a triangle becomes more entrenched, real issues become harder to address. Pastoral ministers should avoid getting hooked into unhelpful relational triangles. It is usually a genuine, but excessive desire to help that leads to trouble. The most difficult job is to let two people find for themselves and manage their own relationship (Lerner 167). Sometimes it feels as though this is contrary to the virtues of Christian vocation.

There are ways, however, to be helpful in sensitive circumstances without getting hooked into a triangle. In her book, *The Dance of Anger*, Dr. Harriet Goldhor Lerner describes three specific strategies (Lerner 183):

■ *Stay Calm.* Try to take low-key approach when confronted with conflict and stress. Avoid fueling the driving force of triangles with more anxiety and intensity.

- *Stay Out.* Resist the temptation to solve their issues. Your advice, analyzing, and lecturing is heeded only enough to keep you entangled in the web. The real solution lies in their managing their own relationship.
- *Hang In.* Maintain emotional closeness with both parties, communicating your care, concern, and confidence that whatever the problem may be, the two of them can work it out.

People do not always realize they are caught in a triangle, but they often sense that something is not right. There are several indicators of relational triangles:

- You find yourself pulling some into a stressful situation to calm things down.
- You feel pulled into a situation for the purpose of calming things down.
- One person is always the main topic of conversation between two others. Or, instead of a person, perhaps they always talk about his job or her health, etc.

Triangles tend to repeat themselves when new struggles emerge. Take note of family members and whose side they choose when tension arises. Triangles do not always include three persons. Sometimes the third party is a job, an emotional issue, etc. Also, if a person or topic is "unmentionable" with another person, that too can be a triangle. The point: triangles are very common and come in all shapes and sizes.

NONANXIOUS PRESENCE

A key concept, or strategy, for understanding and working with emotional family process, is nonanxious presence. The idea here is to be present in the family system to bring about positive change without getting hooked into emotional triangles that stagnate healing and resolution. The term originates from Dr. Edwin Friedman's book *Generation To Generation: Family Process In Church and Synagogue.*

Friedman describes non-anxious presence as the ability to maintain a low level of anxiety in the midst of anxious systems; "to take maximum responsibility for one's own destiny and responsibility" (Friedman 27). " . . . containing one's anxiety particularly regarding congregational matters is crucial. This empowers [a person] to not only be more clear-headed about solutions and more adroit in triangles, but, because of the systemic effect that a leader's functioning always has on an entire organization, a non-anxious presence will modify anxiety throughout the entire congregation" (Friedman 208).

The level of anxiety in any system of human relationships provides the key for effective functioning. In a family, if each person is uptight and walking on eggshells, then the family's ability to function is severely limited. One more minor tension may push them all beyond the breaking point. Likewise, in a congregation or youth program, the leader's anxiety level will be reflected in the entire group's behavior. High anxiety produces negative or blocked behavior. Yet if the leader exhibits low anxiety the group will respond positively even in the face of extremely challenging or adverse circumstances.

Anxiety infuses any system with higher voltage (Friedman 209). A youth minister's anxious presence in the significant life-issue situations of teenagers and their families will have a consistently negative impact, in spite of good intentions. Low anxiety, however, acts as a circuit breaker defusing the high voltage in the system. Even in leadership roles, often the most important thing is to be calmly present. Analyzing, diagnosing, and searching for "content" solutions usually increases the level of anxiety.

Diagnostic thinking always increases the anxiety of the system. When we find ourselves exploring only "content solutions," we are guilty of diagnostic thinking. Exploring content solutions means to relieve the immediate symptom, but its net effect is to shield the real problem from view.

It is easy for youth ministers to get hooked into diagnostic thinking and searching for "content" solutions. A troubled parent wants to know if you've covered all the Church's teachings on sex and sexuality, and if your young people have memorized *The Apostles' Creed*. Or an education board member, inspired by the new document on adolescent catechesis, challenges the curriculum of your catechetical program.

Responses to these concerns must show a knowledge of the "content," but attempt to focus the issue back to the questioner, allowing that person another chance to share his/her deeper feelings about the issue, or person, involved. Keep in mind that the initial "content" question may well be an indicator of a deeper issue. Address the content issue (lest you lose your job), but don't close off a path to the root problem with diagnostic thinking.

In contrast to diagnostic thinking, Friedman describes *playfulness* as the capacity to be paradoxical, a little crazy, etc., which serves as an antidote to the serious, content-oriented nature of anxiety. Playfulness loosens up the seriousness and often dispels enough anxiety to render a possible solution. A well placed word, phrase, or joke can be most effective. Taking a surprisingly opposite stance can have a positive impact.

One must remember that the minister's response to a hostile environment is almost always the key factor that determines how harmful it will be. Neither the "content" issue nor the relational symptom carry as much healing potential as a non-anxious response (Friedman 209-210).

Implications for Youth Ministry

Getting pulled into relational triangles with teens and their parents is a common occupational hazard for youth workers. Sometimes our desire to help and minister is so strong, that we walk right into a triangle with barely a nudge. And then we wonder why, a few weeks later, the problem has not resolved itself. For ministers, our need to be needed is the most dangerous and least helpful of all; especially when working with teens and their families.

There is a difference between *intervention* and getting hooked into a triangle situation. A youth minister may observe a family problem that calls for

action of some sort. To avoid a triangle, the intervention must be done in a neutral, non-anxious way, taking into consideration all persons and relationships.

If a youth minister becomes aware that a household atmosphere appears to endanger the teen (and perhaps others), then intervention is warranted. This intervention should be made only after consulting key people like the pastor, a family therapist, or even local authorities. To avoid a triangle one must remain neutral and employ the efforts of non-anxious presence with both the teen and the parents. This means focusing on process and relationships (vs. content issues) which are keys to healing and reconciliation. If one can create an atmosphere of honest sharing and listening, then a lasting solution becomes possible. One should always suspect that the conflict is rooted deeper than the current issue or struggle. Therefore, remaining calmly focused on relationships and communication allows for deeper healing reconciliation.

Facilitating honest communication in the midst of a problem situation is no small task. If one's non-anxious presence does not produce desirable results, then it is time for referral and perhaps professional intervention. Ministers must know their own limitations, and not let that need to be needed interfere with effective ministry to teens and their families.

CONCLUSION

Family life is very important in the lives of teens. The more in touch we are with the concerns of families with adolescents and their relational dynamics, the better our youth ministry will be. Systems theory gives us insight into the emotional process of family living, and lends understanding to household phenomena that would otherwise be unexplainable. Yet families are still mysterious and unpredictable. Why? Because they are living, organic systems that are constantly growing and changing. Once we thing we've got them figured out, a new wrinkle occurs. Mitch Finley, noted author on family life puts it this way:

> Family living is a comfort, God knows, and family living is a grand and glorious pain. Almost everyday you'd as soon hop

a slow boat to China as stick around.
Almost everyday you'd give your very life
for those ne'er do-well you live with.
Almost everyday you do. God knows.

The principles of systems theory and
emotional family process won't solve all the
mysteries of family living, but they do lend
valuable insight and understanding.

PART II: FAMILY PERSONALITY

Just like individual persons, every family is
unique. But also like individuals, families
have various personality types that, when
named and claimed, can help family
members understand their household
dynamics.

Perhaps you are familiar with the
individual personality types according to
Meyers Briggs: introvert/extrovert,
intuitive/sensate, thinking/feeling,
judging/perceiving. These indicators help
people understand why they react to other
people and situations the way they do.

The same is true for families. They have
different personality types that contribute to
the way family members interact with each
other, and those outside the family. This
chapter explores four family personality
types which indicate how families deal with
change. We will also examine four types
showing how families deal with
togetherness.

Many of these ideas are based on the
"Circumplex Family Model" developed by Dr.
David Olson. In his work as a family
therapist he found that clustering numerous
concepts from family therapy and other
social science fields revealed two significant
dimensions of family behavior. He termed
them cohesion: how the family deals with
being together, and adaptability: how the
family deals with change.

Using scales similar to those described
below, Olson found that a balanced level of
cohesion and adaptability is most conducive
to healthy family functioning. In other
words, too much closeness or too little
closeness is not healthy. Likewise, too much
change or too little change is not good for
the family. Yet there is a wide range of

health between the extremes on both scales.

Olson and his colleagues have made a
great contribution to the family therapy
field with this Circumplex model. It provides
a somewhat measurable indication of how a
couple or family functions, and also
indicates a direction which will lead to
better functioning. If a family is highly
structured, for instance, their therapy
should coach them toward a level of
moderate structure rather than a total
reversal leading to high flexibility, even
chaos. The therapist can provide simple
suggestions to reduce the extreme level of
rigidity in the family.

The value of the Circumplex model to
the non-therapist is important and unique
as well. Quality family life is a key issue,
and often a stumbling block, during
adolescence. What used to purr like a fine-
tuned engine suddenly has fits and starts.
Time together used to be easy and
satisfying; yet now it has become tedious
and trying. As families encounter the
necessary changes of adolescence they must
draw on their natural best resources to
maintain their health and positive outlook.
Helping them discover their family
personality through change and
togetherness (adaptability and cohesion) can
quite possibly give them both the tools and
channels to stay on a healthy course.

FAMILIES AND CHANGE

This concept addresses family adaptability.
Olson describes it as "the ability of a family
to change its power structure, role
relationships and relationship rules in
response to situational and developmental
stress" (Olson). Several family dimensions
are observed: family power structure
(assertiveness and control), negotiation
styles, roles and rules. Again, healthier
families will have balanced levels of
adaptability, particularly when it comes to
role sharing and rule making.

Family communication is key. For
example, these balanced families will have
fewer implicit rules and more explicit rules.
An implicit rule is a family mandate that all
are expected to observe, and yet it has never
been stated, acknowledged, or outwardly
accepted. For example, I know of one

family's implicit rule that the sons will follow in their father's footsteps by attending law school, marrying Irish, Catholic women, and becoming prominent attorneys. That's a tall order to fill, and can only lead to frustration, disappointment, and bitterness.

It should be noted that because of differences in cultural norms, it is possible for some families to operate at the extremes without problems. Yet these extreme patterns are more problematic in the long run for most families who are acculturated to the norms of the North American society (Olson).

Four ways families deal with change are shown in the diagram below. They are actually four points on a continuum, with the extremes at either end being unhealthy. They range from what might be called resistance (to the left) to indifference (to the right). As they grow and mature, all families must change. Some families resist it, while others welcome it. The four points are rigid, structured, flexible, and chaotic.

| Rigid | Structured | Flexible | Chaotic |

On the Structured Side

Generally, the structured family has stable, strong leadership. Discipline is usually democratic with predictable consequences that are firmly imposed and enforced. With respect to problem solving these families find reasonable solutions through structured negotiations. Family roles are stable but may be shared. Rules seldom change and are firmly enforced. Most will be explicit, but there will be some implicit rules (Olson). Most structured families have the tools to be healthy, but they are usually challenged during adolescence.

Too Much Structure Equals Rigid

The extreme of a structured family (moving left on the diagram) is a "rigid" family. This family will often demonstrate passive-aggressive styles of interaction. Leadership is authoritarian, and discipline is autocratic, strict, and rigidly enforced. This family does not solve problems well because negotiation is limited and solutions are imposed. Family roles are often stereotyped and have been

firmly established for generations. Rules abound, and are strictly enforced (Olson).

Flexible Family

Moving across the center line of the diagram we have the "flexible" family. This is usually a more desirable family personality for teens because:

- Parents are more democratic when it comes to discipline. Their leadership is fluid and egalitarian.

- Consequences for bad behavior are logical, rather than arbitrary. For example, if a teen forgets to put gas in the car after a night out, she won't get grounded (arbitrary), but she may lose her privilege to drive the car.

- Problem-solving normally occurs through flexible negotiation and agreed upon solutions.

- Roles and responsibilities are shared among family members. When it comes to kitchen and cleaning work, everyone will be expected to pull their weight.

- Rules in the family can change if situations call for it, and they are usually flexibly enforced.

Sounds great, doesn't it? For the most part it is, but there are a couple of common struggles for teens and parents in flexible families. At times, teens desire stronger expressions of love and support. Most parents become more flexible as their children get older, but occasionally that sends a message of "We don't care. We're tired of parenting. You are on your own." Actually, clear and consistent discipline is a valuable expression of love from parent to teen, and many teens would welcome more expressions like that. Difficulties can also arise when a crisis hits a flexible family. It is not unusual for one parent to suddenly become very structured. This throws everyone into confusion.

Too Much Flexibility Leads to Chaos

Even though this is the opposite from a "rigid" family, the extreme is just as unhealthy. A chaotic family has unpredictable patterns. They will demonstrate both passive and aggressive styles. Leadership will either be erratic or absent, and discipline is inconsistent. Problem-solving often involves endless negotiations followed by impulsive solutions. Roles can shift dramatically, even with complete role reversals. Rules can be the same way, and they are arbitrarily enforced (Olson). A teenager in this house never knows what to expect.

FAITH AND FAMILY CHANGE

Family personality will certainly have an impact on faith expression. If the family is on the structured/rigid side of the scale, one might find it hard to give up childlike expressions of prayer and faith, and develop a more mature faith. When there is resistance to change, sometimes faith remains rooted in childhood experiences. One's vision of God may be that of a Father who loves and cuddles his little children. Or, one might see God as the almighty lawgiver, and upholder of truth and justice—God maintains a high level of structure in the world.

If the family is on the flexible/chaotic side, one may find faith expression and spirituality constantly in flux depending on emotions. One's vision of God may be something like a teddy bear to be cuddled when needed, and displayed neatly on the bed otherwise. Sometimes we tend to shape God into images that we like.

SUGGESTIONS

Here is some advice to share with adolescents and/or their parents who might be struggling with their current family style of change.

Rigid: Teens in this situation will often hold much anger and resentment toward their parents, teachers and anyone who represents authority. Sometimes they "explode" with rebellion. Other times, they hold the anger inside for years until they become parents themselves, and the unhealthy cycle repeats itself. Teens in these families should seek help from a trusted adult friend or professional counselor.

Structured: If you find yourself struggling in a structured family, these suggestions might help.

- Show your parents one area where you can be trusted. As you show maturity here, it might help them open up in other areas also.

- In seeking a particular privilege, negotiate a certain amount of time (two weeks, a month, etc.) when, if you show your ability to be trusted, you will be granted the privilege.

- Choose a calm time to express your desires for more trust and freedom. Talk to your parents openly and honestly. This is always better than trying to work things out during a loud argument.

Flexible: This is probably the best personality types for families with adolescents because they can tolerate a greater degree of emotional and physical ups and downs. Yet many teens need more structure and predictability in their lives. When people have a lot of confusions on the inside (emotions, self-esteem, etc.), it helps to have some stability on the outside. If your family seems too laid back to provide stability and predictability, then seek it in individual relationships with one or both of your parents, or with another significant adult.

Chaotic: It is not unusual for families with an alcohol- or drug-dependent member to be in chaos. It is a dangerous and unhealthy situation, and teens should seek help from a trusted adult or professional counselor.

FAMILY TOGETHERNESS

The second part of exploring family personality looks at four ways families deal with togetherness or the lack of it. The four points on the continuum are disjointed, separated, connected and enmeshed. The second diagram looks at how some families are close, while others distant. Some families are open to outside relationships, others closed.

Olson defined family cohesion as "the emotional bonding members have with one another." He summarizes this scale as follows.

> At the extreme of high family cohesion, enmeshment, there is an overidentification with the family that results in an extreme bonding and limited individual autonomy. The low extreme, disengagement [for our purposes in this book, we are using the term disjointed], is characterized by low bonding and high autonomy from the family. It is hypothesized that a balanced degree of family cohesion (separated and connected) is the most conducive to effective family functioning and to optimum individual development (Olson).

Again, it must be stated that families of different cultures may operate at the extremes without problems due to their cultural norms. Yet, many will experience difficulty if they assimilate into the dominant culture.

Some of the family traits used to assess family cohesion are: emotional bonding, independence, boundaries, time, space, friends, decision-making, and interests and recreation.

Disjointed	Separated	Connected	Enmeshed

Connected Family

Let's first look at the "connected" family. From a clinical viewpoint, this family will prefer emotional closeness while respecting the need for some separateness. Outside relationships and ideas are controlled but not restricted. Time together is important and scheduled, but time alone is permitted. The family is often involved in individual interests. Shared family space is preferred, but again, private spaced is respected. Most decisions are made with the family in mind, and individual decisions are expected to be shared with the family (Olson).

Connected families have a high level of emotional closeness. There is expression of love, hate, and everything in between. Periods of closeness are wonderful and periods of conflict are turbulent. Loyalty to the family is expected. If you have the choice to go out with friends or attend a

family function, you will be expected at the family function. And friends are shared with the whole family. Your old boyfriend may still be dropping by to visit your parents.

Enmeshed Family

All families need closeness, but when a family becomes too connected, they are "enmeshed." In their extreme closeness, outside influences from people and ideas are restricted. Individual friends are frowned upon, but family friends are encouraged. Generational boundaries between parents and children are often blurred. Time and space together is maximized, while time alone and private space are not permitted. All decisions, both personal and family related must be approved, and nearly all activities and interests are shared by the entire family (Olson).

Enmeshed families are unhealthy because loyalty to the family is not only expected, it is demanded. Individuals are given little or no private space and time of their own. Sometimes you cannot distinguish you from your family. This family is often controlled by one person. Nothing happens without first going through him or her. This is an unhealthy family personality for teens because their biggest need is to come to grips with their self-identity. If the family atmosphere won't allow them to do that, they will likely rebel.

Separated Family

Moving to the other side of the diagram, we have the "separated" family. These families encourage and prefer emotional separateness, but also respect needs for support. They are open to external relationships and ideas, while individual friends are shared with the family. Time alone is important, but they do spend time together as well. Private space is respected. Most decisions are made individually, but they can make joint decisions on important family issues. Individual activities are supported even if other family members do not get involved. Family activities are seldom planned, but will occur spontaneously on occasion (Olson).

Most teens prefer a "separated" family because they enjoy more independence. Yet there are times when teens want more closeness. They might experience loneliness more often in a separated family, especially when dealing with emotional struggles. If your girlfriend breaks off with you, for example, or you don't make the cheerleading team, your family may not give you the support and understanding you might need.

Disjointed Family

When a family is too separated it becomes "disjointed." Everybody does their own thing. Quality family time is unheard of, and family members are on their own for basic services such as laundry, meals, transportation, even money. There is no closeness in the family. Often there is not even much fighting because household members just don't care enough to bother. Individuals make their own decisions without checking with other family members. Outside influences, ideas, and friends are unrestricted leading to no family loyalty whatsoever.

FAITH AND FAMILY TOGETHERNESS

How has your faith and religious practice been affected by this scale? If the family lies on the connected enmeshed side, then one may have grown up always attending the same Mass, always with the whole family, always sitting in the same pew with never a chance to voice opinions about it. God may be viewed as the one who keeps the family together. Has anyone in your family ever said, "The family that prays together . . . "?

If you find yourself on the separated/disjointed side, you may have been encouraged to search your inner self and explore your deepest experiences of life and God. Don't worry, you won't have to make anyone understand your experiences; just go out and experience something deep.

SUGGESTIONS

Here is some advice to share with adolescents and/or their parents who might be struggling with the degree of cohesion in their family.

Disjointed: Living in a disjointed family is a lonely experience. Teens will often act-out with bizarre behavior in hopes that someone

might notice them. A teen should seek someone to talk to, to lean on, who can offer loving, caring support.

Separated: How can you find more closeness in a separated family? Here are a few tips.

- Develop bonds with one person at a time. You probably won't succeed with all household members, but try to get close to one or two. This will relieve some loneliness.

- Risk sharing your emotions. Remember they do love you and have lived with you all your life. When the time is right, take the first step, let down your guard, and show your feelings.

- Write a note. If you cannot bring yourself to say "I love you" out loud, write it in a card or note. Do it for no occasion whatsoever. Chances are you will get some response.

- Rally the family around an issue or activity. Closeness builds in any groups working for a common cause. Call a family meeting to discuss ways your family might contribute to a worthy venture.

Connected: How can adolescents communicate their desires and still keep peace in the family? These suggestions might help.

- Choose the right time and place to tell family members your need for more space, privacy, and independence. An hour before the family reunion is not a good time to discuss whether you have to go or not. Pick a time that is removed from the occasion when everyone can speak and listen calmly.

- If you need more privacy, take a look at your own daily habits. For example, instead of watching TV each afternoon, take some time to yourself to be quiet and alone. If you share your bedroom, arrange a regular time that you can be there by yourself.

Enmeshed: Many teens don't know an enmeshed family is different in an unhealthy way until they see what their friends' families are like. If you think yours is an enmeshed family, find a trusted friend or adult with whom you can talk. Ask them to give you insights on what is normal and what seems unhealthy.

CONCLUSION

Families do not always keep the same personality as they mature through the life cycle. As changes occur, whether sudden or developmental, they may move in any direction on either the change scale or togetherness scale that allows them to function. For example, families with young children are often "structurally-connected" in type, but discover that as their children mature they become more "flexibly-separated." Or a family with a flexible style may become more structured as a result of a serious trauma such as a death or divorce. This shift allows them to deal with the serious problem and still maintain family identity.

The two scales operate simultaneously in every family. This means their "family personality" is comprised of their characteristics from both scales. When the scales are overlapped there are 16 different types in the Circumplex model. Four types reflect balanced levels of both adaptability and cohesion, and these are seen as most functional to individual and family development:

> flexibly separated
> flexibly connected
> structurally separated
> structurally connected

When both dimensions are balanced, the family is most functional. Balance is the key factor. For example, children require a balance of parental support and control. Too much or too little is detrimental. The optimum level of support and control is moderate (Olson).

The four extreme types reflect very high or very low levels of adaptability and cohesion, and are seen as most dysfunctional to individual and family development. These types are:

chaotically disjointed
chaotically enmeshed
rigidly disjointed
rigidly enmeshed

It must be noted here that it is possible for extreme family types to be functional at some times for families. Extreme emotional closeness might be just what a family needs after experiencing a crisis such as a death in the family, or after a significant addition such as the birth of a child.

However, if this becomes the predominant style of relating in the family, they will experience problems once the pain of trauma has subsided or the newness of birth has worn off. In another instance, the extreme family type of being rigidly enmeshed might be functional for taking care of an infant, but would certainly not be healthy when the child becomes an adult (Olson).

Another interesting factor about the extreme type is, according to Olson, couples and families with extreme levels (high or low) of cohesion and/or adaptability will not have problems as long as all members of the family like it that way (Olson).

There is great value in these family personality types not just for therapists, but also for youth ministers and others who work with teens and their families. Family life is extremely important to teens, but also it can be a source of stress. An understanding of family personality may help the youth worker give teens more concrete advice and direction for living in his/her family. It will also help the youth minister have a broader understanding of why teens and their families interact the way they do. He or she will be better equipped to offer assistance either through pastoral presence or referral to a professional.

WORKS CITED

Braun, Mary, Lecture on Family Systems Theory. Regis College, June 30, 1987.

Durka, Gloria. "Family Systems: A New Perspective For Youth Ministry." *Readings in Youth Ministry*. Ed. John

Roberto. Washington, DC: NFCYM, 1986.

Friedman, Edwin H. *Generation To Generation: Family Process in Church and Synagogue*. New York: The Guilford Press, 1985.

Guarendi, Ray. *Back To The Family: How To Encourage Traditional Values In Complicated Times*. New York: Villard Books, 1990.

Lerner, Harriet Goldhor. *The Dance of Anger*. New York: Harper and Row, 1985.

Olson, Dr. David. "Circumplex Model of Marital and Family Systems." *Family Process* 18 (1979): 1-28.

Power, Thomas A. *Family Matters: A Layman's Guide to Family Functioning*. Meredith, NH: Hathaway Press, 1989.

CHAPTER 2

A Family Life Cycle Perspective

Nydia Garcia Preto

The adaptations in family structure and organization required to handle the tasks of adolescence are so basic that the family itself is transformed from a unit that protects and nurtures young children to one that is a preparation center for the adolescent's entrance into the world of adult responsibilities and commitments. This family metamorphosis involves profound shifts in relationship patterns across the generations, and while it may be signaled initially by the adolescent's physical maturity, it often parallels and coincides with changes in parents as they enter midlife and with major transformations faced by grandparents in old age.

These changes take place within a larger social context, which has become increasingly complex. In highly technological societies, such as the United States, the family no longer functions as a comprehensive economic unit and has become dependent on external systems for teaching children, setting limits on them, and finding them employment. Whereas in the past the family was able to offer practical training to children in the form of jobs, it must now provide them with the psychological skills that will help them differentiate and survive in an evermore rapidly changing world. As a result the family's major function has been transformed from that of an economic unit to that of an emotional support system.

This essay focuses on the overall transformation that families experience as they try to master the tasks of adolescence. Most families, after a certain degree of

confusion and disruption, are able to change the rules and limits and reorganize themselves to allow adolescents more autonomy and independence. However, there are certain universal problems associated with this transition that can result in family dysfunction and the development of symptoms in the adolescent or in other family members. Clinical cases will illustrate some of the blocks that families experience during this phase, as well as factors that may contribute to family disorganization or symptomatic behavior, and therapeutic interventions that may be effective with these families.

THREE-GENERATIONAL VIEW OF TRANSFORMATION

Adolescence demands structural shifts and renegotiation of roles in families involving at least three generations of relatives. Adolescent demands for more autonomy and independence tend to precipitate shifts in relationships across generations. For instance, it is not uncommon for parents and grandparents to redefine their relationships during this period, as well as for spouses to renegotiate their marriage, and for siblings to question their position in the family.

Because adolescent demands are so strong, they often serve as catalysts for reactivating emotional issues and they set triangles in motion. The struggle to meet these demands often brings to the surface unresolved conflicts between parents and grandparents or between the parents themselves. Requests for greater autonomy and independence, for example, often stir fears of loss and rejection in parents, especially if during adolescence, they felt rejected or abandoned by their own parents. In families with adolescents, triangles generally involve the following players: the adolescent, the father, and the mother; the adolescent, a parent, and a grandparent; the adolescent, a parent, and a sibling; or the adolescent, a parent, and the adolescent's friends.

As the adolescent enters into conflict with a parent, efforts to ameliorate the tension often repeat earlier patterns of relating in the parents' family or origin. Parents who have made a conscious effort to raise their children differently by avoiding the same "mistakes" their parents made often have a particularly rude awakening. when their children reach adolescence, they are often surprised to observe similarities in personality between their children and their parents. The following caption from a cartoon by Jules Feiffer illustrates this well (Heller):

> I hated the way I turned out . . . So everything my mother did with me I tried to do different with my Jennifer. Mother was possessive. I encouraged independence. Mother was manipulative. I have been direct. Mother was secretive. I have been open. Mother was evasive. I have been decisive. Now my work is done. Jennifer is grown. The exact image of my mother.

Parents in this situation may react with extreme confusion, anger, resentment, or in many other ways. In fact, there appears to be a reciprocal chain reaction of meeting and making demands across the generations that is precipitated by the adolescents of the younger generation. Parents, while responding to the adolescent's demands for greater support and autonomy, may themselves get in touch with similar needs, and, in turn, make the same requests of their own parents or each other.

Families during this period are also responding and adjusting to the new demands of other family members, who themselves are entering new stages of the life cycle, In most families with adolescents, the parents are approaching middle age. Their focus in on such major midlife issues are re-evaluating the marriage and careers. The marriage emerging from the heavy caretaking responsibilities of young children may be threatened as parents review personal satisfaction in the light of the militant idealism of their adolescent children. For many women this may actually be the first opportunity to work without the restrictions they faced when the children were young. Many women may be starting a career at this point whereas men are involved with maximizing their professional careers (Prosen, et al.). The normal stress and tension posed to the family by an adolescent are exacerbated when the parents experience acute dissatisfaction and feel compelled to make changes in themselves. At the same time, the grandparents face retirement and possible moves, illness, and death. These stressful events call for a renegotiation of relationships, and parents may be called upon to be caretakers of their own parents or to assist them in integrating the loses of old age.

What often forms is a field of conflicting demands, where the stress seems to be transmitted both up and down the generations. So, for example, the conflict between parents and grandparents may have a negative effect on the marital relationship that filters down into the relationship between the parents and the adolescent. Or the conflict may travel in the opposite direction. A conflict between the parents and the adolescent may affect the marital relationship, which ultimately affects the relationship between the parents and grandparents.

TASKS OF ADOLESCENCE

The origins of this family transformation are the adolescent's developmental tasks that begin with the rapid physical growth and sexual maturation during puberty. As a result of sexual maturation, moves toward solidifying an identity and establishing autonomy from the family (which are really lifelong developmental processes) are accelerated during adolescence. Changing and often conflicting social expectations about sexual roles and norms of behavior are imposed on adolescents by the family, school, peers, and the media. Their ability to differentiate from others depends on how well they handle the expected social behaviors for expressing the intense emotions that are precipitated by puberty. To establish autonomy they need to become gradually more responsible for their own decision making and yet feel the security of parental guidance.

Flexibility is the key to success for families at this stage. For instance, increasing the flexibility of family boundaries and modulating parental authority permit greater independence and developmental growth for adolescents. However, in an attempt to lessen the conflicts generated during this period, many families continue to reach for solutions that used to work in earlier stages. Parents often try to tighten the reins or to withdraw emotionally to avoid further conflict. Or they either blindly accept or reject the adolescent. Adolescents, on the other hand, in an effort to win their way, resort to temper tantrums, withdraw emotionally behind closed doors, turn to grandparents for support, or present endless examples of friends who have more freedom.

This section focuses on the normal challenges and typical fears or blocks that parents and adolescents experience during this transition.

SEXUALITY: TRANSFORMATION OF THE PHYSICAL SELF

Puberty brings about a great number of changes that not only transform the physical self but also signal the beginning of the psychological transition from childhood to adulthood (Hopkins, 1983). There are variations in the age at which it begins, but it generally starts earlier for girls than for boys. Also, there has been a trend toward earlier maturation for both girls and boys, referred to as the "secular trend." Menarche, for instance, has shown a regular trend toward earlier occurrence since the 1800s. The average age for onset of menstruation is now 13, whereas in the 1800s it was over 16 (Hopkins).

The physical and sexual changes that take place have a dramatic effect on how adolescents describe and evaluate themselves, and radically alter how they are perceived by others. Coping with this upsurge in sexual thoughts, feelings, and behaviors is a major task for all family members. It is not uncommon for family members to experience confusion and fear when adolescents begin to express their new sexual interests. The Lornes illustrate a familiar pattern observed in families coping with these changes.

> Mr. and Mrs. Lornes had always been proud of their 14-year-old daughter, Sandra, who was an excellent student, active in the school band, a gymnast, and a dancer. When they discovered that she was interested in older boys who drank, drove, and had the reputation of being "jocks" at school and in the community, they reacted with fear and confusion. Their initial response was to monitor all her calls and outings and to drive her to all activities. She, confused by their reaction and frightened by her own feelings, began to lie and "sneak around."

The Lornes' initial reaction was similar to the way many parents respond when they first become aware of a daughter's increased sexuality. Parents want to protect their daughters from the dangers of the world, fearing the possibility of sexual exploitation, rape, or an unwanted pregnancy. Although a daughter may be physically mature, parents fear that she is unable to protect herself from the reality of her environment. These fears are not unfounded, since sexual abuse, rape, and teenage pregnancy are problems that seem to be on the rise in this country (Dickman). Worries about male children are somewhat different. A boy's parents may worry more about sexual interests distracting him from his studies and jeopardizing his future than about sexual exploitation.

Usually parents who are comfortable with their own sexuality are more able to accept the heightened sexuality of adolescents and to convey their acceptance.

Also, when the home has been a place where information is openly shared, the possibility is greater for setting realistic, sensitive limits and for tolerating minor transgressions. This provides adolescents with an accepting framework within which to express and experiment with this new and important aspect of their lives. In contrast, if the adolescent's growing sexuality is denied, ignored, or rejected by the parents, the possibility for the development of a positive sexual self-concept is diminished. The probability of increased feelings of alienation between adolescents and their parents is greater and risks of premature, excessive, or self-endangering sexual activity are increased.

Personal experiences with sexuality influence the way in which parents set limits and expectations and affect the extent to which they include the adolescent in the process of establishing rules. In general, parents who had positive experiences at home and with peers during their own sexual transformation are more likely to provide a similar experience for their children than parents who were neglected, rejected, or sexually abused. This does not imply that all parents who had these negative experiences will repeat the pattern, but it is not uncommon to observe in families the repetition of abuse, neglect, or rejection, as well as the recurrence of teenage pregnancy and children born out of wedlock.

In fact, incestuous impulses between the adolescent and the opposite-sex parent are likely to increase with the adolescent's emerging sexuality. The energy and unacceptability of these urges easily develop into heightened conflict. Perhaps adolescents act so obnoxiously to make it easier for parents to let them go, and perhaps parents become difficult to make it easier for adolescents to want to go. A previously special and loving relationship between father and daughter may rapidly evolve into a mutually hostile one, with the father being possessive and punitive and the daughter being provocative. Mothers who are especially close to their sons may experience confusion and conflict when sons begin to demand more privacy and distance from them. The mother's request for closeness may be met with aggression and rejection, and mother, feeling hurt, may react in a similar manner.

Parents and children of the same sex, on the other hand, tend to become involved in struggles that are more competitive. One assumption that has been extensively discussed, especially in psychoanalytic theory, is that they compete for the attention and love of the opposite-sex parent (Freud; Blos). Another assumption, however, is that they compete over their conflicting perceptions of appropriate gender roles. Since adolescents appear to be more stereotyped in their view of sex-type behaviors for men and women than any other age group (Hopkins), it seems natural that they would confront and challenge parental behavior that does not conform to their perceptions. It follows that the overall struggle during adolescence may be more intense with the parent of the same sex, who usually serves as the primary role model during childhood. To be certain much of the conflict between parents and adolescents reflects differences in the way each generation interprets the stereotypes and double standard about sexual roles that exist in this society.

Although the general trend is toward a breakdown in the double standard, adolescent girls continue to exhibit more emotional commitment in their sexual experiences than do boys (Peplau; Schulz, et al.). However, among adolescents of both genders the trend seems to be toward earlier sexual experiences. This implies that most parents of adolescents will need to review changes that will better fit increasing liberalized sexual norms. For many parents this may be a very difficult task, especially if their values fit the more traditional double standard.

IDENTITY: TRANSFORMATION OF THE SELF

Identity refers to a person's private view of those traits and characteristics that best describe him or her. This self-structure undergoes its greatest transformation during adolescence (Marcia), when it seems to become more abstract and psychologically oriented.

Attempts to understand this process have been primarily based on Freud's and Erickson's theories. Freud focused on sexual drives and on the process of individuation (Blos), while Erickson identified adolescence as a period when individuals experience an identity crisis, which, when resolved, leads to commitments to sociopolitical conceptualizations and occupation.

One critical issue that these theories neglect is that, apart from the obvious physical characteristics that distinguish males from females, there are basic differences in the way that both sexes structure their identities. Few studies address this issue, but those that do seem to support the general assumption that females rely more on the relationships and connections they made and maintain whereas males place the emphasis on separation and individuation (Chodorow; Gilligan). Based on studies of men, most developmental theories assume that male patterns are the norm. This has created a double bind for women in this society, since traits that characterize the concept of "ideal women" are different from those that describe the "ideal adult" (Broverman, et al.). The "ideal adult" is seen as having more of the traits that characterize the "ideal man." This inconsistency in role expectations makes gender consolidation especially difficult for females during adolescence when this process seems to be accentuated. Male adolescents who do not have strong sex-typed identities may also experience more difficulty than their more "masculine" counterparts.

Regardless of differences in theoretical frameworks and in gender, the sudden and dramatic acceleration of identity formation that takes place during adolescence can become a source of excitement and energy, but also of conflict, for adolescents and their families. A new-found ability to formulate intellectual hypotheses expands adolescent creativity and feelings of mastery (Inhelder and Piaget). They become amateur philosophers and moral judges of social values and mores, often acting as ambassadors between home and community, bringing new ideas and attitudes that serve as catalysts for other family members to make changes. Their propensity for questioning and challenging rules and standards tends to precipitate transformations at home, at school, and in the community.

The struggle to gain a separate, clear, and positive self-image can also cause confusion and immobilization for adolescents and their families. New experiences in the world may subject them to anxiety, disappointment, rebuff, and failure. As with clothes and hair styles, roles may be tried on, prized briefly, and then discarded or clung to in an attempt to anchor a sense of self. While some of these roles are consistent with family values, they frequently challenge, if not assault, the mores of the family.

While attempting to establish self-identity, adolescents often disagree with parents about ideas, beliefs, and values. Comments such as, "My parents are so old-fashioned, they can't understand me," or "I never want to be like my parents, they are so boring" are familiar to those who work with adolescents. Also easily recognizable are parental comments such as, "I was so different at that age," "I didn't dare question my parents," or "I can't believe how girls call boys and initiate going out with them." These differences tend to create conflict among the generations, and sometimes lead to struggles over rules, roles, and relationships. Fears of conflict may inhibit the adolescent's asking questions or sharing ideas, and this creates distance and lack of trust.

Parents with a strong sense of self can be expected to be less reactive to adolescent challenges. This is not to say that they will not experience confusion or fear, but they may personalize their reactions less. Rather than feel attacked or threatened by criticisms, they will be more likely to ask questions, listen to explanations, and share feelings—methods that help parents and adolescents negotiate differences and conflicts (Offer, et al.)

Since gender has always been an integral aspect of self-identity, during adolescence same-sex, child-parent relationships have a powerful effect on the process of gender identification. Adolescent views about who they are will be greatly connected to their feelings about being male or female. Relationships with opposite-sex parents are just as influential in validating the adolescent's sense of gender identity, and to a certain extent serve as a program for shaping future relationships with the opposite sex.

Although there are always exceptions, as a rule daughters learn how to be female from mothers, and sons learn from fathers how to be male. Unfortunately, in their attempt to provide positive role models, parents often teach ideals about sexual roles rather than communicate to their children the value of their own experience. Betty Carter clearly describes this pattern:

> Mothers in an effort to fulfill their responsibility, namely raising perfect children, routinely tell their daughters what they think would be helpful, instead of how they really feel, especially if the latter would convey the mother's doubts, fears, struggles and uncertainties. So, trying desperately to be "good mothers" and to guide their daughters, mothers withhold their *deepest personal experience* and try to convey to their daughters *how it should have been* and *how they want it to be for their daughters*—instead of how it *really is or was for them* (Carter 16).

Striving for ideals themselves, adolescents often experience their parents as hypocritical and angrily reject advice. A similar pattern takes place between fathers and sons. In other words, what parents say is often not what they do. Inconsistencies in this process are as unavoidable as the conflict that emerges when adolescents confront and challenge the differences.

AUTONOMY: TRANSFORMATION OF DECISION MAKING

Adolescents need to venture out of the home to become more self-reliant and independent. Alliances outside the home increase and the influence of peers becomes stronger. While needing nurturance and acceptance to develop strong separate identities, they also need permission and encouragement to become more responsible for themselves. Autonomy does not mean disconnecting emotionally from parents, but it does mean

that an individual is no longer as psychologically dependent on parents and has more control of making decisions about his or her life.

Certainly, from an adult perspective, the adolescent's decisions in a rapidly expanding era of behavioral choices can leave much to be desired. The distinctions between choices that are merely unwise and self-defeating and those that are self-destructive or even life-threatening, are often hard to determine. Uncertainty concerning when and how to act is common for parents of adolescents.

It has been found that adolescents are more likely to move toward autonomy in families where they are encouraged to participate in decision making, but where parents ultimately decide what is appropriate. In this type of family, adolescents are also likely to model their parents and to seek parent-approved peers. In contrast, adolescents raised in families where participation in decision making and self-regulation is limited tend to become more dependent and less self-assured (Newman and Newman). As the researchers note, these findings pose an intriguing paradox: "The same conditions that foster a sense of independence also build a bond of closeness and affection between parents and children."

Retaining control while being objective, supportive, and democratic is not an easy task for most parents to accomplish, especially when they feel judged and criticized by their own children. Parental tolerance will tend to be low if they have not been able to achieve emotional autonomy from their own parents. Also, if parents have unresolved conflicts with each other, their ability to accept the adolescent's desire for autonomy becomes impaired. The adolescent may then be triangled into power struggles between spouse or between parents and grandparents, which will complicate the process by increasing tension, dissatisfaction, misunderstanding, and conflict for all.

Although adolescence is a time when both boys and girls move steadily toward autonomy from parents, differences have been found in the way each accomplishes the task. Douvan and Adelson, in a dated but still relevant study, found that boys appeared to be behaviorally dependent for a longer period than girls. However, boys seemed to achieve emotional autonomy at a much faster rate than girls. Their findings also imply that independence is a more important concern for boys than for girls, and that parental expectations seem to reinforce that pattern. More recent studies seem to indicate that differences may still be valid (Gilligan).

Gender role expectations certainly influence adolescents as they become involved in making decisions about life goals. Traditionally, families have given males greater encouragement than they have females for educational and occupational advancement, independent living, and financial self-sufficiency. Recently, females have been demanding the same opportunities as families with female adolescents find themselves making choices that challenge the values held by previous generations. When there are no prototypes to provide role models, the conflict and confusion that are normally experienced during this phase may increase dramatically for families with female adolescents.

For adolescents to master the developmental tasks that have been discussed, the family must be strong, flexible, and able to support growth. This is often easier with each successive child, and particularly difficult if the marital dyad is severely threatened.

ATTACHMENT, SEPARATION, AND LOSS DURING ADOLESCENCE

All transformations threaten previous attachments. The task of adolescence precipitates feelings of loss and fears of abandonment in most families. As adolescents strengthen their alliances outside, their decreasing participation at home is often experienced by other family members as a loss. Indeed, the transition from childhood to adolescence marks a loss for the family—the loss of the child. Parents often feel a void as adolescents move toward greater independence because they are no longer needed in the same way and the nature of their caretaking needs to change.

The difficulties inherent in the task of separation are greater when the parental support system is not working or is unavailable and there are no adults who can provide assistance. Under such conditions parents are likely to become overwhelmed and to respond either by attempting to control their adolescents arbitrarily or by giving up control completely.

Attempting to control adolescents may arbitrarily lead to serious symptomatic behavior. This type of control is often seen in families where, as Stierlin suggests, centripetal forces operate to keep members from leaving the system. For instance, families that have experienced early losses and rejections tend to become overprotective, and parents may try to exert control by reinforcing excessive childlike behavior. The message given is that separation is dangerous, and strenuous efforts are made to protect members, especially children, from outside threats. Through mystification, or by demanding such strong loyalty ties that extreme guilt is induced when separation is considered, the families that are so tightly bound attempt to meet each other's needs, but fail to promote growth. As a result adolescents may become stuck when they feel the urgency to grow, but stay home to meet their parents' needs. Parents experience a similar dilemma when fears of loss interfere with their attempts to help the children grow. The dilemma is often solved by adopting symptomatic behavior.

Often families find themselves caught in ongoing struggles that only seem to reach resolution with a premature separation. Parents who are overwhelmed by the tasks of adolescence may give up all responsibility and call outside authorities to take control. Frustrated and feeling hopeless about changing the behavior of delinquent or emotionally disturbed adolescents, they may ask courts, social agencies, or hospitals to take them out of the home. Adolescents may also marry precipitously, go to live with friends or lovers, and at times run away in an attempt to escape the conflicts at home. At the extreme, there are those adolescents who are essentially expelled from their families. In those families, as Stierlin suggests, there seem to be centrifugal forces that impel the adolescent from the system.

For example, parents who themselves were abused or neglected tend to abuse and reject when they lose control and feel helpless. Especially when parents are emotionally disturbed or substance abusers, adolescents may be forced into premature autonomy.

The expulsion of adolescents (Sager, et al.) may lead to a permanent family rift. This type of separation, while less intense than that following death, has significant and traumatic ramifications. For the adolescent who is cast out or runs away, the casualty rate due to other-inflicted or self-inflicted violence (including drug overdose) is high. Vulnerability to exploitation is also high. Unemployment, underemployment, prostitution, and involvement with an abusive partner are more likely outcomes for the adolescent without family supports. The remaining members of the evicting or deserted family are likely to confront heightened guilt, mutual blame, self-reproach, bitterness, continued anger, depression, and unresolved feelings of loss. The family's capacity to move ahead along its own life cycle course may be severely compromised. Both parents and other adolescents, or soon-to-be adolescents, in the family are significantly affected by the experience as they attempt to negotiate their own transitions.

All change implies the acceptance of loss. Sometimes parents, unable to cope with the loss of the dependent child, experience serious depression. Likewise, the adolescent must deal with the loss of the childhood self and the family as the primary source of love and affection. The loss of an early romantic attachment can also trigger depression in adolescents.

Early loss in a parent's history can make this stage difficult. A number of studies have found life cycle connections between early loss or life cycle disruption and later development of symptoms (Orfanidis; Walsh). They also found a correlation between the death of a grandparent at the same time of the birth of a grandchild and that child's patterns of symptom development during adolescence.

SOCIOCULTURAL FACTORS INFLUENCING THE FAMILY

Social class, education, race, ethnicity, sex, and place of residence strongly influence the life cycle of families. For example, the experience of poor families with adolescents is significantly different from that of middle-class and upper-class families. Adolescents from poor families usually leave school earlier to look for jobs in an attempt to become financially independent. Unfortunately their lack of skills makes it difficult to succeed. Resultant frustration, combined with the pressure of living in a home with limited resources, may lead them to leave precipitously, or the family to throw them out. Parents in these families often have difficulty with their own role definitions and are not able to provide the guidance and control that would assist their children in mastering adolescence. The possibility of becoming involved in crime, prostitution, drug addiction, and alcoholism is very high for this group.

In recent years more attention has been given to the significant role that ethnicity and culture play in the lives of families. Relationship patterns are deeply influenced by ethnic values and attitudes that are passed down through the generations. Ethnic groups differ remarkably in the rituals used to facilitate life cycle stages. For instance, British-Americans tend to promote the early separation of adolescents and their transition into adulthood (McGill and Pearce). Unlike most Italian, Hispanic, and Jewish families, they do not struggle to keep their adolescents close to home. McGill and Pearce observe that British-Americans are good at promoting separation, but more provide insufficient guidance and support for adolescents.

In contrast, Portuguese families, while also expecting adolescents to make an early transition into adulthood, handle separation very differently. Adolescents are encouraged to find employment and to make financial contributions to the home, just like adults. However, socially and emotionally they are expected to remain loyal and under the supervision of their parents (Moitoza). They are expected to live at home until they marry. Leaving home before marriage involves the risk of being ostracized by the family. When these expectations are challenged, serious conflicts between parents and adolescents can occur. Parent-adolescent interaction and contact may substantially diminish or decrease. Such cut-offs obviously interfere with healthy transitions to adulthood.

Another factor influencing adolescents and their families is the kind of community in which they reside. For example, the pressure and expectations experienced by families living in rural areas are different from those experienced by families in urban areas. Adolescents who grow up in cities tend to be less dependent on their families for recreation. With public transportation and a greater concentration of recreational options, their potential for independent activity increases. Generally they are exposed to a greater diversity of life-styles and role models, both positive and negative. This may increase the distance between parents and adolescents and escalate the normal conflicts of that stage. Parents may be less able to keep track of their children's friends and their whereabouts, or be less concerned about doing so, than their suburban or rural counterparts.

By contrast, adolescents in suburban and rural areas, due to geographic distance, may find themselves isolated from their peer group and dependent on the family for transportation and social stimulation. Greater dependence on the family may intensify the normal adolescent struggle for independence or slow down the growth process. The acquisition of a driver's license and availability of a car represent a transitional event that permits a major increase in independent actions by the adolescent.

Divorce is another social factor that has a tremendous effect on families with adolescents. Peck and Manocherian describe some of the patterns that emerge in families where adolescents are unable to maintain appropriate emotional distance from parental conflicts after divorce or separation. The change in family structure may cause a blurring of boundaries and an intensification of bonds between parents and adolescents. Adolescents may assume adult roles in an effort to replace the missing spouse and support the remaining parent. Single parents who do not have a network of peers sometimes lean inappropriately on their children for emotional support.

CONCLUSIONS

Adolescents grow up to become adults, have children of their own, and tend to adopt values and attitudes that reflect their parent's beliefs, unless while growing up they were seriously injured psychologically. Families handling the tasks of adolescence experience transformations in structure and organization, which are initially disruptive and create confusion. Most families, however, adjust to the changes without major difficulty and move on in the life cycle, but some, unable to make the transition, become symptomatic. In therapy unlocking the system to allow movement becomes the goal.

Assessing how families are coping with adolescent tasks is crucial to understanding the problems they bring to therapy. To diagnose what they present, therapists must broaden their perspective to consider not only the multiple ways in which families function, but also external factors that have an impact on them. Usually, without a relatively stable social framework, families have more difficulty providing the flexibility and protection that adolescents need to grow.

Interventions that take a life cycle approach to adolescents and their families and that are three generational in scope, tend to precipitate transformation in the system. Reframing the family's conceptions of time, working with subsystems, and proposing rituals that promote traditions or imagination are interventions that promote change in the system's organization. Tracking relationship patterns across the generations and connecting present conflicts to past unresolved conflicts allows families to be more objective about their interactions with each other. By offering new connections, the therapist can help families negotiate relationship shifts that must take place during adolescence, and to view the future in a less dangerous way.

WORKS CITED

Blos, P. *The Adolescent Passage: Developmental Issues*. New York: International Universities Press, 1962.

Broverman, J. K., D. M. Broverman, and F.E. Clarkson. "Sex Roles Stereotypes and Clinical Judgements of Mental Health." *Journal of Consulting and Clinical Psychology* 34: 1-7. 1970.

Chodorow, N. "Family Structure and Feminine Personality." *Woman, Culture and Society*. Eds. M. Z. Rosaldo and L. Lamphere. Stanford, CA: Stanford University Press, 1974.

Carter E. A. "Legacies, Intergenerational Themes." *Mothers and Daughters*. Eds. E. Carter, P. Papp. O. Siverstein, and M. Walters. Washington, DC, 1980.

Dickman, J. R. *Teenage Pregnancy: What Can Be Done?* Public Pamphlet No. 594, 1983.

Douvan, E., and J. Adelson. *The Adolescent Experience*. New York: Wiley, 1966.

Erickson, E. H. *Identity: Youth and Crisis*. New York: Norton, 1968.

Freud, S. *Three Contributions to the Theory of Sex*. (A. Brill, trans.) New York: Dutton, 1962, originally published 1905.

Gilligan, C. *In a Different Voice: Psychological Theory and Women's Development*. Cambridge, MA: Harvard University Press, 1982.

Heller, S. *Jules Feiffer's America: From Eisenhower to Reagan*. New York: Knopf, 1982.

Hopkins, J. R. *Adolescence: The Transitional Years*. New York: Academic Press, 1983.

Inhelder, B. and J. Piaget. *The Growth of Logical Thinking*. New York: Basic Books, 1958.

Marcia, J. E. *Handbook of Adolescent Psychological*. "Identity of Adolescence." Ed. J. Adelson. New York: Wiley, 1980.

McGill, D. and J.K. Pearce. "British Families." *Ethnicity and Family Therapy*. Eds. M. McGoldrick, J.G. Pearce, and J. Giordano. New York: Guilford Press, 1982.

Moitoza, E. "Portuguese Families." *Ethnicity and Family Therapy*. Eds. M. McGoldrick, J.G. Pearce, and J. Giordano. New York: Guilford Press, 1982.

Newman, B. M., and P. R. Newman. *An Introduction to the Psychology of Adolescence*. Homewood, IL: Dorsey Press, 1979.

Offer, D., E. Ostrov, and Howard K. I. *The Adolescent: A Psychological Self Portrait*. New York: Basic Books, 1981.

Orfanidis, M. *Some Data on Death and Cancer in Schizophrenic Families*. Paper presented at the Symposium Meeting of the Georgetown Symposium, Washington, DC, 1977.

Peplau, L. A. "Impact of Fear of Success and Sex Role Attitudes on Women's Competitive Achievement." *Journal of Personality and Social Psychology* 34:561-568, 1976.

Prosen, H., J. Toews, and M. Martin. "The Life Cycle of the Family: Parental Midlife Crises and Adolescent Rebellion." *Adolescent Psychiatry: Developmental and Clinical Studies*, vol. 9. Eds. S.C. Feinstein, J. C. Looney, A. Z. Schwartzberg, and A. D. Sorosky. Chicago: University of Chicago Press, 1981.

Sager, C. J., H. S. Brown, H. Crohn, T. Engel, E. Bodstein and L. Walker. *Treating the Remarried Family*. New York: Brunner/Mazel, 1983.

Schultz, B., G. W. Bohrstedt, E.F. Borgatta, and R. R. Evans. "Explaining Pre-marital Sexual Intercourse Among College Students. A Casual Model." *Social Forces* 56:148-165., 1977.

Stierlin, H. *Separating Parents and Adolescents: A Perspective on Running Away, Schizophrenia and Waywardness*. New York: Quadrangle, 1979.

Walsh, F. "Concurrent Grandparent Death and the Birth of a Schizophrenic Offspring: An Intriguing Finding. *Family Process* 12:179-188, 1978.

CHAPTER 3

A FAITH DEVELOPMENT PERSPECTIVE

Gary Chamberlain

FAITH DEVELOPMENT IN ADOLESCENCE: AN OVERVIEW

John Roberto

The research of James Fowler has produced a very helpful framework for understanding faith growth through the life cycle. In general, the faith stages of Fowler do not behave like other development stage theories, which are more discrete and sequential. Different faith stages or styles can coexist in the same age group with one or more in ascendancy. Here is an introduction to the patterns of early adolescent and older adolescent faith growth.

Early Adolescence: Many early adolescents derive their faith, beliefs, and values mainly from parents and family through earlier experiences and parent role modeling. This style of faith can be called *experienced faith*. Other early adolescents seek their faith-identity in the authority of the faith community's understandings and ways—experiencing belonging and active participation in the life of the faith community. Through these experiences they establish a set of beliefs, attitudes, and values, learning who and whose they are. They are dependent upon the community for the content and shape of their faith. This style of faith can be called *conventional faith*, since it is the faith of the community that the individual makes his or her own.

Older Adolescence: Some older adolescents still derive their faith mainly from parents and family (*experienced faith*) and/or through the community's faith (*conventional faith*). Many older adolescents begin to reflect on their own life and its meaning so as to establish their own faith identity. Through doubt and questioning, there is a breakdown of the conventional faith and a restructuring of faith as more personal to oneself. They begin the process of taking responsibility for their own faith life, commitments, lifestyle, beliefs, and attitudes. This process can be called *searching faith*. In addition, older adolescents also construct their faith interpersonally, developing a more personal relationship with Jesus: a belief in Jesus as important through his teaching and his example and as present in one's life. God becomes a personal God, who knows, accepts, and confirms them deeply. This can be called a *personal faith*. Relatively few older adolescents grow in faith to the point of making a firm commitment to a personally owned faith through their own decision. This personally-committed or *owned faith* is more characteristic of the young adult and adult years.

The following essay by Gary Chamberlain provides a description of *Conventional Faith* and *Individuative Faith* as developed by James Fowler. In broad strokes, and with many exceptions, the description of Conventional Faith provides insight into the faith style of early adolescents, while the description of Individuative Faith provides insight into the emerging faith style of older adolescents. These patterns are descriptive and are intended to be a guide to understanding the faith journey of adolescents.

FAITH GROWTH IN ADOLESCENCE

Gary Chamberlain

CONVENTIONAL FAITH

The key to understanding the person's faith growth at a Conventional Faith stage lies in the focus around personal relationships. "Social stories" or conventions of a social group now form the structure of the daily world in which the conventional way of understanding faith operates. The world is structured in interpersonal terms, and the critical personal question becomes "Who am I?" Parents, peers, and church leaders, political and cultural authorities all reflect back to the adolescent in these years the possibilities he or she can become, must reject, would dream about. While the conventional stage describes the period of adolescence most aptly, the dynamics of this stage also describe many adults whose faith is lived out at the conventional level, especially if the guiding theology of their church life calls for unquestioning or even begrudging acceptance of the dominant patterns of life.

In this interpersonal world not only is society held together by the people who fulfill the social roles, but the individual's self-understanding is constituted by the expectations of significant other people and of important groups. Thus a basic unrelenting question, whether conscious or unconscious, is what would "the gang" expect, what would grandmother expect, what would *they* say at church or school. The task of faith and of the quest for personal identity is precisely to find the ways in which these various expectations can be held together.

In search of an answer to the questions of "Who am I?" and "What will I become?" the adolescent tries on different roles to see how well they fit, how comfortable they are, how much security they bring. These roles are worn by adults who both prove

themselves trustworthy and lovable to the adolescent and at the same time confirm that he or she is a trustworthy and lovable person. The search for identity focuses upon models who exemplify faith in the form of fidelity, a trusting commitment of one person for another.

At this stage of faith growth, the individual is able to undertake abstract thinking, examine hypotheses, and develop reflective skills to some degree. The adolescent's sense of world order is only a budding one. The "system" which holds the world together at this point is generally an unquestioned one. Questions are certainly asked, but they can be answered by the "conventional understanding" of one's faith community.

The increased ability to take others' perspectives into account often leads to the dramatic character of this stage and to the predominance of feelings over thought. "I see you seeing me" reflects the overwhelming awareness of others which shapes the view the person has of self. The person comes to rely upon people who make the self feel most comfortable and accepted and who reflect the interpersonal virtues of sincerity, loyalty, authenticity, and friendliness as criteria of truth and value. When these values can be discovered in one person who acts as model for a particular viewpoint, the faith of the adolescent or of the group at this stage can be conformed or challenged.

In this conventional stage the group serves as the source of the individual's identity and faith. The individual and even the community have not yet taken on the burden of personal and social responsibility for ideas, actions, and life choices. Responsibility rests instead upon authorities outside the self.

Finally symbols emerge as the mediating force between daily realities and the realm of ideals, values, and truths. Symbols achieve a pervasive, metaphorical quality with various meanings but are not turned into abstract ideas. In the Christian context, God becomes real in terms of the affective and personal qualities of love, closeness, intimacy. God now becomes father while Jesus is seen as friend, companion, trusted confidant.

In terms of our discussion of the characteristics of faith growth at this stage, central needs emerge for growth in faith. Among these are involvement in community, a participation in family and community life, realistic role models of faith, occasions to share faith stories, experiences of challenge and conflict, an exploration of the roots of the Christian life in Scripture and theology, and particularly a method of understanding symbols which carries beyond the literal meaning. Literalism, the root of all fundamentalism, results from the confusion of the symbol with the reality symbolized, and the consequence is that God's mysterious, varied ways are reduced to "one way."

Because perspectives will also be shaped by the interpersonal view of the world, personal involvement in service will be an important way to develop a critical perspective and sense of justice. Even the dynamic of friendship can be extended across racial, religious, and national boundaries to include people in groups and countries different than one's own. This exposure to other people's cultures and values can expand the boundaries of social awareness of capacities for perspective-taking so important to a vision of social justice at the Individuative Faith stage.

The Conventional Faith view can be nudged into an individuating mode in several ways. The clash of images and symbols engendered by exploring different cultures, different social groups and religious traditions along with opportunities to articulate a personal faith history, to listen to those of trusted others, to ask serious questions and have them taken seriously by an admired representative of a faith tradition—all can lead to the self-conscious appropriation of a personal faith stance. Teachers, parents and mentors can also serve as models of faithful people who went through the same questioning and have developed powerful, life-giving world-views, ideal self-images, goals, and centers of ultimate loyalty. Perspectives can be broadened through education and travel. And finally the opportunities to take responsibility for others, whether in volunteer service or through a job, can develop the sense of personal worth and value which lead to an individuative faith stance.

INDIVIDUATIVE FAITH

The central characteristics of Individuative Faith are a keen sense of owning one's personal beliefs and actions, a developing, strong self-identity, the powerful pull of the world of ideas and ideals, and the realization that the views and outlooks the individual takes demand some justifications. Strengths emerge from this meld of self-identity and an identifiable worldview such as greater self-reflection; a sense of system to thinking; a strengthened personal authority for beliefs, attitudes, and values; firmer realization of the demands of peace, love, and justice along with an articulate basis for the criticism of existing social structures, and a delineation of the ways one's faith is different from earlier times and from other people's faith views. "Make it your own" or "Don't buy a used system" might be the slogans of this stage.

But there are weaknesses too, such as the tendency to fit a complex reality into a "clear and distinct" set of ideas, the attraction to an ideological viewpoint which distorts other perspectives and the imposition of one's own perspective upon other people and groups. In the midst of this dynamic form of faith, the central question which emerges for the Christian churches is what ideal community do we have to offer and how is that ideal community made real in practice.

In general at this stage a person has developed the thinking capacities to utilize abstract thought in rather advanced ways. The ability to differentiate ideas clearly from others' perspectives leads to the acceptance of personal responsibility for beliefs, values, and actions. Yet often the differences between viewpoints tend to be "dichotomized" into an "either/or" framework. This is especially true of some of the basic relationships between self and others, the individual and community, or truth and error. If the person at a Conventional Faith tends to validate reality and meaning on the basis of feelings, the person at stage four tends to allow thought to dominate feeling.

Even more deeply concerned with persons, the person of Individuative Faith becomes aware of the ways in which complex social realities shape and control persons. The individual can often begin the tasks of understanding entire perspectives different than his or her own. The authority for one's faith life, then, lies in one's own outlook. This movement toward greater autonomy in faith life and in personal identity is essential to the development of the mature Christian. Thus, the sense of "calling and responding," of surrendering one's will to God in love, of becoming a disciple rather than an imitator of Christ— all depend upon the development of a sense of self which leads then to service with others.

The bounds of social awareness, too, have extended in dynamic relation to the capacity to take authority for one's own beliefs and actions. Thus the ability to step outside one's own perspective and the perspective of one's own group to understand the worlds of others is an essential characteristic in the ability to identify with the struggles of oppressed peoples. Such concepts as "kingdom of God," justice, freedom, equality, liberation, shalom become the goals of new understandings of what it means to be human. New possibilities of the social order are entertained, and new social identities are fostered. Action relates to the structures of society, the patterns which guide relationships. Sin includes sinful structures, and liberation of the self is entwined with liberation from oppressive social situations.

This ability, in turn, leads to more complex and varied moral thinking. The ability to use categories of equality, fairness, and care allows people to evaluate the rules and regulations of any particular society or group in terms of more universal norms. Yet precisely because of the distortions arising from their abilities in perspective-taking, the principles used often have a class or group bias. This leads to the danger of premature universalization, namely the belief that our perspective is the one true viewpoint which should be extended universally to all others. Yet while some may tend to absolutize their own perspective, others may adopt a principle of relativity in moral thinking, borrowing such phrases as the late Fritz Perls' "You do your thing, and I'll do mine."

Finally, the symbol-making capacity takes an interesting and ironic twist. In one sense symbols often lose their power to evoke the realities they symbolize. In the process of critical thinking the unconscious, affective dimension of symbols may be set aside from the concept or content which animates the symbol. Such a process robs symbols of their power to invoke imaginatively the reality beyond reason and reduces the evocative, emotional aspect of the symbol to a pale reflection of itself. Thus while the decline of uses of incense, large amounts of candles, Gregorian chant and the Latin language seems a step forward in making Roman Catholic congregations more participants in worship than observers of a spectacle, the power of those realities to evoke the divine has not been captured by what has replaced them.

Important concerns for the religious educator, parents, and minister center around how well the traditional belief system can be reinterpreted in light of the new questions. How can the Gospel be related to questions of justice and to the structural evil in institutions? How can we legitimate and foster models of community in parishes, religious communities, study groups? Can we recognize the need for a movement in prayer toward an awareness of God's personal presence and God's liberating action in the everyday world? Will we offer exposure to differing perspectives along with the developing awareness of the limitations of any particular perspective? Will we support these searchers' efforts with care, be with them through failure, and offer encouragement to try again? Churches in the recent past have been more relieved not to have such questioners around. And in some cases, even today, the most creative response we might have is to say with a great deal of grace, "You might need to leave us for a while, but we'll always be open when you return."

FOSTERING THE FAITH GROWTH OF YOUNG ADOLESCENTS

Early adolescence reflects the emergence of more conventional modes of faith as these adolescents move into the beginnings of more critical thinking and the development of strong feelings. In addition the capacity for real friendship is growing while the early adolescent begins to feel the pressures of many different individuals competing for his or her allegiance.

Once again stories play a prominent role in the faith life of early adolescents. Yet now the stories involve the real person who can articulate the developmental needs of the student in an increasingly complex world. The arrival of puberty or its increased intensity for those who experienced its arrival earlier means that the readiness for friendship in which the needs of another can be subordinated to personal needs is coupled with a growing and confusing sexual self-awareness. The models whom the student encounters as teacher, minister, community leader need to become sensitive to the questions which early adolescents may not even vocalize to adults but which plague their feelings and thoughts. Most of these questions center around how "I" appear to others who are significant to me—too tall, too short, too thin, too fat, too intelligent? And the list goes on.

In faith development terms, the basic question around imagination and symbols concerns the literalism which has served to ground the appreciation of concrete reality for the child. This focus upon language would seem academic were it not for our understanding that the language we use forms and shapes the realities we understand, and the ability to envision different meanings to worlds and concepts is related to our ability to pass beyond literalism to symbolic understandings.

For the religious educator and minister one approach to the problem of literalism is a view of Scripture which moves from the discussion of events to the stories of Joseph and his brothers, of Esau and Jacob, of Saul and David, of Ruth and Esther, the multiple relationships of Jesus to his disciples, to Mary Magdalene. All serve to raise questions of friendship, sexuality, personal identity, and family patterns. These stories can begin the discussion for early adolescents whose boredom with Scripture is easily read in glazed eyes and tortured expressions because they are so familiar with the "exploits" of biblical characters. They have emerged from the stage of narrative heroes and heroines and need to look at the lives of real models who exhibit some of the same concerns arising in their own lives. Utilizing the relational patterns found in scripture would be one way to capitalize on the rich texture of Scripture in light of their needs.

Similarly perspective-taking takes on a new dimension during these transition years. The burst of self-awareness among early teens often coincides with an ability to take multiple perspectives into account. Initially this becomes an agonizing realization as the young person struggles with the knowledge that so many different people are looking at him or her in so many different ways *and* expecting so many different things. Parents, teachers, ministers, the peer group, trusted friends, "the opposite sex"—all these individuals and groups confront the seventh and eighth grader's conflicting images of the self. As these struggles emerge more completely into Conventional Faith, the "conventions" and rules of those groups become both guides for acceptable behavior and restraints upon a growing self-awareness.

The feelings for friends offers an opportunity to extend early adolescent's concerns to others outside their own group across ethnic, religious, and even class lines. There are many stories and films which are excellent for this purpose. Again letters and exchanges through international agencies to "pen pals" or school peers in other lands can become ways to overcome stereotypes and the ethnocentrism which each culture develops. Since friendship is emerging for these young people as the most dynamic manifestation of God's love, then speaking of friendship relations even among nations can become a way in which early adolescents can appreciate the idea of uniqueness and self-development of all peoples.

On the level of personal awareness an increased ability at perspective-taking allows students to share faith stories with greater empathy. And it is equally important for the teacher and minister to share at least part of their own stories, both as models of developing Christian lives and as evidence of trust in these young people. In addition reading about the faith journeys of people of other faiths reinforces the sense of God's universal love and of the legitimate differences among peoples in being "faithful" to the transcendent dimension in life.

At the same time the teacher and minister can help students grasp injustice through sharing stories of the pain and suffering of peoples in the United States and the world over. Those presentations can challenge the student to ask the questions of why those sufferings happen and continue. A careful reading of biblical material with emphasis upon the prophets' and Jesus' concern for the poor and oppressed will help students forge the link between their Christian faith and the doing of justice so essential to the full Gospel vision.

Working to enlarge the perspective of the early adolescent also impinges upon their own sense of participation. Not only must they be encouraged to take the perspectives of other members of their immediate and global communities, but opportunities for active participation must emerge if faith is to become a lived reality. Under the guidance of the teacher or minister, early adolescents can be led to develop their own rules about cheating, stealing, cleaning up, helping, and so forth in ways in which build up community. Shared decision-making and greater responsibility for carrying out decisions not only enhance the sense of being trusted but help early adolescents establish themselves in their own eyes and in the perspective of their peers. In an environment of trust and respect early adolescents can support one another in times of trial and can openly confront conflict with each other in ways which lead toward resolutions based on love and justice.

Within the strictly "religious" context, early adolescents can take a much larger share of responsibility for planning and carrying out worship services. Once again, their involvement in worship becomes a way of developing their imaginative understandings of symbols as well as providing direct participation in the central events of the worshiping community. In view of their growing self-awareness of their own needs, they can begin to replace patterns of formal prayer with personal prayers, both as part of the worship service as well as in their own times for prayer. This corresponds to the development of a sense of Jesus as friend beyond this wonder-working which was so powerful at earlier stages.

Certainly some service component will be an effective factor in the movement toward a well-developed Conventional Faith. While the opportunities for community service are endless, teachers or ministers should spend time with the early adolescents in discussing what the service meant to them, how it reflects that Jesus asked them to do, how those helped respond to the service, and a host of other questions. In addition, early adolescents can begin to make the connections in some cases between the social ills they see in their service—poverty, hunger, malnutrition, and so forth—and the causes of those conditions.

FOSTERING THE FAITH GROWTH OF OLDER ADOLESCENTS

Beset by peer pressures, conflict with parental and societal values, the highs and lows of emotional life, the discovery of sexual attraction and romance, encounters with prejudice and stereotype, new ideas and ideals, sudden conversions and loss of faith, the adolescent struggling with new questions about identity and loyalty enters a region of uncharted and often tormenting conflicts. Faith development theory indicates that within this swirling vortex of questions and conflicts adolescents are involved in the difficult transitions from the literalism of childhood through dependence upon conventional understanding of faith (Conventional Faith) on to at least the beginnings of independent faith (Individuative Faith). Now that the adolescent is pulling away from the home environment and developing strong peer relationships, the supports for faith shift dramatically. Within this mobile world of interpersonal relationships and intense feelings, the church can provide a "nurturing environment," continuity and challenge for negotiating some of the difficult transitions of teen years. In this sense the school or parish setting offers much more than a series of classes.

In addition to the conflicts mentioned above, the adolescent experiences new physical development, increased intellectual understandings in early abstract thought, and heightened emotional life. In the area of faith these developments often mean conflicts with the religious understandings of childhood as well as distrust of the structured and seemingly cold patterns of adult beliefs and practices.

At the same time, researchers note that adolescence is a time of deep religious awakening and strong response to the evocative power of symbols, images, and myths. In addition, often during the high school years young people make a decision for or against the religious faith in which they have been socialized. The task for the teacher and minister serving the adolescent is to shape an adult faith to fit the needs and developments of adolescents.

In her provocative study of high school students, Dr. Margaret Gorman found that a functional literalism served as a hindrance to later stages of faith development. In particular such literalism centered around the perceived opposition between religion and science and the literal understanding of biblical materials. What seemed to help in this transition were activities and courses involving an understanding of myth, symbolism, science, evolution, and religion. The strictly cognitive dimensions of these courses could be supplemented by retreat experiences, exposure to older people whose faith life has developed to Conventional Faith and beyond, the powerful experiences of liturgy in which such symbols as light, water, bread, wine, incense are explored. Without such challenges and experiences, the symbolic realities of word and sacrament may be locked in confining literalism.

In addition, the adolescent must develop the ability to step outside his or her own perspective and work to understand the world as others understand it. Certainly one of the most important tools which enables students to take other perspectives is cognitive conflict. Exploring other perspectives within a student's own tradition or looking at other religious traditions through classes, visits, and speakers can serve as ways of helping students articulate their own faith concerns as well as experience different understandings of faith questions from other traditions. Raising critical questions about the ways in which our social structures are arranged or who profits from existing arrangements can challenge students to examine social issues in a broader context and in light of Gospel values. In Dr. Gorman's study, teenagers felt that their teachers and ministers did not address their own faith concerns. In response to questions on death, suffering, injustice, and values, students stated: "Nobody ever asked me about these before." Certainly a fundamental dimension of faith growth from adolescence on is the opportunity and *encouragement* to articulate a personal faith understanding without being judged and the chance to hear the faith stories of others without imposing judgment.

In this context the faith community should offer all participants the opportunity to articulate their faith journeys while listening to those of other community members. Biographies of committed individuals who demonstrate their faith in their own lives can be utilized. And students could be encouraged to write statements of faith which in their senior year they could share with one another in a seminar, in liturgies, or on retreats as testimony and witness to their own growth and faith.

Another aspect of perspective-taking involves the creation of a trusting environment in which such sharing and conflict as described above can take place. In particular that involves the legitimation of conflict and disagreement and the exploration of skills to articulate those disagreements as well as to resolve them. The entire context demands a growing sense of responsibility for one's own ideas and feelings and a care for the ideas and feelings of others.

Certainly students should be involved in the planning and leadership of youth programs as much as possible. Adolescents will feel trusted and thus trusting, when they *experience* being trusted with responsibilities. Besides the obvious example of liturgy in which they choose the readings, prepare the music and carry out much of the service, adolescents should be encouraged to assume responsibilities in leading, preparing classes, teaching other youth, leading retreats, and so forth. This kind of community recognition and support strengthens the emerging self-identity and fidelity necessary to the independent faith stance of the mature, committed believer.

A second dimension of participation involves the growing practice of involving teenagers in programs of community service. From the point of view of faith development, such programs are particularly important inasmuch as they expose adolescents to perspectives and lifestyles different from their own and provide confirmation for personal faith. Furthermore such programs involve the teenagers in a sense of justice on a level at which they can understand the meaning of justice best, that is, in terms of fairness in interpersonal relations. Adolescents also gain a strong sense of responsibility for and with others from these experiences. The teenager's overriding concern with self expands to include the problems of others and the problems of the world at large.

To further serve growth in faith, the program must also incorporate some reflection upon service experiences. Through discussion, adolescents can support one another, analyze their successes and failures, see the relationship of their work to the larger framework of the Church's mission, and begin to develop a more critical understanding of the ways in which those whom they serve are not being served by the larger society and why.

If faith in the early high school years is emerging from the narrative, literal form and searching for an embodiment in real adult models, then every adult leader becomes a faith model, of "bad faith" as well as "good faith." Placing the total responsibility for youth ministry upon the "religious teacher" or "youth minister" misses the complex ways in which teenagers perceive the reality of church. Further if the adults in those settings are models of faith, then those models must be seen as worthy of the trust and loyalty of the adolescent and must show in their lives that they trust in and are loyal to the God of the Christian tradition.

Just as importantly, the religious educator and youth minister as models of faith are carriers of faith histories and visions which can be shared with one another and with young people. If we accept the findings of a recent study of faith development that biographies served as an important element in the development of faith, especially in the movement toward stage four, then we can understand how the examples of people who have a sense of their own identity and who are faithful to their visions provide powerful faith models for others. In addition, younger teenagers could benefit from hearing the faith stories of the older teenagers who are themselves models. Such sharings would provide confirmation of faithfulness in a variety of ways and would stimulate the challenge to an individual's faith perspective which is necessary for any development.

A note of cautious realism creeps in at this point. For a fundamental question concerns the operative concepts of church which inform the educational program. If the primary image is that of church as embodiment of rules and regulations which foster loyalty to the institution, then the faithful person is one who conforms to those rules. Violation of the rules and disloyalty to the institution constitute "unfaithfulness." The painful and difficult transition from Conventional Faith to Individuative Faith will not find nourishment in such a conforming environment. In this regard a faith "rebellion" or lapse into "a-theism" may be a response of an independent faith style against the constrictions of a very conventional, dogmatic faith.

If we turn to the model of church as community, a different process for faith emerges. Church in this sense would mean the web of relationships which confirm and challenge the adolescent. Here the community provides for the older adolescent a support for the kind of individual challenging of the conventional "faith" world which leads to an independent faith in young adulthood. Further this concept of the Church as community also implies that students must be trusted to make decisions governing their own relationships. The faith development model demands an even greater context of trust on the part of religious educators and youth ministers and calls for a faith-sharing dimension which could permeate the classroom, retreats, liturgies, and decision-making processes.

CHAPTER 4

Perspectives on the Changing American Family

Richard P. Olsen and Joe H. Leonard Jr.

We write on behalf of the changing American family. Our belief is the Church can vitally serve the wide diversity of family types in our society. It can also help families adjust to changes yet to come. We believe this will be a marvelous extension of the mission of the Church. In turn, changing families will enrich the life of the Church immeasurably.

At present, opinion is mixed regarding the dialogue between church and changing families. Some families bear witness to the sensitivity their church showed them when they experienced change. However, all too few families feel this way. More often, churches that offer much to families in general become paralyzed when dealing with some of the newly evolving family types. This paralysis stems from two sources: lack of comfort with the expertise about each family type's unique dynamics and needs, and uncertainty about faith perspectives on changing families.

To respond to the first of those uncertainties, we will explore many of these changing family types and their unique needs. We will identify ministries with these family types that have been undertaken and will make suggestions for other possibilities.

However, as we do this, we need to explore some other questions. What are the facts about families in America today? How did their present situation come about? What are their Christian responses to these facts? How does one apply biblical teaching about family life to the present scene? We

need both a historical perspective and a biblical-theological perspective. This essay is our effort to provide them.

A number of changes have taken place in families over the last century or two. Each is important; taken together, their impact is powerful. All these changes interact with one another, but for purposes of discussion we shall isolate them. What are these changes?

URBANIZATION

First of all, the family moved from the farm to the city. In 1790, the rural population (farmers and nonfarmers) of the United States was nearly 95% of the total population. The U.S. Bureau of the Census did not begin distinguishing farmers from rural nonfarmers in its reports until 1880. Their figures from that time on reveal the extent of this change. In 1880, 43.8% of Americans were farmers. By 1920 this had shrunk to 30.1%. It was 23.2% in 1940 and 8.7% in 1960 (U.S. Bureau of the Census 457). By 1980 it was 3.3%. In two centuries, the settings for the American family changed from 95% rural to 97% predominantly urban (or at least nonfarm)! Events of the 1980s indicate that the farming population will shrink even more. Further, farming itself has changed tremendously over this period. Once a labor-intensive occupation, where the efforts of many family members were needed, farming today is a capital-intensive venture, requiring the labor of very few family members.

CHANGING NEEDS AND EXPECTATIONS

The change from a rural to an urban population leads to a second observation. The needs and expectations of family members have changed. Some family tasks and roles have evolved, some have vanished, and others have become more prominent. In those earlier farm settings, the needs, tasks, and roles of husband and wife were separate and quite definite. The man was expected to provide the raw materials for creating a home, food, and clothing. He was to protect the family. The woman was to preserve and cook food, weave and sew cloth, care for the home, and bear and raise children. For the most part, the test of an effective family was functional: Were the needed tasks for family survival performed? If so, it was a successful family (Barbeau 2).

Much of this had changed by the twentieth century, when persons increasingly contracted marriages for personal and emotional needs. Warm community and communication, an atmosphere for personal growth (for the couple, the family, and its individual members), a supportive emotional climate, a satisfying romantic-sexual relationship—these were some of the hopes for marriages. At the same time, it was expected that families would be places to experience personal freedom, individualism, and sexual equality. Some family functions and expectations decreased; others rose dramatically, although potential partners were offered little preparation in the interpersonal task of fulfilling such high hopes for marriage.

SELF-SELECTION OF MARRIAGE PARTNERS

Third, the process of mate selection changed. To be more accurate, the changes in this area that began to emerge in

preceding centuries continued and accelerated. Both historically and cross-culturally, the family network had influenced or controlled the choice of marital partners for young adults. While this was already on the decline in Europe in the eighteenth and nineteenth centuries, the decline accelerated greatly on American soil (Shorter 65). Family influence over mate selection was offered informally, and even this waned. As time passed, more and more young adults moved away from their families of origin. Work, education, or military service took them to new settings. There they selected their own marital partners, based on friendship, compatibility, romance, and sexual attraction.

DEMOGRAPHIC CHANGES

Fourth, changes in death rate and life expectancy had an impact on families. Infant and child mortality declined through the nineteenth and twentieth centuries. One study showed, for example, that a baby's chance to survive its first year rose from 80% in the late eighteenth century to 99% in the late twentieth century (Greeley 21). Therefore, it was not necessary for parents to have many children in order to assure the survival of a few. With growing knowledge of contraception it was possible to control fertility. Women began having fewer children and having them later.

The life expectancy of both men and women increased. For men, the expected life span increased by about 14 years from the mid-nineteenth century to the mid-twentieth. For women, the life expectancy almost doubled (Reuther 1984, 29).

All these demographic facts had an impact on the family. Couples spent less of their lives together raising young children. In the late-twentieth century couples spent only 18% of their married life raising young children, compared to 54% a century before (Bane 25). A lifetime commitment to marriage became a bigger, longer responsibility. In the eighteenth century, a typical young couple (groom age 25 and bride age 20) had a 57% chance of both surviving for 25 years of marriage. By the late twentieth century, a similar-age couple had a 92% chance of both surviving. The average possible duration of a marriage nearly doubled from about 25 years to about 50 years (Sullivan 20). This meant that couples had a better chance of surviving to "empty nest" years after children had left.

Increased life expectancy also meant there were fewer orphans. (Many institutions created for orphans found it necessary to find other uses.) This also meant that more persons lived to be grandparents thus adding that dimension to family life. The larger number of elderly persons in society brought about another development. Their status changed—from socially honored to burdensome on society (Greeley 18ff; Bane 25; Reuther 29).

THE SEPARATION OF SEX AND REPRODUCTION

Fifth, both the technology and behavior of sex changed. Sex had always had a double purpose—personal enjoyment and perpetuation of the human race. Technology separated these two purposes, at least in part.

Scientific advances promised the possibility of sexual intercourse without fear of pregnancy. To replace older, cruder methods of birth control, new ones were developed. For many, the pill and the IUD increased the convenience and aesthetics of the sexual experience. There was even research into a "morning after" pill. Increasing numbers of those desiring permanent freedom from pregnancies chose tubal ligations and vasectomies. An option for those whose methods of first-line birth control failed was the legalization of abortion in 1973. Though this alternative was stridently debated and severely attacked, it was widely used. In the 1980s there were about 1.3 million abortions a year in the United States.

It must be noted that these various birth control methods and their use were far from perfect in effectiveness. In the 1980s there were a half million out-of-wedlock births a year. Most of these, according to the mothers, were unwanted and unplanned.

For a time, the effectiveness of antibiotic medicines in curing venereal diseases reduced yet other fears. This trend ended rather abruptly with the appearance of new diseases for which no cure existed. One of these, herpes, was rather mild in consequences; the other, AIDS, was not. A painful, costly illness followed by death was the grim prospect for those in whom this virus became active. Still, a good many people trusted the technology of their culture to provide safe, curable, childless sex.

At the same time, technological options were being made available for persons who desired conception without intercourse. Or, more accurately, possibilities of conception were offered for those for whom intercourse with a partner had failed to produce a pregnancy. In vitro fertilization, surrogate mothers, sperm banks, and artificial insemination offered promise to persons with problems of infertility. It was soon discovered that none of these were ideal solutions. A whole new body of law began to emerge over the rights of surrogate mothers and the persons with whom they might make contracts. While the number of persons using these options was rather small, media coverage increased public awareness and consideration of them as options.

Such changes occasioned these questions: If intercourse can be separated from conception and conception from intercourse, what is the meaning of the sexual experience? At what stage in one's life may it begin? Between whom may it take place, appropriately and responsibly? Is the decision to engage in it as serious a matter as it once was? What religious norms are available to guide us in this changed situation? What are the values that apply in this age? Historian Edward Shorter, who has studied European and American families over recent centuries, perceives a compelling drive toward liberation from the sexual controls that family and community formerly imposed on young persons. By the 1960s "the chances were very high that young people who felt attached to each other would extend their relationship into the sexual domain" (Shorter 119). This trend has accelerated. A Lou Harris poll in the late eighties revealed that, by age 17, 57% report having had intercourse.

GAINS FOR WOMEN

Sixth, the women's movement gained increased strength and vigor, and many values from this movement also made their impact on the family, such as the four that follow.

1. Women are not "biologically destined" to be only in the mother-homemaker role.
2. All aspects of society and all occupations should be open equally to men and women. Full development to the extent of one's potentialities should be available for all.
3. When both husband and wife are employed, there is no predetermined role prescription for the division of labor among them. Child-rearing, food preparation, and house care and maintenance should be negotiated between the couple on an equal basis.
4. All persons should be free of violence in sexual and domestic situations. Rape, incest, sexual abuse, and physical-emotional-spiritual abuse should be squarely faced. Victims should be protected and abusers detected, prosecuted, restrained, and cured, if possible.

The most widespread factor contributing to these changes was the increased presence of women in the work force. In the year 1900, 5.6% of all women were formally employed. This grew to 50% by 1975 (Stearns 118). It is estimated that by 1995, women will account for 60% of the labor force (*Wall Street Journal* 11/26/85, 1). The widespread presence of women outside the home brought a need for adjustment in child care arrangements, in distribution of power in the family, and in male-female roles.

CHANGING VIEWS OF MARRIAGE

Seventh, organized religion and other institutions experienced diminished influence as a stabilizing influence on marriage. In the twentieth century there has evolved increasing tension between two views of the married state. Is marriage basically dedicated to the welfare and stability of society? Does it have divine blessing and divine sanctions? Or is it a private agreement between two people for their enjoyment and satisfaction? The famed Lutheran theologian and martyr Dietrich Bonhoeffer wrote from his prison cell to those contemplating marriage, "Your love is your own private possession, but marriage is more than something personal, it is a status, an office" (quoted in Barbeau 39). Increasingly, however, couples saw marriage as a two-person contract that could be terminated when either party desired.

SHRINKING FAMILY SIZE

Eighth, the average size of families decreased considerably, from 5.76 children per family in the late nineteenth century to 3.06 in the 1970s (Bane 45). By 1986 the U.S. Bureau of the Census reported that the size of the average household—adults and children living together—was 2.71 people, the lowest since the start of census records. This in turn brought about other directions in family life. The smaller number of children makes more care possible for each child. Infants were given much more attention in the twentieth century, on the average, than in preceding centuries. Children are often valued for themselves, rather than as part of a large family work force. Children today are much more apt to be raised by parents and other adults than by siblings.

NEW STUDIES OF THE FAMILY

Ninth, the body of knowledge about children and families increased. Reliable information about how children develop and what their needs are was more widely disseminated. A new discipline, family therapy, emerged. This discipline saw an individual's problems as likely to be symptomatic of an entire family system. Thus treatment was offered for the whole family, not just an "identified patient." The topic of effective communication—within the family and without—was researched and taught. Childhood development, communication, and family therapy are still young and developing disciplines. Nevertheless, they now offer more helpful information and assistance than most families have the time and energy to use. Excellent tools for family ministry are emerging.

INCREASE IN NUCLEAR FAMILIES

Tenth, American families have become increasingly mobile. Family historians do not entirely agree that in earlier times there was more emphasis on extended families. However, it cannot be questioned that with many extended families today spread over several states or nations, there must be increasing reliance on the nuclear family. Not only may grandparents and other kinfolk live at a distance, friendships are often disturbed as the nuclear family uproots itself in pursuit of a better job, education, or other opportunity. As one observer noted, America has become a nation of strangers (Packard).

GROWTH OF THE MASS MEDIA

Eleventh, several new media forms were invented and invaded the home. Radio, television, movies, video and audio cassettes, records, and tapes, as well as books, magazines, and newspapers, exerted powerful influences on families. As media pioneer Marshall McLuhan noted, "The family circle has widened. The whirlpool of

information fathered by electronic media . . . far surpasses any possible influence Mom and Dad can now bring to bear. Character is no longer shaped only by two earnest, fumbling experts. Now all the world's a sage" (quoted by Marx and Quesnell 43–44).

RESULTING CHANGES IN FAMILY STYLES

Scholars of family life, aware of these influences, debated whether family life would endure beyond the last quarter of the twentieth century. While they were discussing this possibility, families muddled into an amazing variety of family styles. Here are nine notable changes.

1. The "traditional" American family— intact marriage, father employed outside the home, mother not, at least two children—has shrunk to about 10% of all families.

2. Persons who marry have a lesser chance that they will stay married till death. The Skolnicks noted that "the freedom of modern family life is brought at the price of fragility and instability in family ties" (12). On the other hand, as some observed, approximately the same percentage of married partners experience premature separation as in earlier centuries. The only difference is that death used to be what separated couples. In the twentieth century, it is more likely to be divorce.

3. An increasing number of persons raise children as single parents. At the same time, a larger percentage of children live with at least one parent. In earlier times, a single parent was more likely to put children in a home for foundlings, an orphanage, or a foster home. In the twentieth century single parents raise children themselves.

4. Divorced partners are more likely to hear the court assign joint custody of children. This means that two adults who feel they can't live together will

still have to meet regularly. They need to make joint decisions about their children and transfer them back and forth between two homes.

5. A large proportion of those who divorce marry new partners and enter into stepfamilies. Frequently such persons leave one difficult family relationship and enter into one even more complex. Two contracting partners might come with children, varying ties to ex-spouses, ex-in-laws, and more. A larger, extremely complex network of persons will need to start all over again to build a family-type community.

6. In the vast majority of couples, both partners are employed. Skills are needed in negotiating the use of those scarcest of family resources, energy and time. Many employment situations (health care, police, fire protection, sales in shopping malls, factory shift work) have invaded family schedules. As a result, there is less time to be together. Persons in career military service have learned to adjust to constant changes in togetherness and separation. Married persons who discover that career opportunities call them to different places become commuter couples.

7. A significant number of people marry partners from other religions, ethnic groups, or nations, thus adding still other dimensions to their marriages. Some adoptive parents welcome international or special-needs children into their home.

8. Many couples delay having children, have fewer children, or decide against having any at all. Such couples have begun to redefine marriage without children.

9. Some people elect singleness as a choice. Others, single or married,

admit other people's children into their families, permanently or temporarily.

These changes are not passing fads. They are part of the social landscape in the last decade of the twentieth century and beyond.

WORKS CITED

Bane, Mary Jo. *Here to Stay: American Families in the Twentieth Century.* New York: Basic Books, 1976.

Barbeau, Clayton C., Ed. *Future of the Family.* New York: Bruce Publishing Co., 1971.

Greeley, Andrew, Ed. *The Family in Crisis or in Transition: A Sociological and Theological Perspective.* New York: Seabury Press, 1979.

Marx, Paul and Jack Quesnell. "Family Life: The Agony and the Ecstasy." *Future of the Family.* Ed. Clayton C. Barbeau. New York: Bruce Publishing Co., 1971.

Packard, Vance. *A Nation of Strangers.* New York: David McKay Co., 1972.

Reuther, Rosemary. "Feminism, Church and Family in the 1980s." *American Baptist Quarterly*, 13 (March 1984): 21–30.

Shorter, Edward. *The Making of the Modern Family.* New York: Basic Books, 1975.

Skolnicks, Arlene and Jerome H. Skolnick. *Intimacy, Family, and Society.* Boston: Little, Brown, and Co., 1974.

Stearns, Peter N. *Be a Man!* New York: Homes and Meier Publishers, 1979.

Sullivan, Teresa. "Longer Lives and Life-long Relations: A Life Table Exegesis." *The Family in Crisis or in Transition: A Sociological and Theological Perspective.* Ed. Andrew Greeley. New York: Seabury Press, 1979.

U.S. Bureau of the Census. *Historical Statistics of the United States, Colonial Times to 1970.* Washington, DC: U.S. Government Printing Office, 1975.

CHAPTER 5

A Perspective on Teenagers and Divorce

Randy Smith

Divorce is a crisis event for children of all ages. Divorce is usually preceded by painful and disturbing experiences in the family. When we began ministering to children of divorcing families, we learned to expect an emotionally intense and challenging experience.

When you begin to deal with children of divorce, you come face to face with sin and sickness in our society—selfishness, affairs, violence, alcohol and drug abuse, and more. You also encounter the intense emotions of pain, anger, and fear that go with these problems.

After years of listening to teens tell their stories, we learned that divorce experiences are as diverse as families, ranging from quiet to raging, from proximate to scattered throughout the country, from reasonably calm to painfully violent. To get a balanced perspective on the teen's experience of divorce and to help us remember that divorce is merely one part of an ongoing process, we talk about divorce as an experience of pain, of gain, and of change.

DEALING WITH PAIN IN DIVORCE

No matter what the details of the story, we have noticed that to one degree or another teenagers are hurt and disillusioned by divorce. Divorce brings pain and the pain of divorce takes many forms. Most children, whether perceived to be handling a divorce

well or not, feel abandoned, neglected, abused, and smothered when their parents divorce. They are also left with a dysfunctional model of marriage that can set them up for marital failure themselves.

ABANDONMENT

When a significant person in a teen's life just leaves, that teen experiences an intense feeling of loss. Commonly a child's father moves away after the divorce and rarely visits his children. Perhaps his employer transfers him, or maybe his new wife wishes to live elsewhere. Sometimes a man tries to escape feelings of pain or guilt by putting physical distance between himself and his teenagers and ex-wife. The cause is not as important to them as the fact that they feel they have been abandoned.

NEGLECT

Another experience common to children of divorce, neglect, happens when parents are so caught up in their conflict that they don't pay enough attention to their teenagers' developmental needs for affirmation, nurturing, correction, and guidance. Parents sometimes neglect even their children's fundamental needs for food, clothing, shelter, and medical attention.

The process of a marriage breaking down and the subsequent divorce drains energy from the adults, energy that is normally expended in parenting. Parents obsessed and worn down by their conflict are emotionally unavailable for their teenagers. Even if they are handling it well emotionally, a parent who manages a single-parent home and works full-time has less energy for nurturing children. For many teens the parent who most often feels overwhelmed in the divorce is Mom. She is often depressed and overloaded, and neglect commonly occurs, despite her best intentions.

ABUSE

Whether behavior as routine as yelling at children, an act as denounced as sexual molestation of a child, or anything in between, abuse escalates during the stress of marital conflict. Abuse is a parent being mean to a child. It can include yelling at children, harshly criticizing them, calling them names, hitting or slapping them in a passion, allowing children to see adult sexual behavior, or actual sexual molestation by the parent. Because of the complex web abuse weaves around the entire family, we often refer to a professional counselor abused teens who hint of their circumstances during the workshop.

During the stressful breakdown of a marriage, adults sometimes regress into inappropriate, abusive behavior. Major fights can erupt, leading a parent to scream at and even hit a teen. Sometimes the teen hits back, and a major fight ensues. We have worked with adolescents who have been beaten, kicked, and even thrown through glass doors.

Parents who don't yell and hit their children may abuse them in other ways, such as not shielding their own promiscuous sexual behavior from them. If Mom or Dad brings dates home to spend the night, for instance, they may neglect or refuse to be private during sexual encounters. Some parents even attempt to relate sexually with a child as a way to escape their own feelings of loneliness, fear, and inadequacy.

OVERCONTROL OR ENMESHMENT

In their loneliness or anxiety about divorcing, parents often pursue inappropriate closeness with a young person, displaying emotions that overwhelm the teen, in an effort to manipulate the teen into comforting or taking care of them. Parents may turn to a child instead of themselves or a spouse of a friend to meet their primary emotional needs. The parent may overly restrict the child from peer activities as a way of insuring time with the child. Hurting parents also may pursue a best-friend relationship with the young person. Such a relationship sacrifices appropriate distance and authority.

Or, in trying to protect a child from the emotional pain and feelings of failure they themselves are experiencing, parents may smother or overprotect the child. Parents try to make up for the divorce by making everything perfect for the child. When parents respond to the stress of divorce by tightening their control over the children and demanding perfection of them, rules become rigid and school grades and other "performances" become crucial and pressured. It is as if parents try to cope with the failure of divorce by making sure their children succeed for them.

DYSFUNCTIONAL MODELING

Children learn powerful lessons by witnessing their parents' behavior. The way their parents treat each other is a young person's primary model of an intimate relationship. Unfortunately, children of divorce often see dysfunctional patterns of communication, physical assaults, unfaithfulness, betrayal, deception, and aggressive litigation. It hurts children to see someone they love being hurt. When parents hurt each other, they teach their children that hurting each other is okay.

The above patterns of pain in divorce—feeling abandoned, neglected, abused, enmeshed, as well as witnessing a dysfunctional marriage—leave children of divorce with powerful pain, fear, and hurt. The bottom-line message they receive through a divorce is that they don't really matter to their parents. They begin to question their own value—"If I were really worth loving and protecting, my parents would stop the fighting and the divorce, because they must know it's tearing me up inside." Since the fighting doesn't stop and the divorce becomes final, low self-esteem emerges in a young person.

DEALING WITH GAINS IN DIVORCE

Most stories of divorce that we hear from teens fit the above painful patterns. Yet that is not the entire picture. Some teenagers also report patterns of gain—advantages that emerge from the divorce.

PEACE AND SAFETY

The most common positive report we hear from young people is that divorce has separated them from the troubled, hurtful parent. Children who with their mother move away from a violent, alcoholic father, for instance, celebrate the relief from his abuse. Even though the separation may not have been easy, the children say they feel grateful and happy that it is over. We hear this response most often from teenagers who clashed with a stepparent whom the mom married impulsively. When he is finally gone, they are glad.

For some children it is not so much separation from abuse directed at them that relieves them. It is experiencing what the young people simply call peace. The war between their parents is over—or at least it is no longer in their face every day. If the battle continues, it happens in the courts or over the phone.

BETTER PARENTING

Another gain we often hear is that some parents actually make changes in themselves through the process of divorcing, and after separation they each become better parents to their children. Fathers in particular sometimes make an effort at improved parenting when they are on their own. When they visit their children they actively listen to them, communicate with them, and enjoy doing things together with them—which is a new experience for many fathers and teens. Some adults value their children more highly since they are "all they have."

Parents sometimes grow personally in ways that can be helpful to teens. They may seek counseling, attend self-help workshops, or go to church. The loss they feel because of divorce may propel them into personal evaluation and both emotional and spiritual growth. Consequently they become more mature adults and better parents, models, and companions.

FUNCTIONAL FAMILIES

A final gain that sometimes comes out of divorce is the addition of a positive stepparent and/or siblings through remarriage. Some adults do make better choices the next time around, and some teens do get new families they really like and with whom they bond. Though the percentage is small, this gain is real for those young people.

Gains, however, are often mixed with and overshadowed by the patterns of pain mentioned previously. Teens feel confused that one day they hate the divorce and the next day they are relieved it happened. We try to help them see that divorce is not black or white, that there can be both gains and pains, and that they can accept their experiences and feelings instead of fighting with them.

DEALING WITH CHANGES IN DIVORCE

Divorce brings changes. Among the adjustments that adolescents must navigate are changes in parent-teen relationships, changes in family communication, and changes in environment.

CHANGES IN PARENT-TEEN RELATIONSHIPS— THE CUSTODIAL PARENT

Children of divorce end up living with one parent, called the custodial parent; the other parent becomes the visiting parent. (While the practice of split custodial parenting is increasing, it is still relatively uncommon.) When teens begin to live with a custodial parent (usually Mom), they often take responsibility for the chores Dad used to do—lawn-mowing, taking out the trash, cleaning the garage. And since Mom generally has to start working outside the home, added chores might also include housecleaning, caring for younger siblings, and cooking.

Most teens resent these extra duties, but some feel pride and satisfaction in helping out and gaining more competency. Teens need help to accept willingly some extra responsibility in a single-parent home without having to miss too many of their age-appropriate activities. After-school sports and dating should not be automatically out of the question because of the divorce.

Teens in a single-parent home not only take extra responsibility around the house, they also assume some of the emotional roles of the departed spouse. The custodial parent may lean on his or her children for emotional support, reassurance, affection, counsel, or companionship. While teens sometimes welcome the added closeness in a time of loss and stress, too much emotional responsibility can become an inappropriate burden for a teen to carry, frequently provoking withdrawal on the teen's part and even defiance in response to a perception of smothering.

Teens need help learning how to care about their parents' feelings without assuming a comforter role more appropriate for an adult peer, such as a friend, pastor, or counselor. Brief talks and affection are enough for teens to give their parents. Adolescents need to learn to express their feelings of discomfort if their parents cross the line from appropriate companionship to smothering dependency.

CHANGES IN PARENT-TEEN RELATIONSHIPS— THE VISITING PARENT

A teen's relationship with a visiting parent (usually Dad) is changed as well. The bond is now based on periodic visits that are often complicated by conflicting schedules, competition, or logistics (where to sleep in Dad's tiny apartment, for example). The bond may be challenged by fear of abandonment, pain of separation (especially when the pair are separated by a long distance), resentment toward him for leaving home, and discomfort and anxiety because of a growing alienation. Teens most successfully overcome problems with the visiting parent when they say plainly what they are feeling and what they want the arrangements for visits to be. Along with asking for what they need, teens must also give and take on the arrangements in light of their parent's needs and limits. We try to help the teenagers tell the difference between significant needs and changes that they can live without. Things like having their own room with a few of their things at Dad's place, being able to see him without his new girl friend, or doing things with their own friends while staying at Dad's rank among the significant needs teens should discuss with their parents.

CHANGES IN FAMILY DIALOGUE— COMMUNICATION TRIANGLES

When parents who separate have a communication breakdown, they commonly convey verbal and emotional messages to each other through their children. There are three ways in which teens get caught in these communication triangles.

As messengers: "You tell your dad for me..." followed by an angry message. Threats or messages about money or feelings should be communicated directly between parents or through an adult third party, such as an attorney.

As spies: "Who's your mom seeing tonight?" might be followed by third-degree questioning. Parents may try to garner information about dating patterns, spending habits, moral behavior, and more. Children ought to be left out of any issue that is part of the parents' ongoing warfare.

As dumping grounds: "If you only knew what she did to me. Let me tell you..." Many times parents vent their pain and anger in front of their children. Since teens still need and love both parents, it hurts them when one parent puts the other one down. It can also create loyalty battles for the child, as if each parent is trying to get the child to love him or her most.

The role of intermediary is stressful for teens, because the messages are usually full of intense hostility and distrust. If the parents need a mediator, it is a role better assumed by adult peers or professionals. Teens need help escaping communication triangles.

Petite Amy, a seventh grader, was Mom's money collector. Each visit with her dad on the first of the month was completed only when he handed her the check to bring to Mom. Being the check carrier pressured Amy into feeling resentment toward both parents. On one hand she felt that her mother used her to communicate a subtle message of disdain intended to hurt her dad. On the other hand her dad sometimes put her off and said he would mail the check in a couple days, just to show her mom he was still in control. We encouraged her to let Mom know how pressured she felt and to ask Mom to procure the support money some other way.

CHANGES IN ENVIRONMENT

Divorce almost always requires that teens adjust to new homes, neighborhoods, schools, parents, and siblings. They have to get used to how much money is now available for needs and discretionary spending, which relatives they won't be visiting any more, and what's okay to tell the custodial parent about their visit with the other parent (and what will only start a fight) and who their parents are dating. Endings and beginnings abound in this time of transition.

Change, whether good or bad, brings stress. Multiple changes increase stress. And unwelcome, uncontrolled change adds even more stress. Bad stress generates anxiety, fear, fatigue, and the feeling of being overwhelmed. In our workshops we teach teenagers to recognize the amount of change and therefore the amount of stress that they have in their lives. They brainstorm a list of losses and gains they have experienced because of the divorce. Then we tell them that anyone going

through that amount of change experiences anxiety and irritability. We talk about handling stress through proper rest, food, recreation, and, most of all, through dealing with their feelings.

DENIAL AND SHAME: AVOIDING THE EXTREMES

Two mistakes sidetrack effective divorce recovery for teens: the first is minimizing the impact of the divorce; the second is overemphasizing the experience. Adults minimize the divorce by saying things like, "The divorce simply has to be, so keep busy and don't let it bother you." Some people choose to believe that divorce is no big deal, that they will roll with the punches, get through the experience, and move on. Parents who will not deal adequately with their own divorce experience often hold this view. They want their children to share in their own denial of the painful effects of divorce. The truth is, divorce is a dramatic crisis that significantly shapes the life of a child.

Overplaying the effects of the divorce is the opposite error. Adults, even Christian leaders, tend to think of a child as ruined or badly scarred by divorce. These well-meaning people perceive split families as key evidence of the decline of our culture. Children of divorce are thus shamed in a way similar to incest survivors or children of alcoholics. In our workshops we neither shame teens nor pity them. We do not use the term "broken," for instance, when we refer to families. Families in divorce are not broken in the sense that they cease to function—they continue to work, love, argue, communicate, celebrate Christmas, and so on. Families are living, breathing entities that require loving care and spiritual nourishment to thrive. Although the impact of divorce is significant, children from divorced families don't deserve to be pitied, shamed, or labeled as hopeless. Children of divorce can and do recover to health and wholeness.

In *Surviving the Breakup*, Judith Wallerstein, the principal investigator of the Children of Divorce Project, describes her study of the effect of divorce on children and teens. This study, which did much to remove the sense of hopeless doom often associated with children of divorce, followed a large sample of children of divorce over a period of several years. By the end of the study period, one-third of them recovered to a normal, positive development. A second third struggled, but seemed to work through to resolution with good and bad times. A final third continued to have significant struggles for years.

So two-thirds of these children of divorce worked through the crisis successfully. Why did many young people do well? Part of the answer is that some intact families can be more abusive and destructive to children than divorced ones. Divorce brings loss and abandonment, but ongoing dysfunctional families bring continuous abuse—emotional, physical, or both—to children. Separation from an abusive or self-destructive adult or family system can actually help a child's development. (Of course, divorce does not always bring the relief of resolution. Some families maintain the pain in the changed family formation.)

Divorce is a big deal, and it hits young people dramatically; but it is not determinative and crippling. They can and do deal with it. They grow, learn, and move on—especially when they receive appropriate help and assistance.

Wallerstein's more recent book, *Second Chances: Men, Women and Children a Decade After Divorce*, reinforces the troubling, long-term effect of divorce on the children she studied. She notes what she calls "sleeper effects" (hidden problems that appear later). Being unable to trust and unwilling to be intimate, experiencing low self-esteem, and fearing failure are some of the significant struggles of these children later in life. But many made significant breakthroughs and growth through the hidden problems as they sought help to confront the issues.

DIVORCE: A PROCESS NOT AN EVENT

Children from divorced families not only need to recover form the impact of the event of a divorce, but from living—often for years—in a painful family system. A divorce usually begins with years of often intense marital discord and family conflict, leading to a separation, the subsequent unraveling of two adult lives, and the establishment of two new family systems. Children are impacted each step along the process. We are not dealing with divorce alone, but also with the effects of dysfunctional family systems, single-parent families, and blended families. This means the range of issues for young people is broad.

SUMMARY

Knowing what teens experience and feel because of their parents' divorce helps you effectively walk with a teen through divorce recovery. Teenagers go through similar patterns of pain—abandonment, neglect, abuse, over-control, and witnessing a failed marriage. But they are willing to acknowledge gains as well as losses—things like peace, better relationships with parents, and sometimes positive stepfamilies. Divorce brings changes to parent-teen relationships, family communication, and the young person's environment. To be most helpful to teens in divorce, neither minimize nor overplay the effects of the divorce on children, and treat divorce as a process that includes living in a painful family system, the divorce event, and the pressures of the altered family structure.

WORKS CITED

Wallerstein, Judith. *Second Chances: Men, Women and Children a Decade After Divorce*. New York: Ticknor & Fields/Houghton Mifflin, Co, 1989.
_____. *Surviving the Breakup: How Children and Parents Cope with Divorce*. Hobart, IN: Basic Books, 1982.

CHAPTER 6

A Perspective on Remarried Families

Richard P. Olson and Joe H. Leonard Jr.

Remarriage has become an important new reality of family life in the late twentieth century. The sheer number of such families compels our attention. The complicated dynamics of the blended family units that result where there are children deserve sensitive pastoral care and support.

Of all marriage now being contracted, 46% include at least one person who was previously married. In 1970 the comparable figure was only 30% (U.S. Bureau of the Census 83). Frank Furstenberg notes, "Given present levels of remarriage—about three-fourths of all females and five-sixth of all males reenter marriage after divorce—it seems likely that no less than a fourth of all adults will have wed more than once by midlife" (Furstenberg 444). If the rate of divorce does not decline, the probability that an individual will live in a remarried family either while growing up or as an adult is close to, if not greater than, one in two (Furstenberg 444). It is estimated there are 15 million stepchildren under the age of 18. One observer notes that 35% of all children in America will live some part of their lives in a stepfamily (Sukosky 14).

Remarriage today is different from remarriage in the past. Throughout history there have been numbers of remarriages, but until this century almost all remarriages followed widowhood. For example, in the Plymouth Colony about one-third of all men and one-fourth of all women who lived full lifetimes after the death of a spouse remarried. There was little divorce in that colony. Even as late as the 1920s, in the United States, more remarriages occurred among widowed people than among the divorced (Cherlin 637). But by 1984, at least three-fourths of all remarrying brides and remarrying grooms had been previously divorced (U.S. Department of Health and Human Services Table 1–28.) The existence of living ex-spouses is a relatively new factor in remarriages.

The statistics on the fragility of remarriages are equally staggering. One pair of observers notes that the divorce rate is 30 to 40% for first marriages, 60% for second marriages, 80% for third marriages, and 90% for fourth marriages (Houmes and Meier). Other estimates are a bit more optimistic, but all would admit that those observations are not far off the mark. Yet another pair notes that 40% of all second marriages end in divorce within four years! (Visher and Visher 1980, xix). Persons in remarriages face a most difficult task, and particularly so in the early years of that remarriage.

Such information may be hard to believe for the faithful church leader. Perhaps one does not note anywhere nearly that proportion of divorces and remarriages among the members of one's congregation. There might be several reasons for this. Persons often drop out of sight when marital breakup occurs. They may go to a different church or to none. If so, they may lose the support of the church family through that difficult time. People who join a church may well not publicize the fact that they are a remarried family because of the stigma of divorce and the fear of rejection. Many remarried families are entirely churchless. They may not believe that any church has a place for them or anything to offer them.

METAPHORS FOR REMARRIED FAMILIES

What is the situation for remarried families? We will attempt to describe it by using a series of images. These images are not meant to demean persons or remarriage. We have the highest respect for those couples who have persisted to make their remarriages happy and enduring unions—they are among the pioneers of our society, and we have much to learn from them. Rather, these images suggest complex tasks for remarrieds and note that support for these families is often inadequate.

A SHAKY BUILDING WITH SOME OF THE PILLARS MISSING

Remarried families are deprived of some very important supports: a language to talk about themselves; legal precedents; parenting patterns; and supportive societal norms.

In noting this fact, one sociologist, Andrew Cherlin, calls remarriage an "incomplete institution" (634–650). By institution the sociologist means those enduring, predictable, habitual, reliable behaviors that exist in a relationship. (One's social setting teaches and reinforces these behaviors, until everyone "knows" how you are supposed to act.) For example, we all know what a mother is and what a father is, and how they are supposed to behave, with what authority and power. While there are variations, the roles are quite clearly defined in our society. The presence of such habitualized patterns contributes to family unity. The most important psychological gain is that the family has fewer decisions to face. By routinizing everyday life in family living, there will be fewer points at

which the family must struggle over how to conduct family life (Cherlin 636).

In the remarried family, this habitualization of family life is often absent—particularly in the early years of remarriage. And when the patterns are established, the family has had to struggle for much of this themselves. This family type has had little help from the society in which its members live.

There are several areas in which this phenomenon makes remarriages more difficult. One area is language. At first thought, this might seem fairly minor. However, when no adequate terms exist for such important roles as stepfather, stepmother, or stepchild, there is both confusion and lack of societal support (Cherlin 643). We do indeed lack adequate, universally accepted language. We don't know what to call this family unit. The term "stepparent" (literally, grief parent) originally meant a parent who replaced a dead one, not a parent stepping into a partial role also occupied by a divorced parent. The term "step-" carried negative connotations. There is no widespread agreement on alternate terms for the unit, such as "blended family." There are no adequate terms for what children should call their parents' new spouses. With vagueness in terms, there is also vagueness in rights and duties of members of this new family unit.

Another area of difficulty is that of law. Implicit in law is the assumption that the marriage in question is a first marriage. Quite commonly in most states, there is no provision for several problems of remarriage. Issues needing attention include balancing financial obligations of husbands to their spouses and children from current and from previous marriages, and defining the wife's obligations to husbands and children from new and from old marriages. When a death occurs, there is little legal guidance for reconciling the competing claims of current and former spouses for rights to a portion of the estate. Legal regulations concerning incest and consanguineous marriage need to be redefined for families of remarriage (Cherlin 644).

Still other vaguely defined areas include the proper disciplinary relationship of a new spouse to the partner's children. How should parenthood be shared in the new household? And how should one relate to one's former spouse and former in-laws, including the grandparents of one's children? What is the proper etiquette, or courtesy, for treating one's former spouse when he or she comes to pick up or return the children? Is such a person invited in? offered drink or food? treated on a social basis? And what about that ex-spouse's family network? One sociologist calls these people "quasi kin." What contact should be maintained? Should they be involved in major events in the lives of the children?

The incompleteness of the institution of remarriage is at least one factor in contributing to the tremendously vague, uncertain feeling that clouds many early remarriages. Persons have expressed this feeling in some vivid metaphors. Becoming a stepparent in a remarriage is like "trying to follow an unfamiliar path in the dark . . . The path seems lonely even though there are millions of others walking down the same trail" (Visher and Visher 1982, 2). It was like trying to learn to swim by jumping in the deep end, rather than the shallow end, of the pool; parachuting into an unknown territory and being expected to perform effectively, even when you don't know the language, the customs, or the rules; or stepping into a play already in progress—you know that somehow you are involved, but you don't know the plot, you don't know who all the cast members are (and there are many), and nobody seems to give you a script for your part! (Olson and Della Pia-Terry 64).

The institutional supports of which we speak emerge slowly in a society. For the foreseeable future, remarried families themselves will need to struggle with much too wide a range of decision-making. They will need to build their own expectations, rituals, habits, and customs as a family.

WHEELS WITHIN A WHEEL

There are still other ways to look at the new stepfamily. One might be as "wheels within a wheel." We are not referring to Ezekiel's vision or the delightful spiritual we sing to celebrate that. Rather, we speak of one large circle or "wheel"—the new, remarried family—and of the many little "wheels" within that larger one. This understanding comes from family systems theory. Practitioners of that discipline speak of the family "system" and the "subsystems" within. We will appropriate their insights using our own metaphor. Jamie Kelem Keshet identifies several "wheels" (subsystems) within the stepfamily (520–524).

First is the ex-spouse wheel, which once included many bonds (residence, mutual conversations, sexual relations, coparenting, for example). By the time of divorce this has become a relationship that is "held together primarily by past history, legal and financial obligations, and a common commitment to child-rearing."

Second is the parent-child wheel, which includes both the resident and the nonresident parent. The residential parent-child wheel may have grown very strong as children live with the fears of losing a remaining parent. The remaining parent may also cling more closely to the child. In later, more stable stages, this grouping may have become a self-sufficient unit with a strong outer boundary. This may well be a unit very difficult to integrate into a stepfamily. Its members may not be eager to share their newfound intimacy and equality with new people. Visiting parent-child wheels, on the other hand, will vary widely in their effectiveness and cohesiveness.

The new-remarried-couple wheel is the newest subgroup and is often the most fragile. This relationship may initially form somewhat apart from the other partner's children. In this courtship period, a bond is formed and the decision to marry is made. Thus, a fledgling couple relationship finds itself encountering and engaging several sturdy, long-standing "wheels" as they attempt to combine into a functioning stepfamily unit.

As Keshet notes, the new stepfamily system threatens each of these relational units, and they in turn threaten the new stepfamily. At the same time, there is also a possibility that the interrelationship can be one of mutual strengthening.

The remarriage can affect the ex-spouse relationship both negatively and positively.

It may enable the ex-spouses to recognize and do the work of separating emotionally. But it may also make cooperation as postdivorce parents of the same children even more difficult.

The stepfamily interacts with the parent-child "wheel" by challenging the tightly closed circle. This new family asks for admittance of another person or persons. At the same time it can relieve children of responsibility for the parent's emotional well-being, and perhaps for some practical household tasks. This may in turn free the child for more autonomy and for more energy for relationships with peers and with siblings. The new adult (stepparent) may be very slowly admitted as a resource adult. On the one hand, the new couple may find their relationship threatened by their large responsibilities and by conflicts over appropriate involvement in the various relationships whirling around them. On the other hand, a shared life both with a spouse and with one's children can be a strong source of satisfaction.

Keshet notes it is quite logical that these various groupings will compete for scarce resources such as time and finances and that the negotiating of these needs can be a beneficial process. She points out that some stepfamily members will hold membership in more than one of these "wheels." These persons are the pivotal persons in resolving their conflicting needs.

After Keshet has analyzed the step-family, she draws these hopeful conclusions

> The individual members and subunits of a stepfamily can, however, learn together to reach common goals and to enjoy common satisfactions. The development of this unity within the stepfamily is facilitated by 1) resolution of conflicts within the subsystems, 2) negotiations between subsystems for fulfillment of competing needs and distribution of resources, 3) weakening of boundaries between subsystems, 4) recognition that the stepfamily cannot duplicate the nuclear family model, and 5) a strong fulfilling couple relationship which enables the partners to cope with the complications of the stepfamily. (530–531).

A CROWDED VEHICLE

In a vivid paragraph, Morton Hunt has written, "Unlike the young who come to each other relatively empty handed, the divorced (or widowed) man and divorced (or widowed) woman come with all the acquisitions of the years—their individual histories, habits, and tastes, their children, friends, and chattels. Love can be a rickety vehicle, loaded with much of life's baggage" (Hunt 269).

We might add that this vehicle of which Hunt speaks is often extremely crowded. For example, consider the experience of a friend and sometime writing partner who went into a bank and said to an official, "I'm Carole Della Pia-Terry, and I'd like to open a new account here." The official responded, "That sounds more like a corporation than a person!" As Carole reflected, "He was much more accurate than he knew. There are 31 people who, so to speak, own a piece of me. And those are just the main ones. There are many more persons in this family structure."

Or as another man put it, "I didn't marry my wife, I married a crowd. There are my three sons who give me the silent treatment when they see me every other weekend, *and* the twin ten-year-old daughters of my new wife Carolyn, who frankly are often a pain . . . *and* my new in-laws, who cold-shoulder me, *and* Carolyn's ex-husband, who spoils the kids rotten when he sees them, *and* my ex-wife, who is still bad-mouthing me to my kids, *and* the Bank of America's Credit and Loan Department" (Krantzler 219).

Those persons have put it well. Remarriage can well be a crowded and rickety vehicle.

OVERABUNDANCE OF FAMILY LEGACIES

Furthermore, a remarried family will have many past experiences—family legacies, if you will—that shape their ideas of what a family is and how it should function.

For example, consider the new family of Phoebe and Rick. Phoebe was married seven years and had two children before she divorced. After three years of being a single parent she married Rick, a widower who had one son and who had functioned with him as a single parent. When these folks began their new family life together, at least six different family heritages influenced the family's decisions:

1. The family in which Phoebe grew up;
2. Phoebe's first-marriage family;
3. The single-parent family of Phoebe and her two children;
4. The family in which Rick grew up;
5. Rick's first-marriage family;
6. The single-parent family of Rick and his son.

When this family comes together and begins its life, there may be at least six opinions about "when to go to bed, where to put the television, how to light a fire, bake cookies, make pancakes, drive a car, and celebrate holidays" (Visher and Visher 1982, 7–8).

A MULTIDIRECTIONAL TUG-OF-WAR

Persons who enter a remarriage frequently speak of experiencing a good bit of strain, particularly in the early years. Members of the new unit sense that they are pulling against a number of resistances to bring this new family experience into being. Virtually all members of the new remarried family will feel this. But the question is, who are the pullers, and who are the pulled, and in what direction are persons pulling?

The new stepparent may see the spouse's children as the resisters. And these children may well feel a prime loyalty to their biological parents and to the first marriage. Some stepparents may suspect that children are attempting to sabotage the new marriage so that original parents can get back together. Children may feel it is disloyal to biological parents to express love and acceptance of stepparents, likable though those stepparents may be. Further, children may be socialized to trust biological parents and distrust other adults. The newly remarried couple may sense that they are pulling in the direction of family unity. They may feel that the children of either or both

spouses are the pullers against such unity.

The children, however, may feel more like the pulled. Sometimes they may even feel like the tug rope between unaccepting ex-spouses. At other times they may find themselves confused by their changed place in the family, both in regard to parents and in regard to siblings and stepsiblings. (For instance, a child who once was the youngest may, in the restructured family, have become a middle child.)

At the same time, the whole family is pulling against unrealistically high expectations. Family members may have a hard time sorting out normal family stresses from those special to the remarried family. Sometimes they are also contending with the normal problems of building a new family unit.

Patience and communication are the keys to arriving at the discovery that they are all on the same side. When that happens, the new family is born.

A REVOLVING DOOR AND A REVOLVING CHARGE ACCOUNT

One symbol of the remarried family is the revolving door—the resident membership of such a family does not remain constant.

Many family courts are moving in the direction of granting joint custody of children to divorcing parents. For some children this means spending almost equal time in each of two parents' homes—parents who no longer live together. For others it means going from one parent's home to the other for shorter stays. It might be school week in one home, weekends in the other; school year in one home, summers in the other; or part of vacations, weekends, and holidays in one home and part in the other.

If each remarried partner brings children from a previous marriage, their home may sometimes shelter children from both marriages, or from either of the previous marriages. Each combination has its possibilities for relating, cooperating, and competing.

All family members may have problems with entry and exit when the members of the family scene change constantly. All will need to learn to deal with loneliness when someone leaves and discomfort when someone reenters.

Remarried families need to develop special skills and styles to let the occasional family members know that they have a place. Those who come and go need to know that they belong, whether present or absent. The families need to learn how to let children go and welcome them back.

But along with the symbol of the revolving door, an equally appropriate one might be the revolving charge account. For as children come and go within the remarriage, so does money. A stepfather might have financial obligations for the raising of his biological children who live elsewhere. A mother might be receiving child-support payments from an ex-husband. In each case, financial decisions need to be faced: How do we handle the costs for this medical or dental need of a child? What about music, instruments, increased education, or cultural opportunities? What about inflation and the increased expenses of growing children? There are many decisions that will need to be made about how much money should stay, how much money should come in, and how much money should go out. These decisions also involve negotiating with a wide number of people.

THE SHAKE-AND-BAKE FAMILY

Dan Houmes and Paul Meier (103–114) describe Bill and Mary, who met in a grocery store and quickly discovered a commonality of faith, family situation (divorce), and loneliness. After a ten-month whirlwind romance, they married and Bill moved into Mary's house with her three extremely active children, ages 16, 14, and 12. In addition, Bill's son and daughter occasionally came for visits of several days.

Very early in the marriage, Mary's children's needs seemed to grow and Mary became ever more involved with them. While Bill felt a vague discontent about this, work demands were claiming extra time from him as well. Much too quickly, the joy and satisfaction they had felt in their earlier courtship was dissipating.

Houmes and Meier call this the "Shake-and-Bake" family—that is, the instant family. It suffered from:

- Too little time, and no time at all as a couple before children were present;
- Too little bonding between stepparents and children, so the stepparent may be tempted gradually to withdraw;
- Too many responsibilities—work, time, financial, parenting, kin, marriage;
- Too many complications, such as reconciling conflicting needs and schedules;
- Too few adjustments.

Every marriage needs time for adjustment, recommitment, and stabilizing. And yet the instant demands placed on the remarrying couple may render time to do that difficult or impossible.

There is need for skill in negotiating the scarce resources of a remarriage so the couple may find strength to make it go. Such families might well benefit from expressions of support—such as offers to take the children for a weekend or an afternoon.

A TEMPLE

Tom and Adrienne Frydenger offer a beautiful image of the stepfamily drawing close together in bonding. They first recall the baby that was born to their union and the bonding that occurred during the time of the pregnancy, the birth, and immediately after birth. Quite naturally, this led to shared experiences with their new baby. They ask, if an adult comes into children's lives after as a stepparent, how can some bonding take place? They suggest the image of Solomon's Temple, with its three different areas.

First there was the outer court, bustling with activities. They suggest that just as anyone could enter the outer court, so anyone can enter into activities with children. These activities are a safe place for bonding to begin between stepparent and stepchild. This should be initiated by the stepparent and should center on the child's interests. The purpose is to provide opportunities for the child to have fun and to associate those good times with a stepparent.

Secondly, there was the holy place. This implies bonding through the exchange of ideas. And just as a sign above the holy place might have read PRIESTS ONLY, NO ONE ELSE ALLOWED, so the sign posted between a child's activities and that child's thoughts and feelings might say, FRIENDS ONLY, UNCARING PEOPLE STAY OUT. Faithfulness in shared activities may occasionally allow the stepparent entrance into this part of the child's life. The goal of bonding through the exchange of ideas is not a lecture. It is rather to hear what is going on in the child's life.

Third and last there was the Holy of Holies, and this implies bonding at its deepest level. The Frydengers note that the Old Testament priests entered the Holy of Holies only once a year on the Day of Atonement. The stepparent, if fortunate, may have about the same number of chances to enter into spiritual bonding with the child. They suggest that since these opportunities are so infrequent, it is important to use them sensitively and well. They suggest (113–114):

- Walk in softly, slowly, and follow your stepchild's leading.
- Be sensitive and realize that the situation and the child's feelings are important.
- Be available. Though it may sound simple, being available is one of the biggest commitments you can make. You can judge your availability by your willingness to put down the paper, to go shopping, or turn off the football game when your attention is needed . . .
- Be sure your motivation for helping is pure . . .
- Be secure in yourself. Don't feel angry or threatened when your stepchild talks to you about your spouse's ex-mate.

With such sensitivities, the Frydengers suggest that the stepparent may be

admitted into the Holy of Holies of an occasional spiritual bonding with a stepchild.

SUMMARY

The Vishers have summarized what we have said by noting five structural characteristics of remarried families in which they differ from the first-marriage nuclear family: 1) Virtually all members of these new families have sustained the loss of a primary relationship; 2) where the remarriage was preceded by a divorce, one biological parent probably lives outside the current family unit; 3) the relationship between the adult couple in the household is predated by the relationship of parents to biological children; 4) role definitions are weak; and 5) usually the children in remarried households have membership in more than one household (Visher and Visher 1979).

Remarried families face an extremely complex set of tasks that must be accomplished if they are to succeed as an enduring and satisfying family unit. The difficulty of their tasks will vary widely from family to family. Circumstances that reduce the complexity are: having only one spouse with a previous marriage; having children from only one member of the new couple; children being younger, rather than older, at the time of the second marriage; and the children and other extended family members viewing the new union with enthusiasm. But virtually every remarried family will face some struggle in adjustment.

WORKS CITED

Cherlin, Andrew. "Remarriage as an Incomplete Institution." *American Journal of Sociology* 84.3: 634–650.

Frydenger, Tom and Adrienne Frydenger. *The Blended Family*. Grand Rapids, MI: Zondervan, 1984.

Furstenberg, Frank. "Reflections on Remarriage." *Journal of Family Issues* 1.4 (December 1980): 443–453.

Houmes, Dan and Paul Meier. *Growing in Step*. Richardson, TX: Today Publishers, 1985.

Hunt, Morton M. *The World of the Formerly Married*. New York: McGraw-Hill, 1966.

Keshet, Jamie Kelem. "From Separation to Stepfamily: A Subsystem Analysis." *Journal of Family Issues* 1.4 (December 1980): 517–532.

Krantzler, Mel. *Learning to Love Again: Beyond Creative Divorce*. New York: Thomas Y. Crowell, 1977.

Olson, Richard P. and Carole Della Pia-Terry. *Help for Remarried Couples and Families*. Valley Forge, PA: Judson Press, 1984.

Sukosky, Donald G. "Making the Most of Blended Families." *Family Life Educator* 4.2 (Winter 1985): 14–17.

U.S. Bureau of the Census. *Statistical Abstract of the United States: 1988* (108th edition). Washington, DC: U.S. Government Printing Office, 1987.

U.S. Department of Health and Human Services. National Center for Health Statistics. *Vital Statistics of the United States 1984*, vol. 3, Marriage and Divorce. DDHS pub. no. (PHS) 88–1103 (Public Health Service). Washington, DC: U.S. Government Printing Office, 1988.

Visher, Emily B. and John S. Visher. *Stepfamilies: A Guide to Working with Stepparents and Stepchildren*. New York: Brunner/Mazel, 1979.

_____. *A Stepfamily Workshop Manual*. Stepfamily Association of California, 1980.

_____. *How to Win as a Stepfamily*. New York: Dembner Books, 1982.

CHAPTER 7

A Pop Culture Perspective

Reynolds R. Ekstrom

DOMINANT CULTURE: CHANGING AND COMPLEX

Is there a dominant culture in North America today? To use a term like "dominant culture" in a meaningful manner, one would have to grasp the complexities of the term culture. What is a culture? Obviously, it is not people themselves. After all, people create cultures. Thus, a culture must be the overall way of life shared by a people, encompassing their beliefs, dreams, stories, hopes, histories, and laws. Culture, though, also includes a people's religion(s), artworks, and products.

A classic definition of culture would maintain that people shape their culture and it, in turn, reshapes their lifestyles. A traditional notion about culture would hold that cultures are handed on (transmitted) by older generations to their young, for the happiness and well-being of the young.

Some analysts of culture challenge us today to think seriously about the current condition of affairs in American life. Some speak, in fact, about our dominant culture as if it were a pop culture—not a traditional culture, nor an adult culture, nor a youth-oriented culture. After all, are not most of us, really the creators of the dominant stories, personal dreams, consumable products, and artworks laid out there for almost everyone to desire?

Some cultural observers note that media tell us our stories, shape our wants and values, and in general educate us about who we should be and how we should look. In other words, video and other media (including print media, such as magazines) are the chief storytellers, teachers, and sellers, modern commercial messengers all.[1] Therefore, some thinkers believe people, young and old, are fast becoming consumers of culture, not primary producers of it. Just how many individuals, young or old, do you know (or you have heard about) who try hard to remake themselves in the images and likenesses of what they see and want on TV, or in the movies, or in fashion magazines? Here is the power of culture—*culture can create people*. It can influence the values, identities, and worldviews of people. Now that's power!

Pop culture. The phrase implies that our society is to be characterized by words like accessibility, disposability, enthusiasm, energy, quick-pacing, colorfulness, constant changes, and, ultimately, surface emotionalism, surface values, style over substance, and insincerity or phoniness. It is pop culture if it is something or someone who fits nicely with the phrase "new and improved."

At its best, a culture is to be passed on from one (mature) generation to the next for youth's well-being and for the conservation of the tangible and intangible treasures crafted by a people. Yet, some social analysts claim that many things that pass for culture today among Americans are crafted and marketed for profit, disposability, and power over individuals' fancies and purchasing whims.

Thus, writers like Todd Gitlin and others do not view the average American citizen as a co-creator of a distinguishable, traditional culture. Rather, many people today seem to be joined tenuously by the things they buy and possess as consumers in the dominant culture and by ideas they hear and believe uncritically through media, an arid, and stale form of community or shared life. Some liken this to fusing trees at the branches and leaves, not the roots. At the most basic level, then, these are vestiges of a widespread, spiritual malaise creeping into Western society and thus finding their way into family lifestyles too. When traditional values and spiritual roots are eroded, something must take their place. Liberation theologians, such as Gustavo Gutierrez, in the spirit of the ancient prophets, have pointed out, for some time now, that "something" often is a consumer hunger, and it must be brought under control.

AMERICAN FAMILIES TODAY: CHANGE AND DIVERSITY

Using quite broad strokes, we have been trying to describe some of the apparent characteristics of and a bit about the personality of contemporary pop culture. In an analogous sense, a society has a personality, just as an individual does. In a similar sense, each family has a personality or character too.

Leif Kehrwald, in Chapter 1, has described types of families, or family personality and identity traits, to indicate how families today deal with togetherness, change, and daily existence. He names these family personality patterns as: rigid, structured, flexible, and chaotic. In our society, many would have us believe that the norm for family life and family interaction is chaos, or at least an unhealthy condition of hyper-flexibility. No rules, no clearly defined roles, lots of dysfunctions and substance misuse, constant flux, an anxious situation in which it's every man, woman, adolescent, or child for himself or herself.

A common stereotype about contemporary American families would have us trust that there is so much change and so much diversity in family lifestyles that redemption and happiness, according to the good old ways of doing things, is out of the question. Does this kind of stereotyping match your observations, your firsthand experiences and insights, about the many types of families today? Is the stereotype true according to your own family experience?

Current cultural creeds on individualism, self-reliance, and the relentless pursuit of the American "good life" make the survival and strength of the family in the U.S. most amazing. At its heart, family stands for loving relationships and hope, bonds which unite family members. At its best, family stands for interdependence and complete acceptance. This traditional sense of family represents, though, "a historically older form of life" (Bellah 87).

Marriage and family fulfill social functions. In North American history, they have offered individuals committed, stable relationships and have connected individuals to the wider culture.

However, there are tensions now. Spontaneous intimacy and short-term involvements are idealized in pop culture. Longings to "find myself" and "to be somebody" lead many on individualized quests for self-fulfillment. In searching for personalized happiness and quick-fix intimacy, in a non-traditional pop culture, family roles and obligations "may be viewed negatively, as likely to inhibit such intimacy" (Bellah 85; Verhoff 140). An irony there, to say the least, wouldn't you say?

Change and diversity are fundamental words that should be used to describe the condition of family lifestyles in our society today. These words are much more accurate in describing the broad economic, socio-logical, and multicultural variations we find among families in our country. They are more fair and universal than terms such as chaotic, dysfunctional, rigid, separated, connected, or other terms that might be used in negative-judgmental ways.

Nevertheless, the American family remains resilient as an American institution in the face of change, despite mounting signs of personal and interpersonal stress. There have been dramatic shifts in family life patterns in recent decades—increased divorce, remarriage, cohabitation, lone living, and single-parenting, to name a few. So, changing and diverse are benchmark terms for families in pop culture. An ever-changing, pop cultural kaleidoscope presents the contemporary family, rigid, flexible, or otherwise, with unanticipated pressures and interesting opportunities. U.S. Church leaders see the modern family as standing at a crossroads, confronting fundamental challenges (*Family Perspective* 4).

Research indicates that Americans believe strongly in family life and community. Yet, contemporary American lifestyles in pop culture often produce the language and practice of individualism. A paradox there, of course, but one we can understand. People seem to easily "develop loyalties to others in the contexts of (new) families, small communities, religious congregations, and . . . lifestyle enclaves" (Bellah 250). Family life and marriage seem somehow more fragile, more vulnerable, more difficult to sustain in our contemporary pop culture. In a sense, some observers note, they have become optional, matters of personal choice in modern society.

In the U.S., we have become more tolerant in recent decades of those who turn their backs on marriage as an institution and as a way of life. In a more tolerant pop culture atmosphere, for example, "alternate forms of committed relationships long denied any legitimacy, such as those between persons of the same sex, are becoming widely accepted" (Bellah 110).

There is no longer a typical American family personality or a typical American family way of life, made in the image of the '50s TV shows like "Father Knows Best," or "The Donna Reed" clan, or even the blended, '60s "Brady Bunch" ensemble. In a changing society, one more tolerant of and hopefully more accepting of social and multi-ethnic diversities, each family must be seen as unique.

Families in North America differ greatly in their structures, needs, and responses to various social trends. Families experience many kinds of socio-economic standings and inherit many kinds of cultural, ethnic, and religious traditions (*Family Perspective* 28). Many Catholics in the U.S. have blended into this dominant, multiethnic American mosaic. Catholic families in America reflect the conditions, stresses, changes, achievements, and consumer "good life" desires of the American family in general.

This pattern can be very different for ethnic families. Ethnic adolescents often live in two different cultures: one at home and one at school or in the broader society. These adolescents have to balance the conflicting demands and values of these different cultures. Often times what they do is to adopt the external features of the dominant culture.

Complex social changes and the complexities of trying to live together as a family, in a society that professes a doctrine of individualism, have reduced the average family household's ability to "tie individuals securely into a sustaining social order" (Bellah 110).

Our cultural creeds and hymns urge individuals to take personal control in finding what they want, and for finding relationships (temporary or lasting) that will meet their changing needs. Thus, it is difficult today for parents to say honestly that members of their families always do thus and so. In pop culture, family members have many options to pursue. The varied lifestyles which result often reflect, necessarily, individual preferences and dissimilarities (Glick 871).

Some cultural analysts note, wisely, that the family is "no longer an integral part of a larger moral ecology tying the individual to community, church, and nation" (Bellah 112). Actual research indicates that families and households created during 1985–2000 may not much resemble the American households of yesterday (Exter 46). This is a critical issue to which family life specialists, pastoral ministers, especially religious educators and youth ministers, and family therapists ought to pay vigorous attention.

Desires for personal fulfillment, self-stroking, sudden intimacy, consumerism, undue wariness toward others, and escalating needs for personal support, in a harried pop culture environment, are taking their toll on the individual and on the family in America. Those particularly concerned about how the family of origin transmits its faith, moral values, and cultural norms should further examine the moral ecology issue soon. How will we (or maybe that should read, Will we) ever reintegrate the individual, the family, the wider community, the church, and the dominant culture? Robert Bellah and his colleagues have framed a most ironic commentary on this:

> The family (today) is the core of the private sphere, whose aim is not to link individuals to the public world but to avoid it as far as possible. In our commercial culture, consumerism, with its temptations and televisions, augments that tendency . . . "Taking care of one's own" is an admirable motive. But when it combines with suspicion of and withdrawal from the public world, it is one of the conditions of despotism . . . (Bellah 112).

What do we make of family life, changing and diverse, in the 1990s? We might recall the 1950s as a sentimental time of family and tradition. The 1960s? A decade for social upheaval and youthful rebellion. The '70s? A time of rootlessness and the dominant birthing of "me-first" journeys. The 1980s were often described as a period in which many put down some roots and reclaimed some traditional values. But here in the brave, new '90s, many demographic trends "belie a (sentimental) return to the traditions of the 1950s." This decade is better characterized, when it comes to family life and many other cultural matters, as an overall time of great diversity.

Current family patterns reflect this trend. Dominant cultural habits and American families are changing, in some cases, at this very minute. Solutions to problems we encounter today can't be found among '50s social records (Russell and Exter 22). There are warning signals mixed in with glimmers of hope.

Will it prove possible to hand on effectively social and religious values to the youth of 1990s families? Is it inevitable that young people will inherit the contemporary pop culture and its ways? "Each decade shapes the next," some sociologists say. "And there is never any going back." In transition yet resilient, American families in this decade, with or without the help of church and family-serving agencies, will struggle with key issues: how to cope and grow as a community system; how to fulfill personal and social responsibilities; and whether to withdraw from or choose to interface, in a healthy and productive way, as basic Christian communities, with the wider society.

THE FAMILIES WITH ADOLESCENTS/ POP CULTURE INTERFACE

A crucial question must be explored in the 1990s. Can we possibly reconnect and reintegrate families (and thus, family members) with the wider church and wider social community? Given the tenor of the times, it is not surprising that we would find Americans exhibiting, in general, much independence in their religious ways.

Many in the U.S., for example, say they view their faith and their central values as something between God and them only. During the 1980s, one-third of the American people, consistently, reported an individual religious experience or a moment of spiritual insight which had changed their lives. Yet, even today, many seem to rely on themselves or the righteous lifestyles they lead for true self-fulfillment and personal happiness, rather than organized religion (Gallup and Castelli 252).

While many in the U.S. see religion as an individualistic matter, some do belong to larger church organizations. However, if any organizational loyalty comes into play, the chief setting for most Americans remains the local congregation or parish church. Ironically, many report that local church affiliation is significant to them but the local church is not equated, usually, with religion.

Many in the U.S. today see religion as something going beyond the boundaries of the ordinary local church body or the ordinary individual. Religion is a topic readily handed over, by countless Americans, to those specialists who claim to comprehend and enjoy it. A Gallup survey in 1978 found that four of five respondents believed that each "individual should arrive at his or her (own) religious beliefs independent of any churches or synagogues" (Hoge 167).

There are many people, young and old alike, in our dominant culture today who think more independently or individualistically than during past generations, especially when it comes to matters of faith and values. This kind of post-modern thinking has had major impacts on family life, on family religious ways, and on family relationships, particularly in family households that include children. It has added fuel to the fire burning at the heels of a long-held cultural Christianity in all of Western society.

Without doubt, there are so many research pieces available to inform us about contemporary families in our society, particularly families with children, it is hard to sort out the meaningful from the mundane. Numerous trends, statistics, and fads could be cited. Yet, which among these are truly important when it comes to comprehending the hurdles faced by families in pop culture today?

EMERGING PATTERNS

There are a few emerging, observable patterns that should be named. Note how many are media-related and what these trends imply about the overall spiritual/religious condition of life in American families with children today. Note also what the following imply about the possibilities for reconnecting and re-integrating family members with the wider social community for the survival and well-being of our shared Western culture.

1) In general, family members spend less time with each other nowadays than in past times. Children tend to spend less time with grown-ups than in the past (e.g., note adults' typical work and social habits; teens often have jobs with other peers supervising; more entertainment media and media personalities are available today than ever before, especially for young people who spend time alone at home or elsewhere). Many people experience significant bouts of loneliness or isolation. This is very true for children and adolescents.

2) In times of social change and much family stress, young people are often left on their own—thus, as social beings, they are drawn toward each other for companionship and understanding and help with pressures.

3) Many individuals (young and old) seem very career-oriented and more concerned nowadays, in general, about making money, getting it all, and achieving success. This is consistent with the me-first and "good life" values many have been taught, since birth, by parents, school, other adults, and pop culture education sources, such as television. These attitudes have been tacitly agreed to or, at least, tolerated by many church bodies. Young people in families, generally, seem to be adopting and believing uncritically in these "good life" values.

4) Generally, what unites persons (a provocative thought) in our society, more so than a ubiquitous religious sense or moral vision, more so than a cultural Christianity, are merely the things they buy, possess, and plug-in as consumers, little more. Some say this is most true about pre-adolescents and teenagers today (What types of things "unite" teenagers today? Walkmans, TVs, music, clothing, language, MTV, etc.). Ironically, possessions do not unite anyone with anybody. In reality, personal possessions and material things only serve, ultimately, to isolate individuals even more (Gelman 10–16). Thus, in contemporary pop culture, there really is no uniform youth culture nor adult culture, or American cultural consciousness. There is a consumer-driven pop culture, however.

5) Media personalities appearing on TV, radio, movies, and elsewhere are becoming like an alternative family or (cynically speaking) an alternative community of friends for many who experience loneliness, isolation, and confusion in our dominant pop culture. Of course, many of these modern

media creations are not "friends" at all. They are entertainment characters, cartoon beings, and commercial agents targeted toward selling and otherwise influencing vulnerable, unquestioning adolescents and adults in need of spiritually satisfying relationships.

6) Individuals today, like many in the 1980s, grow up quickly in a pressured society. They experience many freedoms, choices, and pressures unthinkable just several generations ago. Countless young people, frequently, are expected to deal with these concerns with little sense of structure or guidance from parents and other voices of authority. Yet, many adults also feel stressed and confused today by modern complexities and face such obstacle course events without much family support or the security of caring community. Feelings of anger, frustration, betrayal, and/or the run-away impulse can be the response.

Your idea of the typical family today may take a shape like the wholesome, yuppie Huxtables of "The Cosby Show." Or it may resemble more the exasperating Bundys—Al, Peg, Kelly, and Bud, the '90s family from hell brought to us on the Fox Network's show, "Married . . . With Children." The Huxtables are too-together and too-polished to be authentic, but they are frequently quite funny and teach basic moral lessons. The Bundys embody, as satiric stock characters, all the dramatically negative traits of contemporary families, sharply pointing out the absolute worst of parental flaws and the perversion of traditional values in particular. The Bundy clan, also, is usually entertaining (The Simpsons, Bart, Homer, and crew could also be used as an example here).

Both the Bundys and the Huxtables are meant to instruct us about how their creators see the condition of family life and family interactions in America today. Whichever TV clan you might think to be more accurate, according to your own perceptions about modern American family ways, quite likely the actual state of the American family today lies somewhere in between "The Cosby Show" and "Married . . . With Children." Almost all families are touched, in some way, by each of the six trends named above. Daily

interaction with our dominant culture almost guarantees that no family will escape untouched or unchanged by these emerging social trends.

As direct results of these patterns now taking shape, what else could we validly observe about contemporary families with children in pop culture? You sometimes now hear both serious commentators and pundits speaking of U.S. homes as becoming quite child-centered, or child-run, rather than adult-centered and parent-run. Some observers call young people who care for themselves, during after-school hours and at other times, "self-nurturing" (a cynical term to a great degree). Of course, the irony in such remarks cannot be lost on perceptive hearers.

In the U.S. now, teenagers have over $75 billion annually at their disposal. Half of this money comes from parental sources and is targeted for family and household-style purchases. Those between the ages of 9 and 12, in the United States, have about $4.7 billion more given to them annually, to spend as they see fit. About 50% of American teenage girls do at least some of their family's grocery shopping each week, especially as the percentage of working mothers increases. (About 65% of all U.S. moms of pre-teens and teens now work outside the home.) Many young people, ages 5–18, these days, report in surveys they also cook for family members at least once a week or more, typically preparing microwave or easy step, easy-prep entrees, like Kid Cuisine, pizza, and frozen foods.

The money to do such grocery shopping comes, usually, from overall family funds. Yet, young people who do the choosing at the supermarket (a task previously reserved to parents mostly) are also making other key family-spending decisions nowadays. More than one pundit has noted, sardonically, that some parents are so consumed by making money (some out of sheer economic/family-survival necessity, others out of sheer compulsion) they often don't have time to spend it.

Adolescents purchase things besides clothing, cologne, compact discs, and candy. They do not influence family purchases at the supermarket alone. Adolescents are buying more and more big-ticket, durable items, including autos, household appliances, and family wardrobes. Findings by the respected research institute, Teenage Research Unlimited, located near Chicago, indicate that 29% of driving teenagers own their own cars. About 45% of all adolescents possess their own VCRs. About 70% have significant say in family vacation choices. About 60% of adolescents own a calculator. About 28% have their own telephones. About 50% possess a personal-use TV (Miller 30).

All this, quite likely, will increase as the teenage population in North America rises during the 1990s. Peter Zollo, president of T.R.U., has noted accurately that some parents today consider their kids to be experts when it comes to certain kinds of purchases and technological products. Take cars, CD players, word processors, and VCRs, for instance.

Adolescents listen to the radio about 20 hours per week. They average about 20–25 hours of commercial TV, which includes therefore two or three hours of advertising, about one-fifth of TV-viewing time. (About 33% of adolescents under 17, in fact, watch move than five hours of TV a day.) Interestingly, research by the Gallup organization, in the 1980s, consistently pointed out that parents and adults mainstreamed into pop culture habits and lifestyles listen to a little less radio than the average adolescent, per week, but watch about 20% more TV!

Many young people seem to have inherited and claimed, as their own, a 1980s consumerist mentality from parents, media, and the multilingual, pop culture voices speaking to them from the adult world of marketing and advertising. By the late 1980s, U.S. teenage females were spending, on average, about $55.50 a week, while U.S. teenage males spent about $48.80 weekly, on average. By 1988, about 7.7 million youth, about one-third of all U.S. residents between the ages of 14 and 19, were working in some kind of job. In some places today, employed school-age youth make $200 or more per week. A commentator on such trends, Laurence Steinberg, believes young people are more motivated by luxury tastes than economic need. Some put money away

for college or save their dollars in responsible fashion, but they tend to be the exception rather than the norm (Miller 29).

And what about those "good life" commodities or the daily survival tactics adopted by some children, like pilgrimages to the supermarket because the family (especially the kids in the household) has to eat and clean up and keep the home lamps burning despite the decreasing presence of parents and other adult figures? Let's look at the CDs, fashions, rock videos, Air Jordans (at $100 per sneaker), and the performers, movies, and magazines made for America's children. Typically, these are identified by adults as youth culture elements. We could, of course, name many more. Adolescents tend to be blamed by parents and other adults for their attraction to the things of pop culture.

Yet, adolescents do not produce the things of contemporary pop culture. They do not film the rock videos, write the cosmetics ads, or set the prices at the Foot Locker or other shopping mall outlets. Adults do. Pop cultural shifts among parents and adult institutions have created youthful malljammers, rock videovogues, and latchkey youngsters. Young people inherit (and often buy into enthusiastically) the things of "pop culture." Yet, they are not the chief crafters and shapers of the stuff of our dominant social existence, the products, ideas, values, attitudes, "looks," and material things we see as central to the American way of life.

Is censorship of pop culture's voices in the home any answer? The old saying goes, "What you see is what you get." Yet, in pop culture, what you hear and what you read is what you get too. Some concerned advocates claim that children's TV and rock music habits should be radically curtailed because pop culture puts youth at-risk. Do you know any parents who have tried to ban cable or heavy metal or rap music tapes from their homes, for example?[2]

Ironically, concerned, censorship advocates rarely say much about adults' and parents' TV patterns or other pop culture propensities adopted, at parents' will, in American family households. You rarely hear about intellectual laziness or a creeping, unconcerned cultural illiteracy as problems of average, hardworking adults. These are pinned, usually, only on America's children. Censorship-style concern focuses, usually, on the sex, violence, and four-letter type language that many are exposed to today on both commercial and cable television networks, and through rap, heavy metal, and other kinds of pop music. Will labeling compact discs or adding disclaimers to the front-ends of suggestive TV presentations prove to be any solution to the perceived problems?

In a May 1990 issue, *Time* reported, "It's a four-letter world out there: in rock and rap, in movies and on TV, in comedy clubs, and in real life. Many love it, especially kids. Many others hate it or don't get it. Should anything be done about it?" (Corliss 92). In recent months, there has been some intriguing debate in public forums about art and obscenity, and what criteria to use to judge each (Mathews 46–52). Beyond marketing, TV sex, or raunch-mouthed comedians, some see violence as having become dominant today too. The headlines scream, "As America binges on make-believe gore, you have to ask: what are we doing to ourselves?" Welcome to culture of "Sleeping with the Enemy" and the "American Psycho." Have we zoned out into an all-tolerant silence of little lambs?

Some media watchers tell us, firmly, that what we see and what we hear in the 1990s is more than just dirty words, sexual innuendo, and bad-and-bloody movie episodes. In other words, the heated debate over pop culture and pop raunch is illustrative of a struggle basic to life in North America today.

Pop culture is a "feel good" society (at any cost, literally). American families love those funny home videos and Disney World dreams. America loves it smart bombs and antiseptic wars in far-off lands, with conflict and suffering thankfully held at arm's length, courtesy of CNN. Too easily, pop culture lifestyles encourage real human beings to let the gritty, street-life issues slide by painlessly ("Hey, dudes, it's not my problem . . . "). The voices that rise up in pop culture, however, now and then pound with raging screams and shocking (funny) turns

of phrase about what's really going on beneath colorful, plastic, antiseptic illusions.

Of course, quite a few media commentators remind us that much of what we see and read and hear in pop culture is really just meaningless, gross, or phony in a commercial way. Yet, in certain manners, its voices can express loudly, harshly, and (as with the Bundys) humorously, the bitter bite of feelings and edgy resentments held by many who are pushed outside the "good life" shelters in dominant society.

Yes, we live in four-letter world. People in dominant society and average American families use four-letter words, and many other kinds of words too. Many have very real personal problems and confront social ills that pop culture junkies would just as soon not hear about nor see. A literary critic, Leonard Ashely, reminds, "In early years of this century, the tastemakers (of our dominant culture) were the English and the Irish. Now, taste is being defined by different groups. When times get tough for many people, they seek an outlet to give them a sense of freedom. This time, the rebellion is coming in our language and through other pop culture images, sexual, violent, or otherwise."

True art in a people's culture is meant to shock, in a way. True art is much more than the uncritical embrace of the attitudes (and the prejudices) of those who control the power in a culture. Genuine art transcends Jesse Helms and the tastes of society page reporters in the news tabloids.

True art leads human beings to insight, and to the "beauty" in even hard-to-view realities. Not long ago, dominant Americans thought Picasso and Lenny Bruce were obscenely shocking. Are contemporary writers, rappers, and comics simply heralding a new world and signaling the demise of an older, arid culture? Some cultural observers think so. Who knows how we will see all this ten years from now. At least, it seems today, some shocking voices in pop culture are calling it like it is on the mean streets and in the real lives of people in the American dominant. It is up to each hearer and viewer, and a basic decision for each American family, to decide if censorship is any answer.

FAMILY AND CARING COMMUNITY: PASTORAL RESPONSES TO THE POP CULTURE OBSTACLE COURSE

People in ministry, clinicians, therapists, and other family-serving agents are coming to grips with the cultural shifts which have led us toward the spiritual, consumer-oriented malaise affecting individuals, and thus the families of individuals in contemporary Western lifestyles. Social analysts are clearly acknowledging that recent cultural shifts toward individualism and personal choice, as central social values, have caused the family, as an institution, to play a different cultural role and to serve a social function unusual to Western culture (Benson 106–113). Again, in Bellah's words,

> . . . family (today) is the core of the private sphere, whose aim is not link individuals to the public world but to avoid it as far as possible. In our commercial culture, consumerism, with its temptations and televisions, augments that tendency . . . .

Does anybody in the 1990s think it will be possible to reconnect and re-integrate contemporary families and family members with the wider community, church, or anything else? Families with children have been offered some keen insights in recent years.

A wise physician and a writer about contemporary youth and culture, Dr. Robert Coles, points out the obvious and the profound when it comes to adult-child interactions. Youth actually at-risk within pop culture, as well as those young family members just mildly caught up in those six emerging social trends we named earlier, need us. Adults. Parents. You and me. Young people, our children—our biological children, and our spiritual children who are born into our shared human society—need our attention, our concern, and our ongoing emotional and moral support.

Dr. Coles speaks of children and adolescents who would like to find just one strong, good individual to lean on, one who

will not disappoint nor disappear. Even children and adolescents, and yes even adults, doing pretty well in dominant society need parents, relatives, teachers, ministers, coaches, and other adult friends who can be present enough to make a difference. Likewise, they want and need someone to help them experience community on a wider scale with caring others.

Francis A.J. Ianni and other social researchers detect, today, an overarching "search for structure" among American youth. Perhaps we could say the same is true for North American adults and typical families of origin as well. Daniel Yankelovich and colleagues were saying, by the early 1980s, that we should consider and embrace some "new rules" for survival, in a healthy way, in contemporary American life (Yankelovich 1981). For example, seek caring relationships with a few trusted others, rather than spreading oneself too thin over many surface acquaintances or in too many consumer-driven pursuits. Appreciate the value of deeply-affecting emotional encounters or spiritual experiences in small communities of like-minded others, especially in family-style communities.

The sting of loneliness and the uncertainties of the maturation process (an ongoing identity-formation) is felt by young people and adults coming of age in the pop culture of the 1990s. The sting hurts more when young people and adults do not feel connected within a supportive context—a family household or another basic community that cares about its members. The sting, says Ianni, is particularly acute for some children and adolescents today, due to many of the cultural shifts in adults' lives and various media-related factors we have identified in this essay.

Going without the experience of a supportive community (a "community that cares") causes individuals in our society to risk getting roadblocked on the "long obstacle course" toward full human maturity, to echo a phrase by Dr. Coles.

What about the young who seem to develop into maturing, stable young adults, despite dysfunctional home lives or other setbacks? Dr. Ianni notes their resilience but, also, says "We've seen in practically all cases . . . some caring adult figure who was a constant in that kid's life" (Ianni 262). Adults who know about the recovery process from a dysfunction such as alcohol or narcotics abuse will see, readily, that the idea of a recovery sponsor provides the same kind of stabilizing relationship.

Throughout our country, families reflect the social habits and ethnic traits of parents, other adults, and an ever-changing, consumeristic pop culture. Children reflect parental and pop cultural values and desires. As people concerned about the state of family life in American society today, we should be busy in finding ways to help parents and other authorities who serve youth (in school systems, for example) to rekindle a sense of service, sacrifice, and idealism in their own lives, and in children's lives. In other words, rekindle basic and personal Christian values, rather than a single-minded spirit of getting-and-having, a legacy bequeathed to many of America's offspring today.

Young people, adults, and family units become who they become because they live in a world shaped by certain values and attitudes. What will matter for them most, in the end, "is the quality of their home life and school life . . . ," as Dr. Coles has noted.

What will matter most, to put it another way, is how they will or will not resolve the fundamental "search for structure" and caring community in this changing and diverse dominant culture. The ministry-minded continue to search for the best ways to help. Pop culture is not inevitable; it can be reshaped and remolded more in the image and likeness of the best of human values and human wisdom (Warren 29–47). That takes real effort and a sense of shared mission by ministers, educators, and families alike. Dr. Coles once said about the children and adults in our families and society:

> Those who have been lucky not by dint of their (family's) money or power, but (by) their continuous affection and concern, their wish to uphold certain ethical principles and then to live them, rather than merely mouthing them— such (individuals) are well able to handle some of the nonsense and craziness this

late part of the 20th century has managed to offer us all (71)).

END NOTES

1 A full discussion of such issues and some suggested pastoral responses can be found in the book *Access Guides to Youth Ministry: Media & Culture*, ed. Reynolds R. Ekstrom (New Rochelle, NY: Don Bosco Multimedia, 1992).
2 Interesting commentary on this can also be found in "Cable Television Gets Better Grades in Viewers Survey," *Wall Street Journal*, 30 March 1989: B4, and in "The New Puritans Are Very American", *USA Today* 31 March 1989: 8A.

WORKS CITED

Bellah, Robert N. et al. *Habits of the Heart: Individualism and Commitment in American Life*. San Francisco: Harper & Row, 1985.

Benson, Peter L. "Kids Aren't the Way They Used to Be: The Values of America's Adolescents." *Access Guides to Youth Ministry: Media & Culture*. Ed. Reynolds R. Ekstrom. New Rochelle NY: Don Bosco Multimedia, 1992.

Corliss, Richard. "X-Rated." *Time* 7 May 1990: 92–99.

Coles, Robert. "The Long Obstacle Course Called Adolescence." *Youth Worker* 6.1 (Summer 1989).

Exter, Thomas. "The Census Bureau's Household Projections." *American Demographics* 8.10 (October 1986): 44–47.

National Conference of Catholic Bishops. *Family Perspective in Church and Society*. Washington, DC: USCC, 1988.

Gallup, George and Jim Castelli. *The People's Religion: American Faith in the '90s*. New York: Macmillan, 1990.

Gelman, David. "A Much Riskier Passage." *Newsweek Special Issue* (June 1990): 10–16.

Glick, Paul. "Fifty Years of Family Demographics: A Record of Social

Change." *Journal of Marriage and Family* 50.4 (November 1988): 865–890.

Hoge, Dean R. *Converts, Dropouts, and Returnees: A Study of Religious Change Among Catholics*. New York: Pilgrim Press, 1981.

Ianni, Francis A.J. *The Search for Structure: A Report on American Youth Today*. New York: Free Press, 1989.

Mathews, Tom. "Fine Art or Foul?", *Newsweek* 2 July 1990: 46–52.

Miller, Annetta. "Work and What It's Worth." *Newsweek Special Issue* (June 1990): 29–33.

Russell, Cheryl and Thomas F. Exter. "America at Mid-Decade." *American Demographics* 8.1 (January 1986): 22–29.

Verhoff, Joseph et al. *The Inner American: A Self-Portrait from 1957–1976*. New York: Basic Books, 1981.

Warren, Michael. "The Electronically Imagined World." *Access Guides to Youth Ministry: Media & Culture*. Ed. Reynolds R. Ekstrom. New Rochelle, NY: Don Bosco Multimedia, 1992.

Yankelovich, Daniel. *New Rules: Searching for Meaning in a World Turned Upside Down*. New York: Random House, 1981.

CHAPTER 8

A Social Perspective

Francis A. J. Ianni

There is significant congruence between the world views of teenagers and those of the adults in their lives. However, such congruence means that the problems of adolescence are our problems, too.

In March of 1987 two boys, ages 18 and 19, and two sisters, ages 16 and 17, brought national attention to the northern New Jersey community of Bergenfield when they committed suicide in a pact that bound them in death as they had been in their short but troubled lives. All four teenagers had experienced problems with their families. One of the boys had seen his father kill himself a few years earlier. The two girls were having difficulty adjusting to their mother's remarriage and to their stepfather and his children, who had become part of their household. Both boys and the older of the sisters had already dropped out of school, while the younger sister, who had recently been suspended, showed little inclination to return to school.

All four had also been "burnouts," members of a troubled and troublesome peer group addicted to punk fashions and heavy-metal music. Since leaving school, the two young men had been employed only intermittently, and there were indications of frequent drug and alcohol use by these four teens and their friends. According to the local police chief, these were "pain-in-the-ass-type kids" who were "going nowhere fast" ("copycat suicides").

Who was responsible for the uneasy lives and easy deaths of these young people? No one seemed to agree. Some blamed uncaring families that had neglected their children and had not heeded their calls for help; others faulted an insensitive school system that had failed these adolescents at risk. However, many saw the tragedy as yet another example of the excesses of a media-hyped national "youth culture" and of the power of the peer group to pressure its members to conform. Even the experts on teenage suicide could not agree on whether media exposure of teenage suicide only exacerbates the problem by planting the idea of suicide in young minds throughout the country.

Suicide is only one of a variety of social problems, such as pregnancy, drug and alcohol abuse, crime and delinquency, and dropping out of school, that mark adolescence in America as a troubled period of transition to adulthood. The drama associated with these social problems also supplies the forms, the symbols, and the colors with which the popular culture produces its portrait of what most American adolescents are supposed to be like.

Since World War II American teenagers have been portrayed in a number of different ways. In the 1950s, a period of relative peace and prosperity, most were portrayed as clean-cut, materialistic conformists, indifferent to political and social issues. To liven things up there were a few greasers, beatniks, and "rebels without a cause." In the 1960s, a decade scarred by the Vietnam War, urban riots, and political assassinations, the media portrayed teenagers as angry, assertive, hedonistic, idealistic, and anti-materialistic.

Then, in the 1970s, teenagers were shown to be disillusioned by the failure of the activism and reforms of the 1960s and by an oversupply of would-be professionals. In the public mind, at least, young people once again became grade-grubbing, apathetic, and conservative. Still another picture began to emerge in the 1980s. As concern deepened over problems of physical and mental health, sexual and social conduct, and various forms of abuse of self and others among young people, we began to see and hear adolescents described as the "New Lost Generation."

Are such collective characterizations accurate portrayals of what most American adolescents are like? Are teenagers and their peer groups pretty much the same in urban, suburban, or rural areas? Are parents and other adults really so powerless? Are communities, their schools, and other social institutions helpless in the face of some compelling youth culture that seems to shape their peer group no matter where teenagers live?

THE IDEA OF A NATIONAL YOUTH CULTURE

The idea that adolescent society or youth culture is unique emerged most clearly with James Coleman's study of peer behavior in high schools during the late 1950s. Coleman identified the peer group as the major source of socialization for adolescents because "adolescents are looking to each other rather than to the adult community for their social rewards." What Coleman dubbed the "adolescent society" was a separate social system, with a psychosocial unity of its own, that was capable of resisting and even countering the adult society's authority and demands for integration into the general community. Other voices, both before and after Coleman's, have reinforced the idea of a unique "adolescent society."

By the 1960s we were coming to view adolescence less as one of many stages in a continuous path through life and more as a distinct and disruptive sub-society with values, norms, and a culture of its own.

Widely publicized notions of a "generation gap" and a "counterculture" linked the local peer group to a national youth culture—in the popular perception as well as in much of the sociological literature on teenagers. Adolescents supposedly looked to this collective cultural consciousness—broadcast nationally through the lyrics and beat of rock-and-roll music and made increasingly visible as television spread throughout the country—rather than to parents or to local community norms for support and guidance.

The creation of the notion of a youth culture did more than supply an explanation for the mounting social problems of teenagers. *It took both the source of the crises and the hope of their resolution out of the hands of local communities and out of the hands of parents and other adults who were close to the daily lives of teenagers.* The idea that a youth culture was the source of the problems of adolescence moved those problems to a distant national arena. And if the problems were national, then national strategies and resources were required to combat them; local options and the community authority structure were powerless. Lost in this nationalization was the fact that just as communities differ, so do the families, the schools, the workplaces, and other social institutions within them. Moreover, these differences have important and lasting effects on teenagers and the groups they form.

THE DIVERSITY OF THE ADOLESCENT EXPERIENCE

For more than a decade, spanning the 1970s and 1980s, my associates and I observed and interviewed adolescents in ten communities throughout the U.S. We found that the diversity among communities and the effects of local differences on adolescents and on the groups they formed persisted over time. The teenagers in the ten communities we studied were as different from one another as they were from the adults in their own communities. Teenagers live in poverty, in affluence, or someplace in between. They come from broken or intact families, attend good or bad schools, and encounter very different role models in their communities. Adolescent development takes place within a specific community, as the individual teenager's internal resources are nurtured or stifled by what is available.

Just as teenagers differ, depending on where and how they live, so do the peer groups they form. Our comparative data from the communities we studied led us to question whether a "national" youth culture could homogenize all this diversity and come between the social institutions of local communities and the youngsters they teach and enculturate. Indeed, our data convinced us that the local peer groups were not parts of any distinctive and enduring subsociety that isolates adolescents from the adult world while escorting them out of childhood. Peer groups are necessary and effective arenas of social reference that do exert powerful influence, often coupled with considerable anxiety and stress, on their teenage members. But local peer groups grow out of and continue to be related to the adult institutions that sanction them, and they are usually short-lived and dedicated to specific purposes. Although peer groups do provide occasions for interaction among peers and for questioning adult values, few teens ever do completely reject those values.

We tend to talk about adolescence as if it were a single, unified period of life. But teenagers more often experience adolescence at a number of more or less coterminous periods, each structured by such socializing environments as the family, the peer group, the work place, the media, or the criminal justice system. In some of the communities we studied, we found that different rules and roles for adolescents emerge from each of several institutions and that differentiating among them is a difficult process that requires an understanding of societal and personal agendas.

Unfortunately, the adolescent is often left to rationalize these competing and sometimes conflicting ideologies for himself or herself. This is particularly true in those communities in which the family and the school are in opposition, in which the criminal justice system is antagonistic to both institutions, and in which employers berate both institutions for turning out unmotivated and nonliterate youngsters. Conflict and confusion are inevitable when

such social institutions as the home, the school, and the workplace present different standards of adulthood. For example, proclaiming 21 as the minimum age for the legal use of alcohol means that, in some states, young people cannot drink legally until three years after they have been given the right to vote and the young men have been required to register for the military draft. While we are raising the legal age of adulthood for some activities, we are lowering it for others. And despite all we know about individual differences in maturation and development, we continue to think of and treat adolescents as members of a distinctive and age-defined caste.

The sense of identity and the social role of a teenager can change radically with the surrounding social environment, as any parent can attest who has watched a son or daughter who is quiet, withdrawn and perhaps even surly at home suddenly become expansive and outgoing with peers. Consolidating the real and fantasied roles and self-images that adolescents adopt in various social contexts into a more or less integrated representation of self is part of growing up. This conception of self is then internalized and becomes a characteristic style of relating to social environments. However, what adolescents internalize is a function of experience, and different communities offer very different environments to developing youngsters.

COMMUNITY PROFILE: SOUTHSIDE

Southside, one of the ten communities we studied, has all the ingredients to create the serious social problems and personal tragedies that tend to be associated with adolescence. It is one of a number of inner-city neighborhoods in a major eastern city. It is multiethnic, poor, and made up of massive public housing projects and squalid, aging tenements. And it seems to have always been that way. Generations of European immigrants in pursuit of the American dream have lived in Southside and struggled to leave, only to be replaced by new immigrant groups in a seemingly unending process of ethnic succession. Recently, this process seems to be accelerating, and more than a quarter of a million people live out their lives huddled within this two-square mile area, as Chinese and Hispanic immigrants crowd in next to the few remaining European families. Josie is one of the teenagers we observed and interviewed in Southside.

Josie is 16 and has lived in Southside ever since her family came to the U.S. from the Dominican Republic when she was seven. She is the youngest of ten children and the only one who lives at home—though several married siblings live in the same building or nearby in the neighborhood. For Josie, a combination of language, residence, and perhaps even preference makes her peer group and her close friends—male and female—mostly Hispanic and usually Dominican. She attends what is for all intents and purposes a segregated high school, one in which students choose their friends from among those to whom they are bound by language, culture, and ethnicity.

Up before 7 A.M. on school days, Josie dresses, applies some makeup, and eats breakfast in time to meet a girlfriend or two (usually Dominican) for the walk to school. Arriving at school a few minutes before the 8:30 bell, she smokes a cigarette with her friends outside the school in a place frequented by other Dominican students.

Nobody has ever said that Josie or that other Dominicans must congregate in that particular place. Yet the students in Josie's school always group themselves in the same way: blacks congregate on the north side of the school, Hispanics on the west side, and the white and Chinese students on the south side. Such segregation is certainly not school policy, and most of the teachers and administrators try to combat it. But it happens anyway. The bonding of ethnicity follows the students into the school, where they sit together in similar patterns. In classes Josie sits with her fellow Hispanic students, just as most Chinese and black students sit with their ethnic peers.

The members of Josie's family are not greatly involved with what happens in the school—not only because they feel incompetent to deal with education in a new country, but also because they are content, as teachers and administrators put it, to "leave the driving to us." These same teachers and administrators will tell you that the families of Chinese students are very much involved with the school and try to give their children "a positive learning environment." Chinese students and their families, say these educators, are like the Jewish students and their families back in the 1930s and 1940s.

Now the examples begin. The principal recalls the father of a Chinese student, who complained that there was too much class discussion in his son's advanced math course. "My son is here to learn from teachers," he said, "not from other students who don't know any more than he does." The principal was so pleased to have a parent come in and say that he respected what the school and the teachers were trying to do that he thanked the father for his complaint. One of the older teachers remembers a Jewish student who came to class one day without his reader—because his father had fallen asleep trying to learn to read it late at night, after his son had gone to bed. Then the comparisons go the other way, and the teachers compare today's Hispanics and blacks with the Italians of past generations, who always believed that you should not educate your children beyond your own level, lest they forget the family.

In our talks with educators, we found similar perceptions of the lack of parent involvement in each of the inner-city areas and depressed rural areas that we studied. Such perceptions stood out in sharp contrast to the descriptions of community involvement and the complaints of parental interference that we heard about in the suburbs.

COMMUNITY PROFILE: SHEFFIELD

The town of Sheffield, another of the communities we studied, in a small, affluent suburb near the city in which Southside is located. In fact, many heads of Sheffield households commute daily into the business district that lies close to the slums of Southside. Sheffield is not a newly developed suburb; it is actually an old town by American standards, dating to the days before the Revolutionary War. Not only did George Washington sleep there, but he had his headquarters in the town for some time. Today, Sheffield retains its small-town flavor; its streets are lined with arching trees, its houses are painted in subdued shades, and its broad lawns are trimmed with abundant, well-manicured shrubbery. Like Southside, Sheffield is a little more than two square miles in area, but fewer than 10,000 people live there.

If the ethnic diversity of Southside is tangible, in Sheffield one immediately feels the homogeneity of the people and of their lifestyles. Differences of religion and politics do exist, of course, but these distinctions have nowhere near the visibility or power of the ethnic differences that divide Southside. There are virtually no black or Hispanic families in Sheffield. And despite a few affluent Japanese families that have settled in Sheffield in recent years, visible ethnic differences are unknown there.

Families are just as important in the enculturation of children in Sheffield as they are in Southside. But similarity rather than diversity characterizes child-rearing practices and family organizations in Sheffield, because parents have such similar social and cultural backgrounds. Bruce, a high school senior whom we observed and interviewed, moved to Sheffield at age 11, when his father was transferred to the area by the multinational corporation for which he works as a mid-level executive. Bruce's mother, who taught school when the family lived in Michigan, chose not to seek a teaching position in Sheffield, for fear that doing so might detract from the time she could spend overseeing the education and development of Bruce and his two younger sisters. Bruce remembers that both his mother and father—but especially his mother—encouraged him to make friends as soon as possible, so that the family's integration into the community could be facilitated by social contacts with other families. "It wasn't so much that she was a joiner," Bruce recalls. "It's just that we learned in Michigan that families are important for feeling part of what is going on."

In Sheffield, peer association and socialization are organized and directed by the parents, who play active roles on school committees and in the organization of sports and other extracurricular activities at the school. The churches and the school offer a variety of family activities, ranging from family outings to youth clubs with parents advisors. These family-centered groups not only share a common culture and values but they also have similar goals for their children and similar standards for measuring progress toward those goals. Both the present lifestyles and the orientation of Sheffield families toward the future focus on preparing youngsters for college and careers. Peer groups tend to be quite small, and the most common form of interaction is within a small and noncompetitive group of "best friends." Students are also differentiated by a complex system of ability grouping in the schools, and teachers and administrators complain that some parents threaten to send their children to private schools if they are not placed in honor courses. The schools, which reflect community and family expectations, are structured to encourage a competitive spirit, not only in sports but also in academic and social life. People in Sheffield will tell you that the two things you never ask at a cocktail party are a family's income and the Scholastic Aptitude Test scores of the children.

A WORLD STRUCTURED BY RELATIONSHIPS

Differences between growing up in Southside and growing up in Sheffield entail more than the contrast between urban poverty and suburban affluence. These differences grow out of the many ways in which the daily world of the adolescent is structured by relationships that begin in the family and spread out from there into other social environments in the community. The peer group, though often described as emancipating adolescents from the adult community, is subject to the same constraints.

Peer groups, which are important influences in the lives of all children, are particularly important for teenagers. As adolescence proceeds over the course of the teen years, peer groups become social environments in themselves. They are institutional settings for adolescent social development (just as much as families, schools, and churches are), and their influence on adolescents is considerable. However, unlike the more traditional and recognized institutions, peer groups do not have their own physical structures. Lacking a territory of their own, adolescents as groups must either stake out space belonging to one of the traditional institutions, such as the home or the school, or they must find some neutral and usually temporary space in which to meet, outside the scrutiny of adults. Nor do peer groups have the legal status and protection enjoyed by these other institutions. They tend to form and interact, particularly in the early teen years, at the sufferance of one or more of the adult institutions.

Both Bruce and Josie belong to peer groups whose members live in the same neighborhood, come from the same kinds of families, go to the same school, and share other kinds of involvement in their respective communities. Their peer associations are not random choices but are influenced by the families in which they grew up, by the communities in which they live, by the schools they attend, and by the ways in which these institutions relate to one another.

However, the influence of these institutions can work in two different ways: 1) by leading one to accept the attitudes, beliefs, and opinions espoused by members of the institution as one's own, or 2) by leading one to seek social approval from— and avoid rejection by—members of the institution, without necessarily internalizing its values. In the communities we studied, adult influence on teenagers tended to be longstanding, reaching back into childhood. While the teenagers might challenge that influence, it nonetheless continued to shape their basic values.

The peer influence that we observed tended to be of the second type, leading teenagers to seek approval of the group through conformity to its norms. Moreover, peer influence was usually transitory, lasting only as long as the teenager was a member of or continued to accept the norms of the peer group. Teenagers did not

internalize the norms of peer groups to the same degree as they did adult-mediated norms, and usually the norms of the peer group did not cause conflict with adults.

Peer groups were influential without really meaning to be. The individual teenager's willingness—and perhaps even need—to conform, particularly in the early years, rather than any consciously articulated group pressure, had the greatest impact in the groups that we observed. While there were differences among the adolescent peer groups we saw and talked with in each of the communities, there were certain characteristics and feelings that they shared. For example, the most important reason virtually all the teenagers gave for wanting to spend time with their peers was "just to be together." Most of them said that peer association provided them with "understanding." Many said that such understanding was the result of "being the same age," of "wanting the same things," or of "wanting to help each other"; some said that the important thing was "going through the same changes" or "facing the same problems."

Through seemingly random interchanges, adolescents can test their developing abilities and craft socially competent behavior. They learn from their own mistakes and from those of their agemates. They also learn to evaluate what people outside their families say, as they move into the wider and more socially diverse world of the community.

However, for most adolescent peer groups in the communities we studied, we found that association with agemates was not the sole reason that the groups first formed. Instead, a variety of inter-personal relationships with significant adults and even with adult ideological or religious systems first brought the groups together. In most cases, these relationships provided both a setting and a rationale for continuing association. Peer groups are important social settings in adolescent life, but focusing only on teenagers paints a distorted picture of adolescent life and overlooks the significant role of adult guidance in shaping a secure and successful transition from childhood to adulthood. It also masks the vital role that the social institutions of the community—

the family, the school, the workplace, religious institution, and other social agencies—play in determining both adolescent development and the emergence of peer groups.

The vast majority of the teenagers we met, observed, and interviewed were well aware of both adult and peer influences in their lives. There was no question in their minds (or ours) that both kinds of influences helped to resolve doubts about present and future and that the teenagers distinguished between the two kinds of influences. The real question, however, is how near to or far from the local community such sources of influence can be and still have a developmental effect on the norms and attitudes of teenagers.

We did not find any indications of strong, active resistance—on the part of individuals or groups of teenagers—to the preferred norms of communities, as long as the institutions representing the adult authority structure agreed on what teenagers were supposed to be and do, not just on what they were not to be and do. As teenagers mature, they seek to move away from the normative pressures of the adult community. But we found far more congruence than conflict between the world views of parents and their adolescent children.

Children are certainly socialized by their parents, but, as they become teenagers and gain more experience in the world outside the family, they bring what they have learned back to the family and share that knowledge with parents and siblings. While we found some parent-child conflict within families and some teacher-student conflict within schools, most adolescents in the communities that we studied became integrated into the social fabric of their communities—and, indeed, into the mainstream of American society—under the guidance of parents and other adults. In fact, in peer-structured support groups, in adult-developed and adult-mediated peer support networks in drug rehabilitation programs, mental health programs, and programs for runaways, and in scout troops, church youth groups, and schools, we found that teenagers seeking to influence the beliefs and behaviors of their peers quoted

the values proclaimed by adults. We much more frequently heard teenagers preface comments or observations to peers with "my mom says" than with any attribution to heroes or pundits of the youth culture.

Reasserting the continuing importance of parents and other significant adults in adolescent development does not negate the crucial role of peer groups in shaping adolescents' relationships with a community's social environments. Peer groups allow adolescents to explore relationships outside the boundaries of kinship, to test and further develop self-knowledge and self-esteem, and to resolve self-doubts. They also provide an informal support group that provides opportunities for peer counseling and peer tutoring in which both the helper and the helped benefit from the exchange. A variety of programs involving youngsters helping youngsters are already in place in various communities; most are school-based and involve small groups or one-to-one tutoring.

In each of the communities we studied, youths and adults expressed and exhibited a common culture of the community. The notion of a compelling and separatist teenager subculture perpetuates the myth that all adolescents are alike. In doing so, it masks the considerable diversity among adolescents and overlooks their attachments to the cultural, ethnic, and social-class lifestyles of their parents.

For example, family and community combine to provide the dominant influences of socioeconomic status in childhood and adolescence. Backgrounds of poverty impose major developmental hardships on adolescents by restricting their participation in the social and cultural functions of institutions. Youngsters from low-income backgrounds are more likely to have learning disabilities and to record lower educational achievement. They are also more likely to drop out of school, to experience teenage pregnancy and early parenthood, to become involved in criminal and delinquent acts, to be arrested and incarcerated, to be unemployed, and to continue their working lives on the lowest rungs of the work force.

The lives of more affluent adolescents are quite different, but these young people have some problems as well. The pressures to excel are strong in suburbia (Elkind; Elkind and Brooks). We witnessed the stressful effects of such parents and community pressure in many of the suburban schools we studied. We also saw pressure in other areas of adolescent social life, such as sports. We watched early adolescents spending four to five hours a day in an effort to fulfill their parents' dreams that their offspring become sports superstars and bring home Olympic gold medals.

Yet family income alone does not completely determine the character and outcome of the adolescent years for all individuals. Differing parental and community strategies for adolescent development, chance encounters and unique experiences, and the motivation, determination, resilience, and personal belief systems of teenagers themselves make for a variety of patterns of growing up in America.

Communities also differ in the ways in which they structure the patterns of relationships among families, schools, peer groups, and other institutions. And the influence of these relationships can be more important to adolescent development than the effect of any one institution. While each can help or hinder an adolescent's preparation for adulthood, multiple deficits can combine and reinforce one another, with devastating effect. It is possible for adolescents from impoverished backgrounds to succeed; it is possible for them to overcome early educational deficits or association with peers who derogate the schools. But such successes require exceptional intrinsic motivation on the part of the individual adolescent, a family that values and encourages educational attainment, a teacher or school dedicated to success, or some combination of all of these. Many teenagers told me of having met some adult, read some book, seen some film, come in contact with new ideology or lifestyle, "taken up" running or health foods, entered some program, found religion, or discovered some environment that "completely changed" their lives. Indeed, some of the most dramatic of these changes took place in surroundings that were most foreboding and

where more firm and consistent interventions were necessary.

THE CONTEXT OF COMMUNITY

Adolescents do generate their own norms and rules, but this process does not and cannot develop in isolation from the institutional context of the communities in which they live and learn. The norms of adolescents may be in harmony or in conflict with the "ideal" values of the community or of particular institutions, but they can never be independent of them. To that extent, we believe it is not possible to identify some independent "youth subculture." Moreover, the value structures of ethnic groups and social classes also influence the psychological development of adolescents.

However, none of these influences, in isolation, can be said to be the determining factor in the psychological development of adolescents. Rather, we have found that a complex mix of all these factors and of the relationships among the institutions within a particular community establish the pattern. For example, minority status did not have any intrinsic effect on self-regard and was important to self-esteem only to the extent that it was featured in the community's—or more frequently in some component social institution's—ideal identity for adolescents. Daniel Yankelovich has identified the two "truths" that we all know about the self: one is that the self is private and alone and wholly encased in one's body. The other is that one is a real self only to the extent that caring and reaching beyond the self continue (Yankelovich 240). And communities can and should care about and try to help with the self-development of their younger members, as well.

Every community can and should shape the relationships among its various socializing institutions into a network that fosters the learning of its values. Moreover, the messages that each of the institutions send to individual adolescents should be mutually reinforcing, rather than disharmonious or even working at cross purposes. In addition, the opportunity to internalize those values should be available to all children and not just to a fortunate few. The importance of integrating the socializing institutions to provide such a caring structure and the interdependence of the adult and adolescent social worlds in producing and interpreting it were visible in the social and behavioral standards set by each of the communities we studied for its young.

These standards and the expectations they described were not so much a set of rules sanctioned by the community as they were a loose collection of shared understandings that limited the variability of permissible behavior. For example, if we asked a teenager why he or she did or did not become involved in some activity, seek some goal, avoid some risk, or behave in one way rather than another, the reason was seldom said to be because of any specific rule or authority system, such as family or peers. Rather, we heard much more generalized reasons, such as, "I don't know why, but it seemed to be the right thing to do" or "That's the way it is here in Sheffield."

Parents and teachers were equally vague in describing the origins of their expectations of teenagers. In explaining what time they expected a teenager to be home at night, parents would usually cite the general perception of neighbors or community residents that youngsters of a particular age should be home "at about" such and such a time, and we seldom found great discrepancies among families. Teenagers, though they might protest that the times were too early, would usually mention the same general time limits as parents. Teenagers also agreed with parents and with one another on how much leeway they would be granted and what extenuating circumstances their parents would accept. Asking teachers about homework assignments or school administrators about discipline almost always elicited similar references to "what this community expects."

We came to call this unwritten, "sensed" set of expectations and standards the community's "youth charter." While it is nowhere codified, both youngsters and adults usually know the limits set by the youth charter for various kinds of behavior, and the daily lives of the teenagers are governed largely by the conventions that emerge from the shared understandings of the charter.

Like so much else in life, the development of these tacit understandings begins in the family, when the growing child learns from the comments and choices of parents and older siblings to value or devalue individual and group traits, as well as to evaluate the shoulds and should-nots of individual and group behavior. These influences lay a foundation for future reference, and for most youngsters the family continues to be more influential than any other social group.

Beginning in the early adolescent years, peers become increasingly important in spontaneous decision making, but their judgments and opinions are considered along with, rather than as replacements for, parental influences. As the school and other social worlds of the community become increasingly important in the teenager's life, the community establishes a comprehensive frame of reference that both integrates and transcends the influence of any particular institutional sector. Decisions about schooling, for example, involve parental and peer influences and, less directly, the worlds of work and of school. Thus adolescents perceive themselves as interacting within a social environment, and the way in which that environment structures reality becomes their charter for action. Communities can create youth charters that encourage youngsters to move from dependence to interdependence, from the ethnocentrism of early adolescence to the social competence of young adulthood, and from definitions of self provided by surrounding social contexts to those arising from within.

Schools can be instrumental in providing the community and its constituent institutions with a structure for transmitting the expectations and standards that we found most teenagers are desperately seeking. Schools are central to the lives of adolescents—not only because so much of their waking time is spent in them but also because schools have been assigned a role at least commensurate with that of families in the preparation of adolescents for later life. The schools are expected to teach occupational preparation, information about health, a measure of self-discipline, and good citizenship.

Indeed, we have come to see schools—particularly high schools—as the principal remediators of social ills. We include new courses in the curriculum in the belief that this offers our best chance for prevention, as well as for cure. Wide spread drug abuse led to drug education courses, alcohol abuse led to alcohol education courses, and teen pregnancy led to sex education courses. Even so, the specter of Acquired Immune Deficiency Syndrome will inevitably lead to AIDS education courses, however controversial that may be. But the introduction and continuation of such courses is much more a matter of local community sentiment and sensitivity than of any education policy at the state or national level.

The influence of the community on the culture of the schools is so strong that it calls into question the notion of a "school culture" independent of community culture. As part of that interaction, the school establishes networks among adolescents that reinforces the connections between the social organization of the community and the growth and development of individual adolescents. To the extent that the school relies on social, racial, and ethnic identification to sort students' access to educational resources, it confuses and confounds the consolidation of identity. Ethnographers Signithia Fordham and John Ogbu have argued that one reason that black students do poorly in school is the ambivalence and dissonance they experience from "the burden of acting white" (176–206). Fordham and Ogbu found that many academically able black students do not put forth the necessary effort, because they are caught between a school system that fails to acknowledge that black students are capable of academic achievement and a black community that considers academic strive as "acting white."

Once we accept the ability of local peer groups to mediate a variety of external influences and to help youngsters become members of the community of adults, it may even be possible to help teenagers develop peer-group structures that enhance their cognitive and social development. Benjamin Bloom underscored the feasibility of such an approach through the formation of peer groups; he proposed establishing student support groups of two or three students working together to raise the level of learning of the group members (Bloom). Peer groups provide the informal support that can give adolescents access to a vast new set of opportunities for peer counseling and peer tutoring in which both the helper and the helped benefit. As already noted, a variety of programs involving youngsters helping youngsters are already in place in various communities; most are school-based and involve small groups or one-on-one tutoring.

In response to suicide pacts, such as the one in Bergenfield, some schools are setting up peer networks that work with adult counselors to watch for signs of potential suicide and to offer help and care. Similar networks have been tried as ways of dealing with alcohol and drug abuse. Other approaches, such as the Primary Prevention School Program of the Yale Child Study Center, are more broadly based and stress academic competence and help as well.

Adult-mediated peer groups offer a creative means of bringing adult concerns to groups of youngsters who have daily access to one another. But they are largely dependent on adults and on their continuing concern. The more spontaneous and less formal groups that youngsters negotiate for themselves lack the continuity of adult social institutions and tend to respond to changes in adult agendas, rather than to their own agendas or to forces from outside the community. For example, peer groups are one of the social contexts most affected by changes in the structure and functioning of the family. As more mothers have entered the labor market, adolescents have tended to have less adult supervision and have spent more time with peers, becoming more dependent on peer-defined cultural, social, and behavioral norms. This has meant less time for the loving support of parents, which all children need, even when they do not seem to be asking for it. But none of these changes were initiated by any intentional activity of the adolescent peer group.

A COMMUNITY YOUTH CHARTER

When we first undertook our research program, the development of an officially endorsed youth charter was but a dream. We even included a caution in our early proposals and reports, citing Sigmund Freud's *Civilization and Its Discontents*, in which he asks, "What would be the use of the most acute analysis of social neurosis since no one possesses the power to compel the community to adopt the therapy?"

Now, more than a decade later, at least one community is developing precisely such a charter. Sparked both by research and by a number of program initiatives, the city of Seattle has adopted and made explicit a Policy Plan for Children and Youth, which was developed 1) to gain a better understanding of the status of children and youth in Seattle and of current efforts to address their needs and 2) to promote community agreement on goals and priorities in order to establish a clearer understanding of the roles to be played by various jurisdictions and organizations in the service system for children and youth.

This plan, which looks to young people as a community resource rather than as a liability, makes the community's youth charter (what Seattle calls a community youth agenda) clear and available to all. It is designed to 1) help parents better fulfill their responsibilities to their children, 2) improve the health and well-being of children and youth and protect them from harm, 3) prepare young people for a successful transition to adulthood, 4) help young people better understand cultural differences and value the ethnic diversity of the community, 5) project to all young people a vision of high expectations and hope for their futures and a sense of the responsibilities they bear, and 6) involve children and youth as active participants in the community. The plan, which goes on to describe the responsibilities and the rights

of all the constituent social institutions (including those of children), has now become the "official" policy of Seattle and is overseen by a committee of city officials and citizens, including two youths elected by their peers.

The next step that Seattle is taking will convert what is essentially a plan into a charter. Groups of 30 teenagers meet frequently to develop the plan, item by item, into a series of expectations and standards. They have conducted youth surveys to determine how best to disseminate these standards to all youngsters in the city.[1] Of course, it is too soon to call Seattle's plan a success and to assume that this or any other such formalization of a community's adolescent charter will or can be made to work as a new or expanded chance for a smoother and more productive transition to adulthood. However, the experience in Seattle does offer the hope that communities are beginning to accept their local responsibility to treat adolescence as a period in which young people requires a stable and consistent environment in which to grow and develop.

Despite continuing assumptions—both professionals and popular—that adolescents look toward peers and away from the adult community, we found significant congruence between the world views of teenagers and those of the adults in their lives. However, such congruence means that the problems of adolescence are our problems, too, and cannot be explained away by referring to a "youth culture" that we claim adolescents invented. I believe that we have made the adolescent peer group the scapegoat for our own sins, both those that we commit ourselves and those that adolescents learn from us. The use and abuse of drugs, alcohol, and tobacco began as adult problems and became teenage problems only when we introduced young people to them as signs of having reached adult status. Other adult-proclaimed youth problems, such as unemployment and delinquent behavior, follow similar demographic and cyclical patterns among young people as they do among adults. And some, such as poor nutritional and other health habits, are first learned in the family. While we seldom hear about the social benefits of peer groups, they do exist. As we observed the style and the spirit of interaction in peer groups, we found them to offer important ways of allowing youngsters to experiment with and learn about egalitarian relationships and about new and different patterns of representing themselves. The lessons learned in peer groups are sometimes painful, but they are necessary preparation for adult social relations.

The popular picture of a deeply troubled and rebellious generation of young Americans is not the picture we saw emerging during the decade of our research. By the second half of the 1980s, adolescent pregnancy was down to 5.1 per 1000 teenage girls from the 68.3 per 1000 in 1970 and the 89 per 1000 in 1960. While there is some cause for concern in the fact that well over half of these young mothers-to-be were unmarried in the second half of the 1980s, whereas only one-third were unmarried in 1970, it could well be that as a society we are becoming more accepting of the choice to be a single mother. Educational attainment, particularly among blacks, has increased steadily, and the dropout rate has been declining. Eighty-six percent of all 25- to 29-year-olds have earned high school diplomas (twice the percentage of 1940), and 22% are college graduates (four times the 1940 rate). Drug use among young people has decreased significantly, the rate of alcohol abuse among young people has decreased somewhat, and some leveling off has occurred in crime, homicide, and suicide rates.[2]

Teenagers do have time to make choices about their present and future lifestyles, and the adolescents whom we met and interviewed expressed considerable confidence that they could make such decisions, given the time and the adult guidance that they know they need. It was the adults we observed and interviewed who seemed to be in a hurry for teenagers to "settle down" into adulthood—often ignoring or forgetting that developmental tasks and the achievement of a mature identity proceed as much from what the community can provide for guidance and encouragement as from teenagers' own resources and motivation.

With a firm but sensitive set of expectations and standards, undergirded by a youth charter, and with our acceptance of the fact that time is abundant, adolescent crises can become less urgent and can even provide opportunities for learning and progress. This suggests less concern about the prolongation of adolescence and more concern about how we can integrate adolescence into the life course, as a time in which teenagers seek identity rather than interdependence. We can provide an explicit guidance structure within which they can work, rather than offer only benign neglect or outraged moralizing. The transitional role of adults and adult-mediated institutions should be one of patient, guided tutoring. The youth charter seems to be an ideal place to map out the roles of adults and adolescents, since it is more accessible than teenage fantasy for discussion and negotiation—and at the same time has less immediate and less critical consequences than the reality we so often insist that teenagers face. Youth charters and the structure of expectations and standards experienced through adolescent life in the community interact with individual personalities in a variety of social worlds to produce behaviors, motivations, and attitudes that shape the movement to adult status. It is in the harmony of these social contexts that adolescence can—and usually does—become a period of joy and challenge as well as a sentimental journey from what must be left behind in the migration to the new adult world.

END NOTES

1 Personal communication from Robert Aldrich. For an excellent description of the type of data gathering and organization required to move a community in this direction, see Robert A. Aldrich, "Children and Youth in Cities: Seattle's Kidsplace," in Rick Carlson and Brooke Newman, Eds., *Issues and Trends in Health* (St. Louis: C. V. Mosby, 1987), 63–69.

2 See *The Forgotten Half: Non-College Youth in America* (Washington, DC:

William T. Grant Foundation Commission on Work, Family and Citizenship, January 1988).

WORKS CITED

Bloom, Benjamin S. "The Search for Methods of Group Instruction as Effective as One-to-One Tutoring." *Educational Leadership* May 1984: 4–17.

Coleman, James. *Youth: Transition to Adulthood*. Chicago: University of Chicago Press, 1974.

_____. *The Adolescent Society*. Glencoe, IL.: Free Press, 1960.

"The Copycat Suicides." *Newsweek* 23 March 1987: 28.

Elkind, David. *Miseducation: Preschoolers at Risk*. New York: Knopf, 1988.

Elkind, David, and Andree Aelion Brooks, *Children of Fast-track Parents*. New York: Viking, 1989.

Fordham, Signithia and John U. Ogbu. "Black Students' School Success: Coping with the Burden of 'Acting White.'" *Urban Review* 18 (1986): 176–206.

Freud, Sigmund. *Civilization and Its Discontents*. Trans. Joan Riviere. Garden City, NY: Doubleday, 1958.

Yankelovich, Daniel. *New Rules: Search for Self-Fulfillment in a World Turned Upside Down*. New York: Random House, 1981.

CHAPTER 9

An Ethnic-Cultural Perspective

Thomas Bright

CULTURE, ETHNIC TRADITION, FAMILIES, AND FAITH

We live our lives immersed in the culture that surrounds us. Culture affects everything we think and feel, do and say. It is the sum total of all those ways of doing things, of thinking about things, of feeling about things, of believing, that make up the life of a people. On the other hand, culture is not foreordained, a process that we are forced to accept unquestioningly, like it or not. Culture is learned and is subject to change.

At times in the past it was assumed that there was one U.S. culture. The United States was imaged as a melting pot. To be American was to assume one's place in mainstream U.S. culture, setting aside the differences and distinctions that derived from diverse national or ethnic origins. That assumption is being increasingly challenged today as people mix with persons of other countries and cultures, and struggle to affirm or reclaim the values and traditions rooted in their ethnic heritage. The image of the United States is slowly shifting from a melting pot to a multi-hued tapestry. The strength and beauty of the tapestry lie in the diverse colors and textures of its component threads—the varied values and traditions claimed by the different ethnic groups that constitute the people of the United States.

Ethnicity provides people with a lens for viewing the culture in which they live. Even where ethnic and mainstream cultures proclaim the same basic values, ethnic differences can offer a variety of perspectives on how the values are to be lived out at home and in the wider society.

Ethnicity interacts with the family life cycle at every stage. Families differ in their definition of "family," in their definition of the timing of life cycle phases and the tasks appropriate at each phase, and in their traditions, rituals, and ceremonies to mark life cycle transitions. Ethnicity patterns our thinking, feeling, and behavior in both obvious and subtle ways, although generally operating outside of our awareness. It plays a major role in determining what we eat, how we work, how we relate, how we celebrate holidays and rituals, and how we feel about life, death, and illness. Ethnicity impacts our outlook on family life, our expressions of faith, and our faith traditions.

The Church, like all groups in society, is impacted by the cultures that surround it. As Christianity took root in Western Europe in the fourth and fifth centuries, it incorporated many of the ethnic and cultural understandings common to the time into the practice of Christian faith. What began in the earliest days of the Church's life continues in our time. Faith is about relating, about real people encountering and committing themselves to a God made real in past and present history. If faith is to remain alive and dynamic, it must continually adapt itself to the lived history of individuals and of peoples. Ethnicity provides a key not just to understanding ourselves, but also to understanding our

God. "No one group of people has the complete truth and picture of God. Each group can add a different dimension and perspective of God to the rest of Christianity, so that together we gain a fuller picture of God and of God's kingdom . . . Thus culture has the capacity to express faith, and the variety of cultures helps each of us see the true and unique God" (Choy-Wong 139).

DEFINING ETHNICITY

Despite increased talk of "ethnic culture" and the impact of "ethnicity" on family life and values, there has been little consistency in how these, and similar words, have been defined in everyday conversation, media reports, or scholarly articles. Mary Jane Rotheram and Jean Phinney offer the following definitions in their attempt to clarify the meaning of these frequently used terms (Rotheram and Phinney 10–25).

Ethnicity—*Ethnicity* includes group patterns of values, social customs, perceptions, behavioral roles, language usage, and rules of social interactions that group members share. *Ethnicity* is more than ancestry, race, religion or national origin.

Ethnic group—An *ethnic group* is any collection of people who call themselves an ethnic group and who see themselves sharing common attributes. Often the term *ethnic group* has been used to refer to minority groups within a larger culture. It can be argued from a broader perspective than not only minority groups but also the dominant groups in a country, such as white Americans in the United States, are *ethnic groups*. If *ethnic groups* are understood in this way, the distinctive characteristics of each group can be examined and understood in their own terms, rather than as deviations from the "norm" of the dominant culture. Furthermore, the study of *ethnic groups* on their own terms allows the examination of within-group differences that are often ignored when groups are compared only to the dominant culture.

Ethnic identity—Broadly speaking, *ethnic identity* refers to a person's sense of belonging to an ethnic group and the parts of his or her thinking, perceptions, feelings, and behavior that are due to ethnic group membership. *Ethnic identity* is distinguished from *ethnicity* in that *ethnicity* refers to *group patterns*, and *ethnic identity* refers to the *individual's* acquisition of group patterns.

Ethnic awareness—*Ethnic awareness* is the person's understanding of his or her own and other ethnic groups. Awareness involves knowledge about ethnic groups, their critical attributes, characteristics, history, and customs, as well as the difference between oneself and others.

Ethnic attitudes—*Ethnic attitudes* are ways of responding to ethnicity, one's own and others, that may carry either a positive or negative connotation. *Ethnic attitudes* measure people's preferences or likings for their own or another ethnic group, and their negative attitudes toward other groups.

Ethnic patterns—Recent studies of *ethnic patterns* have attempted to document the differences in attitudinal, affective and behavioral patterns experienced in people of different cultures and ethnic traditions. Research suggests four dimensions that are central to differentiating the social behaviors of ethnic and cultural groups: 1) an orientation toward group affiliation and interdependence versus an individual orientation emphasizing independence and competition; 2) an active, achievement-oriented style versus a passive, accepting style; 3) authoritarianism and the acceptance of hierarchical relationships versus egalitarianism; and 4) an expressive, overt, personal style of communication versus a restrained, impersonal, and formal style. Only gradually through the media and direct contact do people learn that some of their behaviors, which to them are the only way to behave in a given situation, are in fact, ethnic in origin.

Reference group—Although children become aware very early in their lives of the more obvious ethnic cues (language, skin color, and so on), they may not realize until adulthood, if then, that they think and behave differently in certain situations from members of other ethnic groups. This awareness of differences leads to the possibility of conscious choice, either to emphasize one's own distinctive patterns, or to adopt the patterns of another group. The group that one chooses consciously to imitate is referred to as one's *reference group*. It is not clear at what age children begin to be able to choose which ethnic patterns they will adopt, that is, which *reference group* they have.

Bicultural or multicultural competence—Children raised in a pluralistic society may, to some degree, be *bicultural* or even *multicultural*, that is, acquire the norms, attitudes, and behavior patterns of their own and another, or perhaps several other, ethnic groups. *Biculturalism* occurs most typically with minority children, but the concept may apply to majority group children who have contact with a minority group, or to two minority groups that interact. *Bicultural* or *multicultural* competence has become the goal of many programs aimed at socializing non-white children into the U.S. culture.

As abstract as these definitions of ethnicity may seem, their implications for family life and ministry are very real. Rotheram and Phinney suggest the following:

1. Ethnic differences go far beyond the obvious differences of skin color, food, and language. They include variations in values, attitudes, and rules of social interaction. Understanding the variations among groups is necessary to work effectively with people of other ethnic traditions.

2. Children's exposure to cultural differences in a pluralistic society can create stress due to conflicting values, particularly for minority group children. It can also increase flexibility and promote an ability to work comfortably in diverse cultures.

3. The impact of ethnicity on children and youth, and the way they understand and deal with it vary significantly with age and developmental level. Beginning in early adolescence, young people become aware that they can make a choice about how closely they will identify with their own groups and their attributes. Attitudes and preferences toward ethnic groups likewise undergo developmental changes, but these shifts are more difficult to pinpoint in relation to age.

4. The impact of ethnicity on children's development is related to whether they are members of a minority or a majority group. Children who are in the minority are more aware of their own ethnicity, and their ethnicity is more evident to other children. Minority children will inevitably be exposed to differences between their own and the majority group. Majority children, on the other hand, may be shielded from an awareness of such differences, or see such differences only stereotypically, as presented by the media or in comments by adults. Majority group children are more likely to be ethnocentric in the sense of being unaware of, or convinced of the inferiority of, attitudes and values different from their own.

5. The immediate and extended family, school, parish, and neighborhood community influence how children and youth grow in their awareness and appreciation of ethnic culture. Young people's sense of their ethnicity is influenced also by the broad social structure, including the way ethnic groups are defined, the coherence of a group and the supports it provides (such as social organizations or churches), the relative status of the groups, and the tensions that exist among them. But the social structure itself changes over time. Recent social movements and an increased focus on cultural pluralism have made minority group children more aware of their own cultural heritage and have made majority children more conscious of diversity in society (Rotheram and Phinney 274–277).

ETHNICITY AND ADOLESCENTS

Tim Tseng and Kathryn Choy-Wong, writing in *Asian Pacific American Youth Ministry*, speak eloquently of the impact of ethnicity on young people of Asian Pacific heritage. What they write of Asian Pacific youth applies equally well to the young people of many ethnic traditions in the United States, and especially those of color. Their thoughts, expanded to apply to youth of diverse ethnic traditions, follow.

Young people who are members of ethnic groups outside the mainstream culture live in at least two cultural settings: American and ethnic. They are often uncomfortable with this experience. This uneasiness is due in part to the way American society is usually portrayed. When the word "American" is used, one usually thinks of white Anglo people and values. The cultural experiences of Asian Pacific, African American, Hispanic, and Native American people are not recognized as a reality in a monocultural society. Thus, ethnic youth often feel alienated from this Western context. Furthermore, many of them, having been raised in this American environment, are also distant from their inherited ethnic cultural contexts. The world in which their parents or grandparents live is equally alienating for ethnic American youth who do not share all the norms and traditions held by their elders. They are caught in the middle. Thus they experience discomfort and even severe stress because of their marginal status.

Of course there will be those in a given group of young people who are either "assimilated" (those who have consciously or subconsciously rejected their ethnic identity and accepted the ways of white American society) or "insulated" (those who have managed in large part to retain ethnic identity. However such clearly defined identities are rare among most youth of color. Most are somewhere along the continuum between culturally ethnic and culturally American and are able to move back and forth. This ability to move back and forth between two cultures in terms of one's behavior and attitudes is called "social adaptivity."

Bicultural young people need to realize that being "socially adaptive" is a gift to be appreciated. In light of the Gospel message, they do not have to act one way or another. This realization carries helpful insights for a dynamic intergenerational church which ministers to both the newly arrived immigrants and the multi-generation members of ethnic groups. As people called to be ethnic Americans, these youth will be encouraged to search more deeply and affirm both their inherited and adopted cultures. Young people need ongoing encouragement to realize the gift of biculturality (Tseng 119).

There are positive values in both white American and ethnic cultures. White America offers the values that youth are important persons in their own right and can contribute to the general society; that each person has a mind of his/her own and has basic human rights; and that each person can make his/her own choices.

Earlier Euro-American generations embraced many of the same values held by new immigrants to the United States, such as the importance of the land and hard work, striving for success, the need for family and community, and responsibility toward others. Some ethnic groups place a high value on the interdependence of persons, group decision making, and honor and respect for elders and authority. Young people who come from a strong ethnic tradition can select and recover the best values in both cultures. They have the opportunity to balance different sets of values and utilize both to benefit themselves and society as a whole. Along with the gift of biculturalism comes the responsibility to share its benefits with others (Choy-Wong 125).

MINISTRY WITH YOUTH IN A MULTI-ETHNIC SOCIETY

The task set before youth ministry today is twofold: to respect and build upon the strengths and riches of ethnic cultures and to promote a multicultural awareness and understanding among all youth.

Marina Herrera describes how youth ministry needs to be multi-cultural:

> I am firmly convinced that youth ministry must have a clear connection with cultural anthropology but not merely with reference to minority cultures but to the cultural patterns and understandings of the dominant groups as well . . . youth ministry should be multi-cultural in two clearly distinct and yet interrelated dimensions: 1) youth ministry must concern itself with the needs of minority youth; and 2) youth ministry must also have a direct multi-cultural dimension when intended for youth from the dominant culture (Herrera 90).

A CHALLENGE TO YOUTH MINISTRY

Two important challenges are set before youth ministry as it attempts to respond to the multicultural reality of our society and Church: 1) Ministering to youth of minority cultures, and 2) Promoting multicultural awareness among all youth. Youth ministry must take its clues from the cultural context as well as the psychological, political, or educational ones. Using these twin tasks as an evaluative tool, one can see that we have much work to do. How effectively do we engage in ministry with minority youth and respond to their personal, familial, social, and institutional needs? How effectively do our training programs prepare us for this ministry? How will the church-at-large work to find the money and resources to support youth ministers and youth ministries in minority parishes and communities? How effectively do we integrate the reality of our multi-cultural society in our programs for youth and leaders of the mainstream culture so that they may see the riches of all cultures and live their lives accordingly?

MINISTERING TO YOUTH OF MINORITY CULTURES

Minority youth must be taken seriously in regard to their numbers, needs, and possibilities. Youth are often the largest single age group in African American, Hispanic, and Asian American ethnic groups. "The needs of minority youth go from the essentials such as housing, food, education, and employment opportunities to the more intangible ones of community acceptance, self-worth, affirmation, recognition, and hope for a better future" (Herrera 92). Youth ministry must recognize the social context and varied needs of youth of minority cultures. This is a critical starting point. In addition ministry must recognize the biculturality of the ethnic experience, cultivating within youth an awareness of the adaptation as well as ethnicity of youth of minority cultures (Mack). Development of identity, and in particular a Catholic identity, means recognizing the dual socialization into the mainstream culture and into an ethnic culture that so many youth of minority cultures experience. As noted above, this dual socialization often creates stress and conflict, especially where there is conflict between the values, images, ideals of the two cultures. To reconcile into one identity values and images that are different, if not diametrically opposed, poses an extraordinary challenge.

Marina Herrera proposes four helpful elements of a ministry with youth of minority cultures:

Element 1: Presence. Being present means outreach to youth in their environment and inviting them to meaningful activities and supportive relationships. Peer ministry can be a most effective approach here.

Element 2: Understanding. Being culturally literate means understanding the history, essential components, and most significant expressions of each ethnic culture and relating well to the special difficulties encountered by youth who are growing up in two different worlds of meaning and values. Cross cultural relations and communication skills are essential here.

Element 3: Affirmation. Providing affirmation to youth of minority cultures means that the minister are is culturally appropriate and recognizes talents and personal assets that may not be valued by the mainstream culture (often times the culture of the minister). Cultural literacy that includes cross-cultural styles of learning, motivation, and reward is essential here.

Element 4: Challenge. Overcoming the prejudices and limitations imposed by the minister's own cultural perspectives so as to be able to recognize the prejudices and limitations of the other cultures. "Educators and ministers of minority youth must be objective in their evaluation of cultural accomplishments of all the groups that are present in society and recognize the shortcomings of the dominant culture. Only then will they be able to call forth minority youth to overcome the shortcomings of their own cultures and bring them to the full potential of their humanity" (Herrera 97).

PROMOTING MULTICULTURAL AWARENESS

Including a multicultural dimension to youth ministry is essential for all youth. Not only is our society multicultural, but the Church is a global community of varied cultures. Developing a multicultural awareness in youth can take place in at least two ways: through awareness experiences with youth of one culture and through cross-cultural experiences in which youth from different cultures can develop relationships with each other and learn about and experience a variety of cultures.

A prime objective of multicultural awareness is to correct ethnic and racial myths and stereotypes by providing youth with accurate information on the histories, lives, and cultures of ethnic groups. In particular, youth ministry needs to deal with racism and prejudice in United States society. "The increased tolerance of racism by such leaders (political leaders, media stars, and figures of import in the culture) has been viewed by many youth as condoning not only the perpetuation of institutional arrangements which work against minorities but also the more direct expression of racial hatred and violence" (Osmer 12).

In order to do this three things are necessary:

1. to acknowledge forthrightly the need for white youth to come to terms with racism in light of the Gospel;
2. to help youth become aware of the pernicious impact of racism in their own communities and the ways it is rooted in large social and historical forces;
3. to involve youth directly in the constructive resolution of community interracial problems through the use of action-reflection models of education (Osmer 12).

A second purpose of multicultural awareness is to correct the mistaken notion that an ethnic group is synonymous with a minority group. There are majority and minority ethnic groups and both kinds should be included in multicultural awareness efforts. Programming should include European ethnics as well as Afro-Americans, Hispanics, Native Americans, and Asian Americans. We all need to learn about: a) our ethnic group as well as the ethnicity of others; b) how ethnic experiences affect our behavior and values and our concepts of self-identity; and c) about the particulars of different ethnic groups' contributions and historical experiences.

A third purpose of multicultural awareness is to facilitate the development of attitudes and values conducive to the preservation and promotion of ethnic and cultural diversity as a value in our society. Youth ministry needs to enhance young people's self-concepts by developing pride in their own and others' ethnic and cultural heritages, and increasing one's sense of cultural identity and ethnic unity. Programming should aim to help young people develop openness, flexibility, and receptivity to cultural diversity and alternative lifestyles; enrich human experiences through the study of different ethnic groups; accept and prize diversity, and reduce anxieties about encountering different ethnic groups, their life styles, value preferences, and behavior patterns.

Cross-cultural experiences provide the context for youth from different cultures to learn and grow in their understanding and appreciation of each other and in developing relationships with each other. Youth ministry needs to encourage, plan, and carry out programs which allow young people from different cultural backgrounds to come together to dialogue around issues which are important to them and to experience the richness of each other's culture. Youth of minority cultures and youth of the mainstream culture must be offered the skills for cross cultural communication if cross-cultural experience are to be positive ones. Cross-cultural experiences provide an opportunity for liturgical and social celebrations that express the spirit and traditions of the different cultural groups present in the community, especially on occasions linked to their particular histories. "Action in common is the best test of the fruitfulness of cross-cultural dialogue. When youth groups are able to join hands across cultural or racial barriers and give witness to their hope for a more just and peaceful world, then multicultural ministry will have come of age" (Herrera 101).

A CHECKLIST OF PRINCIPLES FOR PROMOTING MULTICULTURAL MINISTRY WITH YOUTH

Felipe Salinas offers the following principles for integrating a multicultural perspective into ministry with youth. They can serve as a checklist for weighing present and future efforts at making our ministry truly multicultural.

CULTURE

1. Culture is a gift from God and an essential expression of our humanity.
2. The creative tension between cultural differences and church unity must be affirmed and preserved.
3. The youth minister should be committed to learning about culture, specific cultures in his or her geographical area, and cultures in general.

MINISTRY TO MINORITY YOUTH

4. Young people's search for cultural identity should be encouraged, supported, and affirmed.
5. The importance of the family in young people's search for cultural identity should be recognized.
6. The language, cultural, and material needs of recent immigrants should be advocated for and provided by parishes.
7. Youth ministers should be familiar with the styles of communication and learning of the cultures in which they minister.

MULTICULTURAL YOUTH MINISTRY

8. An awareness of culture and of the need for a multicultural approach in society and church should be infused into our ministry with youth.
9. Youth ministry should bring young people into regular contact with people of other cultures for service, learning, worship, and celebration.
10. Coordination of youth ministry in multicultural settings should include people of the various cultures.
11. Prejudice among youth is an issue which should always be confronted and countered based on Gospel values.

GUIDELINES FOR CULTURAL SENSITIVITY IN MINISTRY WITH FAMILIES AND YOUTH

The research, reflections, and principles included above provide general background on ethnicity and culture and how they impact ministry with families and youth. The brief essays which follow go one step further, providing guidelines for the

Church's ministry with people from specific ethnic groups: African Americans, Hispanics in the United States, Native Americans, and Pacific Asian Americans.

WORKS CITED

Choy-Wong, Kathryn. "The Role of Culture in Faith." *Asian Pacific American Youth Ministry.* Ed. Donald Ng. Valley Forge, PA: Judson Press, 1988.

———. "Faith in our Setting." *Asian Pacific American Youth Ministry.* Ed. Donald Ng. Valley Forge, PA: Judson Press, 1988.

Herrera, Marina. "Toward Multicultural Youth Ministry." *Readings in Youth Ministry.* Ed. John Roberto. Washington, DC: NFCYM Publications, 1986.

Mack, Faite R-P. "Understanding and Enhancing the Self-Concept in Black Children." *Momentum* (February 1987): 22–25.

Osmer, Richard. "Challenges to Youth Ministry in the Mainline Churches: Thought Provokers." *Affirmation* 2.1 (Spring 1989): 1–25.

Phinney, Jean S. and Mary Jane Rotheram. *Children's Ethnic Socialization— Pluralism and Development.* Newbury Park, CA: Sage Publications, 1987.

Tseng, Tim. "Being Socially Adaptive." *Asian Pacific American Youth Ministry.* Ed. Donald Ng. Valley Forge, PA: Judson Press, 1988.

CHAPTER 9:
GUIDELINES

Working with
African American Families

Eva Marie Lumas, SSS

Any serious discussion of African American families must be prefaced with four considerations: 1) The current crisis of the African American family is indicative of the social, political, economic and ethical crises that pervade all of contemporary American life. African American families are thus in the process of reorganizing themselves to find effective ways of dealing with the larger societal situation in which they live. 2) Much more research on African American families remains to be done regarding cultural traits, organizational structures, functional roles of family members, and interactive patterns. 3) The "average" African American has not studied the research that does exist. Much of their family cultural norms, organizational structures, functional roles, are done instinctually or consequent to unspoken directives within the culture. 4) The diverse approaches utilized to study African American families, requires those who attempt to address African American family life to cite their sources so that their bias can be readily identified. Apropos to this, I have attached a bibliography at the end of these guidelines to indicate the research and theories that have influenced my thinking.

1. The principal functions of the African American family are to provide subsistence (care for physical needs), nurturing, guidance, support, protection, and mobility for its members. In addition, the African American family teaches its members how to overcome the handicap of their inferior social

status, the lack of equitable access to resources within society at large, and the general hostilities of personal and institutional racism.

THEREFORE, ministers should be sensitive to the general and the specific functions of African American families. And, they should develop policies, programs, and strategies in collaboration with Blacks that support and enhance the principle functions of African American families by influencing public policy and developing other means of helping African Americans to achieve equality in the areas of economic development, education, employment, housing, health care, and legal representation.

2. The organizational structure of African American families serves the functional needs (psychological, social, emotional, cultural, and spiritual) of Black people.
   a. Black family life is not a deviant expression of white family life.
   b. The organizational structure, functional roles, interactive patterns and values of African American families reflect the nature and circumstance of being Black in America.
   c. Some characteristics of African American families are carry-overs from Africa; some are adaptations of family life within America's dominant culture, and some characteristics are adaptations of African family life which offer

alternatives to the family life of America's dominant culture. The following examples illustrate the point:

- African carry-over: When an older Black person resides in the home of one of their children, the elder person is usually regarded as the head of the household.
- Adaptation of family life in the dominant culture: Blacks do not perceive a single-parent family as a "broken" family. As long as the adult who is present in the nuclear-family home, and the extended family network can provide the necessary care and nurturing required, the single-parent family is considered to be whole (i.e., healthy).
- Alternative to family life of dominant culture: The well-being of the extended family network has primacy over the nuclear family to which a person belongs.

THEREFORE, ministers need to be sensitive to the fact that African American families must be understood within the context of their own values, conceptual framework, and organizational structures. Also, ministers need to develop policies, programs, and strategies that enable African Americans to name and better appreciate their family experience.

3.   African American family structures, operational functions, interactive patterns and values carry the influence of its African roots. It is not simply a construct of American slavery.

    a. African Americans did not come *from* slavery; they came through slavery, steeped in the values and traditions of Africa.
    b. Contemporary research on African American families reveals that slavery did not completely destroy the cultural legacy of Africa.
    c. The following examples illustrate the inherent influence of Africa

within African American families:

- Extended family networks resemble African tribal kinship networks.
- The ability of African Americans to utilize flexible gender roles is consistent with the African value of cooperative work and responsibility.
- High esteem given to elders.
- Naming children after a favored or deceased member of the family resonates with the African notion that a person lives as long as their name is remembered.
- Shared responsibility for the extended family is consistent with the African value of cooperative sharing of resources.
- Children are regarded as the family's greatest wealth.
- A "broken family" is a term that refers to a breach within the extended family network; not to absence of one of the spouses in a nuclear family unit.
- A "poor family" refers to the inability of an extended or nuclear family to provide for the basic physical, social, psychological, and spiritual well-being of its members. It is believed that once these needs are met, the rest (i.e., higher education, economic stability, etc.) will come in time.
- While husbands in most African societies commonly had authority over their wives, women had considerable control over what they earned from their own labor.

THEREFORE, ministers need to remember that even though some of the behavioral characteristics of African Americans appear to be consistent with the behavioral norms of other ethnic and cultural groups, no simple assumptions can be made about the origin or meaning of behavior. The meaning and expected outcomes of the African American family structures, operational functions, interactive patterns, and values are rooted in an African psyche and African Americans must be allowed to describe and define their own experience.

4. African American families have traditional strengths:

    a. Strong kinship bonds: African Americans are highly relational. They tend to relate to a greater number of their relatives on a regular basis than do other ethnic and cultural groups. Strong kinship bonds afford an individual family member considerably more resourcefulness than he or she would have otherwise (Hill).

    b. Strong work ethics: The disenfranchisement of African Americans from the resources and benefits of the larger society has reinforced their need to be self-generating and self-reliant (Hill).

    c. Adaptability of family roles: African Americans generally share the same gender-role definitions as the dominant culture; however, they expect family members of both sexes to participate in role performance to the extent that they are able.

    d. Strong achievement orientation: African Americans share the human need for productivity, recognition, and personal efficacy to control the details of life. In addition to this, however, the African American's orientation to achievement includes the need to provide for their own people those resources and services that they cannot receive from the larger society (Nobles).

    e. Strong religious orientation: African-American people have found tremendous strength and courage from their belief in a supreme being who knows their

hardship, affirms the righteousness of their efforts toward justice, and is actively engaged in opposing the forces of their oppression. Black families have taught their members that there are no permanent constraints to their ability to achieve their just ambitions as long as they are true to the will of God (Nobles).

    f. Legitimizing the personhood of its members: Familial relationships have nurtured positive self-images and senses of self-worth in the family's members to counteract the effects of their being treated as objects or commodities within the institutional and social structures of American life (Nobles).

    g. Provision of a family code: The family provides its members with guidelines and values that govern their ability to interpret and manage familiar and unfamiliar situations and relationships (Nobles).

    h. Provision of information and knowledge: The insights gained from family members' experiences are shared so that each member of the family has the benefit of the group's resourcefulness in managing the events of their lives.

    i. Concrete mediation of the existential circumstances and conditions of its members: Besides buffering the individual stresses of family members, this function provides group collaboration for problem solving and the assurance of recognition for achievements. In addition, this feature of the family provides collaborative decisions regarding the distribution of the family's resources.

    j. Determination of interpersonal interaction: Interaction within the family is governed by the principles of mutual respect, responsibility, reciprocity, and individual restraint. (Restraint may take the form of self-sacrifice for the benefit of another person.) (Sudarkasa).

k. Provision of sociopsychological safety: The family serves as a sanctuary that counteracts the ill-effects of racism and social hostilities.

THEREFORE, ministers need to develop policies, programs, and strategies that affirm the strengths of African American families and the role that these family strengths have had in the survival and success of blacks within American society. At the same time, ministers need to develop policies, programs, and strategies that address the ills of African American families with the purpose of reinstating the historic health, goodness, wholeness, and holiness of Black family life.

5. The special characteristics of African American families (Nobles):

a. Comprised of the residents of multiple households who are primarily related by blood.

b. Elastic in the sense that they may include persons and households who are not related by blood, but who share the same hopes, struggles, pains, etc. Persons who are considered to be family, although they are not related by blood, are often given familial titles, namely, uncle, aunt, sister, brother.

c. Child-centered system rather than systems based on the conjugal relationship between spouses.

d. Composed of close networks of relationships between families. Blacks may regard their aunts and uncles with the same esteem as they do their parents. Also, Blacks may regard their cousins with the same regard as they do for their siblings.

e. Able to maintain flexible and interchangeable role definitions and performance.

- The roles of nurturer and provider for the family have not been traditionally linked to the male or the female, but to the person who could best perform the needed function.
  - The concept of mutual responsibility for caring for the needs of the family, mitigated against rigid adherence to traditionally defined gender boundaries.

f. Multiple parents and interfamilial consensual adaptations.

- The extended family network may sometimes operate in a manner that makes the eldest member of the family (male or female) the head of a number of households.
- The care and supportive functions of a family may be provided by multiple households who share the responsibility for providing for the entire family network.

THEREFORE, ministers need to be aware of ways that their own family experience biases their understanding of "the family" and avoid trying to understand or describe Black families by comparing them to families of other ethnic and cultural groups. Ministers also need to develop policies, programs, and strategies that encourage intergenerational interaction, extended family participation, and flexible gender performance.

6. There are many characteristics common to African Americans as a group. However, the African American community is not monolithic, and, African American family life is influenced by a variety of factors:

a. Each African American family carries the influence of its geographic origin: Rural United States, Urban United States, Northern United States, Southern United States, Eastern United States, Western United States,

Georgia Sea Islands, South Carolina Sea Islands, Caribbean Islands, Central American, and South American.

b. Each African American family carries the influence of its socioeconomic class, that is, lower, middle or upper class.
   - These socioeconomic class distinctions are often poor indicators of a person's esteem within a family. For example, persons who live at a low socioeconomic level may be regarded with high esteem due to their wisdom or insightfulness. On the other hand, persons who have risen to the upper class may be regarded with contempt because of their lack of generosity or their criticalness of other, less fortunate family members (Dodson).
   - These varying socioeconomic classes will often affect how Black people view their social status; their awareness of Black oppression and their interpretation of its consequences; the degree to which they aspire to assimilate within the mainstream of American life; and the degree to which they personally identify with the Black struggle for liberation.

c. Each African American family carries the influence of its educational level.
   - While African Americans have historically believed that education is a necessary means of achieving freedom and equality, formal education is not regarded as the full measure of a person's intelligence or worth and it is not the fulcrum of a person's ability to achieve.
   - A high level of formal education does not automatically award a person high esteem within a family.

People who forget or reject the folk wisdom of their people are regarded as "educated fools."
   - Highly educated people who do not use their learning or the benefits it generates for the good of their people are believed to have exploited or sold out their people.

THEREFORE, ministers need to be conscious of the characteristics that are common to all African American families and attentive to the uniqueness of each African American family. Ministers must avoid stereotypical or generalized concepts of African Americans. At the same time, ministers need to facilitate opportunities for African Americans to tell their own story and the meaning they have ascribed to that story.

7.   The extended family network of African American families are based on consanguineous (blood) relationships rather than conjugal bonding patterns.
   a. The extended family serves to buffer the effects of unmet needs in the nuclear family. In addition, the extended family expands and reinforces the effective resources of the nuclear family.
   b. Blacks regard their extended family to be primarily, but not exclusively, comprised of those persons who are related by blood.
   c. The spouses and children of blood relatives are incorporated into the extended family to the extent that these persons comply with the foundational principles and general priorities of the group.
   d. Divorce does not necessarily sever the extended family's tie to the spouse of a blood relative as the family may empathize with the spouse.
   e. The children and/or step-children of blood relatives are not excluded from the extended family due to the divorce of the parents. They are still regarded as "the family's children."

THEREFORE, ministers need to develop policies, programs, and strategies that reinforce the "corporate identity" of African Americans. When African Americans gather as a faith community during times of tragedy or celebration, ministers should address the family's need to strengthen its bonds and heal its divisions. During the normal course of the family's participation in the Church, ministers should find ways to involve whole families into church ministries, programs, and events.

8. African American families are person centered, yet community oriented.
   a. The family network can make allowances for the individual styles, personalities, contributions, conditions, and/or circumstances of its members.
   b. The idiosyncratic and novel aspects of individual personalities are generally encouraged and appreciated, especially when they add to the general well-being of the group.
   c. The family expects individual members to occasionally compromise their personal preferences and/or styles for the good of the group.
   d. An individual's personal identity is strongly rooted in his or her corporate identity as a member of the family.

THEREFORE, ministers need to remember that African Americans are often caught in a dilemma in the Church: Blacks are expected frequently, rather than occasionally, to compromise their perspectives or desires for the "good of the larger church community." Ministers who are generally not willing to value the Black person or Black people over the norms, traditions, or rules that benefit others will quickly lose their credibility with Blacks. The uncompromising attitudes of these ministers will result in their being labelled as having an uncaring attitude. Policies, programs, and strategies need to be developed that encourage African Americans to contribute their insights, styles, talents, preferences, and personalities to the Church.

9. African American families suffer immense pressure from Black male-female conflict due to displaced anger resulting from institutional racism and an attempt to adopt the gender role definitions of the dominant culture.
   a. African Americans generally embrace the traditional American ideologies of male-female roles within the family. However, Black men and Black women are not provided with the means of implementing their ideals.
      - Most Black men are excluded from the socioeconomic systems that maintain America's notion of "manhood." As a result they cannot perform the traditionally prescribed masculine family roles.
      - Unable to find a sufficient number of Black men who have attained the prescribed notions of "manhood," most Black women who marry will assume masculine family roles (i.e., they become the provider), or they give up on the attempt to marry at all.
   b. Saddled with unrealistic expectations of each other, Black men and Black women are primed for conflict with each other.
      - The alleged Black matriarchy is the invention of those who choose to blame Black women for the continued decimation of Black men in American society. However, Black women do not control the legal system, social structures, economy, schools, or propaganda networks that debilitate Black men.
      - The propagation of Black male stereotypes that depicts them as socially violent, domestically indifferent, interpersonally callous, and socioeconomically inept, acts as a self-fulfilling prophesy that erodes their self-esteem

and undercuts their relationships.

c. The high incidence of female-headed households are the direct consequence of America's institutional structures. There is a direct relationship in the level of Black male unemployment and number of Black female-headed households.

d. The particular circumstances of being Black in America have placed African American women in positions that are socially prescribed for men:

- Social institutional structures put large numbers of Black women into the workforce, even though most of their jobs were once domestic. As early as 1900 almost half of all Black women in America were in the labor force. At the same time, Black men were barred from the economic means necessary to assume the socially prescribed masculine role as the family provider.

- The socialization process of Black women teaches them to aspire to traditionally prescribed male-females relationships. At the same time, it also prepares them for self-sufficiency and independence due to the precarious conditions of Black men.

- Black culture's approbation of adaptability in family roles has engaged African-American women in endeavors that are generally regarded as the domain of men. For example, Black women have conducted family business that is external to domestic chores or the running of their households.

e. The particular circumstances of being Black in America have systematically and consistently suppressed the potential of Black men:

- The educational system has left approximately 50% of the Black male population ill-equipped to function successfully in a technological society.

- Only half of all Black men are in the labor force.

- A disproportionately high number of Black men are incarcerated.

- Many Black men have incomes significantly lower than their wives.

- Negative social-psychological images of Black men comprise the bulk of media attention given to them. It is ironic that Bill Cosby's portrayal of Dr. Cliff Huxtable is renounced as an incredible role model for Black men, while Redd Fox's depiction of Fred Sanford is received without criticism.

f. Negative, distorted representations of the African American family (e.g., the Moynihan Report) are more widely publicized within the Black community and within American society at large, than are positive, self-reflective research of Black social scientists. This must be understood as a deliberate institutional attempt to corroborate the bias of the destructive forces that continue to assault African American family life.

THEREFORE, ministers need to develop policies, programs, and strategies that encourage African American men and women to examine and reclaim the strengths of traditional Black male-female relationships which enabled them to build stable conjugal relationships. Such an endeavor would unleash the potential for Black men and Black women to develop relationships characterized by self-sufficiency and networking, assertiveness and negotiation, mutual responsibility and empathy, and nurturance and support.

10. The values and expectations regarding parents and parent-child relationships in African American families generally focus on providing children with (1) the skills necessary to survive in a hostile society and (2) the hope of succeeding in the society in spite of the hostilities.

a. Black children have a dual socialization process that teaches them the ways of the Black community and the realities of a white-dominated society.

b. In deciding how to have a task completed, most Black families will not consider a child's gender. If a child of either sex has the competence to perform a task, the child is expected to do so. Apropos to this, an older child of either sex is expected to care for the younger children in his or her family.

c. Most Black families do not use psychological methods to discipline a child, such as making a parent's affection conditional to the child's performance. Black families are generally very direct and physical in the correction of a child.

d. Black families of all socioeconomic levels attempt to reinforce similar positive values in their children: personal values (i.e., generosity and fairness), racial and cultural pride, sound morals, self-control, and the need for an education.

e. Black families of all socioeconomic levels suffer race-related stress in the rearing of their children:

   ■ They must teach their children how to participate effectively in the Black community so that they will not be displaced within the society. And, they must teach their children how to effectively participate in the white community so that they will not be disenfranchised from the society.

   ■ Because of their general feeling of vulnerability, they will often choose not to directly or publicly confront a racially motivated affront to a child unless the effects on the child are extreme. The family may simply tell the child to ignore the incidents, the family may over-simplify the incident with explanations or excuses, or the family may distort the incident to camouflage the racial intent. In any of these scenarios, the child learns not to look to his or her family for protection. The child learns to doubt his or her right to be protected. Finally, the child may learn to deny or distort the reality and ill-effects of racial assault.

f. African American children who are taught to identify and confront racial incidents develop more healthy self-concepts, self-confidence, and group identity.

g. Black men and Black women share the responsibilities of decision making and care for their children.

h. Black parents expect emotional support from Black grandparents and other members of their extended families for the rearing of children.

i. Child-rearing within single-parent homes is strained when extended family networks breakdown or when the parenting is being done by a teenager.

j. African American families of all socioeconomic levels experience stress in child-rearing due to their children's exposure to and adoption of the prevailing negative values of the society, namely, individualism, self-determined decision-making regarding the use of money, early sexual activity, and the prominence of substance abuse.

k. Most Black parents regard religion to be a primary resource for child-rearing.

l. The participation of African American youth in the Church is strained:

- Black youth often do not perceive the Church's understanding of the realities of their lives.
- Black youth often do not perceive the Church's youth ministry programs to be equivalent options to the events and relationships that engage them within the larger society.
- Black youth often do not perceive the Church to have a critical or credible impact in the quality of their lives or their future.

THEREFORE, ministers should develop policies, programs, and strategies that foster healthy parent-child relationships, alleviate part of the stresses of child-rearing, address the social ills that undermine positive family (and human) values, and establish meaningful ways to manifest the Church's investment in the life of Black people: adults, children, and youth.

11. Integration has contributed to the erosion of traditional African American family structures, functions, and stability.
    a. The relatively high geographic mobility of African Americans within American society has caused Blacks to experience a new "Diaspora" (scattering of peoples).
- Upwardly mobile Blacks are often isolated within predominantly white residential areas, schools, and places of employment.
- Those Blacks who are "left behind" in the old neighborhoods do not have sufficient access to positive Black role models or to the resources gained by the successes of some of their family members.

    b. African Americans who have had high levels of exposure to and interaction with whites in the last 25 years are constantly reminded that they know more about whites than whites know about them.
- Those Black people who have high levels of exposure to and interaction with whites in residential communities, schools, and places of employment have often tried to manage these situations by cultural assimilation (rejecting their own culture). In other instances these Blacks are assaulted by cultural accommodation (being tolerated, but not understood or appreciated, by the dominant culture).
- Many Black children who attend integrated schools have learned to cope with their inferior status by attempting to assimilate with their white peers. The developmental need of youth for peer approval, coupled with the isolation of these youth from their extended families with their histories, values, norms, and world view, make these Black youth particularly susceptible to cultural confusion.

    c. The Civil Rights Movement of the 1960s sought to give African Americans greater access to the resources of American society and more equitable share of their benefits. But, the resistance of the dominant culture to relinquish its privileged status has resulted in limited achievements on the part of Blacks:
- Social-class stratification is more pronounced among Blacks than ever before.
- The majority of America's Black population is no better off.
- The educational system continues to undereducate and miseducate African-Americans.
- Social services are still inadequate, and when these services are accessible,

African-Americans are still treated with condescension.

- The political and legal systems continue to ignore the enduring devastations of institutional racism. Isolated, individual experiences of racial justice and cultural pluralism are cited as sufficient reason not to address racism as an institutionalized aspect of American life.
- Religious institutions spend more time discussing the basic human similarities between Blacks and whites rather than developing an appreciation for their respective cultural differences. But, a people's similarities is not the source of their conflict. And, more than that, the need to reduce people to their lowest common denominator is, itself, a means of domination and control.

THEREFORE, ministers need to develop policies, programs, and strategies that encourage African Americans to maintain and share the Afro-centric strengths, values, traditions, and insights inherent in their cultural heritage as a resource created by God for the benefit of the whole society.

12. The two most powerful and life-giving institutions in the life of African Americans have historically been the family and the Church.

a. The basic values of African American family life were recognized, clarified, sanctioned and reinforced within a Christian framework through the Church.

b. Historically, the Church functioned as an extended family that provided spiritual, emotional, educational, social, economic, and political support to African Americans.

c. Along with the supportive programs that all Christian churches provided to their predominantly Black congregations, the Black Church was also the storehouse of culture for African Americans.

- Within the Black Church, African American culture was respected and normative for its members.
- Within the Black Church, African American culture and spirituality united to address the realities of Black life.

d. Historically, the Black Church enabled African Americans to develop resources (i.e., leadership skills, monetary resources, clarify of purpose, etc.) and strategies to combat racism and facilitate the ability of African Americans to move into the mainstream of American life.

e. African American Catholics have not experienced their Church's direct involvement in the Black community's effort to combat racism.

- African American Catholics have historically believed that the Catholic Church's educational programs have assisted them in overcoming some of the effects of racial oppression.
- Although African American Catholics have relied on the spiritual resources of their Church for the inspiration to persevere in their struggle, they have persistently requested the Church to aid them with other concrete systematic approaches to combat oppression.

f. African American Catholics have begun to appreciate the relationship between culture and faith (including spirituality, theology, liturgy, etc.).

g. Both Protestant and Catholic African Americans now have a growing concern for their Church to apply its institutional resources to combat the persistent problem of racism within the Church and the society at large. Fueling this

concern are the beliefs that:
racism contradicts the Christian
faith as it is a denial of the
inherent human dignity, worth
and rights of every person, and
the Christian Church's inactivity
regarding racism is believed to be
an implicit and an explicit
communication of the Church's
consent or at least its
indifference.

THEREFORE, ministers must develop
policies, programs, and strategies that
explicitly declare the Church's opposition to
racism and any forms of oppression;
embrace Black culture and the Black
experience; and, further the Black
community's noble ambition for justice
within the Church and society.

BIBLIOGRAPHY

Bowman, Sr. Thea (Ed). *Families: Black and Catholic, Catholic and Black*. Washington, DC: United States Catholic Conference, 1985.

Cheatham, Harold E. and James B. Stewart. *Black Families*. New Brunswick, NJ: Transaction Publishers, 1990.

Lyke, Most Reverend James P. *The Family in the Black Community*. Cleveland: Catholic Archdiocese of Cleveland, OH, 1986.

Martin, Elmer P. and Martin, Joanne Mitchell. *The Black Extended Family*. Chicago: University of Chicago Press, 1978.

Mathis, Arthur. "Contrasting Approaches to the Study of Black Families", Nobles, Wade W. "Toward and Empirical and Theoretical Framework for Defining Black Families", McAdoo, Harriette Pipes. "Factors Related to Stability in Upwardly Mobile Black Families" in *Journal of Marriage and the Family* (Special Issue: Black Families). November, 1978. Vol. 40, No. 4.

McAdoo, Harriette Pipes (ed). *Black Families*. Beverly Hills: Sage Publications, Inc., 1981.

Roberts, J. Deotis. *Roots of a Black Future: Family and Church*. Philadelphia: Westminster Press, 1980.

Smith, Wallace Charles. *The Church in the Life of the Black Family*. Valley Forge: Judson Press, 1985.

What We've Seen and Heard: A Pastoral Letter on Evangelization, from the Black Bishops of the United States. Cincinnati: St. Anthony's Messenger Press, 1984.

CHAPTER 9:
GUIDELINES

Working with Hispanic Families

Elisa Rodriguez, SC and Gelasia Marquez

1. Family ministers ought to apply themselves to understand the situations within which marriage and family are living today in order to fulfill their task of serving.

   a. Pope John Paul II and the National Conference of Bishops of the United States have recognized: 1) the multicultural composition of the Church; 2) the inalienable dignity of every human person, irrespective of racial, ethnic, cultural, or national origin, or religious beliefs as well as the unity of the human family; and 3) how the differences between the members of the Church, should be used to strengthen unity, rather than serve as a cause of division (*Origins* 18.29).

   b. In our ethnically diverse U.S. Catholic Church, where there is no primary ethnic group numerically, the consideration of ethnicity and culture as essential components of family life structure and interactions is determinant in developing programs, policies, and services.

   c. These principles are important when ministering culturally different families:

      ■ Family differences must be understood rather than interpreted and evaluated— what is considered "peculiar" behavior in one cultural setting may be viewed as proper and necessary in another culture.

      ■ Common experiences/variables that apply to all families must be identified and studied under the umbrella of general characteristics; thus, main areas of differences can be categorized and the varying values and customs of each ethnic group can be highlighted.

      ■ Family ministers must have sensitivity and flexibility to discover and to understand the uniqueness of each family situation as a result of its own history, structural characteristics, ethnic and racial heritage, socioeconomic status, level of acculturation to the mainstream culture of each one of its members, etc.

      ■ "Optimal family functioning" and levels of family life satisfaction cannot be equated with the presence of so-called "strengths"—or positive characteristics—nor with absence of "negative" features, but, with the ability of individual family members to fulfill their own psycho-social developmental tasks and with the ability of the family itself to rearrange its own structure, to work out its transactional patterns and to re-negotiate its dynamics so the family continues performing its tasks as well as insures some sense of historical continuity and cultural and ethnic traditions.

2. The number of Hispanic families increased by 59% from 1980 to 1989. By the year 2080, Hispanics are expected to number 59.6 million, therefore, Hispanics (Latinos) in the United States make up a significant part of American society and the Church. Hispanics (Latinos) are from many nations and from a variety of cultures.

a. Hispanics (Latinos) with a long history in the United States include: Spanish Americans, descendants of Spanish settlers during the colonization of the Southwest by Spain, Mexican Americans, descendants of Mexican citizens residing in the Southwestern and Western states at the time of the Texas Revolution and the Mexican-American War. These immigrant descent families have retained not only their identification for many generations after immigration but also their ethnic values (Greeley).

b. Hispanics (Latinos) immigrants to the United States include: Mexican Americans descendants of Mexican immigrants, residents and/or naturalized citizens; Puerto Ricans; Cuban Americans residents and/or naturalized citizens; Dominican Americans, residents and/or naturalized citizens from the Dominican Republic; Central American immigrants and descendants from the following countries: Costa Rica, El Salvador, Guatemala, Honduras, Nicaragua, Panama, and South American immigrants and descendants from the following countries: Argentina, Bolivia, Chile, Columbia, Equador, Paraguay, Uruguay, and Venezuela,

These immigrant families may belong to one of these two major groups:

- the recently arrived families—family energy is spent largely on the development of basic survival skills for work, housing, and relating in the new land;
- families with immigrant parents and American born children or immigrant children who are being raised and/or educated in America.

This second group of families experience a great degree of cultural conflict between parents and children. The perception of these conflicts and its internal factors is also affected by where in the acculturative continuum the family members are located.

c. There has been a steady immigration of Hispanics into this country due to economic, religious, and political reasons. Regretfully we cannot assume that all Hispanic families migrated to the United States in a planned fashion or in optimal conditions. Therefore,

- members who immigrated at different points in their lives may have different definitions of who and what they are due to the fact that persons who migrate during adolescence or later, come with a particular value system and psychological frame of mind imposed by the language, educational system, and the historical, cultural, and political trends of their native country (Rodriguez and Villa);
- previous life cycle issues may not get adequately resolved or are still pending; and
- the family life growth cycle may be stopped or interrupted to deal with specific, urgent issues, such as procuring housing, work, learning a language, etc.

d. Hispanics are not only diverse in places of origin but also very diverse culturally, racially, socially, and politically, even from within the same national group, so it is impossible to categorize them in general.

3. Hispanics immigrated to the United States at various times in history and for varied reasons.

a. Given the diversity of geographical origins, languages, backgrounds, norms, socioeconomic status, and immigration status in developing programs, policies, and services, special attention must be given to assess:

- migration patterns. Migration occurs for diverse reasons, and the adjustment of the family depends on the extent to which its original expectations compare with present reality and whether it has a positive connotation or not.

- country of origin and its political, economic and educational situation. The Mexican migration may be seen as a natural outgrowth of moving to areas that Mexicans perceive to be culturally theirs; Central American immigrants usually migrate as a means of running away from their countries in civil war or in poverty struggles, but they are unable to benefit from main institutions due to their undocumented status; Puerto Ricans do not need any documentation to enter or exit from the United States, therefore, their pattern of migration reflects repeated ruptures, reinstatement, and a dismantling of familial and communal networks (Garcia-Preto); finally, Cubans' sense of temporary uprootedness helped them to develop a "frozen" culture in which energies were spent not in

acculturation but in maintaining the values/morals of the homeland.

- age and developmental stage of family members at the time of migration in order to understand what experiences are stored in which language (Inclan).

- socioeconomic status and educational background of family members prior to migration—although a poor person may have a sense of pride about previous achievements and life styles that may be more influential than their current status.

- availability of support systems, especially friends, religion, and ethnic group.

4. Hispanics have very deep cultural roots in the United States.

a. Hispanics were preceded in occupying this country only by Native Americans.

b. In one way or another Hispanics are within two different cultural environments and are dealing in one way or another with a process of acculturation.

c. The process of acculturation involves the whole life of the child/adolescent/young adult/adult. Therefore, Hispanic families are in continuous need of doing a selective adaptation and undergoing a process of differentiation in order to make decisions and choices for a healthy accommodation to two different socioeconomic-cultural context, and for their internal identity adjustment in ways of thinking, feeling, and acting.

d. Different modes of adaptation of migrant ethnic families have been described. Common patterns observed are the following:

- denigrating the old culture— some families sever the old ties and deny their cultural origin by adopting the external features of a stereotyped American family; habits and perceived values—often materialistic—are copied;

- denying the new culture—families turn inward, associating only with members of their own background and attempting to reproduce a micro-culture similar to the one in the home country, though, the children in these families, due to contact with the outside world through schools and friends, become acculturated and conflicts frequently develop in the next generation; and

- becoming able to bring the two cultures together and tolerate the conflict and anxiety of crossing cultural boundaries by maintaining important attachments to ethnic culture along with a productive adjustment to the host culture.

e. For many Hispanic families the immigration and adaptation process is a painful one:

- Many of them must go "from extended to nuclear families, from group existence to individual existence, as they lose their roots through migration; as church, religion and community become unfamiliar and unresponsive" (Paredes).

- Families are often caught in a state of helplessness without appropriate support systems. Resources on which they would have relied in home countries are often not found in the United States, while the existing resources may appear alien to them. In addition to various adaptational problems faced by legal immigrants, illegal aliens encounter a number of obvious social, psychological, and legal problems.

f. Family coping mechanisms are particularly threatened by poverty and discrimination (Minuchin). A great number of Hispanic families live at poverty levels, are more vulnerable to disease, posess lower self-esteem, and have daily stresses that are quite pervasive and negatively influence their children.

g. The loss of ability to use native language and a corresponding greater fluency in English on the part of the children generates poor communication between generations. Also, children become the main source of guidance, control, and decision making when they have to translate for their parents when they are unprepared developmentally to handle those duties.

5.   As members of a minority group, Hispanics have experienced:
   a. being ignored
   b. being taken advantage of
   c. being pushed out of school and jobs
   d. being slighted, ridiculed, and harassed
   e. being overworked, underpaid, underemployed, etc., and
   f. being considered ignorant because of language difficulties.

Hispanics have responded in various ways to this oppression:
   a. by giving into the societal pressure to assimilate and changing their names, giving up all traces of cultural differences;
   b. by assuming some of the dominant cultural values but keeping those values which are important to family and community;
   c. by gathering into neighborhoods (barrios) where they can be themselves without outside interference, and basically

rejecting society's efforts to assimilate them; and

d. by entering a process of re-evaluation, which often leads them to reclaim their lost cultural values and traditions.

In developing programs, policies, and services for Hispanic families, leaders need to understand the different levels and processes that families go through in their adjustment to the host culture and respect the place where people are without making assumptions or being judgmental; while taking positive steps towards creating an environment of healing and acceptance.

6. The fundamental institutions for Hispanics are God, family, and community.

a. Hispanics have no doubt about "God who cares" and around this belief they develop their practices and spiritual values.

b. Hispanics tend to personalize their relationship with God and the saints. Mary, the saints, and souls in purgatory are members of their extended family. Hispanics argue with them, ask them favors, tell them jokes, include them in popular songs, and keep pictures or images of them alongside of the portraits of the family and best friends.

c. Faith has made Hispanics a joyful and providentialistic people. In their fiestas they celebrate the mystery of life that, in its successes and failures, joy and sadness, birth and even death, is a gift from God.

d. Religiosity also gives Hispanics a more spiritual dimension in life. Hispanics emphasize spiritual values and are willing to sacrifice material satisfaction for spiritual goals. For them *being* is more important than *doing* or *having*.

e. The family is the foremost institution in Hispanic culture. For Hispanics, family includes not only relatives by blood and marriages but also relatives by association, such as godparents

and relatives by friendship, and out of respect, such as other hometown or elderly neighbors.

f. The family is the first school of love, tenderness, acceptance, discipline, and respect. In their homes, Hispanics have come to experience the bonds of friendship, mutual support, concern for one another, and the presence of God. In times of stress, Hispanics turn to their families for help; their cultural expectation is that when a family member is experiencing a crisis or has a problem, others in the family are obligated to help, especially those who are in stable positions.

g. Hispanic families enmesh their members in a system of help-giving exchanges, which has the force of a sacred obligatory norm; it is sustained by the double edge of guilt and gratitude. That is, not to help a relative in need evokes feelings of sinful guilt; in turn, to be helped by a relative induces feelings of gratitude. The norm applies through time because the person is bound permanently to his or her family of origin. The norm applies also through space, because relatives who are separated by geographical distance behave in accordance with what they have learned.

h. Celebrations of life stages are cherished by Hispanics and form significant Church-family events. Some of these stages are baptisms, first communions, quinceañeras, weddings, and funerals.

i. Mutual help and a sense of hospitality crisscrosses blood and affinal relationships to include neighbors, friends, and the community at large, fostering principles of true solidarity among Hispanics.

7.   The fundamental values of Hispanics differ significantly from the values of the dominant society.

    a. Whereas dominant culture values constant activity, control of oneself, of others, of nature, Hispanics practice passive acceptance, seek harmony within oneself, among others, and with nature.

    b. Whereas the dominant culture espouses planning and efficiency (business), Hispanics value spontaneity and the personal (friendships).

    c. Whereas the dominant culture values "having" (possessions) and promotes materialism, pragmatism, and technical progress, Hispanics value "being" (communion) having human relationships, beauty, and tradition.

    d. Whereas the dominant culture views success in terms of upward mobility of the individual and admires ambition, motivation, and competition, Hispanics view success as stability of the group, and admire stability in a person, perseverance, and cooperation.

    e. Whereas the dominant culture determines that respect is due to those who earn it, Hispanics understand that respect is due because a person exists.

8.   In communicating Hispanics visualize and experience the world as a totality, using symbols, gestures, sounds, dance, poetry, music. They communicate in indirect and discrete ways which often include a great deal of diplomacy. Hispanics prefer to communicate person to person.

In conclusion, in developing programs, policies, and services, leaders need to be sensitive to the strength and inspiration of Hispanic Christian values.

WORKS CITED

Garcia-Preto, N. "Puerto Rican Families." *Ethnicity and Family Therapy*. Ed. M. McGoldrick, J. Pearce, and J. Giordano. New York: The Guildford Press, 1982.

Inclan, J. "Variations in Value Orientations in Mental Health Work with Puerto Rican Clients." *Psychotherapy*, Vol. 22 No. 2: 325–334.

Minuchin, S. *Family and Family Therapy*. Cambridge, MA: Harvard University Press, 1974.

Paredes, Mario. "Ministering to the Migrant and Alient Families," The Bishop and the Family—The Church Addresses Her Future, 1985 Workshop.

CHAPTER 9: GUIDELINES

Working with Native American Families

Michael Galvan

1. North American society provides a multicultural context for the experience of the Roman Catholic Church.

    a. Assimilation is no longer the guiding principle among the various racial, ethnic, and national groups in our society.

    b. The preservation and practice of one's own culture, traditions, and languages are a primary value.

    c. North American society is a blend of various groups, each maintaining their own identity while together producing a North American tapestry.

    d. Native Americans hold a unique place in this tapestry as the original inhabitants of this land.

    e. While Native Americans are a minority, their cultures, languages, and traditions have equal value with other racial and ethnic groups in a multicultural society.

    f. The Roman Catholic Church exists in this multicultural society.

The value and integrity of all racial, ethnic, and cultural groups must be respected. North American society is not the assimilation of all groups into one, but the experience of a community of communities.

2. Native Americans are diverse in their own cultures and traditions.

    a. The primary identification of Native Americans is with their village, tribe, or nation.

    b. North of the Rio Grande, there are over 300 extant Native languages and cultures.

    c. The cultural differences among Native peoples are as diverse as other cultural groups, such as Europeans and Asians.

Native peoples must be viewed through their own cultural tapestry. Programs must avoid an attempt to present a monocultural understanding of Native Americans.

3. Native Americans have had a variety of experiences of European contact.

    a. Some Native Americans had their initial European contact almost 500 years ago. Others have had substantial contact only in the last 150 years.

    b. The experience of European contact varied partially because of the different European groups (English, French, Spanish, Russian) and their different approaches to colonization.

    c. A number of Native American peoples had their primary European contacts with Americans of European descent who no longer considered themselves to be immigrants.

    d. The experience of initial conversion to Catholic Christianity also differs from over 400 years to less than 100 years.

The variety of Native American histories with Europeans needs to be taken into account in programs and policies.

4. Native Americans have a diversity of experiences of living in a multicultural society.
   a. Some Native Americans live among their own people on their own land (reservations).
   b. Some Native Americans have grown up on their reservations and have migrated to an urban setting. For most, this is a real and dramatic experience of immigration.
   c. Many urban Native Americans (who constitute at least half of the Native population) maintain some contact with their cultures through urban Native centers and/or visits to their reservations.
   d. In urban areas, there will be Native Americans who are native to the area and others who have migrated there from other parts of North America.
   e. Not all Native Americans have reservations. Some urban Natives belong to landless tribes. Their primary community is the multicultural urban experience of North American society.

The variety of reasons why Native Americans live where they do in our American society needs to be understood and appreciated. Programs need to reflect their pluralistic experience.

5. Native Americans have a variety of experiences in regard to their own culture and the dominant North American Culture.
   a. After European contact, a number of Native American tribes lost their cultures and languages through the destruction of their villages. Some tribes disappeared while others continued with a few survivors.
   b. Through the experience of Christian missionization, some Native Americans lost their own culture and language and adopted European ones.
   c. Some Native Americans maintained a strictly divided two cultural life: one for the village or reservation and the other for the larger society and often for the Church.
   d. Some Native Americans have lost their culture and language because of the governmental assimilation efforts of previous years.
   e. There is presently a revival of Native cultures, traditions, and languages occurring. Many are regaining their culture.

The many diverse ways in which Native Americans relate to their own societies and to North American society must be appreciated in any program.

6. Native Americans continue to experience racial stereotyping and racism.
   a. Through centuries of contact, certain stereotypes have developed around Native Americans. The media has played a significant role in dispersing and supporting these stereotypes.
   b. Native Americans experience among themselves various forms of racism through tribal prejudices.
   c. Due to the experience of reservations, Native peoples have known the experience of forced segregation. The reservation system developed as a consequence of the Native peoples being a conquered people.
   d. Some Native Americans have a mistrust of the institutions of the dominant culture, such as governmental agencies, and the Church.

The reality of centuries of prejudice, racial stereotypes, and racism needs to be acknowledged. Programs need to develop and support trusting relationships betweenNative Americans and the larger North American society.

7.   Among Native Americans, the understanding of relationships provides some shared elements and a means to embrace them in a pluralistic society.
   a. Native Americans arrive at their self-identity through the various relationships in which they share.
   b. How Native Americans experience these primary relationships will help an understanding of a particular cultural group. These relationships are with word, time, land, and all creatures.
   c. Native Americans view themselves as living through these relationships in a sacred and spiritual world.

Programs need to appreciate the deeply spiritual world of Native Americans. An understanding of Native peoples' primary relationships will be of help in this area.

8.   Native Americans' relationship with language.
   a. The spoken word has a higher value than the written word. The use of story has primary importance since through the telling of one's tribe's stories, the people are given and sustained in life.
   b. The speaker's personal integrity gives credence and value to the words he or she speaks.
   c. The value of words lessens with their quantity. Some Native Americans may appear reticent when in fact they are respecting the value of the conversation.
   d. Silence has an intrinsic value. It is important to spend time in silence with people.

Any program must appreciate the Native relationship with words and must rely more on the spoken word than on the written word.

9.   Native Americans' relationship with time.
   a. The primary understanding of time is how it relates to the days, months, and seasons of the world. Time is the expression of one's unity and harmony with the world.
   b. While the understanding of time used in the dominant society by hours and minutes has importance, it is secondary to the Native understanding of time.
   c. Through the use of ritual, one can place oneself more in harmony with the rhythm of the world. History is not seen as linear but rather as how it reflects the movement of the world, of the seasons.
   d. Through the respect for one's elders, this appreciation of one's history is reflected. For the elders carry in their bodies, the traditions and values of the people.

The Native understanding of time needs to be appreciated to avoid confusion. History is not viewed as a chronicle of past events but rather as a reflection of living with the universe.

10.   Native Americans' relationship with land.
   a. Native Americans view the world on which we live as Mother Earth: the giver and sustainer of life.
   b. In the faith expression of Native Americans, Catholic Christianity needs to be inculturated in the Native traditions and cultures. Otherwise, the adoption of Catholic Christianity would mean the loss of one's culture.
   c. Native spirituality and Catholic Christianity are compatible with one another.

Catholic Christianity needs to be inculturated in the various Native traditions and cultures which are deeply spiritual. Such an approach reflects the acceptance of the pluralistic world in which we live.

Working with Pacific Asian American Families

David Ng

1. The contemporary North American Church and society are multicultural.
    a. Church and society are no longer a "melting pot" into which all racial, ethnic, and national groups are blended into a single culture.
    b. Church and society are no longer monocultural societies into which minority groups are assimilated into the majority group (minority racial and ethnic groups assimilated into the majority white group).
    c. Church and society today can move toward a "mosaic," or "tapestry," or "tossed salad" form of society in which many diverse groups are included in the mix but continue to maintain their individual group identity and culture.
    d. Pacific Asian Americans (or, Pacific Asian North Americans, if Canadians are included) are a part of the multicultural society which is a "mosaic."
    e. Pacific Asian Americans are numerically a minority group in North America but they have equal status with every racial/ethnic group in the multicultural society.

THEREFORE, in developing programs, policies, and services, leaders need to affirm our multicultural society and avoid any implication that one racial, ethnic, or cultural group is superior to the others.

2. Pacific Asian Americans are themselves multicultural and diverse.
    a. Pacific Asian Americans could be described or categorized in various ways, for example, by region and national origin:
       - Pacific Islands—Filipino Americans, Hawaiian Americans, Samoan Americans, Tongan Americans, Micronesian Americans (such as Marshallese, Palauans, etc.), and other islands, such as Guam, Midway;
       - East Asian—Indian (East Indian Americans), Pakistani Americans;
       - Asian—Japanese Americans, Chinese Americans, Korean Americans, Taiwanese Americans, and Okinawan Americans;
       - Southeast Asian—Vietnamese Americans, Cambodian Americans, Thai Americans, Burmese (Myamar) Americans, and Hmong Americans,
    b. Pacific Asian Americans, because of their diversity, cannot be or described easily, using only one frame of reference or one physical,

social, psychological, historical, or religious stereotype.

THEREFORE, in developing programs, policies, and services, leaders need to affirm the variety of nationalities, cultures, and experiences among Pacific Asian Americans, and avoid treating all of them in a monocultural, stereotypical fashion.

3.   Pacific Asian Americans have had a variety of experiences of immigration.
    a. Some Pacific Asian Americans are the third, fourth, fifth, or later generation in North America. Some of these Pacific Asian Americans are thoroughly assimilated into American culture.
    b. Some Pacific Asian Americans are first generation, may be recent immigrants, and may have only a small degree of assimilation into the North American culture. Some speak only their native language and not English.
    c. There are a variety of reasons for Pacific Asian American immigration into North America, including poverty, education, economic opportunity (wealth), politics, and family. Not all Pacific Asian Americans are wealthy or have skills in business.

THEREFORE, in developing programs, policies, and services, leaders need to be aware of the variety of reasons that Pacific Asian Americans are in North America, and be particularly sensitive to those who are having difficulty adjusting to a culture that is different for them.

4.   Pacific Asian Americans have experienced a variety of national approaches to assimilation, such as:
    a. cultural annihilation (slavery, genocide, etc.)
    b. cultural alienation (segregation)
    c. cultural substitution (rejecting one's own culture)
    d. cultural assimilation (adopting the majority culture)
    e. cultural accommodation (being tolerated by the majority culture)

THEREFORE, in developing programs, policies, and services leaders need to be aware of the North American society's and the Church's blemished history of race, culture, and ethnic relations. Leaders need to foster creative, positive efforts aimed at developing an accepting and harmonious multicultural society.

5.   Pacific Asian Americans continue to experience condescension, racism, and institutional racism.
    a. Some Pacific Asian Americans find it difficult to trust people and institutions of the majority culture.
    b. Some Pacific Asian Americans prefer to associate primarily or only with their own ethnic or national group.
    c. Some Pacific Asian Americans will participate in activities with other ethnic groups only when someone from their group facilitates the participation.

THEREFORE, in developing programs, policies, and services, leaders need to be sensitive to the possibility that some Pacific Asian Americans have endured prejudice against them and may still harbor painful memories or feelings about how they have been treated by other persons and groups in North America. To develop trusting relationships with Pacific Asian Americans who have been hurt by prejudice will require patience, understanding, tact, and a willingness to listen to Pacific Asian Americans.

6.   Pacific Asian Americans can be "assimilated" through a process of cultural pluralism that assumes church and society to be multicultural and all racial/ethnic groups to be a part of the general society while maintaining individual cultural identity.

THEREFORE, in developing programs, policies, and services, leaders need to develop and exhibit an affirmative attitude about multicultural society, and be creative in incorporating into existing and new programs positive experiences of multicultural activities and learnings.

7.   Pacific Asian American families may be quite different than Euro-American families. Pacific Asian Americans may exhibit male-dominant, patriarchal family and group relational patterns, but for differing reasons.

   a. Some Asian groups follow Confucian values and social relationship patterns that emphasize respect for elders, respect for (or reverence of) ancestors, filial responsibility, and hierarchical relationships, including the superiority of males over females.

   b. Some Pacific Island cultures follow values that reflect small village social patterns, such as the authority of the chief, the superiority of males over females, and the village as an "extended family."

   c. Most Pacific Asian American cultures emphasize family membership and loyalty. The role of the individual is established in the context of the family, and decisions are made with family expectations in mind.

   d. The roles of children and adolescents differ between Pacific Asian American cultures (and differ from the roles in majority American culture). For example, children and adolescents in some Pacific Asian American cultures have few rights and must accept the authority of elders, particularly of the father. Unlike the freedom of expression afforded in majority American culture, many Pacific Asian American young people are not to make independent decisions or commitments. School and career choices are to be made in light of family expectations and needs.

   e. Pacific Asian American adolescents often face "double and triple stress" as adolescents, as racial/ethnic minority persons,

and as persons caught in cultural clash. They need help in being "bicultural" or "amphibious."

   f. Pacific Asian American families often need help or extra understanding regarding family relationships and family life. They may not be able to do the same activities expected of majority American culture families, because of language difficulties, different cultural values, and different ways of expressing roles and authority in families.

THEREFORE, in developing programs, policies, and services, leaders need to take into account a wide range of attitudes and actions of Pacific Asian American families, such as their original cultures and traditions, experiences of immigration, strategies for assimilation, communities for residence, economic status, religious commitments, relationship between parents and children, etc.

Leaders often need to be understanding of the cultural conflicts often experienced by Pacific Asian American families, particularly those with young persons.

8.   Pacific Asian Americans tend to be communal rather than individualistic.

   a. They tend to establish their identities in relation to the family or group.

   b. The peace and harmony of the family or group is viewed as more important than individual happiness.

THEREFORE, in developing programs, policies, and services, leaders can affirm the sense of corporateness and interrelatedness of Pacific Asian Americans and understand and appreciate the different values that inform and motivate them.

9.   Pacific Asian Americans often practice styles of thinking that are different than "Western styles of thinking."

   a. Pacific Asian Americans do not necessarily prefer rational, logical, scientific styles of thinking; some (perhaps many) have been brought up with preferences for intuitive thinking, acceptance of mystery and non-rationality, and a mixture of subjective and objective thinking.

b. Affective and global thinking is practiced, in contrast to cognitive and detailed or analytical thinking favored in Western cultures.

c. Objective, factual information is not necessarily separated from personal, subjective feelings. Thinking and learning may be impressionistic, aesthetic, or holistic.

THEREFORE, in developing programs, policies, and services, leaders need to be sensitive to the different forms of expression and different styles of thinking that are a part of the rich, varied ways to thinking and acting among Pacific Asian Americans.

10.　Pacific Asian Americans often practice styles of communication that are different than "Western styles of communication."

a. Communication often is formal or formalized and mindful of protocol.

b. Some communication is indirect and contextual and seems ambiguous to those who are accustomed to precision and directness.

c. Personal feelings may be suppressed.

d. Especially among Asian Americans, body contact is avoided as well as eye contact.

e. Especially among first generation Asian Americans, a show of affection may be avoided.

f. Deference is seen as a virtue rather than a weakness.

g. Oral tradition and story forms are preferred over written forms and fact-based forms, by some Pacific Asian Americans, especially Pacific Islanders.

THEREFORE, in developing programs, policies, and services, leaders can be appreciative to the variety of styles of life and ways of thinking exhibited by Pacific Asian Americans and can encourage them to share their differences as gifts to the entire group.

11.　Pacific Asian American religious tradition does not necessarily reflect Judeo-Christian tradition.

a. Pacific Asian American religious tradition will reflect historical, regional, and cultural tradition, and is as diverse as are Pacific Asian American cultures.

b. For example, Pacific Asian American cultures have observed and practiced Islamic, Christian, Buddhist, Shinto, shamanist, Hindu, animalistic, and other religious traditions, and Taoist or Confucian philosophies.

c. Within families there may be conflicts over the practice of religious rituals and celebrations.

d. Pacific Asian American parents may expect their children to observe certain religious rituals and celebrations, in order to preserve cultural values and traditions.

e. Some Pacific Asian Americans will view Christianity as a "Western religion."

f. Not all Pacific Asian Americans are committed to a religion or particularly to Christianity.

g. Some Pacific Asian Americans, including many Chinese, Koreans, and Japanese, maintain Confucian social values and ethics. For them religion and social ethics are parallel areas of life and religion does not necessarily require commitment and corporate membership in the same ways they are required in Christianity.

h. Many Pacific Asian American families include members who practice different faiths or belong to different denominations. For example, a family may include parents who are Buddhists, children who are Baptists, Roman Catholics, and non-religious. Such families may not be able to do any religious activities together or discuss Christian concepts together.

THEREFORE, in developing programs, policies, and services, leaders need to be sensitive to the variety of religious expression that may be present in a Pacific Asian American family and to feelings of conflict or confusion that are sometimes experienced. In presenting the Christian faith, leaders need to be clear, loving, and humble; they need to be open-minded about religious truth and to non-Western forms of Christianity.

SECTION 2

Developing a Family Perspective in Youth Ministry

CHAPTER 10

Affirmations for Faith Growth and Faith Sharing in Families

John Roberto

The *Catholic Families Project* has developed a series of affirmations, which have guided the development of the five-year project and of the *Catholic Family Series*. These affirmations serve as a conceptual framework around which each book is built and the goals toward which the *Catholic Families Project* is committed. These affirmations focus on the importance of the family in nurturing and sharing the Catholic Christian faith and in living out this faith in the family and world. They bring a family perspective to the process of faith growth and to the church ministries charged with responsibility for fostering faith growth. Each affirmation is grounded in a broad *understanding* of the role of the family, which is drawn from a variety of sources, including developmental research, social science research, family systems theory, theological reflection, and pastoral practice. Each of these affirmations reinforces our belief that it is of the *highest priority* that the family be respectfully understood, critically assessed, and pastorally assisted by the Church today. You will find that *Families and Youth* develops and deepens your understanding of these central affirmations, while using these affirmations to develop the key content areas for the learning program.

AFFIRMATION 1: THE FAMILY IS A COMMUNITY OF LIFE AND LOVE IN SERVICE TO GOD'S KINGDOM IN HISTORY WITH A SPECIFIC IDENTITY AND MISSION. IT HAS THE SAME FUNCTIONS AS THE REST OF THE CHURCH, BUT IT IS THE CHURCH IN A FAMILY WAY. IT IS THE *DOMESTIC CHURCH* OR THE *CHURCH OF THE HOME*.

There is a great diversity in definitions of the contemporary family. In order to focus our work, the *Catholic Families Project* utilizes the definition of the family developed by the United States Catholic Bishops in *A Family Perspective in Church and Society*:

> . . . the family is an intimate community of persons bound together by blood, marriage, or adoption, for the whole of life. In our Catholic tradition, the family proceeds from marriage—an intimate, exclusive, permanent, and faithful partnership of husband and wife. The definition is intentionally normative and recognizes that the Church's normative approach is not shared by all (19).

While this definition may be restrictive in some senses, it also proposes a broader view of the family in the following ways: a) it includes multiple generations and extended family members; b) it recognizes that many persons are involved simultaneously in several families; c) it includes single persons, since they have families of origin; d) it recognizes that there are other covenantal relationships in the family besides marriage (parent-children, siblings); and e) it recognizes families that are created by adoption.

Our approach to the contemporary family also recognizes the great diversity of family structures with nuclear, extended, single or multiple generations, two-parent, single-parent, single-earner, dual-earner, childless, blended, and separated families. We also recognize the diversity in family structures within particular ethnic groups in which the family may be viewed as the entire extended network of relatives, as a wide informal network of kin and community, or as all the ancestors and their descendents.

The Church teaches that the family has a unique identity and mission that permeates its tasks and responsibilities. This identity and mission is shaped by a Christian vision of family life—family life as sacred and family activities as holy. The Church sees the family at the service of the building up of the Reign of God. As such the family can be called the *domestic church* or the *church of the home*. The family as a *domestic church* means that the family itself is part of the church.

> It has the same functions as the rest of the church, but it is the church in a family way. . . . Evangelization, catechesis, worship, and ministry will all have their family expressions, but because of the earthly character of family life, they will be rather secular in appearance. . . . For it is the life of the family itself which is its basic spiritual resource. And it is the way in which the love of God and neighbor are joined together in the family that gives it its most fundamental charge (Thomas 16–17).

AFFIRMATION 2: THE MISSION OF THE FAMILY IS TO BECOME AN INTIMATE COMMUNITY OF PERSONS; TO SERVE LIFE IN ITS TRANSMISSION, PHYSICALLY AND SPIRITUALLY; TO PARTICIPATE IN THE DEVELOPMENT OF SOCIETY; AND TO SHARE IN THE LIFE AND MISSION OF THE CHURCH.

AFFIRMATION 3: SHARING THE CATHOLIC CHRISTIAN FAITH IN FAMILIES INVOLVES CELEBRATING OUR FAITH THROUGH RITUALS, TELLING THE CATHOLIC FAITH STORY, ENRICHING FAMILY RELATIONSHIPS, PRAYING TOGETHER AS A FAMILY, PERFORMING ACTS OF JUSTICE AND SERVICE, AND RELATING AS A FAMILY TO THE WIDER COMMUNITY.

AFFIRMATION 4: WE ENCOUNTER GOD IN THE EXPERIENCES AND EVENTS OF EVERYDAY LIFE—IN OUR WORK, IN OUR RELATIONSHIPS, IN OUR FAMILY LIFE—*AND* IN THE CATHOLIC CHRISTIAN STORY—IN THE SCRIPTURES, IN TRADITION, IN PRAYER, IN THE SACRAMENTS. FAMILY LIFE IS A PRIVILEGED LOCALE FOR ENCOUNTERING GOD IN EVERYDAY LIFE EXPERIENCES *AND* IN THE CHRISTIAN STORY.

The mission of the family as a *domestic church*, a community of life and love in service to God's kingdom in history, is realized through four very specific tasks. One of the primary goals of the *Catholic Families Project* is to empower families to undertake and realize these tasks as well as to assist the variety of church ministries and their leaders in their work of empowering families. These four tasks provide the nucleus around which the Catholic Families Series is built. Each resource seeks to promote the development of these four tasks in the lives of families. These tasks can be briefly summarized in the following manner:

> **Task 1: The family is an intimate community of persons.** This community is manifested in mutual self-giving by the members of the family throughout its life together. This community also calls for the respect of each family member's uniqueness and dignity.

> **Task 2: The family serves life in its transmission, physically, by bringing children into the world, and spiritually, by handing on values and traditions as well as developing the potential of each member at every age.** It is the duty of parents to create a family atmosphere inspired by love and devotion to God and their fellow persons, which will promote an integrated, personal, and social education of the child. It is the responsibility of all

members of the family to promote the development and potential of each member at every age.

Task 3: The family participates in the development of society by becoming a community of social training, hospitality, and political involvement and activity. How family members learn to relate to each other with respect, love, caring, fidelity, honesty, and commitment becomes their way of relating to others in the world.

Task 4: The family shares in the life and mission of the Church by becoming a believing and evangelizing community, a community in dialogue with God, and a community at the service of humanity. As the basic community of believers, bound together in love to one another, the family is the arena where the drama of redemption is played out. The dying and rising with Christ is most clearly manifested. Here, the cycle of sin, hurt, reconciliation, and healing is lived out over and over again. In family life is found the *church of the home*: where each day "two or three are gathered" in the Lord's name; where the hungry are fed; where the thirsty are given drink; where the sick are comforted (*Family Perspective* 20, 21, 22).

These four tasks point to specific ways that we can empower families to share the Catholic Christian faith. The *Catholic Families Project* has identified six specific ways that families share faith and promote the faith growth of family members. These time-honored ways include: 1) celebrating our faith through rituals, 2) telling the Catholic Faith Story, 3) enriching family relationships, 4) praying together as a family, 5) performing acts of justice and service, and 6) relating as a family to the wider community. Each of these six ways contribute the complex process of promoting growth toward mature faith.

Celebrating our faith through rituals happens when the family celebrates the liturgical year, such as Advent and Christmas, Lent and Easter; celebrates the civic calendar, such as Martin Luther King

Day and Earth Day; celebrates milestones or rites of passages, such as birthdays, anniversaries, graduations, special recognitions; celebrates ethnic traditions which have been passed down through the generations; celebrates the rituals of daily life, such as meal prayer, and forgiveness. These celebrations provide the foundations for a family ritual life in which God is discovered and celebrated through the day, week, month, and year. The family's ritual life is complemented by participation in the ritual life of the parish community with its weekly celebration of the Eucharist; regular sacramental celebrations, such as Reconciliation and Anointing of the Sick; and liturgical year celebrations.

Telling or sharing the Catholic Faith Story happens when parents share stories from the Scriptures with their children, when families discuss the implications and applications of Christian faith for daily living, when a moral dilemma is encountered and the family turns to the resources of the Catholic faith for guidance, when parents discuss the religious questions their children/adolescents ask. The family's sharing is complemented by participation of children, parents, and/or the entire family in the catechetical program of the parish community.

Enriching family relationships happens when the family spends both quality and quantity time together; participates in family activities; works at developing healthy communication patterns to cultivate appreciation, respect, and support for each other; negotiates and resolves problems and differences in positive and constructive ways. Enriching family relationships also involves the parents' developing their marriage relationship or a single parent's developing intimate, supportive relationships in his or her life.

Praying together as a family happens when families incorporate prayer into the daily living through meal and bed times, times of thanksgiving and of crisis; and when parents teach basic prayers and pray with their children. The family's prayer life is complemented by participation in the communal pray life of the parish community, especially through liturgical year celebrations.

Performing acts of justice and service happens when the family recognizes the needs of others in our communities and in our world and seeks to respond. Families act through stewardship and care for the earth; through direct service to others, like the homeless and the hungry; through study of social issues; through developing a family lifestyle based on equality, nonviolence, respect for human dignity, respect for the earth. The family's service involvement is strengthened when it is done together with other families in the parish community.

Relating as a family to the wider community happens when the families join together in family support groups or family clusters for sharing, activities, and encouragement; when families learn about the broader church and world, especially the cultural heritages of others in the community or the world; and when families organize to address common concerns facing families in the community, such as quality education and safe neighborhoods.

AFFIRMATION 5: A FAMILY SYSTEMS PERSPECTIVE PROVIDES A WAY OF SEEING THE DYNAMICS OF FAMILY LIFE AS OPPORTUNITIES FOR FAITH TO MATURE AND FOR THE CATHOLIC CHRISTIAN STORY TO BE COMMUNICATED.

A family systems perspective is central to the *Catholic Families Project* and to the resources in the *Catholic Family Series*. A family systems perspective is a new way of viewing family life. It views the family as a living and developing system whose members are essentially interconnected, rather than a collection of individuals. Through relationships, expectations, and responsibilities people connect the very heart of who they are to other people. The family systems model shows how each person in a family plays a part in the whole system. Since all parts are connected and interdependent, the relationships between the parts are more important than the parts themselves. However, in a family individuals also maintain their own identities, rendering the whole system

greater than the sum of its parts. Often times there is tension between the need for togetherness as a family and the need for individual autonomy.

Family systems have roles for its individual members and family rules which govern family living. Roles, rules, and responsibilities give families balance or equilibrium. All families strive for equilibrium or balance. When change or disruption occurs, the family will always try to come to rest and balance, like a mobile. In striving for equilibrium, families tend to resist change. Change in one family member affects all other members and the whole family.

For all these reasons, communication is the lifeblood of the family. Each family develops a style of communication that can assist or inhibit family functioning, namely, the way the family addresses togetherness and change.

Therefore, when we speak of family as a system we mean the dynamic interplay of relationships within the family as members confront change, maturity, faith growth, and day-to-day life. It is the emotional push and pull within a family that serves as a catalyst for change and growth, but it also provides focal points for struggle and pain. Effective family functioning provides a positive and healthy context for faith maturation.

Utilizing a family systems perspective, we can identify the qualities that assist or inhibit the family from meeting the basic needs of nurturance, autonomy, and intimacy. Family strengths enable families to operate effectively as a system meeting the needs of family members and the family as a whole. Supporting, enhancing, and cultivating the sources of strength in family life, rather than focusing on family problems, positively and significantly affects the quality of family life and the health of family members. The research on family strengths can be briefly summarized in the following categories:

Commitment: an investment of time, energy, spirit, and heart; a strong sense of commitment to stay related during times of transition, difficulty, or crisis. Family members are dedicated to promoting each other's welfare and happiness, and they expect the family to endure. They have a sense of shared responsibility for the family.

Time Together: spend both quality and quantity of time together; share leisure time together. The family has a sense of play and humor.

Appreciation: appreciate and respect and affirm and support each other.

Communication: develop and use skills in communication, negotiating, and resolving problems and differences in a positive and constructive way.

Religious and Moral Wellness: possess a solid core of moral and religious beliefs, promoting sharing, love, and compassion for others. The family teaches a sense of right and wrong. They have a strong sense of family in which rituals and traditions abound. They value service to others.

Coping with Crisis: internally drawing on the above strengths, and developing adaptability; relying on external resources through: social network and community organizations. The family admits to, and seeks help with problems.

Understanding, Affirming Parents and Close, Caring Families: parental harmony, effective parent-child communication, a consistent authoritative/democratic parental discipline, and parental nurturing.

A Personal, Liberating Faith: emphasis on God's love and acceptance, establishing and maintaining a close relationship to God, and empowering people to reach out and care for others; developed through daily interaction, structured times of worship, and works of justice and service as a family.[1]

The *Catholic Families Series* sees the support and development of these strengths as essential to creating both a positive and healthy context and for promoting faith growth and faith sharing.

AFFIRMATION 6: THE FAMILY IS THE PRIMARY CONTEXT FOR FAITH GROWTH AND

FAITH SHARING. THE FAMILY, AND PARENTS IN PARTICULAR, ARE THE KEY VARIABLES IN NURTURING FAITH GROWTH AND IN SHARING THE CATHOLIC CHRISTIAN STORY/TRADITION WITH CHILDREN AND YOUTH. SECOND ONLY TO AN INDIVIDUAL'S FREE RESPONSE TO GOD, THE FAMILY PROFOUNDLY SHAPES CHILDREN'S AND YOUTH'S RELIGIOUS IDENTITY.

At the heart of the *Catholic Families Project* and the *Catholic Families Series* is the belief that the first and primary community for sharing faith and for promoting faith growth is the family. This insight permeates all of the resources and training developed through the *Catholic Families Project*. This insight needs to permeate all church ministries. What makes the family so central is that, sociologically, it is a primary group, charged with particular tasks that can only be met in a primary group.

The family, in its diversity of structures, meets four clusters of needs that are essential for being and well-being: 1) to *belong* and to experience *being irreplaceable*, 2) to experience *autonomy* and *agency* (belonging), 3) to participate in *shared meanings* and *rituals*, and 4) to provide for *bodily well-being*—nurture, wellness, and care. James Fowler observes that the family is the context in which we participate in the forming of a first sense of *identity*—who I am, who I can become, what I am worth or not worth. In the family, we have our first and most formative experiences of love relationships and of relationships in which we participate with loyalty and care. In *The Hurried Child*, David Elkind helps us to see that one of the important elements of early socialization for children is learning the *family's covenant system*: what freedoms will be given children and what responsibilities will be expected from them, what achievements are expected and what support can be counted on, what loyalty will be expected or required from family members, and what commitment will be given by those who require it. This is a crucial part of preschool socialization. It has to be reworked and renegotiated as we move through each of the stages of the personal and family life cycle (Elkind 120). This is what makes families so crucially important for the formation of faith (Fowler).

Research confirms the fact that parents are potentially the greatest influencers of their children's values, religious belief, and behavior. Some of the reasons parents (and the family system) are so important include:

- Parents have a closeness to the child (proximity) over a long period of time (longevity) (Williams).

- The following elements increase the influence of parents (or other significant adults): a) modeling: the effect of example has always been understood to be important; b) agreement: when parents agree on the importance of religion to them and the messages they convey are consistent, the power of influence increases; c) congruence: example is more powerful when parents talk about their actions and when what they say is consistent with what they do (Williams).

- Parents who talk at home about religious activity and motivation are far more likely to have children who have positive attitudes toward religion (Williams).

- The influence of congregations, parents, schools, and peers is best exercised in a warm, supportive environment. In spite of the superior power of parents to influence, if the family relationship lacks warmth, support, and acceptance, most children and adolescents will seek those qualities elsewhere (Williams).

- . . . we can say that there are four different ways the family of origin affects the religious imagination of one of its offspring: 1) the relationship between the parents of the child. . .; 2) the relationship of the parents to one another; 3) the religious devotion of both parents, especially if they are very devout; 4) the perception by the child of the parent as religiously influential, which presumably indicates the parent's explicit attempt to teach religion (Greeley 60).

AFFIRMATION 7: CHRISTIAN FAITH IS A GIFT OF GOD WHOSE GRACE TOUCHES THE INNER CORE OF A PERSON AND DISPOSES

ONE TOWARD A LIVED RELATIONSHIP WITH GOD IN JESUS CHRIST.

A holistic and integrated understanding of the Catholic Christian faith is essential for empowering families to share faith and to grow in faith. Drawing upon contemporary theological understandings, we offer this understanding. Faith as a *gift* invites a free response to share life in relationship, with God who is the very source of life. This response is a personal encounter with God in Christ, which transforms a person's way of life. As a response of the whole person, genuine faith involves an affective dimension, the activity of trusting; a cognitive dimension, the activity of believing; and the behavioral dimension, an activity of doing.

As an *activity of trusting*, Christian faith is "an invitation to a relationship of loyalty to and trust in a faithful God who saves through Jesus Christ by the power of the Spirit" (Groome 75). This activity of faith also involves trust in and loyalty to other persons.

As an *activity of believing*, Christian faith is a particular way of interpreting our experience in light of the Good News and the continuing tradition of the Church so that it leads to a deeper and expanded understanding of living as a Catholic Christian. This activity of faith necessarily involves the gradual development of deep convictions and a fuller understanding of the doctrinal expression of the Catholic faith.

As an *activity of doing*, Christian faith is an active response to the mandate of the God's kingdom—to love God by loving one's neighbor, especially in the living and pursuit of justice, peace, equality, and so on. This activity of faith calls us to transform the world through "a life of loving service on all levels of human existence—the personal, the interpersonal, and the social/political" (Groome 76).

Christian faith is covenantal. It is trust and loyalty, commitment between persons and within groups that is ratified and deepened by a shared trust in and loyalty to God in Jesus Christ. Christian faith as covenantal is a dynamic pattern of personal trust in and loyalty to:

- God as the source and creator of all value, as disclosed and mediated in Jesus Christ, and through the Church, as inspired by the Holy Spirit. As such Christian faith is *Trinitarian* faith.

- The actual and coming reign of God as the hope and power of the future, and as intending justice and love among humankind. In this sense Christian faith gives us a horizon and vision, a horizon of hope grounded in a trust in the actual, present and coming reign of God.

- God, in Christ, as the Loving, Personal Redeemer and Reconciler calling us to repent and freeing us from the bondage of Sin. Christ frees us from anxiety about death, from the threat of separation from love, and from our hostility for and alienation from each other.

- The Church, as Body of Christ, as visible and invisible extension of the ministry and mission of Christ (Fowler 101).

AFFIRMATION 8: GROWTH IN CHRISTIAN FAITH IS A GRADUAL, LIFELONG, DEVELOPMENTAL PROCESS INVOLVING THE INDIVIDUAL AND FAMILY SYSTEM IN A CONTINUING JOURNEY TOWARD MATURITY AS A CHRISTIAN.

Christian faith is a journey, a process of conversion, never a point of arrival. Commitment to and growth of mature faith happens over a long period of time. Growth toward maturity in faith involves both a life-transforming relationship to a loving God and a consistent devotion to serving others. While no complete description of faith maturity is possible, we have identified several core dimensions integral to maturing Christian faith.[2] The Catholic Families Series seeks to actively promote these core dimensions of mature Christian faith:

- Trusting in God's saving grace and firmly believing in the humanity and divinity of Jesus Christ.

- Experiencing a sense of personal well-being, security, and peace.

- Integrating faith and life, that is, seeing work, family, social relationships, and political choices as part of one's religious life.

- Seeking spiritual growth through Scripture, study, reflection, prayer, and discussion with others.

- Seeking to be part of a Catholic community of believers in which people give witness to their faith, support and nourish one another, serve the needs of each other and the community, and worship together.

- Developing a deeper understanding of the Catholic Christian tradition and its applicability to life in today's complex society.

- Holding life-affirming Gospel values, including respect for human dignity, commitment to uphold human rights, equality (especially racial and gender), stewardship, care and compassion, and a personal sense of responsibility for the welfare of others.

- Advocating for social and global change to bring about greater social justice and peace.

- Serving humanity, consistently and passionately, through acts of love and justice.

The process of maturing in faith is both an individual journey and a family journey. Human development, faith development, and the family-life-cycle are all intertwined as a person grows toward maturity in faith. While no theory of human development can explain all the factors that contribute to faith maturing, theories do provide windows through which we can gain a better view of what is happening. The work of James Fowler in faith development studies and of Betty Carter and Monica McGoldrick in family-life-cycle studies, provide useful constructs or frameworks that we are using in the *Catholic Families Project* and in the *Catholic Families Series*. But, they must be taken as descriptive of the maturing process, rather than as prescriptive or normative. For example, there are ethnic and socio-economic variables which have a direct bearing on human development, yet they are not fully addressed in these theories. Individuals and families have unique features which go beyond the interpretive power of any one theory.

The stages of faith—and their life tasks and transitions—provide opportunities to promote faith growth in the individual and in entire family system. The *Catholic Families Series* utilizes Fowler's stages of faith development to describe the faith growth at particular stages of the life-cycle and to propose strategies for promoting individual and family faith growth and faith sharing.

The family-life-cycle stages—and their life tasks and transitions—provide opportunities to promote faith growth in the entire family system across generations. The individual life-cycle takes place within the family-life-cycle, which is the primary context of human and faith development. A family-life-cycle perspective sees the family as a three or four generational system moving through time in a life-cycle of distinct stages with particular tasks to accomplish and challenges to face in order to prepare itself and its members for further growth and development. A family-life-cycle perspective sees the rites of passage that each life-cycle change precipitates as creating opportunities for transformation because the family system unlocks or is more open to change at these times. For example, the Church's basic sacraments revolve around many of these life-cycle changes. The *Catholic Families Series* utilizes Carter and McGoldrick's conception of the family-life-cycle stages to describe family growth and to propose strategies for promoting individual and family faith growth and faith sharing.

Two essays at the end of this chapter outline the stages of development in faith and the stages of the family-life-cycle will orient you to the two theories used in the *Catholic Families Series*. Both theories have been developed and refined across more than 15 years of research.

AFFIRMATION 9: THE PARISH COMMUNITY AND ITS VARIETY OF MINISTRIES ARE TO BE IN PARTNERSHIP WITH THE FAMILY IN NURTURING THE FAITH GROWTH OF FAMILY MEMBERS, IN SHARING THE CATHOLIC CHRISTIAN TRADITION/STORY, AND IN EMPOWERING THE FAMILY TO LIVE THE CHRISTIAN FAITH IN THE FAMILY AND IN THE WORLD. GROWTH IN FAITH THROUGH THE ENTIRE LIFE-CYCLE AND THE SHARING/TRANSMISSION OF THE FAITH STORY IS A COMPLEX PROCESS INVOLVING THE FAMILY, THE COMMUNITY OF FAITH, AND THE MULTIPLE MINISTRIES OF THAT COMMUNITY OF FAITH: LITURGY AND WORSHIP, RITUAL LIFE, RELIGIOUS EDUCATION/CATECHESIS, AND SERVICE TO THE WORLD.

The *Catholic Families Project* calls for an intentional and planned partnership between parishes and families in the process of fostering faith growth throughout the life-cycle. This partnership means bringing a family perspective to the parish's life and ministries as these seek to promote faith growth. We have already identified the six specific ways that families share faith and promote the faith growth of family members. Each of the six family ways need to be complemented by particular parish ministries that are organized using a family perspective. No one ministry or institution bears the total responsibility for nurturing faith growth. *It is the partnership between family and the parish and its multiple ministries that provide the most effective means for nurturing faith growth.*

The role of the parish community is extremely important for faith maturing. The systems perspective that was used to examine the family can be applied to the parish community as well. Looking at the entire parish system, six aspects of congregational life were identified in a recent study as promoting maturity in faith and stronger congregational and denominational loyalty. They were: 1) formal Christian education programs for adults and children/youth, 2) quality of Sunday worship, 3) service to those in need, 4) personally experiencing the care and concern of other members, 5) perceiving the congregation to be warm and friendly, and 6) perceiving the congregation to encourage questions, challenge thinking, and expect learning. The more that each aspect is present in the congregation the greater, the maturity of faith and the stronger the loyalty of the individual member. An additional factor for promoting faith growth is high degrees of faith maturity exhibited by the pastor, educators, and parish leaders (Benson et al.).

Conclusion

The importance of developing, supporting, and encouraging the Catholic faith life of families has never been more urgent. The *Catholic Families Project* is committed to creating new pastoral and educational approaches for fostering faith growth in families and for building an intentional partnership between families and the parish. The *Catholic Family Series* represents a significant contribution toward realizing these goals.

END NOTES

1 This description of family strengths is summarized from Dolores Curran, *Traits of the Healthy Family* (San Francisco: Harper & Row and New York: Ballatine Books, 1983); Nick Stinnett and John DeFrain, *Secrets of Strong Families* (Boston: Little, Brown, and Co., 1985); Merton and Irene Strommen, *Five Cries of Parents* (San Francisco: Harper & Row, 1985).

2 This description of the core components of mature faith is adapted from Peter Benson, Dorothy Williams, Carolyn Eklin, and David Shuller, *Effective Christian Education: A National Study of Protestant Congregations* (Minneapolis: Search Institute, 1990).

WORKS CITED

Benson, Peter, Dorothy Williams, Carolyn Eklin, and David Shuller. *Effective Christian Education: A National Study of Protestant Congregations*. Minneapolis: Search Institute, 1990.

Benson, Peter, and Carolyn Eklin. *Effective Christian Education: A National Study of Protestant Congregations—A Summary Report on Faith, Loyalty, and Congregational Life*. Minneapolis: Search Institute, 1990.

Carter, Betty, and Monica McGoldrick. "The Family Life Cycle." In *Growing in Faith: A Catholic Family Sourcebook*. Ed. John Roberto. New Rochelle, NY: Don Bosco Multimedia, 1990.

Curran, Dolores. *Traits of a Healthy Family*. San Francisco: Harper & Row, 1983.

Elkind, David. *The Hurried Child*. Reading, MA: Addison-Wesley, 1981.

Fowler, James. "Faith Development through the Family Life Cycle." In *Growing in Faith: A Catholic Family Sourcebook*. Ed. John Roberto. New Rochelle, NY: Don Bosco Multimedia, 1990.

Greeley, Andrew. The Religious Imagination. New York: Sadlier, 1981.

Groome, Thomas. *Christian Religious Education*. San Francisco: Harper & Row, 1981.

Stinett, Nick and Defrain, John. *Secrets of Strong Families*. Boston: Little, Brown and Co., 1985.

Strommen, Merton and Irene. *Five Cries of Parents*. San Francisco: Harper & Row, 1985.

Thomas, David. "Home Fires: Theological Reflections." *The Changing Family*. Ed. Stanley Saxton, et al. Chicago: Loyola University Press, 1984.

Williams, Dorothy. "Religion in Adolescence: Dying, Dormant, or Developing." SOURCE 5.4 (December 1989).

ESSAY 1:
STAGES OF FAITH

James Fowler

Primal Faith. We all start as infants. A lot that is important for our lives of faith occurs in utero, and then in the very first months of our lives. We describe the form of faith that begins in infancy as Primal Faith. This first stage is a pre-language disposition, a total emotional orientation of trust offsetting mistrust, which takes form in the mutuality of our relationships with parents and others. This enables us to overcome or offset the anxiety resulting from separations which occur during infant development. Jean Piaget has helped us understand infant development as a succession of cognitive and emotional separations toward individuation from those who provided initial care. Earliest faith is what enables us to undergo these separations without undue experiences of anxiety or fear of the loss itself. We can readily see how important the family is in the nurturing and incubation of this first Primal stage of faith.

Intuitive-Projective Faith. This is a style of faith that emerges in early childhood with the acquisition of language. Here imagination, stimulated by stories, gestures, and symbols, and not yet controlled by logical thinking, combines with perception and feelings to create long-lasting faith images. These images represent both the protective and threatening powers surrounding our lives. If we are able to remember this period of our lives, we have some sense of how important, positively and negatively, it is in the formation of our life-long orientations in faith. When conversion occurs at a later stage, the images formed in this stage have to be re-worked in some important ways.

Mythic-Literal Faith. This faith emerges in the childhood elementary school years and beyond. Here the developing ability to think logically, through concrete operational thinking, helps one to order the world with categories of causality, space, time, and number. This means we can sort out the real from make-believe, the actual from fantasy. We enter into the perspectives of others. We become capable of capturing life and meanings in narrative and stories.

Synthetic-Conventional Faith. This stage characteristically begins to take form in early adolescence. Here new cognitive abilities make possible mutual, interpersonal perspective taking. We begin to see ourselves as others see us. We begin to construct the interiority of ourselves and others. A new step toward interpersonal intimacy and relationship emerges. A personal and largely unreflective synthesis of beliefs and values evolves to support identity and to unite us in emotional solidarity with others. This is a very important stage of faith, one which can continue well into adulthood and throughout our lives.

Individuative-Reflective Faith. With young adulthood or beyond, the stage we call Individuative-Reflective Faith appears. We begin to critically reflect on the beliefs and values formed in previous stages. In this stage, persons begin to rely upon third-person perspective taking. This means constructing a perspective that is neither just that of the self or reliant upon others, but is somehow above them both—a transcendental ego. The third-person perspective brings objectivity and enables us to understand the self and others as part of a social system. Here we begin to see the internalization of authority, that is, the development of an executive ego. This stage brings a new quality of responsibility for the self and for our choices. It marks the assumption of the responsibility for making explicit choices of ideology and lifestyle, which open the way for more critically self-aware commitments in relationships and in vocation.

Conjunctive Faith. At mid-life or beyond, frequently, we see the emergence of Conjunctive Faith. This stage involves the embrace and integration of opposites, or polarities, in our lives. Now what does this abstract language mean? It means realizing, in mid-life, that we are both young and old, that youngness and oldness are held together in the same life. It means recognizing that we are both masculine and feminine, with all of the meanings of those characterizations. It means coming to terms with the fact that we are both constructive people and, inadvertently, destructive people. St. Paul captured this in Romans 7. He said, "The good I would do I do not do, the evil I would not do I find myself doing. Who will save me from this body of death?"

There are religious dimensions to the reintegration of polarities in our lives. Mary Sharon Reilly, a Cenacle sister who specializes in spiritual direction for people at mid-life, titled a paper, "Ministry to Messiness." This messiness has to do with the holding together of polarities in mid-life existences.

In the Conjunctive stage, symbol and story, metaphor and myth, both from our own traditions and from others, seem to be newly appreciated, in what Paul Ricoeur has called a second or a willed naivete. Having looked critically at traditions and translated their meanings into conceptual

understandings, we experience a hunger for a deeper relationship to the reality that symbols mediate. In that deeper relationship, we learn again to let symbols have the initiative with us. It is immensely important to let biblical narrative draw us into it and let it read our lives, reforming and reshaping, rather than our reading and forming the meanings of the text. This marks a second naivete as a means of entering into those symbols.

Universalizing Faith. Beyond paradox and polarities, in this stage, we are grounded in a oneness with the power of being or God. Our visions and commitments seem to free us for a passionate yet detached spending of the self in love, devoted to overcoming division, oppression and violence, and in effective anticipatory response to an inbreaking commonwealth of love and justice, the reality of an inbreaking kingdom of God.

ESSAY 2:
STAGES OF THE FAMILY LIFE CYCLE

Betty Carter and Monica McGoldrick

The family life cycle comprises the entire emotional system of at least three, and now frequently four, generations. Three or four different generations must accommodate to life-cycle transitions, simultaneously. While one generation is moving toward older age, the next is contending with the empty nest, the third with young adulthood, forming careers and intimate peer adult relationships and having children, and the fourth with being inducted into the system. For example, the birth in a new generation corresponds with child-bearing in the parent generation and with grandparenthood in the eldest generation. If we look at the middle years of childhood, we see a settling down— roughly the period of the 30s for the parents; then we see grandparents planning for retirement. In adolescence, we see parents dealing with mid-life transition—a 40s re-evaluation—and we see grandparents

dealing with retirement. Then, as that child comes to the level of being an unattached adult, ready for marriage and courtship, we see parents dealing with issues of middle-adulthood and with renegotiating their marriage relationship. The grandparents, at this point, begin dealing with dependency and late-adulthood.

The Single, Young Adult. In outlining the stages of the family life cycle, we have departed from the traditional sociological depiction of the family life cycle as commencing at courtship or marriage and ending with the death of one spouse. Rather, considering the family to be the operative emotional unit from the cradle to the grave, we see a new family life cycle beginning at the stage of "young adults," whose completion of the primary task of coming to terms with their family of origin most profoundly influences who, when, how, and whether they will marry and how they will carry out all succeeding stages of the family life cycle. Seen in this way, the young adult phase is a cornerstone. It is a time to formulate personal life goals and to become a "self" before joining with another to form a new family subsystem. This is the chance for them to sort out emotionally what they will take along from the family of origin, what they will leave behind, and what they will create for themselves. Of great significance is the fact that until the present generation this crucial phase was never considered necessary for women, who had no individual status in families.

Key Task: Accepting emotional and financial responsibility for self.

Second-Order Changes:

   a. Differentiation of self in relation to family of origin

   b. Development of intimate peer relationships

   c. Establishment of self in work and financial independence

The Joining of Families through Marriage: The Couple. The changing role of women, the frequent marriage of partners from widely different cultural backgrounds, and the increasing physical distances between family members are placing a much greater burden on couples to define their relationship for themselves than was true in traditional and precedent-bound family structures. Marriage tends to be misunderstood as a joining of two individuals. What it really represents is the changing of two entire systems and an overlapping to develop a third subsystem.

Key Task: Commitment to a new system

Second-Order Changes:

   a. Formation of a marital system

   b. Realignment of relationships with extended families to include spouse

Becoming Parents: Families with Young Children. The shift to this stage of the family life cycle requires adults to move up a generation and become caretakers to the younger generation. Parents gain a new sense of themselves as part of a new generational level with specific responsibilities and tasks in relation to the next level of the family. The central struggle of this phase, however, in the modern two-paycheck (and sometimes two-career) marriage is the disposition of childcare responsibilities and household chores when both parents work full-time. In the single parent family the disposition of child-care responsibilities is extremely critical. The shift at this transition for grandparents is to move to a backseat from which they can allow their children to be the central parental authorities and yet form a new type of caring relationship with the grandchildren. For many adults this is a particularly gratifying transition, which allows them to have intimacy without the responsibility that parenting requires.

Key Task: Accepting new members into the system

Second-Order Changes:

   a. Adjusting marital system to make space for children

   b. Joining in childrearing, financial, and household tasks

   c. Realignment of relationships with extended family to include parenting and grandparenting roles

The Transformation of the Family System in Adolescence. Adolescence ushers in a new era. It marks a new definition of the children within the family and of the parents' role in relation to their children. Families with adolescents must establish qualitatively different boundaries than families with younger children, a job made more difficult in our times by the lack of built-in rituals to facilitate this transition. The boundaries must now be permeable. Parents can no longer maintain complete authority. Adolescents can and do open the family to a whole array of new values as they bring friends and new ideas into the family arena. Flexible boundaries that allow adolescents to move in and be dependent at times when they cannot handle things alone, and to move out and experiment with increasing degrees of independence when they are ready, put special strains on all family members in their new status with one another. This is also a time when adolescents begin to establish their own independent relationships with the extended family, and it requires special adjustments between parents and grandparents to allow and foster these new patterns. Families need to make the appropriate transformation of their view of themselves to allow for the increasing independence of the new generation, while maintaining appropriate boundaries and structure to foster continued family development. The central event in the marital relationship at this phase is usually the mid-life crisis of one or both spouses, with an exploration of personal, career, and marital satisfactions and dissatisfactions. There is usually an intense renegotiation of the marriage.

Key Task: Increasing flexibility of family boundaries to include children's independence and grandparents' frailties

Second-Order Changes:
   a. Shifting of parent-child relationships to permit adolescents to move in and out of the system
   b. Refocus on mid-life marital and career issues
   c. Beginning shift toward joint caring for the older generation

Families at Mid-life: Launching Children and Moving On. This phase of the family life cycle is the newest and the longest because of the low birth rate and the long life span of most adults. Parents launch their children almost twenty years before retirement and must then find other life activities. The most significant aspect of this phase is that it is marked by the greatest number of exits and entries of family members. It begins with the launching of grown children and proceeds with the entry of their spouses and children. It is a time when older parents are often becoming ill or dying. This loss, in conjunction with the difficulties of finding meaningful new life activities, may make it a particularly difficult period. Parents not only must deal with the change in their own status as they make room for the next generation and prepare to move up to grandparental positions, but they must also confront a different type of relationship with their own parents, who may become dependent, giving them (particularly women) considerable caretaking responsibilities. This can also be a liberating time, in that finances may be easier than during the primary years of family responsibilities and there is the potential for moving into new and unexplored areas—travel, hobbies, new

careers. This phase necessitates a restructuring of the marital relationship now that parenting responsibilities are deemphasized.

Key Task: Accepting a multitude of exits from and entries into the family system

Second-Order Changes:
   a. Renegotiation of marital system as dyad
   b. Development of adult-to-adult relationships between grown children and their parents
   c. Realignment of relationships to include in-laws and grandchildren
   d. Dealing with disabilities and death of parents (grandparents)

The Family in Later Life. Among the tasks of families in later life are adjustments to retirement, which not only may create the obvious vacuum for the retiring person, but may put a special strain on a marriage that until then has been balanced in different spheres. Financial insecurity and dependence are also special difficulties, especially for family members who value managing for themselves. Further, while loss of friends and relatives is particularlt difficult at this phase, the loss of a spouse is the most difficult adjustment, with its problems of reorganizing one's entire life alone after many years as a couple and of having fewer relationships to help replace the loss. Grandparenthood can, however, offer a new lease on life, and opportunities for special close relationships without the responsibilities of parenthood.

Key Task: Accepting the shifting of generational roles

Second-Order Changes:
   a. Maintaining own and/or couple functioning and interests in face of physiological decline; exploration of new familial and social role options
   b. Support for a more central role of middle generation
   c. Making room in the system for the wisdom of the elderly, supporting the older generation without overfunctioning for them

d. Dealing with loss of spouse, siblings, and other peers and preparation for own death; life review and integration

DIVORCE AND REMARRIAGE

Divorce in the American family is close to the point at which it will occur in the majority of families and will thus be thought of more and more as a normative event. In our experience as clinicians and teachers, we have found it useful to conceptualize divorce as an interruption or dislocation of the traditional family life cycle that produces the kind of profound disequilibrium that is associated throughout the entire family life cycle with shifts, gains, and losses in family membership. As in other life-cycle phases, there are crucial shifts in relationship status and important emotional tasks that must be completed by the members of divorcing families in order for them to proceed developmentally. As in other phases, emotional issues not resolved at this phase will be carried along as hindrances in future relationships. Therefore, we conceptualize the need for families in which divorce occurs to go through one or two additional phases of the family life cycle in order to restabilize and go forward developmentally again at a more complex level. Of women who divorce, at least 35 percent do not remarry. These families go through one additional phase and can restabilize permanently as post-divorce families. The other 65 percent of women who divorce remarry, and these families can be said to require negotiation of two additional phases of the family life cycle before permanent restabilization. (See the essay by Carter and McGoldrick in *Growing in Faith: A Catholic Family Sourcebook*, ed. John Roberto for a description of these additional stages.)

CHAPTER 11

Foundations of a Family Perspective in Youth Ministry

Leif Kehrwald

The preceding sections may have left you wondering, "What concrete, practical application does this information have for my ministry with adolescents? How can I make use of this material right away?" Good questions. Foundational information is important only if it is bridged to the present reality and struggles of the minister.

This section provides a transition from foundational concepts about adolescents and their families to practical application in a variety of youth ministry settings. We will do this by exposing the unspoken assumption we may hold about ministry and family life. We will then take a look at our posture of youth ministry with respect to family life. This will lead to a reflective tool with questions that help you examine your youth ministry efforts through a family lens, and discover possible adjustments. We will conclude our "bridging" process by surfacing a number of practical applications and suggestions for bringing a family sensitivity to youth ministry.

BLIND ASSUMPTIONS IN YOUTH MINISTRY

What are your assumptions about family life as you do youth ministry? Have you ever tried to name them? Sometimes we are not fully aware of the attitudes on which we base our ministry, and which may not be healthy or proper. As soon as we expose them, we realize their folly and can work

toward eliminating them. Below are descriptions of eight common "blind" assumptions that many in ministry hold at one time or another. Review your attitudes toward: adolescence itself, ministry programming, and your vision and praxis for faith formation.

Adolescence is pathological. When you hear the phrase "teenagers and their parents," what words come to mind? Conflict, rebellion, communication gap? If you think of only problem words, then you're probably guilty of this myth: that is, having teenagers in the household always spells trouble.

Yet, if other words like crazy, fun, emotional, busy, friendly, frustrating, trusting also come to mind, then your assumption is probably more balanced and realistic. Adolescence is a highly developmental stage for teens and parents, rendering many families with adolescents somewhat tumultuous and chaotic.

Yet most teens deal with their adolescence (all those self-image questions and relational/emotional ups and downs) with about the same degree of success that adults cope with in day-to-day life. Adolescence is not automatically problematic. But if we expect trouble from them, they will deliver. If we expect growth toward maturity, they will deliver that instead.

Adolescence is transitional. This myth is widely held in our American society.

How often do you hear remarks like, "It's just a stage she's going through. Not much we can do for her now." When a teen experiences a first love lost, severe facial blemishes, or a failed driver's test, it does not feel "transitional" to him or her. These are real (albeit common) experiences for teens which sometimes make the present moment seem like eternity.

Teens have both the need and the right to express the wide range of their emotions. Parents, youth ministers, and the entire community must validate adolescent experiences and the feelings which accompany them. Too often we short-circuit their feelings with, "Don't be sad. It will pass." "You'll be over him, and interested in someone else by next week." These statements may be true, but render injustice to a teen's emotional development.

Adolescence is foundational rather than transitional. All the emotions, mood swings, life questions, ambiguities and rebellions help form the base of maturity essential for adulthood. It's the stuff that shapes individual identity; perhaps the single most important task for adolescents. If these processes are not allowed to take their normal course during the teen years, they will rear their heads in much more challenging ways during mid-life. Adolescence is not just a stage.

More is better. The best youth programs sponsor the most activities, right? That's what I believed as a parish youth ministry coordinator. Some teens in my group were so active they joked about never seeing their parents. That gave me a sense of pride then, but I have since realized more is not always better.

You can have an impact in teens' lives without sponsoring tons of activities that gouge family prime time and burn out volunteer help. When the minister recognizes the family and household limitations of time, energy and space, he or she will be more selective about the quantity and quality of programs sponsored. If you filtered all your activities through a family lens, would they all be necessary? Careful planning which recognizes family limitations will yield a balanced and dynamic youth program. And you might get a night off!

Effective ministry with individuals obviously benefits their families. This is a common assumption because it seems logical and may actually be true sometimes. Yet if the ministry is solely focused on the individual without respect for household life, then that ministry is quite likely causing stress for the family.

Effective ministry with individuals implies change and growth in their lives. Recall that families, as systems, resist change even if it is positive. Your good work with teens may meet with resistance at home. Yet if you provide "bridger experiences" between your ministry efforts and the households of teens, your efforts will be more effective and will also enrich family life. (More about "bridger experiences" in a following section, "Principles for Bringing a Family Sensitivity to Youth Ministry.")

Effective community building automatically enriches the families of the community. Like the previous assumption, this one seems logical, and, if done correctly, will be true. But if the focus is solely on building community among teens, family life is undoubtedly fragmented in the process.

This fragmentation happens when teens are continually called out of the home for all sorts of activities and when volunteers are drained of energy and motivation with endless demands. Community building efforts can provide positive faith enrichment for teens, but the minister must always keep in mind (and encourage) the faith value of the home. If the church of the home is ignored, then the faith community building efforts in the parish or school will be far less valuable and legitimate.

Parents cannot really pass on faith to their children (especially teenagers). Few ministers would openly profess this statement, but many who work with children and teens continually encounter parents who appear completely apathetic about their child's faith formation. It can cause the ministry to truly wonder about the capabilities of today's parents in transmitting faith. Studies show, however, that the home is often the most powerful faith influence in a person's life. Gather any group of adults and have them reflect and share on the beginnings of their faith journey. The majority will always cite experiences relating to parents, family, or home.

Somehow, faith is transmitted from generation to generation in the home. Some ministers, particularly those who work with teens, fall guilty to this assumption in subtle ways; i.e., believing that we mark the beginning of a young person's faith life or becoming convinced our programs are crucial to the spiritual health of teens. Granted, many parents do not invest themselves in either their child's faith formation or their own for that matter. Yet rather than relinquish them from that responsibility, we must challenge them to accept it. Youth ministry should be done in a posture that seeks a partnership with parents in the faith nature of young people.

Without question, I can certainly transmit faith and values to young people. Perhaps the most dangerous form of youth ministry is the "lone ranger," "guru" approach that attracts young people to a single individual who personally leads them on their Christian journey. Personal relationships between teens and significant adults is very important to faith nurture, yet we must always remember that our Christian faith is communal in nature, not isolationist and individualistic. The significant adult in a teen's life must lead them into a relationship with the community as well as a personal relationship with Jesus Christ.

Again, we cannot forget the value of the household as Christian community. God is fully present in our homes, just as God is present in Church on Sunday morning, and at our youth catechesis programs. The more we can bridge these forms of Christian community together, the more effectively we will transmit our faith to the next generation.

Do any of these assumptions hit home for you in your work with adolescents? Just naming the attitudes out of which we minister can sometimes reveal our shortcomings. Be sure to take the time to work through the questions in "Youth Ministry and Families: Reflective Tool" at the end of this essay.

YOUTH MINISTRY POSTURE

In his book, *A New Design for Family Ministry*, Dr. Dennis Guernsey describes four approaches to ministry in relationship to household life. These approaches lie on a continuum from negative and self-serving to positive and relational. The four approaches are described below. Check your posture of ministry in your work with teens and their families.

On the far negative side of the continuum, Guernsey describes the **parasitic** approach to ministry. This posture demands unfailing commitment to all programs and activities. As a result the virtue of service gets turned around: families serve and sustain the programs, thus allowing the minister to feel needed and successful. This approach may even go so far as to equate one's level of Christian commitment with his/her participation in the programs.

Few, if any ministers are blatantly parasitic in their work. Yet when the minister becomes so enthused about a particular program, movement, or renewal, recruitment efforts may take on this characteristic.

The **competitive** approach is less severe but far more common in all parish programming, particularly youth ministry. Picture the calendar as battlefield over which we skirmish for the best nights for activities and programs. Working around school, sports, and community events, we schedule our programs during remaining family prime time, because "that's when we can get them to show up." Families are caught in the middle and feel frustrated. If they want quality time together, they are forced to "do battle" with all the institutions that are supposed to be serving their needs: school, community, parish.

Before long, family motivation begins to wane, and participation dwindles. Ministers find themselves asking, "Why don't folks come to our programs? We're doing good things." Program quality isn't a problem, but quantity and posture may be. If the minister continually feels cynical toward parents and families while conducting programs, that is a good indication of a "competitive" approach to ministry.

Moving to the positive side of the continuum, we come to the **cooperative** approach which attempts to work within the rhythms and dynamics of family life. It recognizes that the individuals in any given program have strong connections to family and household members, and those connections will influence the program. It attempts to learn about these family influences and adjust the program accordingly. At times, just a slight schedule change or personal encounter can make the difference between success or failure.

Guernsey uses the image of "friendship" to describe the cooperative approach. A friend is someone you know well enough to know how to ask them to be involved or lend some assistance. For example, in recruiting volunteers a cooperative approach may place more emphasis on tapping the gifts and talents of the folks than filling the vacant job slots. Another point here is that a friend can say "no" without feeling guilty. Too many people agree to participate only to avoid feeling bad for saying "no." And too many ministers capitalize on that.

On the far positive side is the **symbionic** approach to ministry. Here there is a mutual interdependence between program and the families involved in the program. The health or illness of one is reflected in the other. Granted, this model is idealistic, but it can be experienced in small groups where there is less distinction between minister and those ministered to. Efforts in peer ministry programming can reflect a symbionic approach.

What is your ministry posture? Where do your activities lie on the continuum line? How can you move them farther to the positive side? You may reflect on these questions, and pertinent others, when you get to use the Reflective Tool at the end of this essay.

PRINCIPLES FOR BRINGING A FAMILY SENSITIVITY TO YOUTH MINISTRY

A family sensitivity in youth ministry means looking at our ministry and service efforts through a "family lens," and making appropriate adjustments. It means doing all we can for teens and their families without creating new programs. Pope John Paul II in his Exhortation on the Family, *Familiaris Consortio*, captured the essence of family perspective when he wrote, "No plan of organized pastoral work at any level must ever fail to take into consideration the pastoral area of the family."

More specifically, a family perspective in youth ministry seeks to do three things.

1. It seeks to sensitize the minister to the realities of marriage and family life.

Today's family is not what we were raised to believe it should be. Nearly every household has been influenced by divorce, remarriage, dual careers, high mobility, and/or a serious family dysfunction. There is a myriad of family forms present in our parishes: blended families, single-parent, two career, etc. Youth ministry leaders are generally aware of these trends, and yet some youth ministry programs fail to fully involve folks from non-traditional family forms. At times we tend to label all but a small minority of families as "broken." When actually, all families are broken and wounded in one way or another—which means all households deserve to be embraced and accepted.

How can parishes and youth programs respond to the realities of marriage and family life today? One parish provided *Family Background Sheets* for all their catechists and youth ministers. The sheets indicated how many students were from single-parent families, or blended families, or dual career, how many were oldest or youngest in the family, etc. The idea was to provide information about students and their families so the catechist could tailor the lessons to their lived experiences at home.

Other parishes have used a simple strategy called *Family Life Awareness Raising*. This involves using the various forms of parish communication to raise parishioner consciousness of everyday household realities. Through means such as the Sunday bulletin, prayers of the faithful, notes home through students, and even pulpit announcements, parishioners are exposed to the many forms and functions of family in our society.

2. A family sensitivity in youth ministry seeks to sensitize those who serve individuals to broaden their perspective by viewing the individual through the prism of adolescent household life.

Here we must remember a couple of key principles of family systems theory. All families seek a balance of relationships. This means there are particular patterns for interacting with each other as well as those outside the family. Also, there are particular "roles" that family members play. This balance is called *homeostasis*. Whether healthy or not, most families resist anything that might upset their particular "balance."

When one family member experiences change, all others must adjust in order for that change to be lasting. In other words, the whole family must seek a new balance to accommodate an individual's change. Most families will try to change the individual back the way he or she was, rather than seek a new balance.

The primary goal of youth ministry is to help individuals respond to God's activity in their lives, that is, *change*! Most of the programs and activities are focused on individuals: retreats, confirmation preparation, informal counseling, catechetical classes. This is not wrong. On the contrary, it is appropriate and necessary. The challenge, however, is to help families adjust to the changes the programs are trying to encourage in the lives of individuals. Families resist change, even if it is a positive one. If ministers cannot help them adjust, then the changes for individuals will not be lasting.

How do we do this? The obvious answer would be to involve the entire household in the program in which the individual is enrolled. Some gallant efforts are being made here, particularly in the areas of family catechesis.

Yet, for many aspects of youth ministry, it is just not realistic for the whole family to participate. Therefore, some parishes are working to create *Bridger Experiences*. They provide exercises designed to "bridge" the experience of the particular youth program with the individual's home life. Family members can adjust to the changes in the individual if they can be kept abreast of, and connected to the progress of the ministry activities.

One parish developed a very effective *Bridger Experience* for young adolescents preparing for Confirmation. They were given a 50 question review of the Catholic Faith, and told to take it home and ask anyone to help them answer the questions. The catechists were not so interested in correct answers as they were in spurring dialogue about our Catholic Christian faith in the home. The strategy worked beautifully.

As another example, a parish youth ministry program designed a *Retreat Re-entry* session for parents of teens returning from the youth group retreat. Their goal was to sensitize parents and family members to the powerful faith experiences which occurred on the weekend, and give practical advice on nurturing on-going growth at home.

These *bridger experiences* can connect the evangelizing and catechetical work of youth ministry to the delicate balance of home life.

Along these lines, families will also benefit from opportunities to draw support and encouragement from others having like experiences. Families find it easier to adjust to the change and growth of an individual (finding a new balance) when they interact with other dealing with similar tasks. For this reason, parish like-to-like support groups are extremely valuable, particularly at the adolescent stage of family life.

3. A family perspective in youth ministry helps families with adolescents become better partners with the many institutions they deal with regularly . . . including the parish itself.

There was a time in generations past when the family maintained both responsibilities and control over the most important human functions: education, religious formation, health care, recreation, work, child bearing and rearing, personal nurturing, etc. In the agrarian society of 200 years ago, the family, in conjunction with the small community, fulfilled all these major functions.

With the dawning of the Industrial Revolution, families moved into the cities and employment was found outside the home and family farm. Families were fragmented when the work place was separated from the home. This fragmentation has only escalated as society has shifted from industrialism to high technology and vast information exchange. As our lives have become computerized, so our lifestyle has become compartmentalized. In our high mobility, our household numbers have shrunk. Consequently, we have created institutions to fulfill the functions families used to perform, for example, school sports (recreation), physicians groups (health care), and parish religious education programs (religious formation).

Today, the family has held onto only two important functions: child bearing and personal nurturing. Even the personal nurturing function is often shared with child care agencies among single-parent and dual-working families. With all the other functions, the family must *partner* with various institutions of society to receive their services. Coordinating these *partnerships* is a harrying, stressful experience for many households, especially when one or more of these institutions are not particularly family sensitive in their manner of providing service. Complications often arise over issues of scheduling, child care, communication. Does the institution serve the family, or does the family serve to sustain the institution?

Parishes and youth ministry efforts have two challenges here. First, they must look at their own relationship with families. How are the services and ministries of the youth program made available to families? This may sound like an absurd question, but when we focus most of our energy on serving individuals and/or building community among teens in the youth ministry, the question is worth asking because families often become fragmented in the process. When we are more concerned about parish policies than pastoral presence, it is likely that we are not very family sensitive.

From the other side of the coin, families are challenged to fulfill their end of the partnership. When they view the youth catechesis program as just a "sacramental service station" with no real sense of ownership or membership, they hinder faith growth for all. If they contribute to the life and vitality of the community, then they demonstrate their effective partnership.

The second challenge is to support and advocate for families with adolescents in their relationships with other service organizations. The parish can provide a forum for families to gather together and speak as a united voice to the community concerning societal issues facing teens and their families today, for example, drug use, sexual experimentation, unhealthy media exposure.

The youth ministry program can also help create an atmosphere of support for families that helps them prioritize their activities, say "no" to some of society's demands, and rediscover the value of home life. When the minister emphasizes quality home life, it will surely enrich the ministry as well.

PRACTICAL TIPS AND SUGGESTIONS

Below are some first-step ideas for bringing a family sensitivity to youth ministry. They do not call for developing new programs, but rather shifting the posture of your youth work toward a better partnership with families of adolescents.

Meet youth on their "home turf." Contact work with young people is important for developing relationships: going to games and concerts, meeting them at school for lunch, hanging out where they hang out. Have you considered spending time in their homes, getting to know their parents and families? You can learn a lot about a person by simply being in his or her home for a short while. It takes some time and energy, but if you are already doing contact work with adolescents, be sure to include meeting them in their "home turf."

Be involved with parents. Instead of lamenting that age-old question "How can we get more parents involved with our programs?" ask first how you might be more involved with parents. Many parents are struggling through various stages of development just as their adolescents are. They may not be in a position to lend much emotional or practical support to the program. Also, many adolescents send messages that parent participation is not welcome. No wonder it is tough to get them involved.

Yet if the minister shows an understanding of the stresses and struggles of parents, attempts to get to know them personally, and provide opportunities for support, a solid partnership can emerge. The better you know parents, the easier it is to know just how to invite their participation. They will also be more motivated to contribute.

Regularly assess your ministry. Be sure to periodically revisit some or all of the reflection questions in the following section. These may periodically reveal the need for a variety of adjustments in your programs and activities. The questions are best used as you plan the next phase of your youth ministry effort. Ask them of parents too. You may get more advice than you know what to do with.

Parent advisory group. Parents should have a voice in the scope and shape of the youth ministry program. Consider inviting them to be part of a parent advisory group. The role of this group is to help the coordinator and volunteers choose the best ways to meet the needs of adolescents and their families. It may meet only a couple of times a year, but it helps parents stay connected, without having to chaperone dances or drive for retreats.

Parallel needs assessment. If you survey the needs of adolescents in planning your program, consider developing a parallel survey for parents, asking them what topics and issues they would like their adolescents to learn about and discuss. You might want to bring parents and adolescents together for a couple of topics of common concern.

Youth retreat re-entry. A re-entry session for parents of youth following a retreat may help bridge the powerful spiritual experience of the retreat with normal home life. It may also help parents and family members accept whatever changes their teen may have experienced. The re-entry session can be simple; giving parents ideas and suggestions for how they might interact with their teen upon return from the retreat.

Brainstorm ways to bring parents and adolescents together without calling them out to the parish. How many ways can you think of to get adolescents and their parents talking without sponsoring an activity or holding a meeting? For example, sponsor an electricity fast where families are encouraged to spend an evening together without using electricity. You'll be amazed how creative folks can be. If this is too austere, sponsor a "No TV Tuesday," where folks pledge not to watch TV on a given Tuesday night, and spend the evening together.

Family life awareness raisers. Use the parish bulletin to provide interesting facts, statistics, tips, and quotes about family life with adolescents. If done on a regular basis, this simple strategy communicates to all parishioners a genuine concern about adolescents and their families. And you are not asking anyone to volunteer or come to anything, which will certainly stand out in your parish bulletin. You can also do awareness raising through the Sunday Liturgy's "Prayers of the Faithful." Volunteer periodically to write these prayers for the congregation about issues in families with adolescents.

Parent education programs. Organize programs which will address the specific learning needs of parents with adolescents. These programs can include the development of new parenting skills for adolescence; a better understanding of adolescents, the family life cycle, and the key concepts of family systems, especially family change; and the development of skills for communication and faith sharing with adolescents. Be sure to make use of community and church resources to assist you in sponsoring and conducting these programs. Often times it is better to utilize pre-designed programs (print and video) or outside resource people to conduct a program. Be sure to conduct a needs assessment of parents to determine the exact topics and best timing for a program.

Parent education programs would do well to assist parents in strengthening the four essential elements of a close family life as outlined in the research of Merton Strommen: 1) parental harmony—demonstrating love and affection in their relationships with each other; 2) effective parent-youth communication; 3) a consistent authoritative (democratic) parental discipline—valuing both independence and disciplined conformity, and affirming an adolescent's own qualities and style while setting standards for future conduct; and 4) parental nurturing—showing affection and respect, building trust, doing things together, and developing family support systems.

Programs for parents and youth. One way to integrate parents and a family perspective into programming is to design certain programs with built-in parent sessions. For example, a course on human sexuality for adolescents might follow this sequence: a parents-only session, followed by three youth sessions, another parents-only session, then three more youth sessions, and finally a parent-teen closing session.

Other possibilities for programming include: a) family activities and programs which build communication, trust, and closeness; b) parent-teen programs that discuss moral values and promote discussion; c) providing structured times of worship (Sunday worship, celebrations, rituals) in the parish that have a parent-youth focus; d) worship and Scripture resources for parents to use in the home with adolescents; e) justice and service projects that involve the whole family (perhaps at regularly scheduled times during the year); f) parent-youth retreat experiences; and g) home-based Advent and Lenten programs (as individual families or clusters).

Parallel programs for parents and youth. Parallel programs offer the opportunity for parents and youth to experience the same program content but in formats geared to their needs and life stage. For example, parents could take an adult course (like morality or Scripture) while their son or daughter was participating in an adolescent course on the same topic. For many parishes this could be the beginning of an adult education program. Another example of parallel programming can be support groups, which provide parent and adolescent groups on the same topics or crisis situation, for example divorce or separation.

Parent resource center. Parents are realizing that they cannot "go it alone" in today's society. Parents are realizing that it makes sense to draw on the skilled resources of outside experts when problems arise. There are many critical situations that demand outside help today, for example, drug use, alcohol use, sexual activity, suicidal tendencies, child abuse, and other out-of-control behaviors. For parents needing help with critical situations, youth ministry can establish a parent resource center which provides information and videos on adolescent problems, referral assistance to expert and trusted counselling resources, a link to support groups (like AA or Al-Anon), and information on community educational programs that address critical adolescent situations.

These are just a sampling of ideas that you might consider. Hopefully they have stimulated your own creativity. Family perspective adjustments are endless if you continually filter all your efforts through a family lens.

CONCLUSION

Take a moment for reflection. Try to recall the days when you were 13 . . . 15 . . . 17. Who were the key persons in your life? How did you feel about your parents, siblings, and extended family members? How did your family relate to faith nurture, religion, and the Church?

For many, family life has been a place where they encounter holiness, experience Christian community, and discover a call to ministry or service. The church of the home can be the most effective disciple-maker. It stands to reason then that the parish church (and beyond) must partner with the home in this faith-building and disciple-making endeavor. The church of the home can never be the entire expression of Church, but it is an essential link in transmitting faith and values from one generation to the next . . . even for families with adolescents.

Youth ministry in the future will have a stronger multi-generational dimension. It will not isolate teens from their families and parishes. It will bridge the youth program with the homefront, exposing youth to persons and experiences that stretch them beyond the boundaries of their youth culture, and exploring ever more creative ways to bring parents and teens together in the context of Christian community.

In short, a family perspective in youth ministry will not only enrich household life, it will also greatly benefit the field of youth ministry.

WORKS CITED

Guernsey, Dennis B. *A New Design for Family Ministry*. Elgin, IL: David C. Cook Publishing, 1982.

■ Youth Ministry and Families: A Reflective Tool ■

The reflective questions below will help anyone who works with adolescents assess how he or she considers families of adolescents. The questions are based on information in the essay regarding blind assumptions about youth ministry and household life, your posture in ministry, and the three principles for bringing a family sensitivity to youth ministry. These family impact assessment questions will help the minister look at all aspects of service and programming through a family lens.

You may wish to work through these questions by yourself or with your ministry team. They can be particularly helpful if addressed in the process of future planning. One caution: do not be tempted into planning a lot of new programs which incorporate parents and families. Remember, more is not always better. Perhaps the most family sensitive decision you can make is to do less. The questions below are designed to help you look critically at your existing programs, and see what possible adjustments can be made.

1. What is your overall attitude toward adolescence and families with adolescents today?

2. Can you recall an incident when you may have been guilty of assuming that adolescence is pathological?

3. Can you recall an incident when you may have been guilty of assuming that adolescence is transitional?

4. How can your ministry, service and programs better reflect the healthy and foundational nature of adolescence, and the realities of families with adolescents today?

5. How do your programs improve the capacity for families to master the challenging developmental issues of adolescence?

6. Concerning youth ministry programming, have you ever been guilty of assuming that more is always better?

7. Are there any activities or programs that could either be eliminated, reduced, or adjusted with a greater family sensitivity in your youth ministry effort?

8. Have you ever been guilty of assuming that whatever good things you do in ministry for teens will automatically benefit their families?

9. Do your ministry programs have a process for helping teens and their families deal with the change and growth your programs encourage?

10. Do any of your youth community building activities fragment household life in the process?

11. Have you ever been guilty of assuming that parents cannot pass on faith to their teens?

12. How are the parents of teens involved in your program's planning, implementation, and evaluation?

13. Have you ever found yourself assuming that a young person's faith life was completely dependent on your spiritual guidance?

14. Does your work with adolescents show any signs of being the "Lone Ranger" style of ministry?

15. When you consider Guernsey's four postures of ministry toward household life (parasitic, competitive, cooperative, symbionic), what is your posture?

16. Has your ministry posture shifted in the last six months? If so, how?

17. Can you think of any changes in your programs and activities that would help you shift to a more cooperative posture?

18. Does your program address only the adolescent's needs, the needs of the adolescent in relation to his or her family, or the overall needs of the entire family?

19. Are you aware of the different family forms represented by the teens in your program (for example, single-parent, blended, dual career)? Does your program account for these different household situations?

20. What underlying attitudes concerning the family situation are built into your program?

21. Does your program, in any way, advocate for the needs of adolescents and their families within the parish/school community or the civic community at large?

22. How would you respond to these four statements?
    - Our youth ministry program hinders family life when . . .
    - Our youth ministry program strengthens family life by . . .
    - Families hinder the youth ministry program when . . .
    - Families strengthen the youth ministry program by . . .

23. In light of your responses to the above statements, how can you create a better partnership with families with adolescents?

24. What is one immediate adjustment your program can implement to become more family sensitive?

25. What is one long-term goal your program can incorporate to increase its sensitivity to families?

This Interest Finder gives you a chance to make yourself heard about a variety of programs and activities that might be available for you and for your teenager(s).

For each of your children/teenagers, please indicate age, grade level, and school:		
1		
2		
3		

FAMILY CONCERNS

Below are listed some of the concerns faced by families with youth. Please indicate how strong each *concern* is felt by your family.	Put an "x" in the columns below		
	No concern	Minor concern	Major concern
1 scheduling hassles			
2 balancing school, home, and work			
3 lack of time together as a family			
4 poor communications			
5 parental separation/divorce/remarriage			
6 problems with family finances			
7 making realistic rules and expectations			
8 participation in Mass/parish programs			
9 substance abuse: alcohol			
10 substance abuse: drugs			
11 making moral decisions			
12 on moral issues: sexuality			
13 getting along with siblings			
14 living out faith life			
15 prayer			
16 tension between racial or ethnic groups			
17 sharing time in service to others			
18 balancing family and community commitments			
19 other (please specify):			

(Survey continued on next page)

(Survey Continues)

PROGRAM INTEREST

If the parish sponsored programming in the following areas, which would you consider attending? (Mark as many as you like.)

Educational Programs

Enriching Family Relations

	Understanding Adolescent development		Family decision making
	Issues in the life of remarried families		Families, separation, and divorce
	Improving family communications		Parent teen relations
	Handling new needs on the same salary		other (fill in):

Sharing Faith in Families

	Understanding adolescent faith development		Approaches to family prayer and ritual
	Recycling religion: a refresher course for adults		Handling questions of adolescent sexuality
	Helping youth make moral decisions		Helping youth make school and career choices
	Adolescents, alcohol and drugs		Midlife issues for parents with youth
	Coping with the values of pop culture		Planning a family service activity
	Family Bible study		other (fill in):

Recreational/Community Building Programs

	Parent/Youth Family Nights (movies, games, etc.)		Family Picnic
	Family Potluck/Dinner		Talent/Skit Night

Prayer Experiences

	Neighborhood Mass for Families with Youth		Evening of Reflection (Parent & Youth)
	Evening of Reflection (Parents Only)		Family Home Mass
	Overnight Retreat (Parent & Youth)		Overnight Retreat (Parents Only)

Service/Justice Experiences

	Family involvement in a soup kitchen/homeless sheltER
	Christmas gift sharing with a family in need
	Resources for Lenten sharing at home

(Survey continued on next page)

(Survey Continues)

Ethnic/Multicultural Awareness Experiences	
	Ethnic smorgasbord or dinner
	Family participation in local ethnic festivals/programs
	Joint family programs with ethnic parishes/community groups

AVAILABILITY

When is the best time for you to attend activities and workshops?			
Weedays during the day (fill in days):			
Weekdays during the evenings (fill in days):			
	Saturday morning		Sunday morning
	Saturday afternoon		Sunday afternoon
	Saturday evening		Sunday evening

How often would you be interested in meeting for family-related activities or workshops?			
❑ once a week	❑ once a month	❑ every other week	❑ only occasionally

A FINAL QUESTION

If you could ask for one thing from the church to help your family, what would it be?
(Answer below.)

CHAPTER 12

Re-inventing Youth Ministry to Incorporate a Family Perspective

John Roberto

This essay will attempt to "make a case" for incorporating a family perspective in ministry with youth. My reflections will build on the essays in Section One and on the essay in this section by Leif Kehrwald. It is my belief that incorporating a family perspective in youth ministry will take both an attitudinal change (as described by Leif) and a structural change in youth ministry. In effect, I am suggesting that we will need to re-invent youth ministry programming in order to develop a family perspective. I am well aware that to propose re-inventing youth ministry programming to overworked youth ministry and religious education leaders is inviting you to turn the pages quickly to the practical activities in Section Three. However, I am not proposing *more* work or *more* programming; I am proposing *new* work and a *different* approach to programming.

In order to "make a case" for re-inventing youth ministry programming, I will need to examine the inadequacy of many of our current program structures which I believe are one of the greatest obstacles to a family perspective, and, in the long run, to effective ministry with youth. Second, I will use contemporary research to frame the task of youth ministry as promoting healthy adolescent development, which, of course, includes growth in faith and discipleship. This task, I believe, refocuses the role of a parish youth ministry as one socializing agent within a network of socializing agents which include families,

the parish community, schools, community youth and civic organizations. Third, I will offer a systems model of youth ministry which incorporates a family perspective. I believe that this systems model has great potential for re-inventing youth ministry.

PART ONE: THE NEED FOR A NEW DIRECTION

The Church's ministry with youth over the past several decades has been dominated by a set of program structures which are inadequate for the needs of youth and families in today's society. I believe that these structures prohibit the development of attitudes, ministries, and programs that will lead toward effective youth ministry with a family perspective. The very structures that many leaders put in place to promote growth toward maturity in faith may in fact be having the opposite results. I want to examine three dominant program structures that are very common in youth ministry programming and explain why I consider them inadequate for the challenges that are ahead. Briefly these structures are,

- the *schooling* approach which reduces youth ministry to religious education, organizing the parish's catechetical effort into a quasi-school, grouping children and youth into classes which meet one-hour-per-week, 30 weeks per year. The limits of the schooling approach often mean that a young person's experience of church becomes another experience of school!

- the *youth group* approach which reduces a parish's youth ministry efforts to organizing youth activities for a small segment of the parish's youth (10%? 25%? 50%?), while neglecting to address the great diversity of needs, schedules, and interests of youth who are not "youth group members."

- the multiple-year *confirmation program* for youth which supplants a more comprehensive approach to ministry with youth, while consuming enormous amounts of time, personnel, and resources with minimal result. One does not need to take an exit poll to realize that the vast majority of fully initiated, confirmed, young Catholic Christians leave the Church after the celebration of the sacrament of Confirmation.

SCHOOLING MODEL

The parish's ministry with young adolescents, as well as high school confirmation programming, has been dominated by a *schooling* approach to religious education in which the Church's efforts have been modeled on the organization of a school with courses built around a textbook series and classes organized in weekly, one-hour sessions held in classrooms. While many new and exciting approaches to adolescent catechesis/religious education are taking place, the *inadequacy* of maintaining a schooling approach is becoming increasingly apparent. *I strongly believe that catechesis/religious education is an essential and integral element of a comprehensive ministry with youth.* Research shows that quality religious education and the family's socializing influence are the two most important ingredients in promoting faith maturity in adolescents (Search Institute). What I am calling into question is the adequacy of organizing all our efforts in a schooling model.

Let me illustrate several examples of this inadequacy. The schooling approach does not address the wide range of adolescent developmental needs; many times it only addresses doctrinal instruction, which is a need of the Church but not necessarily a need of adolescents. It does not provide the range of programming called for by adolescent developmental needs, nor does it provide a vehicle for meaningful involvement of early adolescents in the life of the faith community and the local community. *The limits of the schooling approach often mean that a young person's experience of church becomes another experience of school!* The schooling approach does not offer a framework for comprehensive youth ministry because it does not address the other essential components: evangelization (especially outreach and relationship building with youth), community life, pastoral care, justice and service, prayer and worship, leadership development (enablement), and advocacy. The schooling model does not assist the Church in ministering with families of adolescents or partnering with families in promoting the healthy faith growth of adolescents.

YOUTH GROUP

It seems like nothing has endured longer in youth ministry than the traditional youth group. In the early days of youth work the youth group model was reflected in the CYO or Teen Club with its four-fold program of social, recreational, cultural, and spiritual activities. In the 1970s, the CYO or Teen Club was replaced by the Youth Group. The program content may have changed, but the concept was the same: build community, have fun, experience your faith. The youth group model is built upon the assumptions that youth's needs can be adequately addressed in a weekly meeting consisting of two hours of program activities and that the youth of a parish constitute one group. Despite the fact that the lives and needs of youth, families, and communities have changed dramatically in the past two decades, the youth group model, like the one hour per week religious education class, continues to be the approach that many parishes take.

The limitations of the youth group model include its inability to address the diversity of youth needs (socially, culturally, developmentally) and diversity in youth's life situation (families, communities, schools, work, urban-suburban-rural). Youth involvement in parish programs is being directly affected by the changing patterns of adolescent after-school commitments like work and school activities. Family changes, like the increasing diversity of family styles (single-parent, two career families), and the increasingly multicultural composition of so many communities and parishes across the country place tremendous stress on the ability of a youth group model to address the major changes which are occurring.

I am convinced that the youth group model is one of the causes of poor youth involvement in many youth ministries. It is simply impossible to minister to the full spectrum of youth in this one program model. In other cases the "success" in organizing youth into a "group" may in fact be alienating young people from their families and from meaningful involvement in the parish community and civic community.

CONFIRMATION PROGRAMS

As I said above, one does not need to take an exit poll to realize that the vast majority of fully initiated, confirmed, young Catholic Christians leave the Church after the celebration of the sacrament of Confirmation. It is an amazing paradox: upon completion of their initiation into the Catholic Christian faith, young people leave the community into which they have been initiated! Proponents of high school confirmation contend that our current practice is leading youth into deeper participation in the Church's life and closer personal friendship with the risen Lord. I don't think so! One of the primary reasons why the vast majority of high school youth are receiving confirmation is that they are being forced. All too often they are learning that faith in Jesus Christ and active membership in the Church are not about freedom and life, but about mandatory participation in courses and counting the correct number of service hours.

What makes all of this tragic is not only the impact that this makes on youth, but that so much time and effort is being devoted to maintaining multiple-year confirmation preparation programs despite the evidence of their ineffectiveness. So many parish youth efforts today are directed exclusively to Confirmation preparation. If the Church were to re-integrate Confirmation preparation and celebration into the initiatory sequence of Baptism-Confirmation-Eucharist (as had been celebrated prior to the 20th century), the vast majority of youth programs in the United States would cease to exist. Outside of two-year Confirmation preparation programs, great numbers of parishes in the United States have no other ministry with youth—before or after Confirmation. Many of these programs are poorly conceived and offer no opportunities for continuing growth after Confirmation. It is no mystery why most youth resist these efforts and never return after Confirmation.

PART TWO: PERSPECTIVES ON ADOLESCENTS

Each of these three program structures make erroneous assumptions about adolescents and adolescent development, which often lead to disastrous results. Re-inventing youth ministry means that we must work from a set of correct assumptions about adolescents and adolescent development. As a starting point, I would like to propose three assumptions or perspectives for viewing adolescents:

1. **View adolescents as resource and hope.**

    Youth are not a problem to be solved. Their energy, vitality, resources, and sense of hope are essential for our communities. We must build upon and empower the strengths that they possess.

2. **View adolescents and adolescent growth holistically.**

    Youth are on a journey with life-cycle tasks specific to young and older adolescence. Their psycho-social development, moral and faith development must be viewed in the context of the whole life span. Youth are integral members of a family system with its own family life cycle tasks, family traditions, family faith and values. They are integral members of our communities: local faith community, civic community (school, youth organizations), and/or ethnic group. Their faith, values, and identity are influenced by these communities.

3. **View adolescent growth as a relationship between providing external support and structure, and the development of internal assets/strengths within the adolescent.**

External support and structure are usually supplied by a combination of the family and the surrounding community. This provides a kind of temporary scaffold around the adolescent in order to support and encourage while the growing adolescent is developing an internal system of supports (assets/strengths) that will see him or her safely into adulthood.

At the heart of the inadequacy of each approach to youth ministry is the view of adolescent development as an individual affair, separate from the socializing influence of the larger community(s) of which the adolescent is an integral member. John Hill gives great credence to this broader view when he writes,

> . . . the impact of the primary changes (of adolescence) on these psychosocial issues does not occur in a vacuum. It occurs in family, peer, school, community, media, church—and, for some, work-settings. The variations in how the issues are resolved stem not only from individuals' past histories but also from their current social relationships. The others who are important in adolescents' lives—whom they encounter in family, peer, school, and community settings—react to the primary changes with modified expectations and norms . . . (Stating it in another way, Glen Elder has observed that adolescents do not experience

society and its values directly but as it is presented to them through their actual social participations in familial, peer, school, and other settings.) (Hill 4).

Such a view is supported by family systems and family life cycle research, faith development research, and social research. Adolescent development must be viewed within the context of the socializing community. In Chapter Eight Francis A.J. Ianni supports this approach.

> Every community can and should shape the relationships among its various socializing institutions into a network that fosters the learning of its values. Moreover, the messages that each of the institutions send to individual adolescents should be mutually reinforcing, rather than disharmonious or even working at cross purposes . . . . The importance of integrating the socializing institutions to provide such a caring structure and the interdependence of the adult and adolescent social worlds in producing and interpreting it were visible in the social and behavioral standards set by each of the communities we studied for its young.

The adolescent is engaged in a *search for structure*, a set of believable and attainable expectations and standards from the community to guide their movement from child to adult status. Young people need a *caring community*—a supportive network of social institutions (family, school, church, youth organizations) which create a community-based socialization. We are challenged to view individual growth within this broader context. *Family is essential to this broader context, and therefore is essential for youth ministry efforts.* Let us now turn to the factors that promote healthy adolescent development within this broader context.

PART THREE: PROMOTING ADOLESCENT DEVELOPMENT AND FAITH GROWTH

GROWING UP HEALTHY—INTERNAL SUPPORTS AND EXTERNAL ASSETS

In 1990 the Search Institute completed a major research study of 46,000 young Americans in grades 6 through 12, entitled *The Troubled Journey: A Profile of American Youth*.[1] The research project studied 20 indicators that placed young people at risk. The study developed a wide range of factors in the family, in the community, in the schools, and within young persons themselves that predispose youth to either healthy or unhealthy growth during their teenage years. As a result, the research is able with considerable certainty to trace a pattern of factors that promote the positive development of youth. These factors, promoted by a young person's family and community provide the structure and context for healthy adolescent development.

The Troubled Journey: A Profile of American Youth reveals two important groups of factors that promote healthy development and reduce the likelihood of adolescents' participation in behavior that puts them at risk. One group identifies *assets external to the adolescent*, but present in family and community. Another group identifies *strengths to be found within the adolescent*.

> When children are growing up, the kind of help they most need is usually supplied by a combination of the family and the surrounding community. The family provides rules, discipline, encouragement, and caring. The community makes available such things as educational experiences, community rules and expectations, friends, recreational experiences, and spiritual nurture. These are the external assets.

> These external assets, taken together, form a kind of temporary scaffold around a child in order to support and encourage while the growing child is developing an internal system of supports that will see him or her safely into adulthood. Their function is much like that of the scaffolds built around buildings during erection or repair to provide a temporary stability until the building is ready to stand on its own. They are there to do what needs to be done while young people are developing their own internal supports—until they develop backbone (April 1991 *Source* 1).

Our focus in this section will be to look at how we can promote the positive through the church's ministry with youth: promoting internal strengths and strengthening external assets.[2]

In a perfect world, these internal strengths would develop gradually throughout adolescence, while external supports were being removed at the same gradual rate. The research shows, however, that, while some internal strengths increase during the teen years, too often the external assets are being removed before adequate internal strength development occurs. Certain of the internal strengths, in fact, are found to diminish between sixth and twelfth grade.

INTERNAL STRENGTHS

The Troubled Journey: A Profile of American Youth indicates 14 elements of the essential internal supports that make positive growth possible for teenagers. Thirteen of the fourteen are positive, a listing of values, attitudes, and skills that caring adults hope young people develop during their adolescent years. They are divided into three categories: commitment to education, positive values, and social competence. Only one (values sexual restraint) implies a "just say no" message.

Educational Commitment

The first essential component of internal support is enthusiasm for the educational process, now and well into the future. Four elements were identified in the study:

1. *School Performance*: working at above average performance

2. *Achievement Motivation*: caring about their school performance and wanting to do well

3. *Homework*: spending six or more hours each week on homework

4. *Educational Aspiration*: hoping to go on after high school either to college or technical school

Positive Values

The second essential component of internal support is positive values—values that center on caring about others as well as oneself. Four elements were identified in the study:

5. *Values Sexual Restraint*: postponing sexual activity as a personal goal, "just say no"

6. *Values Helping People*: being of help to others

7. *Is Concerned About World Hunger and Poverty*: expressing a desire to better the circumstances of those who are hungry and in poverty

8. *Cares About Other People's Feelings*: attending to the well-being of others

Social Competence

The third essential component of internal support is social competence and social skills—success in interacting with others, in learning how to work in groups, in "holding your own" against opposition, and in anticipating what is coming. Six elements were identified in the study:

9. *Self Esteem*: having a reasonable sense of one's own value

10. *Assertiveness Skills*: standing up for what one believes—explaining your understandings and needs clearly and firmly, without being angry or abrasive in doing so

11. *Decision-making Skills*: dealing with increasingly complex decisions and selecting the things to which one will "just say no."

12. *Friend-making Skills*: mastering the skills for making and keeping friends

13. *Planning Skills*: being able to map out one's future over the next days, months or years and being able to delay what seems most attractive right now in order to complete the less-desirable but necessary task

14. *Positive View of Personal Future*: feeling positive about the future and their own future

EXTERNAL ASSETS

One of the major contributions of the *The Troubled Journey: A Profile of American Youth* is that it identifies those elements in the family and in the community that appear, in effect, to protect teenagers against the kinds of trouble most feared by parents, teachers, and others who work with adolescents. The more assets a given teenager reports being present in his or her life, the fewer the at-risk behaviors that teenager displays.

These 16 external assets provide the kind of interest, care, and structure that are essential if an adolescent is to progress through the teenage years relatively untroubled. They supply a necessary network of support while adolescents develop internal supports firm enough to carry them successfully into adult life.

Eight of these external assets lie mostly within the control of individual families. The remaining eight are community-based, requiring the cooperation or initiative of persons or groups outside the family. Thus it is evident that neither the community nor the family can assume the entire responsibility for the support of adolescents. They have to work together.

External Assets: Support

The first essential component of external assets is support, creating an atmosphere of appreciation and encouragement that provides young people with experiences of being loved, successful, and worthwhile. Thus equipped, one can survive the inevitable temporary failures and defeats of daily life. Of the seven external assets included under external assets: support, the first four assets are almost entirely family-generated and the remaining three depend largely on institutions outside the family.

1. *Family Support*: providing high levels of love and support

2. *Parent(s) as Social Resource*: viewing parents as people one can go to for advice, comfort, and encouragement

3. *Parent Communication*: having frequent, in-depth conversation with parents

4. *Parent Involvement in Schooling*: continuing to show interest in the nature of their children's school work and success in school

5. *Other Adult Communication*: having frequent, in-depth conversations with adults other than parents

6. *Other Adult Resources*: knowing non-parent adults to go to for advice and support

7. *Positive School Climate*: caring, encouraging school environment

External Assets: Control

The second essential component of external assets is controls on behavior—learning how to exercise some self-discipline, to develop willpower to complete projects, to allocate time to life's demands according to carefully-thought-through priorities rather than momentary impulse. These are essential capacities that most adults absorbed by having certain controls imposed throughout adolescence. While the first four elements of this category are largely parent-controlled, the final one is related to circumstances largely beyond family control:

8. *Parental Standards*: making expectations of behavior and the penalties for inappropriate behavior known to adolescents

9. *Parental Discipline*: disciplining adolescents for violating family rules

10. *Parental Monitoring*: knowing where the adolescent is going when he or she leaves the house, with whom, and for approximately how long

11. *Time at Home*: insuring that the adolescent goes out for fun and recreation no more than three nights a week

12. *Positive Peer Influence*: developing friends who approve of and model responsible behavior

External Assets: Structured Use of Time

The third essential component of external assets is the development of a disciplined structure—working at a task to meet given deadlines, not at one's own convenience or whim. Four elements fit into this category of external assets. All of them, though partly dependent on family decision, largely depend on activities provided and supervised for youth by adult members of the community.

13. *Involved in Music*: spending one hour or more per week in music training or practice

14. *Involved in School Extra-curricular Activities*: spending one hour or more each week participating in school-related sports, clubs, or organizations

15. *Involved in Community Organizations or Activities*: spending an hour or more each week participating in organizations or clubs outside of school

16. *Involved in Church or Synagogue Activities*: spending an hour or more per week attending worship services or participating in church activities

The 14 internal characteristics together with the 16 external assets, make up a network of interior and exterior strengths that has remarkable power to *shield* adolescents against at-risk behaviors and *promote* positive teenage development. They equip adolescents to make wise choices.[3]

Both deficits and assets, as measured in this report, strongly influence at-risk behaviors. The more assets one has, the less at-risk behavior. Conversely, the more deficits one has, the greater the at-risk behavior. A two-pronged approach—to prevent deficits and to promote assets—is necessary to alter the frequency with which adolescents make choices which compromise their health or jeopardize their future.

Since most adolescents experience at-risk behavior in several areas, communities must offer effective prevention and intervention programs that address behavioral areas and equip young people with multiple internal and external assets. This kind of effort helps strengthen families, schools and other institutions to provide strong support and control and to nourish in young people the kinds of commitment, values and competencies that lead to healthy choices (April 1991 *Source* 3).

ADOLESCENT FAITH GROWTH

What are the family and congregational factors that help promote an adolescent's growth in faith? Many studies have been conducted which seek to trace a pattern of factors that promote the faith growth of youth. This brief summary provides a research foundation to the central conviction of this essay—that youth ministry needs to move to a more comprehensive approach involving families and the community.

Parental/Family Influence Factors

1. In examining the religious biographies of youth, the two experiences most associated with higher faith maturity are the level of *family religiousness* and the amount of *exposure to Christian education* (Benson and Eklin).

2. Influence related to religiousness transfers slowly. During the period of adolescence, both schools and families make the maximum impact on a person's later religious life when two ingredients are present: *proximity* and *longevity* (Williams).

3. Parents are potentially the greatest influencers of the adolescents' religious belief for reasons, if for no others, of being close to the child (*proximity*) over a long period of time (*longevity*) (Williams).

4. These elements increase the influence of parents (or other significant adults):

    a. *modeling*: the effect of example has always been understood to be important;

    b. *agreement*: when parents agree on the importance of religion to them and the messages they convey are consistent, the power of influence increases;

    c. *congruence*: example is more powerful when parents talk about their actions and when what they say is consistent with what they do. (Williams)

5. Parents who talk at home about religious activity and motivation are far more likely to have children who have positive attitudes toward religion. (Williams)

6. . . . we can say that there are four different ways the family of origin affects the religious imagination of one of its offspring: 1) the relationship between the parents of the child . . .; 2) the relationship of the parents to one another; 3) the religious devotion of both parents, especially if they are very devout; 4) the perception by the child of the parent as religiously influential, which presumably indicates the parent's explicit attempt to teach religion (Greeley 60).

7. Life experiences are strongly associated with maturity of faith. Having family and friends are two near-universal experiences that have impact on one's growth in faith maturity. Ask these experiences increase, so also does faith maturity. Many of these factors are within the scope of congregational programming. By incorporating an emphasis on parent education as well as by offering opportunities for young people to discuss their faith with their best friends, churches can encourage some of these experiences for their young people. Specific experiences with family and friends that are significantly associated with maturity of faith include: (Benson and Eklin)

    + Frequency of talking with one's mother and faith about faith and about God

    + Frequency of talking to other relatives about faith and about God

    + Frequency of family devotions

+ Frequency with which one's family does things together to help other people

+ Frequency with which one talked to one's best friends about faith and God

+ The degree to which one's current three or four best friends are religious

Congregational Factors

1. In examining the religious biographies of youth, the two experiences most associated with higher faith maturity are the level of *family religiousness* and the amount of *exposure to Christian education* (Benson and Eklin).

2. Faith maturity and the two forms of loyalty (congregational and denominational) are strongly tied to the characteristics of the congregation one belongs to. The research shows that the more each of the following six aspects of congregational life are present in a congregation, the greater the maturity of faith and the stronger the loyalty of both youth and adults. Of the six, the factor with the greatest potential to increase loyalty and maturity of faith is the *effectiveness of Christian education* (Benson and Eklin).

   + *Effectiveness of formal Christian education*—resulting from particular kinds of processes, content, leadership, and administrative foundations. Effective religious/ education not only teaches insight and knowledge (educational content), but also allows insight to emerge from the crucible of experience (educational process).

   + *Climate: Thinking*—the degree to which members perceive their congregation to encourage questions, challenge thinking, and expect learning.

   + *Climate: Warm*—the degree to which members perceive their congregation to be warm and friendly.

   + *Worship*—the quality of Sunday worship

+ *Service to Others*—the success a congregation has in getting members to provide volunteer service to people in need.

+ *Receiving Care (sense of family)*—the frequency with which members personally experience the care and concern of other members.

3. . . . a constellation of parish characteristics predicts community and commitment (among parishioners): (1) the opportunity to participate in parish organizations that serve a wide variety of human needs, (2) responsibility for some part of the parish's life, (3) the quality of the pastor's concern and affirmation, (4) the quality of friendliness and concern expressed by fellow parishioners, and (5) liturgies that celebrate the community gathered around the sacrament, that encourage participation in music and liturgical responses, and whose sermons offers insights that can be applied to daily life. What is so striking in the data is the call to a common responsibility and service is the principal ingredient in the sense of community and commitment (Leege).

4. The influence of congregations, parents, schools, and peers is best exercised in a *warm, supportive environment*. In spite of the superior power of parents to influence, if the family relationship lacks warmth, support, and acceptance, most children and adolescents will seek those qualities elsewhere (Williams).

5. Family factors are also important, particularly in the high school years. Students whose parents are involved in their parish religious education program and students who experience engagement with faith issues as part of family life are more likely than other students to report favorable outcomes (on tests of religious behavior, beliefs, values, and influences). This is an important finding which affirms that families and church-based programs constitute an important partnership. The suggestion here is that programs best affect students when the family is considered part of the religious education team. . . . The family that practices faith

models a mature faith, and the message does not escape our children. (Kelly, Benson, Donahue).

IMPACT ON YOUTH MINISTRY

This research serves to strengthen the importance of family in providing the external support and encouragement so necessary for healthy adolescent development and faith growth. It relocates a parish youth ministry into the broader life of the parish community and the civic community. A parish *must* become a partner with parents and the broader community because it is only one of the socializing agents within this broader network of families, schools, and community youth and civic organizations. No parish can "go it alone" when it comes to promoting faith growth and healthy adolescent development. Young people need a *caring community*—a supportive network of social institutions (family, school, church, youth organizations) which create a community-based socialization. *Family is essential to this broader context, and therefore is essential for youth ministry efforts.*

PART FOUR: A SYSTEMS MODEL OF YOUTH MINISTRY

THE VISION

The model for youth ministry with a family perspective already exists in an embryonic form in the 1976 national paper, *A Vision of Youth Ministry*, which offers an *integrated, holistic,* and *comprehensive vision* of ministry with youth. In *A Vision of Youth Ministry*, the goals and the framework of youth ministry are drawn from the mission of Jesus Christ and his Church: *Word* (evangelization and catechesis), *Prayer & Worship, Community Life, Justice & Service, Pastoral Care* (guidance & healing), *Leadership Development* (enablement), and *Advocacy. A Vision of Youth Ministry* transcends the narrower approaches of a schooling model, a group model, or a

confirmation model of ministry. Yet, many leaders in youth ministry and religious education *still* reduce this comprehensive vision to one programmatic expression. We must overcome this problem if we are to experience the richness of youth ministry in today's Church.

If we are going to attend to the twin concerns of promoting internal assets and enhancing external, community supports then youth ministry must adopt a *dual* focus. The *Vision* is quite clear in this regard. Youth ministry is a ministry *within* the community of faith as we minister to the needs of young people through our ministry efforts and programming. Youth ministry is, however, more than what happens within the four walls of the church building. Youth ministry is a ministry *to* the broader community as we serve youth in our communities through outreach and as we collaborate or partner with families, youth organizations (like scouting), and schools in promoting healthy adolescent development. While many in youth ministry have emphasized ministry within the faith community, youth ministry also addresses the broader community context. In the style of Jesus' ministry *to* people by healing, preaching, teaching, forgiving, and serving, youth ministry brings a ministry to youth beyond the confines of our in-parish youth programs.

Supporting this dual focus is the contextual or systems approach advocated by the *Vision*. This contextual approach is an essential ingredient in the new directions proposed in this essay. This contextual approach seeks to view young people as part of a number of social systems which influence their growth, values, and faith, rather than as isolated individuals. "In all places, youth ministry occurs within a given social, cultural, and religious context which shapes the specific form of the ministry" (*Vision* 10). Among these systems are the family, society, the dominant culture, youth culture, ethnic culture, school, and local church community. Attention to the impact, positive or negative, of each of these systems on youth, and a ministry to these systems are essential for effective youth ministry.

Our ministry with youth is directed toward three goals:

Goal 1: Youth ministry works to foster the total personal and spiritual growth of each young person. (*Vision* 7) The first goal emphasizes *becoming*. Our understanding of the unique life tasks and social-cultural context of adolescence provides direction for fostering their growth in discipleship and Catholic identity. This goal challenges us to promote the internal assets of young people through personal guidance and specialized programming, as well as to strengthen the external supports that provide support and encouragement for this growth.

Goal 2: Youth ministry seeks to draw young people to responsible participation in the life, mission, and work of the faith community. (*Vision* 7) The second goal emphasizes *belonging*. Active engagement of youth in the Christian community's life and mission provides an important context for growth and overcomes the danger of marginalizing youth in the church, segregating them from the real centers of power, responsibility and commitment in community life. This goal challenges us to provide the meaningful participation youth require, broadening our ministry to support family life and to integrate young people into the life of the faith community.

Goal 3: Youth ministry empowers young people to become disciples of Jesus Christ who live their faith by living and working for justice, peace, and human dignity. This third goal emphasizes *transforming* and *serving*. Helping young people realize that their faith in Jesus Christ calls them to serve others and work toward a world that is built on the values of the Reign of God is an essential task for youth ministry. Our challenge is to help youth use their considerable energy and efforts in positive ways.

Prosocial behavior covers a wide range of human actions—helping people in distress, donating time or energy to voluntary service organizations, attempting to reverse political, economic and social injustice or inequality. The common thread among prosocial behaviors is the desire or intent to promote the welfare of others.

When it comes to raising healthy children, promoting prosocial behavior is as important as preventing antisocial or health-compromising behavior. Acts of compassion help develop social competencies, positive values and a sense of purpose in life. Furthermore, prosocial behavior may actually reduce risky choices. Students who engage in helping behavior on a weekly basis are shown in this study to be less likely than non-helpers to report risky behaviors. (*The Troubled Journey*)

There is nothing that can compare with the increase in sensitivity to others, sense of personal value, and compassion that adolescents develop when adults provide concrete structures to channel teenagers' energy. Combined with this involvement is reflection which brings them to new insights and a more positive view of themselves, their world, and their future

A SYSTEMS MODEL OF YOUTH MINISTRY

In Chapter One Leif Kehrwald describes the family as a system, outlining several key characteristics of systems thinking. In many ways what I have been suggesting throughout this essay is the need for a total systems approach to promoting healthy adolescent development and faith growth. In past decades, the Catholic school system, in tandem with parish communities and families, provided that systems approach to faith growth and adolescent development. This system no longer exists for the vast majority of adolescents across the United States today. However, we have not replaced that system with a new system; instead, what we have done is try to replace it with one hour a week religious education classes or youth group meetings or multi-year confirmation programs. And we have found that approach wanting. We always will when we replace an entire system of faith formation with one-hour-a-week programming. The system for socialization, promoting adolescent development and faith growth that has served us well for many decades cannot be replaced with a one-hour or two-hour-a-week program. It has to be replaced with a corresponding systems-approach which involves youth programming, the family, the parish community, and the broader civic community. Unless it is, we will never have an adequate response to promoting young people's growth in faith. We cannot go back to the old system, but we can begin the process of creating a new system, that includes family ministry, comprehensive youth programming, and involvement of youth in the total life of the faith community.

A *Systems Model of Youth Ministry* links all the ingredients which encompass a comprehensive ministry with youth by utilizing the framework of the eight components from *A Vision of Youth Ministry* and by organizing programming around four program settings: *youth programming, family ministry, involvement in parish life,* and *involvement in the civic community.* Each program setting can organize programs in gathered or non-gathered ways. *Gathered Programs* include attendance at organized events. *Non-gathering Methods* provide a way to reach out to youth/families or involve youth/families in programming or ministry efforts without requiring participation at organized events.

Drawn from the mission of Jesus Christ and his Church the components of youth ministry include:

Advocacy: interpreting the needs of youth: personal, family, and social especially in areas of injustices towards or oppression of youth, and acting with or on behalf of youth for a change in the systems which create injustice; giving young people a voice and empowering them to address the social problems that they face.

Catechesis: promoting a young person's growth in Christian faith through the kind of teaching and learning that emphasizes understanding, reflection, and transformation. This is accomplished through systematic, planned and intentional programming (curriculum). Catechesis for younger adolescents includes the faith themes of Church, Jesus and the Gospel Message, Moral Decision-Making, Personal

Growth, Relationships, Service, and Human Sexuality. Catechesis for older adolescents includes the faith themes of Faith and Identity, the Gospels, the Hebrew Scriptures, Jesus, Justice and Peace, Love and Lifestyles, Morality, Paul and his Letters, Prayer and Worship (*The Challenge of Adolescent Catechesis*).

Community Life: building Christian community with youth through programs and relationships which promote openness, trust, valuing the person, cooperation, honesty, taking responsibility, and willingness to serve; creating a climate where young people can grow and share their struggles, questions, and joys with other youth and adults; helping young people feel like a valued part of the church.

Evangelization: reaching out to young people who are uninvolved in the life of the community and inviting them into a relationship with Jesus and the Christian community; proclaiming the Good News of Jesus through programs and relationships that lead young people toward discipleship.

Guidance/Pastoral Care: developing life skills (self-esteem, assertiveness skills, decision-making skills, friend-making skills, communication skills, planning skills); providing youth with sources of support and counsel as they face personal problems and pressures and make important life decisions, like careers; providing appropriate support and guidance for youth during times of stress and crisis; developing a better understanding of their parents and learning how to communicate with them.

Justice, Peace, and Service: guiding young people in developing a Christian social consciousness and a commitment to a life of justice and peace through educational programs and service/action involvement; infusing the concepts of justice and peace into all youth ministry relationships and programming.

Leadership Development: developing, supporting, and utilizing the leadership abilities and personal gifts of youth and adults in youth ministry, empowering youth for ministry with their peers; developing a leadership team to organize and coordinate the ministry with youth; developing program leaders for ministry with youth.

Prayer and Worship: assisting young people in deepening their relationship with Jesus through the development of a personal prayer life; providing a variety of prayer and worship experiences with youth to deepen and celebrate their relationship with Jesus in a caring Christian community; involving young people in the sacramental life of the Church.

Programming in the *Systems Model* is organized around four settings: youth programming (gathered and non-gathered), family ministry (gathered and non-gathered), involvement in parish life, and involvement in the civic community. *Youth programming* focuses around the specific needs of young people in settings with youth and adult leaders. *Family ministry* involves programs and activities geared to developing a family perspective in all youth ministry programming, in developing specific programs and activities for parents, for youth and parents, and for the whole family. *Involvement in parish life* offers young people the opportunities to be participate as integral members and leaders in parish-wide programs, e.g., liturgical ministries, service projects, social activities, etc. *Involvement in civic community* provides a way for a youth ministry to take part in community wide resources and activities, as well as to plan joint activities, programs, and meetings with the different youth-serving organizations in the life of a community (e.g. other churches, schools, scouting programs, youth agencies, etc.). Programs in each of these four settings can be developed as gathered or non-gathered.

Here are several examples of the four program settings in action:

Catechesis

Youth Gathering: classes, mini-courses, speaker series, retreats
Youth Non-gathering: youth newsletters, books, videos, mentor/tutors, independent learning, scripture study
Parent/Family: Advent or Lent family retreat, home study resources, TV recommendations, parent education, parent-teen program or retreat
Involvement in Parish Life: parish-wide Advent or Lenten programming, RENEW program
Civic Community: educational programs for youth and/or parents sponsored by youth organizations or schools, ecumenical religious education programs

Prayer & Worship

Youth Gathering: youth liturgy, Stations of the Cross, prayer services, seasonal worship experiences, celebrating rites of passage (graduation from high school)
Youth Non-gathering: book of young adolescent prayers, prayers for youth concerns at Sunday liturgy, using youth-sensitive music in prayer services so that they will recall the prayer when they hear it again.
Parent/Family: family liturgy involving youth and parents, home prayer books, family or parent-youth prayer night, Advent or Lenten home prayer, celebrating rites of passage (graduation from high school)
Involvement in Parish Life: Stations of the Cross, choir, liturgy planning teams, sacramental celebrations
Civic Community: ecumenical worship services (e.g., Thanksgiving)

Community

Youth Gathering: social events (like movies), sports, scouting, trips/outings, service projects
Youth Non-gathering: birthday cards, newsletters, bulletin board, home visits
Parent/Family: family picnic, parent-youth dance, games night, parent newsletter
Involvement in Parish Life: carnivals, picnics, social activities
Civic Community: social events

sponsored by churches, schools, or youth organizations

Justice and Service

Youth Gathering: courses, classes, speakers on social issues; service projects; social change projects

Youth Non-gathering: international pen-pals, adopting a migrant or refugee family, newsletters, service projects, letter writing (e.g., Amnesty International, political action)

Parent/Family: home discussion guide, Lenten fast program, family service programs, articles on justice issues mailed home

Involvement in Parish Life: working with parish service groups, parish-wide Lenten simple meal program

Civic Community: ecumenical service projects (e.g., CROP walk, week-long service projects)

Guidance/Pastoral Care

Gathering: life skills training program, education programs on drugs/alcohol, sexuality education program, babysitting training, tutoring, preparing for exams night

Non-gathering: printing cards with emergency numbers (for example, runaway hotline), providing a counseling referral list

Parent/Family: parent-teen workshops, providing resources for parents on youth problems

Civic Community: counseling resources, drug education programs, life skills training

(In planning a *Systems Model of Youth Ministry* the grid shown on the opposite page has been a helpful tool.)

The *Systems Model of Youth Ministry* emphasizes multiple program formats with a variety of content offered in a variety of time formats and settings, with multiple forms of participation based on interests and freedom of choice. This comprehensive style of programming is characterized by the following elements:

1. Balance among the components of comprehensive youth ministry.
2. Variety of program formats and schedules (e.g., formats: individualized, small group, large group, events, intergenerational/parent/family, mini-courses/programs; schedules: weekly, bi-weekly, monthly, extended time, full day, overnight, weekend, weeklong).
3. Variety of environments or settings for programming: parish, homes, retreat centers, community centers.
4. Interest-centered programming, based on the needs of youth and families. Programs are designed so that they attract different youth with different interests. This avoids the problem of attempting to create every program "with everybody in mind."
5. Freedom of choice: overcoming the "you have to come to everything" mentality by allowing young people to select the programs that best address their needs in a time schedule and format that best suits their life situation.

There are many advantages of this type of programming:

1. It clarifies the purpose of each program or component.
2. Each program or component meets different needs.
3. Interest-centered programming builds attendance patterns with multiple involvements of youth.
4. Recruiting leaders is much easier since you are asking for a shorter-term commitment with more clearly defined responsibilities.
5. Youth get more involved with adult role models since the group size in each program is smaller.
6. There are more opportunities for expanded youth leadership.
7. Programs can be allowed to die without endangering the rest of your offerings.

A Systems Model of Youth Ministry Grid

(Way program is sponsored) →	YOUTH PROGRAMS		FAMILY MINISTRY		CHURCH COMMUNITY		CIVIC COMMUNITY	
	Gathered	Non-gathered	Gathered	Non-gathered	Gathered	Non-gathered	Gathered	Non-gathered
ADVOCACY								
CATECHESIS								
COMMUNITY LIFE								
EVANGELIZATION								
PASTORAL CARE								
JUSTICE AND SERVICE								
LEADERSHIP DEVELOPMENT								
PRAYER/ WORSHIP								

8. It fits young people's schedules better.

9. Specializing develops the talents and gifts of youth and adults more effectively.

10. Interest-based programs create a natural management system. A youth ministry team representing each component can coordinate the ministries, set policies and directions, and evaluate programming.

For the *Systems Model of Youth Ministry* to be realized there must be collaboration among all those who minister with youth. This is essential for the creation or enhancement of a caring community which provides support and structure for healthy adolescent development. The *Troubled Youth* study expresses this need in the following manner:

Each and every community, regardless of size or location, faces the immense challenge of encouraging positive youth development. Solutions do not come easily. Positive change will require extraordinary commitment to children and adolescents by multiple sectors, including government, business, schools, parents, service organizations, law enforcement, youth-serving organizations and religious institutions.

One of the reasons why it is crucial for communities to develop a multi-sector commission or task force is to help ensure that community, school, family and congregational strategies for positive youth development are integrated and complementary (1991 April *Source* 3).

A Vision of Youth Ministry states the need for collaboration this way,

No one aspect of youth ministry is independent of others; they are all interdependent elements of a unified total vision. The multifaceted nature of youth ministry requires a process of collaboration among all persons involved in it, rather than fragmentation or competition. . . . Part of the vision of youth ministry is to present to youth the richness of the person of Christ, which perhaps exceeds the ability of one person

to capture, but which might be effective by the collective ministry of the many persons who make up the Church.

In all of these developing models (parish, school, diocesan), however, the process of dialogue, collaboration and joint planning is the key to ending fragmentation and restoring a sense of balance to the ministry with youth (*Vision* 24).

CONCLUSION

You are probably asking where do I begin? No one in this parish seems to be working from a family perspective. This does not have to be a reason why you and the youth ministry effort cannot begin. I believe that the key to implementing any change, like the one called for in this essay, is to begin within your own "circle of influence." This means identifying all the programs or activities that are within your responsibility and power to organize and implement. These programs and activities are therefore candidates for change. Don't begin with other people's programs or ministries and don't struggle with issues or concerns that are outside of your "circle of influence." Work from your strengths. Begin now to move away from one of the three dominant structures toward a systems model that incorporates a family perspective. Review again the ideas in Leif Kehrwald's essay in this section. Begin a multi-year effort to move from where you are toward your desired model. By developing a plan of action and moving firmly but carefully toward your designed future, you will build support among youth, families, and a significant percentage of the parish community. You will be educating people as you implement change.

I believe that we have a marvelous opportunity to re-invent youth ministry. The best youth ministries in our country have moved beyond the youth group, schooling, or multi-year confirmation models as their only approach to youth programming. In the 1990s, youth ministry nationally will have to move beyond toward even more comprehensive programming including families, the parish community, and the civic community. The *Systems Model of Youth Ministry* provides an excellent way to begin this movement. My hope is that this essay will provide the basis for re-inventing our ministry with a family perspective.

END NOTES

1   The study reports on more than 46,000 young Americans in grades 6 through 12 and yields information of great significance to all those who are interested in providing youth with a chance to grow up healthy. The students included in this research come mainly from the Midwest; most of them live in communities under 100,000 in population. Ninety percent of them are white. However, in spite of this sample, on key indicators for which representative national data are available (e.g. alcohol use, tobacco use, sexual abuse, involvement in extra-curricular activities, and exposure to television), percentages in this study are remarkably similar to those of national data on in-school youth.

2   Material in this section is drawn from *Source* 6.3 (December 1990) and *Source* 7.1 (April 1991) published by the Search Institute, 122 W. Franklin, Suite 525, Minneapolis, MN 55404. Additional material is drawn from *The Troubled Journey: A Profile of American Youth* developed by Peter Benson of the Search Institute and published by RESPECTEEN, Lutheran Brotherhood, Minneapolis, MN 55415.

3   The study reports that only ten percent of students in this research project meet what the study identified as minimal standards for overall well-being. The criteria used were: having 20 or more of the 30 assets, having 2 or less of the 10 deficits, doing at least one hour per week of prosocial behavior, having 2 or less of the 20 at-risk indicators.

4   Order *The Troubled Journey* or an overview of it by calling 1-800-888-3820. Have this survey administered in your school system. It is available through RespecTeen at no charge, and will highlight important issues for community discussion and action. There is no better way to raise the community's consciousness about youth than through current information about your community's own students.

WORKS CITED

"Backbone: Essential for Survival on the Troubled Journey." *Source* 7.1 (April 1991).

Benson, Peter. *The Troubled Journey: A Profile of American Youth.* Minneapolis, MN: RESPECTEEN, Lutheran Brotherhood, 1991.

Benson, Peter, Dorothy Williams, Carolyn Eklin and David Shuller. *Effective Christian Education: A National Study of Protestant Congregations.* Minneapolis: Search Institute, 1990.

Benson, Peter, and Carolyn Eklin. *Effective Christian Education: A National Study of Protestant Congregations—A Summary Report on Faith, Loyalty, and Congregational Life.* Minneapolis: Search Institute, 1990.

Hill, John. "Early Adolescent Development." *Access Guides to Youth Ministry: Early Adolescent Ministry.* Ed. John Roberto. (New Rochelle, NY: Don Bosco Multimedia, 1991).

Kelly, Frank, Peter Benson, and Michael Donahue. *Toward Effective Parish Religious Education for Children and Young People.* Washington, D.C.: NCEA, 1986.

Leege, David. "The Changing Context of Parish Leadership." *Carriers of Faith.* Ed. Carl S. Dudly, Jackson W. Carroll, and James P. Wind. Louisville, KY: Westminster/John Knox Press, 1991.

"The Troubled Journey: New Light on Growing Up Healthy." *Source* 6.3 (December 1990).

A Vision of Youth Ministry. Department of Education. Washington, DC: USCC Office of Publishing, 1976, 1986.

Williams, Dorothy. "Religion in Adolescence: Dying, Dormant, or Developing." *SOURCE* 5.4 (December 1989).

BIBLIOGRAPHY

To assist you in re-inventing youth ministry program consult the following resources:

Ambrose, Dub and Walt Mueller. *Ministry to Families with Teenagers.* Loveland, CO: Group Books, 1988.

This is an excellent resource that outlines why we need a ministry to families, elements of a successful ministry with families, how to build a ministry with families, and programming ideas for parents and teens, for parents, and for teens. This should be on every youth minister's and religious educator's bookshelf.

Curran, Dolores. *Working with Parents.* Circle Pines, MN: American Guidance Service, 1989.

This is the best resource for learning how to work with parents. Using her vast experience and expertise, Dolores Curran has written a very practical book which examines our assumptions about working with parents, how to develop programming for parents as a group and individually, how to conduct a program for parents, and how to deal with problem parents. This should be on every youth ministers and religious educators bookshelf.

Kehrwald, Leif. *Caring that Enables—A Manual for Developing Parish Family Ministry.* New York: Paulist Press, 1991.

Leif Kehrwald has written a practical resource for developing a family perspective in all parish ministries. He describes three basic strategies that every ministry can use: Family Life Awareness Raising, Family Sensitivity in Parish Ministry, Focus and Invite. The manual includes training sessions that you can use with your volunteers. This is an excellent follow-up to his essay in this section.

Roberto, John. "Principles of Youth Ministry." *Network Paper #26.* New Rochelle, NY: Don Bosco Multimedia, 1989.

This is a brief summary of foundation and pastoral principles which guide our current practice of youth ministry.

Roberto, John, editor. *Access Guides to Youth Ministry: Early Adolescent Ministry.* New Rochelle, NY: Don Bosco Multimedia, 1991.

This may be the most complete resource on early adolescent ministry. In the first section, a variety of authors present contemporary research on young adolescent growth and development and on the social issues affecting young adolescents. In the second section, pastoral direction is given to developing a ministry with young adolescents, including how to take the components of A Vision of Youth Ministry *and program them to address the needs of young adolescents. This should be on every youth ministers and religious educators bookshelf.*

————. *Growing in Faith: A Catholic Families Sourcebook.* New Rochelle, NY: Don Bosco Multimedia, 1990.

The Sourcebook *contains the foundational understandings which undergird the entire Catholic Families Project. Essays explore the contemporary family in the United States, the family life cycle, family rites of passage, family faith development, and the social mission of the family.*

Martinson, Roland. *Effective Youth Ministry: A Congregational Approach.* Minneapolis: Augsburg Press, 1988.

Martinson presents a contemporary understanding of youth and ministry with youth that emphasizes the role of the congregation in youth ministry, thereby moving beyond a simple youth group model. This book presents congregational, peer, and individual youth ministry activities.

CHAPTER 13

Training Design: Understanding Families with Adolescents

Thomas Bright and John Roberto

Objectives

As a result of this session, the participants should be able to:

- understand the important characteristics and dynamics of families with adolescents;
- identify how the changes in adolescence and parents can affect family interaction;
- develop specific ways to introduce a family perspective into their ministry.

Audience: Ministry Leaders: parish staff, youth ministry volunteer leaders, adolescent catechists, teachers, campus ministers

Time: One 3-hour session or two 1½-hour sessions

Materials

- Recommended Participant Handout: *Youth Ministry through a Family Lens*. Leif Kehrwald. Network Paper #40. (New Rochelle: Don Bosco Multimedia, 1991) ($3.50 per copy).
- Participant Handout: Practical Suggestions for a Family Perspective

- Newsprint, markers, and tape

Resources for the Trainer

- Chapter 1: A Family Systems Perspective—Leif Kehrwald
- Chapter 2: A Family Life Cycle Perspective on Families with Adolescents—Nydia Garcia Preto
- Chapter 4: The Changing American Family—Richard P. Olson and Joe H. Leonard Jr.
- Trainer Resource: Young Adolescents, Parents, and Family Interaction— Leah Lefstein
- "The Family Life Cycle." Betty Carter & Monica McGoldrick. *Growing in Faith: A Catholic Families Sourcebook*. Ed. John Roberto. New Rochelle, NY: Don Bosco Multimedia, 1990.
- *A Family Perspective in Church and Society*. NCCB. Washington, DC: United States Catholic Conference, 1988.

Supplemental Resources

Ambrose, Dub and Walt Mueller. *Ministry to Families with Teenagers*. Loveland, CO: Group Books, 1988.

Durka, Gloria. "Family Systems: A New Perspective for Youth Ministry." *Readings in Youth Ministry*.

Washington, DC: NFCYM Publications, 1986.

Farel, Anita. *Early Adolescence: What Parents Need to Know.* Carrboro, NC: Center for Early Adolescence, 1982.

Strommen, Merton and Irene. *Five Cries of Parents.* San Francisco: Harper & Row, 1985.

Overview

Part I: A Family Life Cycle Perspective on Families with Adolescents

1. Activity: Remembering my Family during Adolescence (20 minutes)
2. Activity: Analysis of Families with Adolescents (20–25 minutes)
3. Presentation: Families with Adolescents (20 minutes)
4. Discussion (20 minutes)

Part II: A Family Systems Perspective on Families with Adolescents

5. Activity: Exploring Diversity in Family Structures (25–30 minutes)
6. Presentation and Activity: Family Personality (40–45 minutes)
7. Discussion: Family Perspective (20–25 minutes)

Procedure

1. Activity: Remembering My Family during Adolescence
(20 minutes)

To begin this session, you may want to conduct a brief community building activity to help the participants feel comfortable with each other. Welcome all the participants and introduce the objectives for this learning session.

Form the participants into two groups: parents of adolescents and adolescents. Ask the participants to put themselves into their respective roles for the following activity.

Parent Group: Ask the parent group to name some behaviors, attitudes, and concerns of youth that parents find (a)

encouraging or hopeful, and (b) disturbing, troubling, or confusing. Encourage the participants to brainstorm items quickly, not to discuss the items in detail. They should record their responses on newsprint.

Adolescent Group: Ask the adolescent group to name some behaviors, attitudes, and concerns of parents that adolescents find (a) encouraging or hopeful, and (b) disturbing, troubling, or confusing. Encourage the participants to brainstorm items quickly, not to discuss the items in detail. They should record their responses on newsprint.

Ask each group to post its results. Invite the recorder from each group to summarize, briefly, its report. Leave the lists posted. You will refer to them several times during the session.

2. Activity: Analysis of Families with Adolescents
(20–25 minutes)

Now ask each of the two groups: parents of adolescents and adolescents, to reflect on their lists using the following questions. Ask each group to appoint a recorder who will write down key points.

Parent Group:

a. Why do parents find these behaviors, attitudes, and concerns of youth (a) encouraging or hopeful, and (b) disturbing, troubling, or confusing?
b. What is happening within the life of the parent that may affect parenting adolescents and his or her relationship with the family?

Adolescent Group:

a. Why do adolescents find these behaviors, attitudes, and concerns of parents (a) encouraging or hopeful, and (b) disturbing, troubling, or confusing?
b. What is happening within the life of the adolescent that may affect his or her relationship with parents and the family?

Call for reports from each group. Record the responses of the groups on newsprint.

CHARACTERISTICS OF FAMILIES WITH YOUNG ADOLESCENTS

The following is a basic outline that you can use for your presentation:

A. INDIVIDUAL LIFE CYCLE

The Adolescent Years   **The Middle Adult Years**
Key Task: Construction of an Integrated Identity . . . . Key Task: Generativity & Care
Physical & Sexual Growth: Puberty . . . . . . Concern with Physical Competency & Changes
Intellectual Growth: Formal Operations . . . Life Reassessment: Shifting Time Perspective
Socially: Wider Sphere of Activity . . . . Accommodating the New Generation
Changes in: Autonomy, Attachment, Relationships . . . .

B. FAMILY LIFE CYCLE

Key Task: Increasing flexibility of family boundaries to include children's independence
             and grandparent's frailties

Secondary Tasks:
             a. Shifting of parent-child relationships to permit adolescent to move in and
                 out of system
             b. Refocus on mid-life marital and career issues
             c. Beginning shift toward joint caring for older generation

On the first sheet of newsprint, draw a line down the middle and then record the responses to the first question of the parent group on one side and of the adolescent group on the other side. Proceed the same way with the second question.

Introduce the large group discussion of the reports by saying that the newsprint sheets reflect a view of the dynamics of families with adolescents. Ask the group: What do these profiles say about the family with adolescents? What insights into the family with adolescents do we take from these profiles?

3. Presentation: Families with Adolescents
(20 minutes)

Using Chapter 2: "A Family Life Cycle Perspective on Families with Adolescents" by Nydia Garcia Preto and the Trainer Resource: "Young Adolescents, Parents, and Family Interaction," present a brief overview of the family life cycle as you interweave the key characteristics of adolescent development and adult development. Throughout your presentation encourage the participants to make comments and pose questions. When appropriate, refer to the lists of behaviors,

attitudes, and concerns developed in Movement One. You may want to make transparencies to list the important points of your presentation. You could also create a handout using the Trainer Resource.

Explain that the purpose of the presentation is to examine the adolescent stage of the family life cycle by exploring key characteristics of adolescent and adult development. Introduce the idea that as children enter the adolescent stage of life and the changes associated with adolescence like puberty, adults are often entering middle adulthood and the changes associated with mid-life. How parents see their emerging adolescents is colored by the changes they themselves are experiencing. At the same time, adolescents perceptions of their parents change as they mature physically, cognitively, socially, and emotionally.

Outline: See the outline in the box at the top of this page.

Commentary on Outline

Adolescence ushers in a new era because it marks a new definition of the children within the family and of the parents' roles in relation to their children. In short, family relationships need to be modified to be more in line with the new needs, concerns, and competencies of the individuals involved. In *Growing in Faith: A Catholic Families Sourcebook*, Betty Carter and Monica McGoldrick summarize this new era in the following way:

> Families with adolescents must establish qualitatively different boundaries than families with younger children, a job made more difficult in our times by the lack of built-in rituals to facilitate this transition. The boundaries must now be permeable. Parents can no longer maintain complete authority. Adolescents can and do open the family to a whole array of new values as they bring friends and new ideals into the family system. Families that become derailed at this stage may be rather closed to new values and threatened by them and they are frequently stuck in an earlier view of the children. They may try to control every aspect of their lives at time when, developmentally, this is impossible to do successfully. Either the adolescent withdraws from the appropriate involvements for this developmental stage, or the parents become increasingly frustrated with what they perceive as their own impotence. ...Flexible boundaries that allow adolescents to move in and be dependent at times when they cannot handle things alone, and to move out and experiment with increasing degrees of independence when they are ready, put special strains on all family members in their new status with one another (18).

These changes in the family system during adolescence bring about periods of disequilibrium or imbalance—times when an individual member has changed but the system has not yet fully adapted by altering relationships. A healthy family system will adapt to this new stage in the family life cycle—bringing about balance or equilibrium. These changes in family relationships occur gradually, in a somewhat disorganized fashion, as individuals try on new roles and experiment with new ways of relating to each other. The task for most

families—and it is by no means an easy one—is to maintain *emotional* involvement, in the form of concern and caring, while gradually moving toward a relationship characterized by great *behavioral* autonomy.

The family life cycle portrait of adolescence also includes the transitions happening within the parents. "The central event in the marital relationship at this phase is usually the 'midlife crisis' of one or both spouses, with an exploration of personal, career, and marital satisfactions and dissatisfactions. There is an intense renegotiation of the marriage, and sometimes a decision to divorce" (Carter and McGoldrick 18). It seems that adolescents and midlife parents are simultaneously developing in different directions, causing times of imbalance that the family system needs to adjust to. If this development is not understood and accepted, life together can be filled with confusion, misunderstanding, and disagreement. Family members need to adapt and adjust to their mid-life and adolescent roles.

Recognizing that individual family members' needs and roles change over time and adapting relationships accordingly is a key to positive family life.

4. Discussion
(20 minutes)

In small groups or the large group ask the participants to discuss how the family life cycle perspective helped them to develop a better understanding of families with adolescents. Ask how the family life cycle perspective provides insights into the behaviors of parent and youth.

Then ask the group to completing the following unfinished sentences:

> I learned . . .
>
> I discovered . . .
>
> I was surprised by . . .
>
> I wonder about . . .
>
> I need to know more about . . .

Give them several minutes to do this. Invite the participants to share their reflections with the larger group after the small group discussions are completed. These can be summaries of what was discussed in the small groups. If questions arise, briefly respond to them.

5. Activity: Exploring Diversity in Family Structures
(25–30 minutes)

Diversity is a key element in who we are as church today. The diversity takes many forms, for example, ethnic and cultural backgrounds, socioeconomic status, and family structure. This activity helps those who minister with families with youth to explore the diverse structures that make up family life today, and the implications of diverse family structures for the church's ministry with families and youth.

a. **Family Portraits**

Instruct participants to draw a picture, or create a collage, about their family. Ask that they include in their portraits, words or symbols that indicate how their present living out of family is different from what they experienced, or imagined, when they were younger.

Invite participants to briefly share their family portraits with the group. When the sharing is completed, ask the group to join you in listing the different styles/structures of family life represented in the group. Add to the listing any styles or structures of family life not present in the group but represented in the larger parish community.

b. **A Portrait of Family Life in the United States**

Using the material found in Chapter 4 on changing patterns in family life and Chapters 1 and 6 in *A Family Perspective in Church and Society*, provide a brief overview of the reality of family life today in the United States.

c. **Diverse Structures, Diverse Needs**

Ask the group to explore with you how the different structures that people live in impact the needs they have—as adults and as youth. How, for example, do the needs of young people in two-parent families differ from those in single parent homes where there is little or no contact with the non-resident parent? Or, how do the parenting demands change for a mother who moves from a single parent family with one child to a blended family with two or more children at home?

There are many approaches this exercise could take. You could, for example, do a brief presentation on the experiences common to young people when parents divorce, using the material found in Chapter 5, then ask participants to move in their minds with that young person as she or he adapts to life in a single parent home or becomes part of a new blended family. Or, you could incorporate the learnings of the participants, asking several members, in advance of the meeting, to share from personal experience how their needs and expectations of the church community changed as they lived through separation, divorce, remarriage, or the death of a spouse.

6. Presentation and Activity: Family Personality
(40–45 minutes)

You will be drawing upon material in Chapter 1: "A Family Systems Perspective" by Leif Kehrwald as you present some of the major concepts of a family systems approach to understanding families with adolescents. Throughout your presentation encourage the participants to make comments and pose questions. When appropriate, refer to the lists of behaviors, attitudes, and concerns developed in Movement One. You may want to make transparencies to list the important points of your presentation.

Concept 1: Understanding of Systems Thinking

Use the description in Chapter 1 to describe, briefly, systems thinking. The presentation on the family life cycle gives the participants an understanding of systems. For example, the changes that are occurring within the adolescents or within the adults affect the entire family. As a system that family is affected by changes in its members. Conversely, the family, as a system, also affects its members through family rules, traditions, ways of relating, etc. The family affects the ways its members deal with life changes.

Concept 2: Exploring Family Togetherness

Use the description and examples in Chapter 1 to briefly introduce the four ways families deal with togetherness: *disjointed, separated, connected, enmeshed*. Draw the continuum with the four words on newsprint to illustrate your presentation.

After your introduction, conduct the following activity to help participants apply the four styles of family togetherness.

1. Organize the participants into four groups according to the following four styles: *approaching disjointed, separated, connected, approaching enmeshed*. In these small groups, ask participants to discuss the impact of that particular family personality on adolescents, on their growth and development, on their behavior, etc.
2. Ask for reports from each personality type. Record the responses on newsprint.
3. Ask each personality group to develop advice for teens and/or their parents who live in that family personality type.
4. Ask for reports from each personality type. Record the responses on newsprint.
5. Present several of Kehrwald's suggestions for living in these four family types using Chapter 1.

Concept 3: Change vs. Homeostasis

Use the description in Chapter 1 to describe, briefly, the concept of change vs. homeostasis. Use examples of disruption which occur in families with adolescents to illustrate the concepts. The following activity will help participants understand how families change or resist change.

Concept 4: Exploring Family Personality

Use the description and examples in Chapter 1 to briefly introduce the four ways families deal with change: *rigid, structured, flexible*, and *chaotic*. Draw the continuum with the four words on newsprint to illustrate your presentation.

After your introduction, conduct the following activity to help participants apply the four styles of family change.

1. Organize the participants into four groups according to the following four styles: *approaching chaotic, flexible, structured, approaching rigid*. In these small groups, ask participants to discuss the impact on adolescents of the way their family deals with change. Examine the impact on their personalities, their growth and development, their behavior, etc.
2. Ask for reports from each change style. Record the responses on newsprint.
3. Ask each group to develop advice for teens and/or their parents who live in that family type.
4. Ask for reports from each group. Record the responses on newsprint.
5. Present several of Kehrwald's suggestions for living in these four family types using Chapter 1.

7. Family Perspective
(20–25 minutes)

Begin this section, by asking the participants to reflect on the following question:

One way I can use the insights and ideas on family in my ministry with youth is by . . .

Invite the participants to share publicly their responses. You may want to post these responses on newsprint.

Next, present several ideas for building a family perspective in youth ministry using the Participant Handout: "Practical Suggestions for a Family Perspective" and Chapter 11, especially the sections entitled, "Principles for Bringing a Family Sensitivity to Youth Ministry" and "Practical Tips and Suggestions."

Outline

    a. Principles

        1. A family perspective in youth ministry seeks to sensitize the minister to the realities of marriage and family life.

        2. A family sensitivity in youth ministry seeks to sensitize those who serve individuals to broaden their perspective by viewing the individual through the prism of adolescent household life.

        3. A family perspective in youth ministry helps families with adolescents become better partners with the many institutions they deal with regularly, including the parish itself.

    b. Practical Ideas (see Participant Handout).

Young Adolescents, Parents, and Family Interaction

Leah Lefstein

Young Adolescents (10–15 Years Old)	Parents	Family Interaction
Most Significant Feature		
Experience rapid physical, intellectual, and emotional change.	Experience physical, intellectual, and emotional change.	Becomes temporarily off balance as relationships shift.
Physical Changes		
Develop secondary sex characteristics (e.g., body hair, breasts, broad shoulders, deeper voice).	May worry that they have diminished sex appeal.	Parent may feel both proud and fearful of child's sexual development.
Grow stronger and taller.	Are concerned that they may be less strong, less tall than in their youth.	Child may be bigger and stronger than parent.
Develop ability to conceive children. Menstruation and ejaculation occur.	Women are anticipating the end of the reproductive years (menopause). Men are concerned about their sexual performance.	Parent expects more mature behavior from child.
		Parent develops new relationship with opposite-sex child: "Incest taboo," concern for sexual values and sex education, fear of adolescent pregnancy.

(Table continues on next two pages)

Young Adolescents (10–15 Years Old)	Parents	Family Interaction
### Intellectual Changes		
Begin to think abstractly, to question and test adults' statements and evaluate adults' values. The world expands; ppossibilities, ideas, and dreams are fascinating. Time seems an endless resource.	Become more concerned with the rapid passage of time. Time is measured in terms of how much longer one will live. There is concern for continuity of values and a need to feel that one has contributed to the future.	Child's new ability to think abstractly can improve family communication. However, there may be tension because child is questioning parent's authority and testing parent's values. Differences in time perspective also may cause disagreements.
### Socio-Emotional Changes		
Lose self-confidence and feel inferior to others.	Lose self-confidence and feel inferior to others.	Jealousy, rivalry, or mutual criticism ("clash of inferiority complexes") may occur.
Are more self-conscious and sensitive to criticism.	Feeling less in control of child, parent may be more critical.	Parent and child have mutual desire for respect, reassurance, and approval.
Others view them as moving into highly regarded age group; young adulthood.	Others view them as moving into less highly regarded age group: old age.	Parent feels responsible for giving child guidance and is concerned about child's future employability. Some parents may unconsciously want to relive their own youth through their children.
Begin to consider future work roles and career.	Look back at their employment history. May feel dissatisfied with work and achievements.	Parent-child relationship moves from greater to lesser control, with child gradually given more independence—with limits. Parent or child may feel conflict between "letting go" too early or "hanging on" too late. Parent experiences sense of freedom as child becomes less dependent. Child can accept more responsibility in family.
Need privacy and a degree of independence; are concerned with what friends think; become attached to friends and to adults other than their parents.	Have more responsibilities outside family. May be learning to accept emotional losses (e.g., death or disability of parents or friends, "empty nest" syndrome).	There may be shift in husband-wife roles as new options open to parents (e.g., wife's return to or change in career, husband's increased interest in children).

Young Adolescents (10–15 Years Old)	Parents	Family Interaction
Begin to feel like adult member of the family.	Develop new identity that incorporates their physical, intellectual, and social changes.	Possible changes due to death or divorce. Possibility of shared interests and activities between parents and child.

Leif Kehrwald and John Roberto

Below are some first-step ideas for bringing a family sensitivity to youth ministry. They do not call for developing new programs, but rather shifting the posture of your youth work toward a better partnership with families of adolescents.

Meet youth on their "home turf." Contact work with young people is important for developing relationships: going to games and concerts, meeting them at school for lunch, hanging out where they hang out. Have you considered spending time in their homes, getting to know their parents and families? You can learn a lot about a person by simply being in his or her home for a short while. It takes some time and energy, but if you are already doing contact work with youth, be sure to include meeting them in their "home turf."

Be involved with parents. Instead of lamenting that age-old question "How can we get more parents involved with our programs?" ask first how you might be more involved with parents. Many parents are struggling through various stages of development just as their adolescents are. They may not be in a position to lend much emotional or practical support to the program. Also, many adolescents send messages that parent participation is not welcome. No wonder it is tough to get them involved.

Yet if the minister shows an understanding of the stresses and struggles of parents, attempt to get to know them personally, and provide opportunities for support, a solid partnership can emerge. The better you know parents, the easier it is to know just how to invite their participation. They will also be more motivated to contribute.

Parent advisory group. Parents should have a voice in the scope and shape of the youth ministry program. Consider inviting them to be part of a parent advisory group. The role of this group is to help the coordinator and volunteers choose the best ways to meet the needs of youth and their families. It may meet only a couple of times a year, but it helps parents stay connected, without having to chaperone dances, or drive for retreats.

Parallel needs assessment. If you survey the needs of youth in planning your program, consider developing a parallel survey for parents, asking them what topics and issues they would like their adolescents to learn about and discuss. You might want to bring parents and adolescents together for a couple of topics of common concern.

Youth retreat re-entry. A re-entry session for parents of adolescents following a retreat may help bridge the powerful spiritual experience of the retreat with normal home life. It may also help parents and family members accept whatever changes their teen may have experienced. The re-entry session can be simple; giving parents ideas and suggestions for how they might interact with their teen upon return from the retreat.

Brainstorm ways to bring parents and adolescents together without calling them out to the parish. How many ways can you think of getting adolescents and their parents talking without sponsoring an activity or holding a meeting? For example, sponsor an electricity fast where families are encouraged to spend an evening together without using electricity. You'll be amazed how creative folks can be. If this is too austere, sponsor a "No TV Tuesday," where folks pledge not to watch TV on a given Tuesday night, and spend the evening together.

Family life awareness raisers. Use the parish bulletin to provide interesting facts, statistics, tips, and quotes about family life with adolescents. If done on a regular basis, this simple strategy communicates to all parishioners a genuine concern about youth and their families. And you are not asking anyone to volunteer or come to anything, which will certainly stand out in your parish bulletin. You can also do awareness raising through the Sunday Liturgy's "Prayers of the Faithful." Volunteer periodically to write these prayers for the congregation about family issues.

Parent education programs. Organize programs which will address the specific learning needs of parents with adolescents. These programs can include the development of new parenting skills for adolescence; a better understanding of adolescent development, the family life cycle, and the key concepts of family systems, especially family change; and the development of skills for communication and faith sharing with adolescents. Be sure to make use of community and church resources to assist you in sponsoring and conducting these programs. Often times it is better to utilize pre-designed programs (print and video) or outside resource people to conduct a program. Be sure to conduct a needs assessment of parents to determine the exact topics and best timing for a program.

Parent education programs would do well to assist parents in strengthening the four essential elements of a close family life as outlined in the research of Merton Strommen: 1) parental harmony—demonstrating love and affection in their relationships with each other; 2) effective parent-youth communication; 3) a consistent authoritative (democratic) parental discipline—valuing both independence and disciplined conformity, and affirming an adolescent's own qualities and style while setting standards for future conduct; and 4) parental nurturing—showing affection and respect, building trust, doing things together, and developing family support systems.

Programs for parents and adolescents. One way to integrate parents and a family perspective into programming is to design certain programs with built-in parent sessions. For example, a course on human sexuality for adolescents might follow this sequence: a parents-only session, followed by three youth sessions, another parents-only session, then three more youth sessions, and finally a parent-teen closing session.

Other possibilities for programming include: a) family activities and programs which build communication, trust, and closeness; b) parent-teen programs that discuss moral values and promote discussion; c) providing structured times of worship (Sunday worship, celebrations, rituals) in the parish that have a parent-adolescent focus; d) worship and Scripture resources for parents to use in the home with adolescents; e) justice and service projects that involve the whole family (perhaps at regularly scheduled times during the year); f) parent-adolescent retreat experiences; and g) home-based Advent and Lenten programs (as individual families or clusters).

Parallel programs for parents and adolescents. Parallel programs offer the opportunity for parents and adolescents to experience the same program content but in formats geared to their needs and life stage. For example, parents could take an adult course (like morality or Scripture) while their son or daughter was participating in an adolescent course on the same topic. For many parishes this could be the beginning of an adult education program. Another example of parallel programming can be support groups, which provide parent and adolescent groups on the same topics or crisis situation, for example divorce or separation.

Parent resource center. Parents are realizing that they cannot "go it alone" in today's society. Parents are realizing that it makes sense to draw on the skilled resources of outside experts when problems arise. There are many critical situations that demand outside help today, for example, drug use, alcohol use, sexual activity, suicidal tendencies, child abuse, and other out-of-control behaviors. For parents needing help with critical situations, youth ministry can establish a parent resource center which provides information and videos on adolescent problems, referral assistance to expert and trusted counselling resources, a link to support groups (like AA or Al-Anon), and information on community educational programs that address critical adolescent situations.

SECTION 3

Youth Ministry Activities with a Family Perspective

CHAPTER 14:
Activities for Sharing Faith

Growing in Faith Together

John Roberto

Purpose

This session explores how faith grows and develops through the life cycle. It seeks to help parents and/or youth understand that growth in faith proceeds through stages or styles, and recognize that differences in styles of faith are acceptable and healthy.

Audience: This session can be conducted with parents-only, adolescents-only, or parents and adolescents.

Time: 1½ hours

Session Overview

1. Introductory Presentation: Faith Is . . . (15–20 minutes)
2. Activity: Faith Growth of Parents; Faith Growth of Adolescents (30–40 minutes)
3. Presentation and Discussion: Growing in Faith (30 minutes)
4. Conclusion and Closing Prayer (if you are using this as a independent session)

Materials Needed

- Flipchart, newsprint, tape, and markers (or chalk and chalkboard)
- White paper, pen or pencil, and crayons or markers for each participant
- Overhead projector (if you choose to use transparencies for your presentation)

Session Plan

1. **Introductory Presentation: Faith Is . . .**
   (15–20 minutes)

Introduce yourself as the workshop leader. To introduce a contemporary understanding of faith, invite the participants to brainstorm responses to the question, "Faith is . . ." After five minutes, call time and present a brief overview of faith using the information below from *The Challenge of Adolescent Catechesis*. The key concepts you want to address include: a) faith as gift and relationship, and b) faith as believing, trusting, and doing. Throughout your presentation, encourage the participants to make comments and pose questions.

> Christian faith is a gift of God inviting people to a living relationship with God in Jesus Christ. In the years since

Vatican II, the Church has reiterated its belief that faith has affective (trusting), cognitive (believing), and behavioral (doing) dimensions. We remain firmly convinced that Christian faith must be lived. Catechesis that take the Christian faith as its purpose intentionally promotes all three dimensions—trusting, believing, and doing.

An Activity of Trusting

Christian faith is a response to an invitation to a loyal and trusting relationship with God. Developing and deepening the adolescent's relationship with God in Jesus requires particular attention to and catechesis on the activity of personal and communal prayer. Catechesis attempts to dispose young people to awe, reverence, and wonder at the goodness of God. The loving relationship adolescents develop with God will shape and be shaped by their relationship with other people. The affective dimension of the Christian faith helps young people develop and deepen their sense of belonging within the faith community. Catechesis has the task of enabling adolescents to develop friendship-making and maintenance skills. Such a catechesis seeks to promote in adolescents a deep and abiding bond of friendship and good will toward the whole human family.

An Activity of Believing

The cognitive dimension of Christian faith—the activity of believing—requires that we provide opportunities for youth to deepen and expand their understanding of the scriptural/doctrinal expression of our faith tradition in ways appropriate to their readiness and maturity. We do this by showing the reasonableness of assenting to Catholic Christian beliefs, by helping youth draw on the wisdom of the Catholic Christian tradition to give meaning to their lives, and by enabling youth to think for themselves about matters of faith. We help them to articulate their understanding of the tradition in a language appropriate to their generation (see *GCD* 88).

An Activity of Doing

Christian faith requires a catechesis that promotes a life based on the values of the Reign of God. This means that we present the Christian story as Good News, thus enabling young people to live as a Christian people—joyfully, hopefully, peacefully, and justly. Catechesis challenges young people to respond to God's love by living a life of loving service to others and by working for peace and justice on all levels of human existence—the personal, the interpersonal, and the social/political. The "doing of faith" leads to a deepening of faith. Faith leads to doing and doing leads to renewed faith.

2. Activity: Faith Growth of Parents; Faith Growth of Adolescents
(30–40 minutes)

Explain that the purpose of the activity is to explore how faith grows throughout the life cycle, especially in adolescence and in adulthood. (If you have conducted the Activity: Families with Adolescents in the Enriching Family Relationships section, be sure to refer back to the important concepts about development raised in this activity.)

Each participant will need two pieces of white paper, a pen or pencil, and a crayon or marker for this activity.

ROUND ONE

The following activities use parents-only and youth-only groupings. The richness of each others' stories can be lost in this arrangement. You may want to group parents and youth of different families together for discussion. This will promote intergenerational learning.

Activity for Parents

1. Remembering Adolescence

   Ask the parents to recall their adolescence. Invite them to describe characteristics of their faith during adolescence. What was it like being a Catholic? What did their faith mean to them? Why was it important or unimportant? What were their faith struggles as an adolescent? Ask them to write several key characteristics on one piece of paper, making sure they leave room for further work later.

2. Faith Today

Now ask them to think about their faith today. What is it like being a Catholic today for them? What does their faith mean to them today? Why is it important or unimportant? What are their struggles in living their faith today? Using a second sheet of paper, ask them to draw a **symbol** or an **image** that best describes their faith today.

Discussion: In small groups of four, invite the parents to share their responses to the remembering activity and to share their symbol or image.

Activity for Adolescents

Ask the adolescents to think about their faith today. What is it like being a Catholic today for them? What does their faith mean to them today? Why is it important or unimportant? What are their struggles in living their faith today? On the first piece of paper ask them to write several key characteristics on their piece of paper, making sure they leave room for further work later. Then on their second piece of paper ask them to draw a **symbol** or an **image** that best describes their faith today.

> **Creative Expression**: An alternative to the reflection questions is to give each person a piece of clay or similar creative material. (You can substitute a paper cup, building blocks, drawing materials, collage materials, etc. for clay.) Ask the participants to shape the clay into a symbol or image of the meaning of Christian faith for them.

(Since the adolescents will finish discussing their questions before the adults, it is recommended that you use the creative expression activity with adolescents. The creative expression will use more time in the preparation phase, thereby compensating for the shorter youth discussion time.)

Discussion: In small groups of four, invite the adolescents to share their responses to

the activity and to share their symbol or image.

ROUND TWO

If you are conducting this session with adolescents-only or parents-only, select the appropriate audience and lead them through the questions. If you are conducting this session with adolescents and their parents, ask them to divide into two groups of parents-only and adolescents-only. Have a facilitator work with each group separately. List the responses on newsprint or the chalkboard. Encourage the participants to brainstorm items quickly, not to discuss the items in detail. Provide the following instructions:

> **Parents**: Ask the parents to respond **as if they were adolescents** by naming some of the characteristics of faith in adolescents: their values, struggles, concerns. What does their faith mean to them today? What are their struggles in living their faith today?

> **Adolescents**: Ask the adolescents to respond **as if they were parents** by naming some of the characteristics of faith in adulthood: their values, struggles, concerns. What is it like being a Catholic today for them? What does their faith mean to them today? What are their struggles in living their faith today?

After about 10–12 minutes, summarize the items listed on the newsprint sheets, pointing out similarities and differences between the two lists and citing examples of how the lists come from two very different perspectives. Leave the lists posted. You will refer to them several times during your presentation.

3. Presentation and Discussion: Growing in Faith
(20 minutes)

Using Chapter 3: "A Faith Development Perspective" by Gary Chamberlain present a brief overview of faith development, with a special focus on the key characteristics of adolescent development and adult development. For additional resources use:

Chamberlain, Gary. *Fostering Faith—A Minister's Guide to Faith Development*. New York: Paulist Press, 1988.

Stokes, Kenneth. *Faith is a Verb—Dynamics of Adult Faith Development*. Mystic, CT: Twenty-Third Publications, 1989. (An essay on faith development from this book is contained in the Catholic Families Series publication, *Families and Young Adults* by Ronald M. Bagley, CJM.)

Introduce your presentation by stating that it might be difficult for people to think that faith grows and develops. Explain that for some, faith is an absolute, a given that does not change; it is outside the individual, and one must either accept or reject it. For others, faith is so highly personal that there is no way it can be structured. For most of us who find meaning in the concept of faith development, however, there do seem to be some patterns. We will look at an approach for describing the patterns of faith growth. Keep in mind, however, that these are not *the* stages or styles of faith development; they are attempts by some theologians/psychologists to provide frameworks for understanding the concept of faith development.

Continue by explaining that faith growth is best imaged as the growth exemplified by the rings of a tree. As a tree grows, it adds rings to expand and mature, but the previously formed rings are still present in the central core of the tree's trunk. In essence, our faith journey is a whole, earlier faith styles are integral parts of our current journey. One style is not better than another.

Throughout your presentation, encourage the participants to make comments and pose questions. When appropriate, refer to the lists developed in the preceding activity. You may want to make transparencies to list the important points of your presentation.

4. Conclusion and Closing Prayer

Ask the participants to complete several of the following unfinished sentences:

> I learned . . .
>
> I discovered . . .
>
> I was surprised by . . .
>
> I found _____ difficult because . . .
>
> I found _____ easy because . . .
>
> This helps me understand _____ because . . .
>
> Because of what I learned, I will . . .

Option: Invite parents and youth of the same families to share their answers to the above questions together. Then ask them to share how these new understandings might help them communicate better, have talks about faith questions, and/or share faith with each other.

Growing as Catholic Christians

John Roberto

Purpose

This activity explores the changing nature of Catholic identity and how to share faith in families. It seeks to help parents and/or youth understand the dynamics of Catholic identity, recognize that differences in faith expressions are acceptable and healthy, and identify reasons for being Catholic.

Audience: This session can be conducted with parents-only, adolescents-only, and parents and adolescents.

Time: One 2-hour session or two sessions of 1½ hours and one hour each.

Session Overview

1. Activity: Surfacing Stories of Catholic Identity (30–40 minutes)
2. Presentation and Discussion: Reflections on Catholic Identity (20 minutes)
3. Intergenerational Sharing (20 minutes)
4. Activity: Why Be Catholic (30 minutes)
5. Practical Application: Ways Families Can Grow in Faith (20 minutes)

Materials Needed

- Flipchart, newsprint, tape, and markers (or chalk and chalkboard)

- White paper, pen or pencil, and crayons or markers for each participant
- Participant Handout: "Eight Good Reasons for Being Catholic" by Richard Rohr, OFM and Joseph Martos (*Catholic Update* 0888, Cincinnati: St. Anthony Messenger Press).
- Required Leader Resource: *Perspectives on Catholic Identity*. John Shea and John Nelson. *Network Paper #29* (New Rochelle, NY: Don Bosco Multimedia, 1989).
- Overhead projector (if you choose to use transparencies for your presentation)
- "Catholic Identity" by Joseph Martos and Richard Rohr, OFM. Chapter Eight in *Guide to Christian Faith*, Ed. John Roberto (New Rochelle, NY: Don Bosco Multimedia, 1991)
- *Why Be Catholic*. Joseph Martos and Richard Rohr, OFM. (Cincinnati: St. Anthony Messenger Press, 1989).

Session Plan

Explain that the purpose of this activity is to examine Catholic identity and how we grow as Catholic Christians. This session hopes to bring a greater understanding to the faith expressions of adolescents and of parents; and how these faith expressions can be unique to each generation while still being Catholic.

1. Activity: Surfacing Stories of Catholic Identity
(30–40 minutes)

Introduction

If you are conducting this session with adolescents-only or parents-only, select the appropriate audience and lead them through the questions. If you are conducting this session with adolescents and their parents, ask them to divide into two groups of parents-only and adolescents-only. Have a facilitator work with each group separately.

Each participant will need a piece of white paper, and a pen or pencil for this activity.

The basic process that will be used in this activity is outlined below. This three-step process will be adapted for use with parents and with adolescents.

Process:

1. Name one aspect of Catholic tradition that you prize, one that speaks to you about what being Catholic is all about. (It can be an idea, image, object, behavior or religious practice, people, liturgical activity, or movement.)

2. Write a story about an experience or significant contact you have had with that one aspect of Catholic tradition.

3. Why do you prize or value that aspect of Catholic tradition?

Use the following guidelines for group sharing:

Focusing: Taking turns each person will be the focus person for five minutes. During this period the focus person will share his/her story. Other group members should not let the attention shift from the focus person. While focusing on another's story, hold your own thoughts. This is not the time for a group discussion.

Clarifying: Listen as intently as you can. Try to understand the focus person's story, attitudes, beliefs, feelings. Ask questions to help clarify the focus person's story, but do no allow attention to shift from the focus person to yourself.

Accepting: Try to feel accepting. You can demonstrate your acceptance by listening, smiling, and nodding. Keep eye contact; be warm and supportive. And then listen some more!

Activity for Parents

Ask parents to utilize the three-step process in the following way:

Round One: Use the process to recall what being Catholic was like when they were growing up. Ask the parents to:

1. Name one aspect of Catholic tradition that they prized, one that spoke to them about what being Catholic was all about when they were growing up. (It can be an idea, image, object, behavior or religious practice, people, liturgical activity, a movement.)

2. Recall a story about an experience or significant contact they had with that one aspect of Catholic tradition.

3. Why they did (or still do) prize or value that aspect of Catholic tradition?

Round Two: Use the process to identify what being Catholic is like for them today. Ask the parents to:

1. Name one aspect of Catholic tradition that you prize, one that speaks to you today about what being Catholic is all about. (It can be an idea, image, object, behavior or religious practice, people, liturgical activity, a movement.)

2. Recall a story about an experience or significant contact you have had with that one aspect of Catholic tradition.

3. Why do you prize or value that aspect of Catholic tradition?

Discussion: In small groups of four, invite the parents to share what aspects of Catholic tradition they prize and highlights from their story.

Large Group Reporting: Ask the participants to share in the large group what aspects of the Catholic tradition they identified from their adolescence and what they identified for today. List the responses on separate sheets of newsprint. Encourage the participants to share items quickly, not to discuss any particular item. After the responses have been listed, invite the group to share reflections (no discussion) on what they see on the two lists.

Activity for Adolescents

Ask the adolescents to utilize the three-step process in the following way:

Round One: Use the process to identify what being Catholic is like for them today. Ask the adolescents to:

1. Name one aspect of Catholic tradition that you prize, one that speaks to you today about what being Catholic is all about. (It can be an idea, image, object, behavior or religious practice, people, liturgical activity, a movement.)

2. Recall a story about an experience (or significant contact) you have had with that one aspect of Catholic tradition.

3. Why do you prize or value that aspect of Catholic tradition?

Discussion: In small groups of four, invite the adolescents to share what aspect of Catholic tradition they prize and highlights from their story.

Large Group Reporting: Ask the participants to share in the large group what aspects of the Catholic tradition they identified. List the responses on newsprint.

Round Two: As a large group, ask the adolescents to brainstorm what they think their parents will say about their Catholic faith today. What aspect of the Catholic tradition do they think their parents prize, one that speaks to them today about what being Catholic is all about. Why do they think that these aspects are important for parents?

Post their responses on newsprint. Encourage the participants to share items quickly, not to discuss any particular item. After the responses have been listed, invite the group to share reflections (no discussion) on what they see on the two lists: their list and what they think their parents would say.

Summary for Parent and Adolescent Mixed Group

Post the lists from the parents (remembering adolescence and today) and the lists from the adolescents (their response and their parent list). Summarize the items listed on the newsprint sheets, pointing out similarities and differences between the lists and citing examples of how the lists come from two different perspectives and faith experiences. Be sure to compare the parents' list of today with what their adolescents thought. Ask them to compare the adolescent today list with the parent today list. Are their generational differences? Invite the group to share reflections (no discussion) on what they see on the lists. Leave the lists posted. You will refer to them several times during your presentation.

2. Presentation and Discussion: Reflections on Catholic Identity
(20 minutes)

Using the material by John Shea in *Perspectives on Catholic Identity* (*Network Paper #29*), present an overview of how Catholic identity develops and changes. The key concept is the dynamic nature of Catholic identity with its source in the life, death, and resurrection of Jesus Christ. Just because particular expressions (carriers) of the Catholic faith change, does not mean that faith in Jesus Christ has changed. It is important to emphasize that generational differences in faith expressions do not mean that one person's faith is better or more correct than another person's faith. They are just different. They are different ways to expressing faith in the life, death, and resurrection of Jesus Christ.

Throughout your presentation, encourage the participants to make comments and pose questions. When appropriate, refer to the results (and newsprint lists) from the prior activity for examples to illustrate your presentation. You may want to make transparencies to list the important points of your presentation. If you wish, you can make handouts from the enclosed material.

Outline

1. Catholic identity is relational—it develops in relationship with God.

2. Catholic identity must be Gospel identity. The foundation of Catholic identity is the life, death, and resurrection of Jesus of Nazareth. The event of Jesus of Nazareth originated and continues to give life to the Church.

3. Catholic identity has developed throughout history. The history of the Catholic people is a chronicle of living out a relationship with God in interaction with the culture of the times. This has meant that Catholic identity has grown or evolved through the history of the Church. All these expressions of Catholic identity are culturally indebted and historically bounded.

4. The development of Catholic identity involves the creation and re-creation of countless expressive forms. These forms give expression to Catholic identity and mediate this identity to the next generation. There are at least four categories of expressive forms:

   - Liturgical: Eucharist, sacraments, liturgical year celebrations, rituals
   - Doctrine: beliefs, theological reflection
   - Ethics and Morality: moral values and norms
   - Organizational: Church structures, ministries

5. Today, a clear distinction has developed between the Catholic identity as constituted by a living relationship to God and the various expressive forms which mediate that relationship. We need the expressions to mediate the life, death, and resurrection of Jesus; but because of new situations and needs some of these expressions need to change or be refurbished, some need to be dropped, while others needed to be created. Today, Catholic expressions are being rethought and redirected. New expressions are being developed.

Note: You may want to do a chart on newsprint or transparency which places the life, death, and resurrection of Jesus of Nazareth at the center of the page with four spokes coming out from this center: liturgical, doctrinal, ethical, and organizational. This type of chart will show that all faith expressions seek to mediate the reality of Jesus' life, death, and resurrection. Expressions can change to better mediate or reflect this reality.

3. Intergenerational Sharing
(20 minutes)

At this point in the session you may want to invite parents and youth of the same families or parents and youth of different families to gather for an intergenerational sharing. In these intergenerational groups, invite the adults and youth to share their stories of Catholic identity (from Part 1). The adults should focus on their *current* stories. This storytelling will help build understanding as well as a bridge into the final activity. Remind groups of the three guidelines for sharing: focusing, clarifying, accepting.

4. Activity: Why Be Catholic
(30 minutes)

Begin this section by organizing the participants into a parents-group and a youth-group. Ask each group to brainstorm its own answers to the question "Why be Catholic?" or "Why should I be Catholic?" Ask them to write their responses on newsprint. Ask the group not to discuss or react to any response. After each group has concluded its brainstorming ask each group to select up to eight good reasons for being Catholic. They should circle or check these reasons on the newsprint sheet.

Ask for group reports and then invite the participants to compare and contrast the youth and parent sheets.

Using "Eight Good Reasons for Being Catholic," present the eight reasons for being Catholic developed by Richard Rohr OFM and Joseph Martos. In their essay, Rohr and Martos identify the following characteristics: an optimistic view of creation, a universal vision, a holistic outlook, personal growth, social transformation, a communal spirit, a profound sense of history, and a respect of human knowledge. Correlate your presentation with the participants' responses. Write the eight reasons on newsprint or a transparency. Invite questions and comments during your brief presentation. [You can find the essay, "Eight Good Reasons for Being Catholic," in Chapter Nine of the *Guide to Christian Faith* (Don Bosco Multimedia) or you can purchase it directly from St. Anthony Messenger Press.]

Invite the group to compare and contrast the eight reasons. What was affirming? What was challenging? What new insights did they discover. What would they add or change to their reasons for being Catholic?

5. Practical Application: Ways Families Can Grow in Faith
(20 minutes)

This session will conclude with practical ways families can grow in faith. Ask the participants to develop several specific ways that families can grow in faith during the adolescent years. If you are working with parents and teens, ask family members to join together in small groups. In each family group, ask parents and adolescents to develop two or three ways. Invite reports from the small groups and list the ideas on newsprint.

If you are working with parents-only or adolescents-only, ask them to brainstorm ways in the large group and then list them on newsprint.

Using the introduction to Section Three and the other ideas contained in this section, share with the group ways that families can share faith.

Conclusion: Ask the family groups to select one or two strategies that they will try to implement in the coming weeks and to discuss how they will do it. For parent-only or adolescent-only groups, ask them to select one or two ways that they will try to implement in the coming weeks and to discuss with each other how they can be implemented.

Conclude the session by asking the small groups to share their ideas with the larger group.

Communicating the Good News about Sexuality— A Parent-Teen Activity

John Roberto

Purpose

For many parents and young people, talking together about sexuality is difficult. And it is made more difficult by the different, and often conflicting, messages parents and youth hear about sexuality. Different messages about human sexuality come from varied sources like the family of origin, the Church, the society, ethnic cultures, media, and peers. Because of the diversity of these messages, parents and youth sometimes experience confusion. Making explicit some of the many messages we receive about sexuality and how these messages affect our lives and relationships can be helpful in assisting young people and parents to communicate with each other, as well as to form and clarify values that are consistent with the Catholic Christian view of sexuality.

Audience: Parents and adolescents.

Time: 1½ hours

Session Overview

1. "Voices of Sexuality" Activity (30–40 minutes)

2. Discovering the Catholic Voice (20–30 minutes)

3. Concluding Option 1: Spreading the Word (20–30 minutes)
   Or: Concluding Option 2: Talking to My Parents about Sexuality (20–30 minutes)

Materials Needed

- Newsprint, markers, and masking tape
- Pencils/pens for each participant

Session Plan

1. "Voices of Sexuality" Activity (30–40 minutes)

Introduce the theme of the session as described above. Then organize the participants into youth-only and parents-only groups. Ask the groups to complete the a worksheet like that in the table at the top of the next page. Participants are asked to brainstorm what each "voice" has been teaching or telling them. One person in the group should serve as recorder for the group. Make a large copy of the worksheet on newsprint for all to see.

Call for reports from each group. Record the youth reports and parent reports on different sheets of newsprint. Ask for any

Voices of Sexuality	This Is What I Hear	Example
a. Parents/family		
b. Media (music, films, TV)		
c. Church		
d. Teachers/school		
e. Adolescent female friends		
f. Adolescent male friends		
g. Ethnic culture		
h. Adult leaders (youth programs)		
i. Others (fill in):		

general reflections, but save the indepth discussion for later.

Now organize the participants into smaller mixed groups of youth and parents, but not from the same family. Assign each small groups one the following categories. Determine which apply best in your setting. Feel free to add addition categories. Categories: Parents/Family, Media, Church, Teachers/School, Adolescent Female Friends, Adolescent Male Friends, Ethnic Culture, Adult Leaders.

Ask the participants in each group to discuss the messages that they hear about sexuality from the source that has been assigned. After they have determined the content of the message they hear, ask them to prepare a presentation summarizing the message. This presentation should include at least three statements about what the source says on sexuality as well as a slogan or a part a song that summarizes the entire message.

When all groups have finished, have each small group report to the large group.

After the reports, begin a discussion of the "voices" activity. You can conduct this as a *large group activity* or a *small group activity* (participants can discuss in their work groups from the last activity or return to their youth-only and parents-only groups). Discuss the following questions. Post these questions on newsprint for all to see.

a. What messages from the "voices" of sexuality are similar?

b. What messages are different?

c. Which "voices" are strongest? Why?

d. How do you decide which "voices" you will listen to?

2. Discovering the Catholic Voice
(20–30 minutes)

Present the key teachings of the Church on sexuality by reviewing each teaching and inviting the participants to ask clarifying questions about each teaching. Post the key teachings on newsprint or a transparency. You may want to make a handout out of the teachings.

Introduce the Church's voice by explaining that the Church's teaching is based on Jesus' message of love and promotes respect for all life and that this view often stands in opposition to other voices they are hearing. The following statements can be used as guiding principles in living out the values of the Christian Community. Each statement represents a belief which the Church teaches about sexuality.

A. A Christian person sees sexuality as a gift from God.

We learn from Scripture and the Church that sexuality is something created by

God. Sexuality is not something added to our human nature; it is part of our nature as human beings. We do not need to feel embarrassed or ashamed of our sexuality.

B. A Christian person believes that each person is unique with individual rights and responsibilities.

Each person is created uniquely in the image of God. God establishes a dignity in the human person that is unsurpassed in the rest of creation. The gift of human sexuality carries with it the responsibility to grow into the persons God created us to be. This is a life-long process of saying yes to the way God calls us to mature.

C. A Christian person recognizes and affirms the equality of males and females.

Scripture tells us God created us male and female, and God saw that it was good. We believe as Christians that male and female represent two ways of being in the world, complementing the gifts of each other. Any suggestion that persons of one sex are better or more gifted than the other is a misunderstanding of God's creative purposes.

D. A Christian person respects his/her own body.

To respect our bodies and the bodies of others is to acknowledge that God is present in every person. Scripture tells us that our bodies are to be temples of God. God lives in us and becomes present to others through us. By respecting our bodies, we say thank you to God for creating us.

E. A Christian person builds healthy relationships through commitment, faithfulness, honesty, and a concern for the other person.

The quality of our relationships depends on the values of commitment, faithfulness, honesty, and a concern for the other person. Through the teaching of Jesus we learn about how we should relate to other persons: honor your parents, love your neighbor, forgive your enemies, share your riches.

F. A Christian person believes that sexual intercourse is an expression of love reserved for those in the permanent, life-giving commitment of marriage.

Sexual intercourse, along with the acts of physical affection, is a special way in which a man and woman pledge themselves to one another and to all that their lives together will demand of them. This pledge requires a serious adult commitment. Sexual intercourse is also the expression of love that God has given man and woman to share in the creation of a new life. It is only within marriage that sexual intercourse can be a sign of committed love, and be open to bringing forth new life. Only in this relationship does sexual intercourse find its full meaning.

G. A Christian person has the right to say no to and reject sexual activity for any reason.

Sexual activity is not the same as love. Sexual activity can be a loving expression of commitment or it can be used as a means of force to violate a person's dignity and self-worth. It is wrong to pressure another person with words or actions that do not respect an individual's rights.

H. A Christian person does not use another person merely for his/her own sexual pleasure.

The Catholic Church teaches that to use another person or degrade sexuality is a sin. We violate our relationship with God and others whenever sexual affection is used to manipulate another person or when a person acts impulsively or dishonestly, looking to satisfy his or her own needs without regard for another person's well being. Sexuality is a gift given to us by God. It is meant to express commitment and love, and to bring forth new life.

I. A Christian person does not see abortion as a solution to an unwanted pregnancy.

The Catholic Church teaches that human life is present from the moment of conception. All life is a precious gift from God. Regardless of the circumstances in which a child is conceived, the new life that is created is no less a person and no less precious. This life deserves protection, care, and respect.

After your brief presentation, discuss, as a whole group, which Christian teachings really challenge youth and parents. Next, invite the participants to compare the Christian messages to those they presented in song or slogan earlier in the lesson. How are the messages similar/different? What messages are affirmed? What messages are challenged or questioned by the Christian "Voices"?

3. Concluding Option 1: Spreading the Word
(20–30 minutes)

Ask the participants to join with their intergenerational group (from the earlier activity). Tell each group it has been hired to work on an advertising campaign for the Catholic Church. Their task is to spread the Church's message about sexuality to teenagers and parents. Ask each group to prepare one of the following:

- A newspaper ad
- A 30 second radio spot
- A billboard
- A TV commercial

The session can end with each group sharing its advertisement with the other groups.

Concluding Option 2: Talking to My Parents about Sexuality
(20–30 minutes)

Form into two small groups: parents and youth. Ask each group to respond to the following two items and to list their answers on a sheet of poster paper or newsprint. Be sure to remind them that they should reflect on the learnings from this activity and answer their questions in light of this activity, rather than in general.

Parents:

a. Things I want to tell my son or daughter about sexuality . . .

b. Things I want to ask my son or daughter about sexuality . . .

Youth:

a. Things I want to tell my parent(s) about sexuality . . .

b. Things I want to ask my parent(s) about sexuality . . .

Invite the groups to come back together. Begin by asking the young people to share their responses to "Things I want to tell my parents about sexuality." When the young people are finished, parents are invited to share comments to what youth reported.

Parents are then asked to share their responses to "Things I want to tell my son/daughter about sexuality". When finished, the young people are invited to respond.

Continue the same process with second category: "Things I want to ask my parents (my son/daughter) about sexuality."

Conclude the sessions with learning statements like,

I learned . . .

I discovered . . .

I was surprised by . . .

I found _____ difficult because . . .

I found _____ easy because . . .

This helps me understand _____ because . . .

Because of what I learned, I will . . .

[This activity is adapted from *Human Sexuality* by Janet Drey and Brian Reynolds, New York: Sadlier, 1988.)

Making Moral Choices

John Roberto

Purpose

Adolescents face many pressured, moral choices. Often times the moral choices they make bring them into conflict with their parents. Making good moral decisions involves learning a process that parents and youth can use. This activity presents a discussion of the key steps necessary for making sound moral choices: determining all the influences on a moral decision, educating oneself on the problem or question, consulting reliable authorities, asking for God's help in prayer, deciding—making a moral choice and acting on it, and evaluating the decision.

Audience: This session can be conducted with parents-only, adolescents-only, and parents and adolescents.

Time: 1½ hours

Session Overview

1. Case Study: Moral Dilemma Discussion (10–20 minutes)
2. The Process: Making a Moral Choice as a Catholic Christian (30–40 minutes)
3. Reflecting on Catholic Moral Values
4. Conclusion

Materials Needed

- resources for the case study
- paper and pens/pencils
- audio-visual equipment, if necessary

Session Plan

1. Case Study: Moral Dilemma Discussion
(10–20 minutes)

Introduce the purpose of the activity to parents and/or teens. Begin by asking the parents and youth to brainstorm (with no discussion!) a list of typical adolescent moral issues or dilemmas. These might be areas where parents and youth struggle or disagree. Then, ask each group the following questions. Post the responses on newsprint.

Ask the parents: In your experience, how do youth typically make moral choices?

Ask the young people: In your experience, how do parents typically respond to moral choices you must make?

Explain that the group will first experience a moral dilemma faced by youth through a written case study, role play, or video presentation. Organize the participants into parent-only and youth-only groups or into mixed parent-youth groups of different family members.

Use a case study to present to the group a moral dilemma that youth often face. To find case studies, check adolescent religious education texts on morality. They often contain a variety of case studies for use with youth. If you use the case study option, you can distribute copies to the participants for them to read and/or ask several participants to role play the case study. Another option is to show a film/video from a religious education publisher or to tape a TV show that deals with moral dilemmas. One example of a video resource is *Contemporary Moral Issues* from Brown/ROA (800-922-7696), which deals with issues like honesty, friendship, intimacy, cheating, and justice in short 10–15 minute vignettes. Video resources can often be borrowed from diocesan media centers and public libraries.

After presenting the case study, ask the participants to reflect in small groups on the following questions:

- What decision needs to be made in this situation?
- Who are the key people involved in this situation?
- What values are at stake in this position?
- If you were in the same situation, how do you think you would respond? Why?

2. The Process: Making a Moral Choice as a Catholic Christian
(30–40 minutes)

Present the following D-E-C-I-D-E process for making a moral decision, developed by Audrey Taylor in *Moral Decision-Making* (New York: Sadlier, 1988). You should write each step on newsprint for all to see.

D—Determine all the influences on your moral decision.

Describe and list all the things that are part of the dilemma or problem at hand or that will influence your choices: reason or intellect, family, feelings, freedom, friends, media, beliefs and values, authority figures, society, cultural heritage, past experiences, Catholic faith, relationship with Jesus Christ.

E—Educating yourself further on the problem or question.

List all the ways possible to become better informed about the problem or question at stake. Select the ways that seem like they will offer you the most knowledge and help. Call to mind Jesus' law of love and the moral laws and norms the Church teaches. Spend time thinking and reasoning about options, rather than simply acting on impulse and feelings.

C—Consult reliable authorities.

Talk with those persons who will provide sound advice, new insights, opinions that might not perfectly fit with your own, or the kind of care and support you will need. Pay particular attention to what you can learn from Jesus, the Bible, the Church, and those life-giving people you rely on, like your family. Make good use of the insight or wisdom of others and your own personal reason to decide what is right, what is wrong, and what would be the most appropriate action. There are certain core, Catholic values which should play a part each time we use the process.

I—In Prayer, ask for God's help.

Pray for guidance. Spend time in prayer, alone or with others like your family, before your choice is made. Be open to the Spirit of Jesus and how it will lead you, and support you, as you decide. What would Jesus do in this situation? Ask Jesus to help you be faithful to his Law of Love. Seek the Lord's guidance in Scripture. Ask the Holy Spirit to make you a loving person—helping you to do what is right and reject what is wrong. Listen to what your conscience is saying about the situation. Ask God to be with you in your decision and after it has taken place.

D—Decide; make your moral choice and act on it.

List all the pros and cons in the situation. Look at each reason and decide how important it is. Be sure to reflect on what values are at stake in your pros and cons. How will it influence your life and future, your relationships with other people, and your relationship with Jesus? Using your assessment of the pros and cons go ahead and make a decision. List the ways you will carry out your decision. Identify who you will inform about your decision. Now you are ready to act on your moral choice. Act with the knowledge and faith that you have worked hard to inform your conscience and make the best choice you can.

E—Evaluate your decision.

We evaluate decisions by taking time to think over some important questions, such as: Did anyone get hurt as a result of my choice? Which relationships did it help or did it damage. What basic values were at stake in my decision? How did I act on the core Catholic norms and laws? What have been the chief consequences for myself, my future, others? Am I proud of my choice? Did I do the right thing? Did I really follow my informed Christian conscience?

After your brief presentation, ask each small group to try out the process in making a decision about the dilemma you shared with them. Ask them to discuss each step up to *Evaluate*. One person should serve as a recorder for the group. This activity is best conducted in parent-youth groups.

Call for reports or reflections from each group, focusing on how the process worked, as well as any decision that was reached. Don't evaluate any decisions yet.

3. Reflecting on Catholic Moral Values

Ask the groups to reflect on their decision in light of core Catholic moral values. How central were these values in the group's final decision? What Catholic moral values were at stake in making this decision?

Ask for brief reports from the small groups. Based on this discussion, you may want to present the key Catholic moral value(s) that was at stake in your moral dilemma. Here is a summary list of Catholic moral values that can assist you.

a. **Human Dignity**—We believe that all women and men are created by God and uniquely fashioned in God's image. Created in the image and likeness of God, each person is sacred. No one is expendable. The dignity of the human person does not come from things or status or money; it comes from the Creator. A basic responsibility and challenge for all Christians is to encourage attitudes, behaviors, and structures that value the dignity and worth of every person, regardless of race, ethnic origin, religion, economic class, sex, sexual orientation, age, or degree of ablebodiedness.

b. **Equality**—We believe that all people are equally important members of the Body of Christ, and all deserve equal treatment and a basic attitude of respect. Stereotypes must be recognized, named for what they are, and challenged. Developing healthy racial attitudes, promoting greater appreciation for cultural diversity, challenging racism and stereotypes of women and men, of the elderly, and of people with disabilities are all ways of realizing equality between people and in society as a whole.

c. **Love and Community**—We believe that we are called to love our neighbor as ourselves, that life is meant to be lived in community, in relationships with other people. In community we learn who and whose we are. Relationships are built upon love, compassion, reconciliation, respect for the dignity of people, and equality between people.

d. **Interdependence**—We believe all aspects of God's creation are linked together. We are one human family, diverse and unique, but connected. There is a basic interconnectedness of all life, as evidenced in our environmental problems.

e. **Stewardship**—We believe that God has entrusted us with the duty or responsibility to use the world's resources responsibly. All of the resources of creation are entrusted to us by God so that the needs of *all* people may be met. Promoting conservation of the earth's limited resources, nurturing a sense of reverence for God's creation; encouraging a sense of sharing or stewardship of our personal talents and possessions as well as the earth's resources; and challenging materialism and wastefulness are all ways of realizing stewardship.

f. **Human Rights**—We believe that all human beings are entitled to the minimum conditions necessary for healthy growth. Minimum human rights include sufficient life goods, availability of education and work, cultural acceptance, economic justice, and the right to political participation.

g. **Justice**—We believe that the essential human needs of all people must be met and that Christians are called to address the social problems and social policies which keep people poor and oppressed. As Christians we believe in a preferential active concern for the poor and oppressed, whose needs and rights are given special attention in God's eyes.

h. **Peace**—We believe that people are called to live in harmony with each other and with creation, to realize greater cooperation among peoples. As Christians we are called to resolve conflicts between people and nations with non-violent means.

i. **Compassion and Service**—We believe that we are called like Jesus to have a special sensitivity to human suffering and fragility, to love

and to serve others as Jesus did. We believe that compassion for those that society considers outcasts or worthless or unproductive is to love as Jesus loved. We believe that we are called to serve others in need and work for a world free of poverty and oppression of all kinds.

j. **Relationships and Sexuality**—We believe that the quality of our relationships depends on the values of commitment, faithfulness, honesty, and a concern for the other person. We believe that sexuality is a gift from God, an integral part of our personhood.

4. Conclusion

Based on their learnings in this session, ask the group questions like:

What have you learned about deciding as a moral person?

The steps that seem the most difficult are . . .

In the future, when I have to make big/significant moral choices, I will . . .

The most practical thing I have learned about D-E-C-I-D-E is . . .

I will help others get to know the steps in the D-E-C-I-D-E process by . . .

Conclude by asking youth and parents these questions. (You can discuss these questions in family groups.)

Youth: How has this session helped you in making better moral choices? How can your parents help you?

Parents: How can you help your son/daughter make good moral choices?

Families and Pop Culture

Reynolds R. Ekstrom

Purpose

This activity will help participants examine the impact of pop culture on family lifestyles; and urge participants to consider ways their families could make better choices on how to consume and use various pop media and pop culture materials.

Audience: This session can be conducted with parents-only, and with parents and adolescents.

Time Needed: Two hours

Materials Needed

- Pop culture materials and resources for Experience 1
- Jambox (audio-tape player/FM radio) and music cassette
- Optional: "family room" materials for Experience 1
- VCR and TV monitor; video-cassette of TV sitcom episode
- Overhead projector
- Worksheet copies for Understanding Process 2
- Transparency with key points from Chapter 7
- Materials for Response activity: 8½ x 11 sheets of paper, colored construction paper, scissors, glue, colored markers, masking tape, etc.,
- Closing prayer
- Refreshments for social time.

Background Material

- *Media, Faith, and Families—A Parents' Guide to Family Viewing.* Ed. John Roberto. (New Rochelle,: Don Bosco Multimedia, 1992)
- *Media, Faith, and Families—A Parish Ministry Guide.* Ed. John Roberto. (New Rochelle: Don Bosco Multimedia, 1992)
- *Access Guides to Youth Ministry: Media & Culture.* Ed. Reynolds R. Ekstrom. (New Rochelle: Don Bosco Multimedia, 1992).

Session Design
EXPERIENCE 1

Prior to the beginning of this two-hour session, prepare and set up a display of things drawn from contemporary culture and media with which family members usually come into contact. Note: if possible, have this display arranged in a room or space set apart from where your participants would ordinarily meet, e.g., part of a cafeteria.

In your pop culture immersion display, include collages with images of families taken from current magazines, newspapers, etc., but also incorporate and post around the room the kinds of magazines, posters, clothing, tapes, records, advertisements, and other pop culture stuff that members of families, all ages, might find in their lives. Do not be bashful in developing this experience. Great posters and stand-up, cardboard display materials can usually be acquired by visiting local movie rental and music stores.

Play a Z-Rock radio station or a pre-recorded cassette of rock (and/or rap) music on a jambox, in the background. Play the music kind of loud. If at all possible, make part of your experience here a "family room" scene, e.g., furniture, TV (turned on), VCR, coffee table, stereo (turned on) and other appropriate items. If you were to clutter up this display as a whole and/or to hang certain pop culture items on strings from ceiling fixtures, so they hang down in participants' faces, this should greatly enhance the observers' experience. When all have had time to fully walk through and observe this family-and-pop culture display, move all participants toward a suitable environment for a reflection-and-discussion process that will ensue.

UNDERSTANDING PROCESS 1

Display several unfinished sentences (below) on an overhead transparency, or on a newsprint sheet, for all to see. Have these sentences visible as participants come into the room from the walk-through experience. Play instrumental music on a cassette in the background (use reflective music). Given the previous experience, participants will probably come in slowly, at different intervals. Some will spend more time in the walk-through display than others. Invite all to respond verbally to the following. (If you are working with 12 persons or more, do this response process in small groups of three or four.)

1. In looking over the pop culture display,

   I saw . . .

   I heard . . .

   I started to realize . . .

2. In thinking about all the stuff in the display, I realized that families today

have to deal with . . .

EXPERIENCE 2

Invite all participants to watch a recent episode of a current TV half-hour sitcom that features a "family with children." For example, show them a recent episode (that you have pre-recorded) of "The Cosby Show," "Major Dad" (CBS), "Family Matters," "Beverly Hills 90210" (one hour) (FOX), "Married . . .With Children" (FOX), "Full House" (ABC), "Evening Shade" (CBS), etc. To make this a 20–25 minute viewing experience, edit out the commercials in the TV episode or fast-forward through them on your cassette. Just before you turn on the VCR, ask participants to focus on a reflection question as they watch:

- What are you learning about how to live or how not to live as a family from this TV family situation?
- How will you apply this in your own family experience?

UNDERSTANDING PROCESS 2

Encourage participants to discuss the following reflection questions. (Note: Have the questions on a worksheet, and have one copy for each participant.) Do this in small groups.

- How did this TV show make you feel?
- What were the most memorable scenes or lines of dialogue?
- Which characters were most interesting to you? Were there conflicts/problems acted out?
- What was this show all about? What did it have to say or "teach" about contemporary family life, in your opinion?
- What did you learn about how to live or not to live as a family from this TV show?
- How will you apply such insight(s) to your own family life?

Testing Assumptions: Have participants move now with you to a deeper level of reflection on family life and family change in pop culture. Call for responses to the following in a large group setting (all participants gathered and working together).

1. Given that which occurred in the sitcom family, was the way they handled or resolved the situation true to life as you know it? Why or why not?

2. What are you personally learning about how families or certain members of families (e.g., parents, adolescents, brainy little kids) in particular are often pictured by the media?

3. How would you want your family to be seen by others?

4. How would you want your family members to handle the kind of situation that cropped up in the TV episode (at least on one of your family's better days)?

Lecturette: The chief facilitator or some other competent person should summarize, crisply and succinctly, about six or seven key ideas/themes about families and pop culture found in the Chapter 7: "A Pop Culture Perspective." This presentation should last no more than ten minutes. Note: Try to have the six or seven points visible for all to see on an overhead transparency or sheet of newsprint. Keep on display for all during the ensuing discussion.

Ask participants to discuss the following in dyads (groups of two) or, if you prefer, in their original small groups.

- Which of these key points seem particularly true to you?

- Which do not connect with your own family experience?

- Which is most significant to how families are affected by our mainstream culture today?

- A key point/theme I would add to this list is . . .

Response/Decision: Encourage participants to work individually or in pairs, as quietly as possible, to come up with a symbol (an original drawing, a cutout, a "sculpture," or an item taken from the display in Experience 1 that somehow shows or symbolizes what they will do, following this learning experience, to call their family members to greater awareness of the impact of pop culture and pop media on their family life.

Ask all who are so inclined to share their symbols or artwork with the whole group (or in their small groups) as time allows. Thank all for attending and sharing. Close with prayer and social time.

CHAPTER 14:
ACTIVITIES

Helping Youth Make
School and Career Choices

Thomas Bright

In *A Century of Catholic Social Teaching: A Common Heritage, A Continuing Challenge*, the U.S. Catholic Bishops remind us that "work is more than a way to make a living; it is an expression of our dignity and a form of continuing participation in God's creation." Young people give a lot of time to considerations of job and career, and the schooling needed to get there. They explore their talents and skills, survey the personnel needs of business and industry locally and nationally, check out school and training options, weigh potential job demands against salary and benefits, and try to come up with a mix of ingredients that will help them meet the criteria they've established for personal and professional success. Too often this process takes place without conscious consideration of the values questions involved in career decisions. While most Christians will not be employed *by the church*, all are challenged by the Gospels to work in the world *as church*, consciously doing their part to continue God's creation, to create a world where justice and peace are a reality for all.

How can we help youth (and adults) wrestle with this question for themselves? We can start by providing young people with a broader understanding of what it means to be church in our time. Discussion of what it means to be church can too easily get caught up in internal matters—issues of church discipline and doctrine, practices, and programs. While these topics are important to any discussion of who we are as God's

people, they don't exhaust the subject. The Church exists for the sake of the kingdom, to further the proclamation and actualization of the Reign of God among us. We are church as we celebrate Eucharist together. We are also church as we work in Jesus' name to further justice in our world. Both are essential to the life of Catholic Christians.

A MINICOURSE APPROACH TO DECISION MAKING ON CAREERS

A minicourse designed to help senior high youth explore career options from a Christian perspective can help young people tie these two aspects of church life together. Use the following steps in organizing your minicourse on Careers from a Christian Perspective.

1. Talk with youth and their parents about the kind of career options the young people in your parish are considering. Select the 10 or 12 mostly frequently mentioned careers as the "content" for your course.

2. Invite church and community members who represent the careers identified by the young people and their families to take part as session presenters in the minicourse program.

3. Organize the minicourse in a way that fits the needs of young people and their families. The minicourse, for example, could run on Tuesday nights for 12 consecutive weeks, with each session featuring a distinct career option. Sessions could be done "sandwich-style" hour-long, bag supper sessions sandwiched in between the *end* of school and work commitments and the *start* of evening programs and commitments. Sessions could be doubled up and completed in six weeks, or handled together in a one- or two-week period focused entirely on school and career choices.

4. The minicourse could be opened to all high school youth in the parish and local community. It could be offered for youth alone, or involve parents. Participants could attend all sessions or just sign up for the ones in which they were particularly interested.

5. In a program like this, the choice of presenters is of crucial importance. Presenters should be comfortable talking *about* their job and *with* young people. Presenters should be asked to offer an overview of what their job is like, the skills people should bring to it, and the kind of training or schooling needed to find success in the job market. Presenters should be asked, too, to reflect on their jobs from a Christian perspective. How does their job or profession help people to live better lives, how does it contribute to the work of building the kingdom of God? What ethical or justice issues do they face in their job on a regular or occasional basis? How can their job skills be used outside the work setting, in a volunteer capacity, to touch justice issues in a healing way? Speakers, in summary, should be selected on the basis of professional competence and on the basis of how well and how consciously they integrate their career into their faith life. Such speakers can be great role models for young people.

6. Brief prayer services written for the start or close of the minicourse sessions could draw on Scriptures and Church teachings that speak to the issue of the sacredness of work and the universal call to contribute in our daily lives and tasks to the building of the kingdom of God.

7. Follow-up to the minicourse could include one-on-one or small group meetings with the presenters to continue the dialogue begun during the minicourse. Young people interested in a particular career option could be grouped together and matched up with an adult "mentor" who was a parish member working in the same career field.

The model is not a difficult one, yet could meet the twin purposes of helping youth make better informed choices about career and school and start to view their career choices in light of the Christian call to further God's kingdom in our day and time.

INFORMAL CONVERSATIONS ABOUT CAREER CHOICES

As youth and young adults settle on career directions, sharing some key questions with them can help them reflect again on the call to live out faith in our daily life commitments. These questions could be asked by a parent, a relative, a trusted adult friend, or a parish youth minister. If, for example, a young person has decided on a career in health care, the following questions might be asked:

- Why health care? What will it do for you, and what will it enable you to do for others?

- What aspect of health care are you looking into and why?

- Who is most in need of health care today in our country or world? How will your training help you respond to their needs?

- What schools are you looking into? What kind of on-the-job training does it provide? What kind of clientele would you be working with?

- What languages might you need to be able to do health care well in the cities, suburbs, and rural regions of our country? Is there space in your course work for a language course or two?

- What are health care salaries and benefits like? What kind of lifestyle do you expect to live? How much do you expect to be able to share with others?

- How could your job skills be used in a volunteer capacity? Do you see volunteering in your future? How can you start preparing now to be a more competent volunteer in the future?

- What can we learn from the life of Jesus about the Christian call to healing?

Regardless of the job or profession, similar questions should fit. Helping young people work through the answers can be a great service to them and to the world.

CHAPTER 15: Activities for Enriching Family Relationships

Understanding Families with Adolescents

John Roberto

Purpose

This activity will help the participants understand the normal changes of adolescence and of their adult parents and how these changes may affect family life. This activity helps parents and teens understand the dynamics of families with adolescents and provides them with practical aids for enhancing family communication.

Audience

This session can be conducted with parents-only, adolescents-only, and parents and adolescents.

Time: 1½ hours

Session Overview

1. Opening Activity: What Are Parents and Youth Concerned About? (20 minutes)

2. Presentation on the Family Life Cycle: Families with Adolescents (20-30 minutes)
3. Skills Development: Learning to Communicate in Families with Adolescents (40-45 minutes)
4. Conclusion (5 minutes)

Materials Needed

- Flipchart, newsprint, tape, and markers (or chalk and chalkboard)
- Overhead projector (if you choose to use transparencies for your presentation)
- Background information for this activity and the presentation:
  + Chapter 2: "A Family Life Cycle Perspective on Families with Adolescents"—Nydia Garcia Preto
  + Chapter 4: "The Changing American Family"—Richard P. Olson and Joe H. Leonard, Jr.
  + Chart: "Young Adolescents, Parents, and Family Interaction"—Leah Lefstein (see Chapter 13)
  + "The Family Life Cycle." Betty Carter and Monica McGoldrick. *Growing in*

Faith: A Catholic Families Sourcebook. Ed. John Roberto. (New Rochelle: Don Bosco Multimedia, 1990).

+ "Early Adolescent Development." John Hill. *Access Guides to Youth Ministry: Early Adolescent Ministry.* Ed. John Roberto. (New Rochelle: Don Bosco Multimedia, 1991).

+ "Early Adolescent Development" and "Older Adolescent Development." Laurence Steinberg and Ann Levine. *Guide to Understanding Youth.* Ed. John Roberto. (New Rochelle: Don Bosco Multimedia, 1991).

+ *Five Cries of Parents.* Merton and Irene Strommen. (San Francisco: Harper & Row, 1985.)

+ *You and Your Adolescent—A Parent's Guide for Ages 10-20.* Laurence Steinberg and Ann Levine. (San Francisco: Harper and Row, 1990.)

Session Plan

1. Opening Activity: What Are Parents and Youth Concerned About?
(20 minutes)

Introduce yourself as the workshop leader. Explain that the purpose of the session is to examine the adolescent stage of the family life cycle by exploring key characteristics of adolescent and mid-life adult development. Introduce the idea that as children enter the adolescent stage of life and the changes associated with adolescence like puberty, adults are often entering middle adulthood and the changes associated with mid-life. How parents see their emerging adolescents is colored by the changes they themselves are experiencing. At the same time, adolescents' perceptions of their parents are changing as they mature physically, cognitively, socially, and emotionally.

Option 1: Parents and Adolescents Together

If you are conducting this session with adolescents and their parents, ask them to form into two groups of parents-only and adolescents-only. Have a facilitator work with each group separately. List the responses on newsprint or the chalkboard. Encourage the participants to brainstorm items quickly, not to discuss the items in detail. Provide the following instructions:

Round One

Parents: First, ask the parents to name some behaviors, attitudes, and concerns of adolescents they do not understand or that they find confusing. Second, ask the parents to name several things about their adolescent that they enjoy.

Adolescents: First, ask the adolescents to name some behaviors, attitudes, and concerns of their parents they do not understand or that they find confusing. Second, ask the adolescents to name several things about their parents that they enjoy.

Round Two

Now reverse the questions and write the answers on separate sheets of newsprint.

Parents: Ask the parents to respond as if they were adolescents by naming some of the behaviors, attitudes, and concerns of parents that they think adolescents do not understand or that they find confusing.

Adolescents: Ask the adolescents to respond as if they were parents by naming some of the behaviors, attitudes, and concerns of adolescents that they think parents do not understand or that they find confusing.

Option 2: Program for Parents Only

Lead the group through the following process:

Round One

Parents: First, ask the parents to name some behaviors, attitudes, and concerns of adolescents they do not understand or that they find confusing. Encourage the participants to brainstorm items quickly, not to discuss the items in detail. List the responses on newsprint or the chalkboard.

Second, ask the parents to name several things about their adolescent that they enjoy.

Round Two

Now reverse the questions and write the answers on different sheets of newsprint.

Parents: Ask the parents to respond as if they were adolescents by naming some of the behaviors, attitudes, and concerns of parents that they think adolescents do not understand or that they find confusing.

Option 3: Program for Adolescents Only

Lead the group through the following process:

Round One

Adolescents: First, ask the adolescents to name some behaviors, attitudes, and concerns of their parents they do not understand or that they find confusing. List the responses on newsprint or the chalkboard. Encourage the participants to brainstorm items quickly, not to discuss the items in detail.

Second, ask the adolescents to name several things about their parents that they enjoy.

Round Two

Now reverse the questions and write the answers on different sheets of newsprint.

Adolescents: Ask the adolescents to respond as if they were parents by naming some of the behaviors, attitudes, and concerns of adolescents that they think parents do not understand or that they find confusing.

Summary

After about 10-12 minutes, summarize the items listed on the newsprint sheets, pointing out similarities and differences between the two lists and citing examples of how the lists come from two very different perspectives. Leave the lists posted. You will refer to them several times during the workshop.

2. Presentation on the Family Life Cycle: Families with Adolescents
(20-30 minutes)

Using the outline in the table at the bottom of this page and background material that follows, present a brief overview of the family life cycle as you interweave they key characteristics of adolescent development and mid-life adult development. Throughout your presentation encourage the

---

CHARACTERISTICS OF FAMILIES WITH YOUNG ADOLESCENTS

The following is a basic outline that you can use for your presentation:

A. INDIVIDUAL LIFE CYCLE

The Adolescent Years	The Middle Adult Years
Key Task: Construction of an Integrated Identity	Key Task: Generativity & Care
Physical & Sexual Growth: Puberty	Concern with Physical Competency & Changes
Intellectual Growth: Formal Operations	Life Reassessment: Shifting Time Perspective
Socially: Wider Sphere of Activity	Accommodating the New Generation
Changes in: Autonomy, Attachment, Relationships	

B. FAMILY LIFE CYCLE

Key Task: Increasing flexibility of family boundaries to include children's independence and grandparent's frailties

Secondary Tasks:
   a. Shifting of parent-child relationships to permit adolescent to move in and out of system
   b. Refocus on mid-life marital and career issues
   c. Beginning shift toward joint caring for older generation

participants to make comments and pose questions. When appropriate, refer to the lists of behaviors, attitudes, and concerns developed in Part One. You may want to make transparencies to list the important points of your presentation. If you wish, you can make handouts from the enclosed charts and articles.

Background Resources:

Chapter 2 and the other suggested resources listed at the beginning of this activity will help you to prepare for your presentation. Here is an guide to follow:

Outline

See the basic outline at the bottom of the previous page that you can use for your presentation.

Adolescence ushers in a new era because it marks a new definition of the children within the family and of the parents' roles in relation to their children. In short, family relationships need to be modified to be more in line with the new needs, concerns, and competencies of the individuals involved. Carter and McGoldrick summarize this new era in the following way:

> Families with adolescents must establish qualitatively different boundaries than families with younger children, a job made more difficult in our times by the lack of built-in rituals to facilitate this transition. The boundaries must now be permeable. Parents can no longer maintain complete authority. Adolescents can and do open the family to a whole array of new values as they bring friends and new ideals into the family system. Families that become derailed at this stage may be rather closed to new values and threatened by them and they are frequently stuck in an earlier view of the children. They may try to control every aspect of their lives at a time when, developmentally, this is impossible to do successfully. Either the adolescent withdraws from the appropriate involvements for this developmental stage, or the parents become increasingly frustrated with what they perceive as their own

impotence . . . . Flexible boundaries that allow adolescents to move in and be dependent at times when they cannot handle things alone, and to move out and experiment with increasing degrees of independence when they are ready, put special strains on all family members in their new status with one anothe (Carter and McGoldrick 18).

These changes in the family system during adolescence bring about periods of disequilibrium or imbalance—times when an individual member has changed but the system has not yet fully adapted by altering relationships. A healthy family system will adapt to this new stage in the family life cycle—bringing about balance or equilibrium. "These changes in family relationships occur gradually, in a somewhat disorganized fashion, as individuals try on new roles and experiment with new ways of relating to each other" (Steinberg 13). "The task for most families—and it is by no means an easy one—is to maintain *emotional* involvement, in the form of concern and caring, while gradually moving toward a relationship characterized by great *behavioral* autonomy" (Steinberg 12).

The family life cycle portrait of adolescence also includes the transitions happening within the parents. "The central event in the marital relationship at this phase is usually the 'midlife crisis' of one or both spouses, with an exploration of personal, career, and marital satisfactions and dissatisfactions. There is an intense renegotiation of the marriage, and sometimes a decision to divorce" (Carter and McGoldrick 18). It seems that adolescents and midlife parents are simultaneously developing in different directions, causing times of imbalance that the family system needs to adjust to. If this development is not understood and accepted, life together can be filled with confusion, misunderstanding, and disagreement. Family members need to adapt and adjust to their mid-life and adolescent roles.

Recognizing that individual family members' needs and roles change over time and adapting relationships accordingly is a key to positive family life.

Works Cited

Carter, Betty and Monica McGoldrick. "The Family Life Cycle." *Growing in Faith: A Catholic Families Sourcebook*. Ed. John Roberto. (New Rochelle, NY: Don Bosco Multimedia, 1990).

Steinberg, Laurence. *Understanding Families with Young Adolescents*. Carrboro, NC: Center for Early Adolescence, 1980.

3. Skills Development: Learning to Communicate in Families with Adolescents
(40-45 minutes)

A. OPENING ACTIVITY

Option 1: Communication Is Easier and Harder Because . . .

Most parents and adolescents find that communication is quite different from childhood days. Communication is sometimes harder and sometimes easier in the adolescent years. If you are conducting this session with adolescents and their parents, ask them to form into two groups of parents-only and adolescents-only. Have a facilitator work with each group separately. List the responses on newsprint or the chalkboard. Encourage the participants to brainstorm items quickly, not to discuss the items in detail. Provide the following instructions:

Parents: Ask them for reasons why communicating with adolescents is *harder* than talking with children. Ask them for reasons why communicating with adolescents is *easier* than talking with children.

Adolescents: Ask them for reasons why communicating with their parents is *harder* than when they were children. Ask them for reasons why communicating with their parents is *easier* than when they were children.

After you have listed the reasons on newsprint or the chalkboard, refer to your earlier presentation to point out the changes of adolescence and mid-life that cause communication to be both easier and harder.

Refer to the list of behaviors, attitudes, and concerns that parents and adolescents find confusing about each other (from the opening activity). Suggest that the amount of confusion and misunderstanding that exists between parents and adolescents can be decreased in a number of ways.

Option 2: It's Hard to Communicate About . . .

Most parents and adolescents find that some topics are quite difficult to communicate about in the adolescent years. If you are conducting this session with adolescents and their parents, work with them together. Follow the two steps below:

1. Ask the participants to brainstorm topics that they find hard/difficult to communicate about in the adolescent years. List the responses on newsprint. Encourage the participants to brainstorm items without discussing them.

2. Now ask the participants to share reasons "why" each item is difficult to communicate about.

After you have listed the reasons on newsprint or the chalkboard, refer to your presentation on the changes in families with adolescents that cause communication on these topics to be difficult. Then, suggest that the amount of confusion and misunderstanding that exists between parents and adolescents can be decreased in a number of ways.

B. PRESENTATION: AIDS TO EFFECTIVE PARENT-TEEN COMMUNICATION

Using the following outline and Merton and Irene Strommen's *Five Cries of Parents* (60-67, 77-86), present a how-to lecture on aids to effective parent-teen communication. Be sure to illustrate each point with family examples. Show the participants how they can use effective communication in recognizing that individual family members' needs and roles change over time and adapting relationships accordingly. Effective communication is a means to handle the disruptions that occur regularly in the adolescent family.

You may want to make transparencies to list the important points of your presentation. If you wish, you can make handouts from the enclosed charts and articles.

Outline

1. Four aids to parent-youth communication:

   - Recognize the natural blocks to communication. (e.g., growing self-consciousness of the adolescent, limited verbal skills of adolescents, growing resistance to authority, lack of time of the parents, etc.)
   - Take time to establish relationships.
   - Share thoughts and feelings.
   - Focus on the adolescent's (or parent's) concerns and interests.

2. Listening for understanding:

   In their experience there are three types of listening mistakes:

   - listening with half an ear
   - "Yes, but" listening
   - "I can top that" listening

   They recommend three guidelines:

   - Listen in ways that encourage expression of feelings.
   - Listen to discern the adolescent's (or parent's) perspective.
   - Approach each conversation with a sense of hope.

C. APPLICATION

Ask the participants to develop several specific action strategies to improve communication between parents and adolescents. If you are working with parents and teens, ask family members to join together in small groups. In each family group, ask parents and adolescents to develop two or three ways to improve communication, especially around the changes of adolescence and mid-life that cause communication to be harder (refer back to the behaviors, attitudes, and concerns that cause confusion). If you are working with parents-only or adolescents-only, ask them to brainstorm ways that they can communicate more effectively and to select one or two strategies that they will use this week.

4. Conclusion
(5 minutes)

Ask the participants to complete several of the following unfinished sentences:

> I learned . . .
> I discovered . . .
> I was surprised by . . .
> I found _____ difficult because . . .
> I found _____ easy because . . .
> In the coming weeks, I/we will try to . . .

FOLLOW-UP OPTION

You may want to consider conducting the next Activity, "Parent-Teen Communication" as a follow-up session or activity.

Parent-Teen Communication

John Roberto

Purpose

Learning to communicate effectively is important in all relationships, but particularly in parent-youth relationships. Effective communication helps parents and youth recognize that individual family members' needs and roles change over time and that their relationships must adapt accordingly. Effective communication and problem-solving is a means to handle the changes and disruptions that occur regularly in the adolescent family.

Audience: This session is best conducted with parents and adolescents together, but can be designed as a parents-only or adolescents-only activity.

Time: 1½ hours

Session Overview

1. Activity: Issues and Obstacles to Communication
2. Activity: Ingredients of Effective Parent-Youth Communication
3. Presentation: Effective Parent-Youth Communication
4. Skills Development: Practicing Empathic Communication
5. Conclusion

Materials Needed

- Flipchart, newsprint, tape, and markers (or chalk and chalkboard)
- Overhead projector (if you choose to use transparencies for your presentation)
- Paper and pens/pencils for each person
- Markers and paper for each family group
- The following resource material contains important background information for conducting this activity:
  + *People Skills*. Robert Bolton. (New York: Simon and Schuster, 1979)
  + *You and Your Adolescent—A Parent's Guide for Ages 10-20*. Laurence Steinberg and Ann Levine. (San Francisco: Harper and Row, 1990.) [See Chapter 2, "Family Communication and Problem-Solving"]
  + *Seven Habits of Highly Effective People*. Stephen Covey. (New York: Simon and Schuster, 1989) [See Habit 5, "Seek First to Understand, and Then to Be Understood"]

Session Plan

1. Activity: Issues and Obstacles to Communication

Group Activity

Most parents and adolescents find that some topics or issues are quite difficult to communicate about in the adolescent years, and some of these topics can cause conflict and disagreement, hurting the parent-youth relationship. In mixed groups of parents and youth (or in the large group, depending on size), ask the participants to do the following:

1. Ask the participants to brainstorm topics or issues that they find hard/difficult to communicate about in the adolescent years. List the responses on newsprint. Encourage the participants to brainstorm items without discussing them.

2. Now ask the participants to share reasons "why" each item is difficult to communicate about. Try to identify conflicts or issues that result from the life cycle changes being experienced by youth, parents, and the entire family system.

3. Ask parents and youth to select three or four topics or issues that often cause conflict or disagreement, hurting their relationship.

Role-Playing

Select several of the issues and/or conflicts and ask parents and youth to role play several situations. Organize parents and youth into teams. You can reverse roles so that youth role play the parents role and parents role play the youth roles. Be sure to work with the teams to define roles and give them time to prepare away from the full group. The phases of an effective role-play include:

1. clearly define the situation
2. have learners assume the character roles that will be involved
3. have characters act out the situation
4. stop the action before the role-play is exhausted
5. discuss and evaluate how it went: name central turning points and outcomes in the role-play; ask for insights and feedback in particular from role-players; identify chief issues, new learnings, and/or new directions suggested in the experience; give input on how new

learnings may be further studied or perhaps acted on.

Obstacles to Communication

The group activity and the role-playing should provide plenty of material to draw out the obstacles to parent-youth communication. Ask the large group to identify the most common obstacles to parent-youth communication and give an example of the obstacle. List the obstacles on newsprint.

To supplement or organize the list from the group, here is a sampling of 12 obstacles to effective communication:

JUDGING

1. Judging, criticizing, blaming: "That's really immature."
2. Name-calling, ridiculing: "Okay, you little baby."
3. Interpreting, diagnosing: "You're just jealous of _____."
4. Praising, agreeing: "Well, I think you're pretty/smart/a good player."

SENDING SOLUTIONS

5. Ordering, directing, commanding: "Don't ever talk to me like that!"
6. Warning, admonishing, threatening: "If you do that, you'll be sorry."
7. Exhorting, moralizing, preaching: "You ought to do this . . ."
8. Excessive/inappropriate questioning: "Why do you suppose you hate school?"

AVOIDING THE OTHER'S CONCERNS

9. Advising or giving solutions: "Go make friends with someone else."
10. Diverting, distracting: "Why don't you try burning down the school?"
11. Lecturing, teaching, giving logical arguments: "Let's look at the facts . . ."
12. Reassuring, sympathizing: "Don't worry, things will work out fine."

2. Activity: Ingredients of Effective Parent-Youth Communication

Organize the participants into one parent-only group and one youth-only group. First, ask the parents to develop five or six key ingredients for effective communication with their youth; and ask youth to develop five or six key ingredients for effective communication with their parents. These items should be listed on newsprint. Participants can brainstorm items, and then select their five or six best ideas.

Second, ask the parents to develop five or six key ingredients for effective communication that they expect (or would like) their children to use; and ask youth to develop five or six key ingredients for effective communication that they expect (or would like) their parents to use. These items should be listed on newsprint. Participants can brainstorm items, and then select their five or six best ideas.

Briefly compare and contrast the lists. You will return to this work at the end of the session.

3. Presentation: Effective Parent-Youth Communication

Stephen Covey's book, *Seven Habits of Highly Effective People* provides an excellent approach to effective communication that is not a list of techniques or gimmicks. He calls it empathic communication. The following outline is taken from Habit 5, "Seek First to Understand, and Then to Be Understood" in his book. Refer to this chapter for background and examples for your presentation. Be sure to relate your presentation to the role play situations.

Seek to Understand

We typically seek first to be understood. Most people do not listen with the intent to understand; they listen with the intent to reply. They're either speaking or preparing to speak. When another person speaks we're usually "listening" at one of the four levels: *ignoring, pretending, selective listening, attentive listening*. Very few of us ever practice the fifth level, the highest form of listening, *Empathic Listening*.

Empathic Listening means listening with intent to *understand*—seeking first to understand. *Empathic listening* gets inside another person's frame of reference. You look out through it, you see the world the

way they see the world, you understand how they feel. In empathic listening, you listen with your ears but you also, and more importantly, listen with your eyes and with your heart. You listen for feeling, for meaning. You listen for behavior.

The essence of *Empathic Listening* is not that you agree with someone; it's that you fully, deeply, understand that person, emotionally as well as intellectually

Empathic Listening is so powerful because it gives you accurate data to work with. Instead of projecting your own autobiography and assuming thoughts, feelings, motives, and interpretation, you're dealing with the reality inside another person's head and heart. You're listening to understand. You're focused on receiving the communication of another person.

Common Errors in Communication: Listening Autobiographically

- We *evaluate*: we either agree or disagree
- We *probe*: we ask questions from our world
- We *advise*: we give counsel based on our own experience
- We *interpret*: we try to figure people out, to explain their motives, their behavior, based on our own motives and behavior

How many of these common errors surfaced in the role plays?

Developmental Stages of Listening

The skills, the tip of the iceberg of *Empathic Listening*, involve four developmental stages:

Stage 1: Mimic Content—only reflecting back what people are saying

Stage 2: Rephrase Content—limited to only verbal communication

Stage 3: Reflect Feelings—focusing only on feelings rather than the content

Stage 4: Rephrase Content and Reflect the Feelings—combining stages 2 and 3

What happens when you use fourth stage empathic listening skills is that you authentically seek to understand, as you rephrase content and reflect feeling. You help the other person work through his or her own thoughts and feelings. As the person grows in his or her confidence of your sincere desire to really listen and understand the barrier between what's going on inside the person and what's actually being communicated to you disappears. The person is not thinking and feeling one thing and communicating another. He or she trusts you with his or her innermost feelings and thoughts. Real understanding, created by empathic listening, enables you to get to the real problem.

The skills of empathic listening will not be effective unless they come from a *sincere desire* to understand.

Empathic Listening takes time, but it doesn't take anywhere near as much time as it takes to back up and correct misunderstandings when you're already miles down the road, to redo, to live with unexpressed and unsolved problems.

Seek to be Understood

Seeking to understanding requires consideration; seeking to be understood takes *courage*. Seeking to be understood requires:

- Character/Credibility : Faith people have in your integrity and ability.
- Relationship: Empathic listening to understand the other person's concerns/interests.
- Presentation: Sharing self, ideas, plans in context of what you learned about the other person.

Because you really listen, you become influenceable which is the key to influencing others.

4. Skills Development: Practicing Empathic Listening

Ask the role play teams to present their situations again, but this time to use the skills of empathic listening. Remind them to *seek first to understand* and *then to be understood*. After each role play, discuss how the participants felt about using the skills and review how successful the participants were in using the skills.

5. Conclusion

Conclude the session by developing a parent-youth communication creed. First, review the ingredients of effective communication developed in the second activity. Then ask the parent group and the youth group, if they would add or revise anything on their lists. You may want to reinforce or add ideas to the list using the following ingredients to aid parent-youth communication:

- Recognize the natural blocks to communication, e.g., growing self-consciousness of the adolescent, growing resistance to authority, lack of time of the parents, etc.
- Take time to establish relationships.
- Share thoughts and feelings. Make every effort to be honest.
- Focus on the adolescent's or parent's concerns and interests.
- Make good choices about the timing for communication.

Second, invite parents and youth to join together in family groups. From the list of key ingredients, every family group should develop their own Family Communication Creed. Ask the families to develop "We Believe . . ." statements about effective communication. Tell them it must be things that they believe as a family about effective communication! This will form the basis of improving family communication. Next, ask them to develop "We will . . ." statements that put the creed into action. These should be statements that indicate what they will do as a family to improve communication.

Close the session by inviting family groups to share several beliefs and actions from their Family Communication Creed.

Parent-Teen Problem Solving

John Roberto

This activity should be conducted as a follow-up activity to the "Parent-Teen Communication" activity. If you conduct this as a separate activity, you will need to make a presentation on effective communication prior to using the collaborative problem-solving process.

Purpose

Learning to communicate effectively is important in all relationships, but particularly in parent-youth relationships. Effective communication helps parents and youth recognize that individual family members' needs and roles change over time and that their relationships must adapt accordingly. Effective communication and problem-solving is a means to handle the changes and disruptions that occur regularly in the family with adolescents

Audience: This session is best conducted with parents and adolescents together, but can be designed as a parents-only or adolescents-only activity.

Time: 1½ hours

Session Overview

1. Activity: Issues and Obstacles to Communication
2. Presentation: Effective Parent-Youth Communication (See "Parent-Teen

Communication" Activity)
3. Presentation: Resolving Conflicts
4. Skills Development: Practicing Collaborative Problem-Solving
5. Conclusion

Materials Needed

- Flipchart, newsprint, tape, and markers (or chalk and chalkboard)
- Overhead projector (if you choose to use transparencies for your presentation)
- Paper and pens/pencils for each person
- The following resource material contains important background information for conducting this activity:
  + *People Skills*. Robert Bolton. (New York: Simon and Schuster, 1979) [Chapter 14]
  + *You and Your Adolescent—A Parent's Guide for Ages 10–20*. Laurence Steinberg and Ann Levine. (San Francisco: Harper and Row, 1990.) [See Chapter 2, "Family Communication and Problem-Solving"]

Session Plan

1. Activity: Issues and Obstacles to Communication

Group Activity

Most parents and adolescents find that some topics or issues are quite difficult to communicate about in the adolescent years, and some of these topics can cause conflict and disagreement, hurting the parent-youth relationship. In mixed groups of parents and youth (or in the large group, depending on size), ask the participants to do the following:

1. Ask the participants to brainstorm topics or issues that they find cause conflict or disagreement in the adolescent years. List the responses on newsprint. Encourage the participants to brainstorm items without discussing them.

2. Now ask the participants to share reasons "why" each item cause conflict. Try to identify conflicts or issues that result from the life cycle changes being experienced by youth, parents, and the entire family system.

3. Ask parents and youth to select three or four conflicts or disagreements.

Role-Playing

Select several of the conflicts and ask parents and youth to role play several situations. Organize parents and youth into teams. You can reverse roles so that youth role play the parents role and parents role play the youth roles. Be sure to work with the teams to define roles and give them time to prepare away from the full group. The phases of an effective role-play include:

1. clearly define the situation

2. have learners assume the character roles that will be involved

3. have characters act out the situation

4. stop the action before the role-play is exhausted

5. discuss and evaluate how it went: name central turning points and outcomes in the role-play; ask for insights and feedback in particular from role-players; identify chief issues, new learnings, and/or new directions suggested in the experience; give input on how new learnings may be further studied or perhaps acted on.

2. Presentation: Effective Parent-Youth Communication

(See "Parent-Teen Communication" Activity)

Make this a brief presentation because the focus of this session is on resolving conflicts.

3. Presentation: Resolving Conflicts

Use the following material from *You and Your Adolescent—A Parent's Guide for Ages 10–20* by Laurence Steinberg and Ann Levine (San Francisco: Harper and Row, 1990) in your presentation on conflict and a process for resolving conflicts. This excerpt from their book is written for parents, but can easily be expanded to include youth examples. You might want to write the key points on newsprint or a transparency. Be sure to connect your presentation to the issues raised in the initial activity.

Conflict Is Part of Life.

It's impossible for people to live or work together without ever experiencing differences in values, opinions, desires, needs, and habits. Everyone is aware of the negative aspects of conflict, but we tend to forget the positive ones. Conflict prods us into expressing, rather than suppressing, our feelings. It shocks us out of our passivity, forcing us to think about that we have taken for granted, to change our customary ways of doing things, and to invent solutions to our problems. To go through life avoiding conflict is to confine oneself to superficial relationships and stagnation.

Conflict occurs when:

■ One family member feels that others are threatening his or her values, perceptions, life-style, sense of fairness, or "territory."

■ Family members agree on the final goal but disagree on how to arrive at that point.

■ There is not enough of something to go around. The "something" may be tangible—money, space, telephones—or intangible—time, attention, affection.

- Communication among family members has broken down.

For one or more of these reasons, you have reached an impasse. Unless you get beyond that impasse, hostility and resent are likely to build, and nit-picking, teasing, criticism, yelling, avoidance of one another, and stony silences will increase.

Conflict can improve and invigorate family relationships by helping family members to understand one another better and to be more tolerant of their individual differences, leading them to clarify issues and ideas in a way that clears the air, and forcing them to redefine their goals or set new goals that are more satisfactory to everyone. When conflicts are resolved in a positive way, everyone wins.

Conflict harms family relationships when it takes the form of personality attacks and power struggles. Negative conflicts leads to resentment and hostility; causes confusion, insecurity, and diminished self-esteem; and makes productive, rational discussion of issues and behavior in the future difficult, if not impossible. When family members are at war, nobody wins.

No-Win Solutions

The most common ways parents attempt to resolve conflicts with their adolescents are cracking down, giving in, avoiding the problem, and compromise. Although each of these strategies has its uses, each also has drawbacks. There is an alternative: collaboration, which we will discuss shortly. First let's look at the others.

One way to end an argument with an adolescent is to crack down. Like a military officer pulling rank, parents lay down the law. When parents refuse to consider the adolescent's needs and desires and/or refuse to let her participate in the decision-making process, she is not going to be highly motivated to make the solution work. To the contrary, domination fosters resentment. It should be used only in emergencies, when quick, decisive action is vital (and parents do know best).

A second way to end conflict is to give in to the adolescent's wishes. Giving in or accommodation is appropriate when parents realize that the adolescent was right and

they were wrong: It shows the adolescent that they are willing to listen and to learn, and that they are reasonable. Accommodation is also appropriate when the issue is trivial to the parents but not to the adolescent (for example, how your son dresses for a party). But it shouldn't become a habit. As one psychologist noted, "If you want to hate your child, just let him win all the time. That's a sure formula."

Avoidance is also common: Parents do everything they can to escape a confrontation with the adolescent. When a problem comes up, they change the subject, suggest the family member is making mountains out of molehills, or simply withdraw. Avoidance is useful when the issue is trivial (the adolescent forgot a minor chore), when parties to a conflict are too much under stress to deal with the issue now (the adolescent has an exam the next day), or when they simply need time to cool down. But avoidance doesn't heal wounds; it allows them to fester.

The fourth strategy is compromise: Parents and the adolescent meet each other halfway. Most of us were taught that compromise is the best solution to conflict. This is only partly true. Compromise is useful when the issue is not worth much time and effort (where to eat dinner tonight). It's also useful when time pressures force a quick solution (for example, when you're expecting a long-distance call, the adolescent needs to call a friend, and you compromise by limiting his call to five minutes). But compromise is not a lasting solution to serious differences. Neither party's needs are fully met. Both settle for less than they want.

The problem with all these responses is that they don't resolve the conflict. The issue is left up in the air, and needs and feelings are pushed under the rug. Moreover, with each of these strategies somebody loses. With cracking down, it's the adolescent; with giving in, it's the parent; with avoidance, it's both. Although compromise is preferable to the other three, both parties give up something (what Bolton calls a mini-lose/mini-lose outcome). There is an alternative to these no-win approaches.

Collaborative Problem-Solving

The goal of collaborative problem-solving is to find a win/win solution that satisfies everyone. This approach takes more time and energy than the others we have described. It requires the unhappy family member to confront one another, which isn't always pleasant. But in most cases it minimizes hostility and hurt feelings and maximizes the chances that you will truly resolve the issue.

There are six basic steps to collaborative problem-solving. Again, the formula may seem awkward at first, but after you've used it several times it will begin to seem more natural. This approach works best if you choose a time and place when both you and the adolescent will not be distracted, limit the discussion to a specific issue, and secure in advance the adolescent's agreement to try to work out a solution.

Step 1. Establish ground rules. The ground rules for conflict resolution are essentially the rules of a fair fight. Each party agrees to treat the other party with respect—no name-calling, sarcasm, or put-downs—and to listen to the other person's point of view. Parents can set the stage by stating at the beginning their desire to be fair.

Step 2. Reach mutual understanding. The next step is to take turns being understood. This means that each of you will have the opportunity to say what you think the real problem is and how you feel about it. It's important that you get it off your chest. But it's also important to avoid loaded words and phrases, accusations, and evaluations, and to focus on the issue, not on personalities. Each of you also has the right to be understood. This is where reflective listening comes in. When you've described the problem as you see it, let the adolescent speak her piece. Then rephrase the adolescent's point of view and ask her to restate yours, so that you are sure you understand one another.

Step 3. Brainstorm. The next step is for each of you to think of as many solutions to the problem as you can. The goal of brainstorming is quantity, not quality. At this stage, no idea should be rejected because it's crazy, or too expensive, or one of you thinks it is dumb. Zany ideas can reduce tension and keep creative juices flowing. Set a time limit (five minutes should be enough) and write down everything you can think of.

Step 4. Agree to one or more solutions. The best way to go about this is for each of you to select the options you like best. (Don't discuss each and every option; this can lead to endless, often fruitless, debate.) Then see where your interests coincide. Have you chosen any of the same options? Some give and take, or negotiation, will be necessary at this stage (e.g., a mother may agree to stop nagging if the son/daughter picks up his/her clothes and makes the bed daily). And you need to think through the practical considerations (the family can't afford a maid). But neither of you should agree to something you still find unacceptable.

Step 5. Write down your agreement. This may sound excessively formal, but memory can be faulty. If either of you thinks the other has broken the agreement, you can refer to your contract.

Step 6. Set a time for a follow-up discussion to evaluate your progress. This is as important as the first five steps. One of you might not live up to the agreement, or the solution might not be as elegant as you thought, and you will have to work out the bugs.

This six-step formula can be applied to a variety of situations, from arguments over the adolescent's curfew to decisions about family vacations. In some cases you won't be able to reach an agreement. When it comes to health and safety, parents may have to make a unilateral decision. But adolescents are far more likely to go along with you when they participate in the decision-making process and when they see that you are taking their needs and desires seriously.

4. Skills Development: Practicing Collaborative Problem-Solving

Organize the participants into family groups or mixed groups of parents and youth. Either assign or ask them to select one of the conflict issues from the earlier activity. Ask them to resolve the conflict by working through each step of the collaborative problem-solving process. Remind them to use the skills of empathic listening: *seek first to understand* and *then to be understood*.

An alternative to the above approach is to facilitate the problem-solving process with the entire group using the list of conflicts or to facilitate the process with each role-play team on the conflict issue that they originally acted-out.

Conclude this part of the session by discussing in the large group how the participants felt about using the process and review how successful the participants were in using the process.

5. Conclusion

To conclude ask the participants to complete several of the following unfinished sentences:

I learned . . .

I discovered . . .

I was surprised by . . .

I found _____ difficult because . . .

I found _____ easy because . . .

In the coming weeks, I/we will try to . . .

Exploring Diversity in Family Structures

Thomas Bright

Diversity is a key element in who we are as church today. The diversity takes many forms, for example, ethnic and cultural backgrounds, socioeconomic status, and family structure. This activity helps families with youth explore the diverse structures that make up family life today, and the implications of diverse family structures for the Church's ministry with families and youth. The activity as designed can be done with parents only, or with groups of parents and youth.

FAMILY PORTRAITS

Instruct participants to draw a picture, or create a collage, about their family. Ask that they include in their portraits, words or symbols that indicate how their present living out of family is different from what they experienced, or imagined, when they were younger.

Form the group into mixed teams of four to six to briefly share their family portraits. If the program involves both adults and youth, design the teams so that parents and youth from the same family are not grouped together.

When the team sharing is completed, ask the group to join you in listing the different styles/structures of family life represented in the group. Add to the listing any styles or structures of family life not present in the group but represented in the larger parish community.

A PORTRAIT OF FAMILY LIFE IN THE UNITED STATES

Using the material found in Chapter 4, "The Changing American Family," or the opening chapter in *A Family Perspective in Church and Society*, provide a brief overview of the reality of family life today in the United States.

DIVERSE STRUCTURES, DIVERSE NEEDS

Ask the group to explore with you how the different structures that people live in impact the needs they have—as adults and as youth. How, for example, do the needs of young people in two-parent families differ from those in single parent homes where there is little or no contact with the non-resident parent? Or, how do the parenting demands change for a mother who moves from a single parent family with one child to a blended family with two or more children at home?

There are many approaches this exercise could take. Consider the following:

1. Do a brief presentation on the experiences common to young people when parents divorce, using the material found in Chapter 5, "What Teenagers Go Through When Their Parents Divorce." Ask participants to travel through time with that young

person as she or he adapts to life in a single parent home or becomes part of a new blended family. What new concerns and needs might the young person have? What would the comparable needs of his or her parent look like in these different family structures? Returning to the small teams organized earlier, invite participants to share their reflections. A spokesperson, chosen by each team, would then share the team's thoughts with the full group.

2. Incorporate the participants as panel presenters. Ask members from diverse family structures to share from experience how their personal and family needs, and their expectations of the church community changed as they lived through separation, divorce, remarriage, and the blending of families, or the death of a spouse or parent. These presenters, obviously, should be contacted well in advance of the session and given a clear indication of what is expected of them. Following the presentation with an opportunity for participants to meet briefly in either mixed or same-structure groupings to share any questions they have on the presentation or to swap strategies they have developed to respond to the concerns and needs outlined in the presentation.

3. Post newsprint around the room under the headings of different family styles or structures, and ask participants to move around the room, jotting on the sheets in different colors the special needs or concerns faced by parents (color one) or youth (color two) from that family structure. The process could be followed by large or small group discussion.

IMPLICATIONS FOR MINISTRY

Ask group members to reflect individually on their learnings about family diversity and to list three to five implications of what they have learned about diverse family structures and needs for how the parish ministers to families with youth. Share your comments as a large group.

ACTING ON LEARNINGS

If the group consists of adults only:

From the implications raised by group members, select one or two suggestions that can immediately be incorporated into present program efforts. Decide on an approach for turning the suggestions into reality. This activity can be done in small teams or as a large group.

If the group consists of both adults and youth:

Divide the youth into teams of four to six persons. From the list of implications just developed, ask them to suggest practical strategies for incorporating a better sensitivity to family diversity into parish programs for youth.

Divide the adults into similar teams, asking them to develop strategies for incorporating a stronger sensitivity to family diversity into parish programs for adults and families.

When the teams have finished their task, have them share their ideas as a large group. Following the session, share the group's concerns and suggestions with the appropriate parish leaders.

Resources and Programs for Parenting and Enriching Family Relationships

There are many fine parenting programs available in print and video. Here is a list of selected parenting programs on video that you can use in your setting.

VIDEO PROGRAMS

ACTIVE PARENTING
[Two hours each—six videos, EcuFilm]

Dr. Michael Popkin, founder and director of *Active Parenting*, created this series to help parents find alternative methods for giving their children freedom within limits. It not only helps them make sense out of their child's behavior, but gives concrete guidelines to follow. In addition to the video presentations the *Active Parent Handbook* and *Action Guide* help viewers understand and remember the information and skills shown by the 40 video segments. They contain review exercises, home activities, and family enrichment suggestions.

Titles:

Session I:	*The Active Parent*
Session II:	*Understanding Your Child*
Session III:	*Instilling Courage*
Session IV:	*Developing Responsibility*
Session V:	*Winning Cooperation*
Session VI:	*The Democratic Family In Action*

BOYS TOWN VIDEOS FOR PARENTS
[10–16 minutes each—11 videos, Don Bosco Multimedia]

More and more parents today are seeking help to be better parents. The *Boys Town Videos for Parents* series covers topics from self-esteem and peer pressure to making sure teens and preteens do their homework and help around the house. The tapes are packed with concise information and are lively and dramatic, with true-to-life vignettes that illustrate key points. A booklet with additional information accompanies each video.

Titles:

A Change for the Better: Teaching Correct Behavior
Catch 'Em Being Good: Happier Kids, Happier Parents Through Effective Praise
Homework?: I'll Do It Later!
I Can't Decide: What Should I Do?
I'm Not Everybody: Helping Your Child Stand Up To Peer Pressure
It's Great to be Me!: Increasing Your Child's Self-Esteem
Negotiating Within the Family: You and Your Child Can Both Get What You Want
No I Won't And You Can't Make Me!
Setting Your Child Up for Success: Anticipating and Preventing Problems

*Take Time to Be a Family: Holding
Successful Family Meetings
You Want Me to Help with Housework?
No Way!*

BRIDGING THE GAP BETWEEN PARENTS AND TEENS
[60 minutes each—three videos, Tabor Publisher]

This dynamic, information-packed program can help strengthen relationships and bring about meaningful dialogue between the young people and adults in your family/parish.

Titles:
Series I:	*Talking and Listening with Teens*
Series II:	*Getting Along with Teens and their Friends*
Series III:	*Sharing Faith with Teens*

HOW TO RAISE PARENTS
[60 minutes—two segments, Franciscan Communications]

Clayton Barbeau takes a close-up look at the changing and often frustrating relationships of teenagers and their parents.

I HEAR YOU
[30 minutes, Group Publishing and Mass Media Ministries]

Leading specialists on the family offer practical tips to parents on how to improve communication wit their teenagers. Parents will discover effective listening skills, the secrets of getting their teenager to open up, how to decode their teen's non-verbal messages when not to try to talk with their teenager, and much more. Practical tips from the nation's leading Christian experts on the family. Adapted from the *Parenting Teenagers* video training series.

PARENTING TEENAGERS—SET I AND SET II
[Each set: 30 minutes—four videos, Group Publishing and Mass Media Ministries]

Parents of teenagers need help. Most of all, they need new ideas and insights that can help make family life easier and more enjoyable during these difficult years. In these two series, parenting specialists and real teens discuss the emotional and spiritual needs of maturing young people and how parents can ease the difficult times of transition. The information-packed leaders guides are full of helpful insights, publicity tips and ready-to-copy worksheets.

Parenting Teenagers Set I:
*What Makes Your Teenager Tick?
Parenting, How Do You Rate?
Communicating With Your Teenager
Your Teenager's Friends and Peer Pressure*

Parenting Teenagers Set II:
*Effective Teenage Discipline
How to Talk About Sex and Dating
School: Helping Your Kids Measure Up
Building Christian Faith in Your Kids*

TEENS IN CHANGING FAMILIES: MAKING IT WORK
[26 minutes, Sunburst Communications]

Living in a stepfamily is a fact of life for more and more teenagers. But remarriage brings with it a set of problems that are vastly different from those of first-time families, and many teens have difficulty adjusting to unanticipated pressures.

TEEN-PARENT CONFLICT: MAKING THINGS BETTER
[30 minutes, Sunburst Communications]

Conflict between teens and their parents is almost inevitable, with control at the heart of the issue. This program helps teenagers understand the nature of the conflict and offers specific techniques for dealing with it.

PRINT RESOURCES

PARENTING

Albert, Linda, and Michael Popkin. *Quality Parenting: How to Transform the Everyday Moments We Spend with Our Children into Special, Meaningful Time.* New York: Random House, 1987.

Bolton, Robert. *People Skills.* New York: Simon and Schuster, 1979.

Children's Television Workshop. *Raising Kids a Changing World—Preschool through Teen Years*. New York: Prentice-Hall, 1991.

Curran, Dolores. *Working with Parents*. Circle Pines, MN: American Guidance Service, 1989.

Dinkmeyer, Don, and Gary D. McKay. *The Parent's Handbook: Systematic Training for Effective Parenting (STEP)*. Circle Pines, MN: American Guidance Service, 1982.

_____. *The Parent's Guide: Systematic Training for Effective Parenting of Teens*. Circle Pines. MN: American Guidance Service, 1983

Dinkmeyer, Don, et al. *The Effective Parent*. Circle Pines, MN: American Guidance Service, 1987.

_____. *The Next STEP: Effective Parenting Through Problem Solving*. Circle Pines, MN: American Guidance Service.

Faber, Adel, and Elaine Mazlish. *How to Talk So Kids Will Listen, and Listen So Kids Will Talk*. New York: Avon Books, 1980.

Fassler, David, Michele Lash, and Sally B. Ives. *Changing Families: A Guide for Kids and Grown-Ups*. Burlington, VT: Waterfront Books, 1988.

Gardner, Freda A. and Carol Rose Ikeler. *Active Parenting in the Faith Community*. Atlanta: Presbyterian Publishing House.

Larson, Jim. *Growing a Healthy Family—How to be Christian Parents in a Stress-Filled Time*. Minneapolis: Augsburg, 1986.

Lerman, Saf. *Responsive Parenting*. Circle Pines, MN: American Guidance Service.

McGinnis, James and Kathleen. *Parenting for Peace and Justice*. Maryknoll, NY: Orbis Books, 1990.

_____. *Parenting for Peace and Justice—Multimedia Program*. St. Louis, MO: Institute for Peace and Justice.

Miller, Patricia. *Parent to Parent*. Los Angeles: Franciscan Communications, 1988.

Popkin, Michael. *Active Parenting: Teaching Cooperation, Courage, and Responsibility*. Marietta, GA: Active Parenting, 1986.

Sullivan, Susan K. and Matthew A. Kawiak. *Parents Talk Love—The Catholic Family Handbook about Sexuality*. New York: Paulist Press, 1985.

SINGLE PARENT AND BLENDED FAMILY RESOURCES

Bonkowski, Sara. *Kids are Nondivorceable: A Workbook for Divorced Parents and Their Children*. Chicago: ACTA Publications, 1990.

Bradley, Buff. *Where Do I Belong? A Kid's Guide to Stepfamilies*. Reading, MA: Addison-Wesley, 1982.

Einstein, Elizabeth. *The Stepfamily: Living, Loving and Learning*. New York: Macmillan Co., 1982

Einstein, Elizabeth, and Linda Albert. *Strengthening Your Stepfamily*. Circle Pines, MN: American Guidance Service, 1986.

_____. *Stepfamily Living: Preparing for Remarriage*. Ithaca, NY: E. Einstein Enterprises, 1983.

Ellis, Gordon E. *New Beginnings—Preparing Families for Remarriage in the Church*. New York: Pilgrim Press, 1991.

Evans, Marla D. *This Is Me and My Two Families: An Awareness Scrapbook/Journal for Children Living in Stepfamilies*. New York: Brunner-Mazel.

Francke, Linda Bird. *Growing-Up Divorced: How to Help Your Child Cope with Every Stage—from Infancy through the Teens*. New York: Fawcett Crest, 1983.

Getzoff, Ann, and Carolyn McClenahan. *Stepkids: A Survival Guide for Teenagers in Stepfamilies*. New York: Walker and Co., 1984.

Ives, Sally B., David Fassler, and Michele Lash. *The Divorce Workbook: A Guide for Kids and Families*. Burlington, VT: Waterfront Books, 1985.

Lewis, Helen Coale. *All About Families the Second Time Around*. Atlanta: Peachtree Publishing, 1980.

Mayle, Peter. *Divorce Can Happen to the Nicest People*. New York: MacMillan, 1979.

Monkres, Peter R. *Ministry with the Divorced*. New York: Pilgrim Press, 1985.

Murphy, and Oddo. *Running a Support Group*. Chicago: Buckley Publications, 1987.

Murray, Stephen and Randy Smith. *Divorce Recovery for Teenagers*. Grand Rapids, MI: Zondervan and Youth Specialties, 1990.

Seuling, Barbara. *What Kind of Family Is This? A Book about Stepfamilies*. Racine, WI: Western Publishing, 1985.

Yehl, Suzy, and Medard Laz. *Rainbows for All Children: An Effective School Support Program for Children Who Live in Single-Parent Families, Step-Families, or Families with Painful Transition*. (913 Margret St., Des Plaines, IL 60016).

Visher, Emily B. and John S. Visher. *Stepfamilies: Myths and Realities*. Secaucus, NJ: Citadel Press, 1979.

CHAPTER 16:
Rituals for Adolescence

Rites of Passage for Famililies with Youth

Leif Kehrwald

When I finally passed the ordeal of the written exam and driving test, I was elated to have my driver's license. The ultimate symbol of independence! Even though I didn't have my own car, at least I didn't need my parents to take me around anymore.

That evening our family celebrated my accomplishment. Although nothing special had been planned, the atmosphere around the dinner table was charged with excitement and anticipation. My mother, usually rather reserved, kept joking about all the errands I could now run for her. Taking my little sisters to and from swimming lessons and Brownie Scouts was not my top priority as a new driver.

My father, who had given me driving lessons, kept making "announcements" to warn the citizens of our town to clear the streets, for he could not guarantee the safety of this new driver. He kept going over to the phone pretending to call the radio and TV stations with his important civic "announcement."

My older brother was the only family member who showed little interest in my accomplishment. Perhaps he had not received the same attention 18 months earlier when he got his license. He being the first, my parents were probably too nervous

to joke about it the way they were doing with me.

By the end of the evening, both my parents, by ways of a knowing look and a warm hand on my shoulder, communicated that they were proud and confident in me. The next morning my mother asked me to pick up a gallon of milk after dropping my sister at swim class. Then my whole family knew I was a driver.

My life changed that day I got my driver's license, and that night my family embraced my new self, and initiated me into my new role. Without anyone acknowledging it, they celebrated this important rite of independence with me. They made it OK to be different than I was before, and yet still the same person.

RITES OF PASSAGE/ FAMILY RITUAL: IS THERE A DIFFERENCE?

Not all family rituals signify a rite of passage, and not all rites of passage (particularly for adolescence) are ritualized in the family.

Families develop patterns, habits, and ways of absorbing all that life deals. To that extent, all families engage in ritual. Some families go a step further, and deliberately incorporate faith ritual into their daily living: meal prayers, evening blessings, Sunday worship, seasonal faith celebrations, etc. These rituals provide order, security, and healthy predictability in an often disorderly life. They also provide a faith context to life that is home-based.

Rites of passage signify the periods of major change and transition in life. These events are key growth steps toward maturity. Because these experiences are foundational to maturity, the rites of passage will always occur; yet with an infinite variety of expressions and levels of intensity. Furthermore, they may or may not be explicitly ritualized in the family, youth group or congregation.

John H. Westerhoff describes three stages for rites of passage.

> The first stage is separation. It is followed by a period of transition...during which one learns the skill awareness and knowledge essential to one's newly emerging state or role. In the ordeal of this betwixt and between period a unique sense of community develops, and then one is ceremonially reincorporated into the community (Westerhoff 66).

As an example of these stages, let's examine my driver's license experience. the period of separation probably began a year and a half earlier as I envied my older brother's new found independence and mobility. Suddenly he was separate and superior from me, meaning I was still "Just a kid." The period of transition was most pronounced as I took driver education classes. Then, as I described, I was subtly but "ceremonially re-incorporated" into the family.

The third stage of ceremonial re-incorporation is paramount for the teen and the family to re-adjust their relationships to incorporate the transition. Whether implicit or explicit; whether deliberate or accidental, the rite of passage needs to be absorbed into the family system. Families naturally resist change and transition, but ritual, whether faith-based or purely secular, can greatly assist the full incorporation of the passage.

Another example will help illustrate the point. A teenage girl has been asked out on her first date. While Mother is excited for her, Dad is reluctant. "She's still too young to be dating," he says. When the young man arrives at the door, Dad lets him in and proceeds with the age-old ordeal of interrogation while waiting for his daughter to emerge. Finally, after the two have departed, Dad lets out a long sigh, "My little girl isn't so little anymore."

This brief, uncomfortable ritual helped Dad overcome his reluctance to embrace his daughter's maturity. It also shows that these rites of passage, although adolescent in nature, carry special significance for other family members as well.

RITES OF PASSAGE: AN OPPORTUNITY FOR FAITH REFLECTION

Rites of passage can be categorized into five primary experiences: birth, maturity, life commitment, death, and reconciliation. These categories can be applied to the entire life cycle of a family literally from birth to death. A relationship is "born" when two young adults meet, and somehow they know there's more to this than meets the eye. Months, or years later they make a life commitment through marriage. From then on, all their major life-transitions can be associated with one or more of the five areas.

During adolescence, growth toward maturity implies change. Families who celebrate rites of passage (whether knowingly or not) provide the forum for the life-change to be acknowledged, tried-on, and embraced by all family members. The rite provides the outward experiences for the inward change to become real.

Adolescence provides numerous opportunities for families to celebrate rites of passage. All the necessary ingredients are present: changes occur often and distinctly; life questions are loud and prevalent; identity and belonging needs are paramount; straightforward communication is difficult, lending value to symbol and ritual. Perhaps no other stage is riper for rites of passage than adolescence.

Many families celebrate rites of passage

without ever really knowing it. A change has occurred and the family has somehow ritualized it, yet nothing is ever said. These are implicit rites of passage.

Going back to the driver's license story, no one in my family would have named that experience a "rite of passage," yet, in an informal, ritualistic fashion, they successfully moved me (and all of us) into a new stage of life. Afterward, nobody ever said anything about the change, but we all knew how to incorporate it into our lives. That's exactly the key to a successful rites of passage: it empowers the family or community to embrace the change of one member, and somehow know how to carry on. In a ritualistic way, rites of passage transition the family into a new stage, allowing the system to re-arrange its boundaries and find a new balance. It lessens the family's natural resistance to change.

Implicit rites pass without reflection. When the family does not reflect on the meaning and potential of change, they miss a key *faith* opportunity. Change always provides opportunity for faith growth. We can catch a glimpse of God's activity in our lives, and how we might respond to it. Yet, for adolescents, the moment passes quickly and the window of opportunity fades fast. Personal, familial, and communal reflection on the experience of change leads to the discovery of deeper meaning and perhaps even God's guidance.

Not all spontaneous rites of passage lack the element of reflection. Occasionally, the experience is profound enough (e.g., teenage pregnancy) to stop all family members in their tracks, and cause them to search for God's grace. Or, for some families, reflection and questioning naturally work their way into the process. Even if the rite itself was not planned or anticipated, some families hold a posture that allows them to reflect and see God's activity in their lives.

We should encourage families to be explicit in their rites of passage. Without being phony or contrived, they can embrace change in a deliberate manner, especially when the youth ministry effort models good, simple, effective ritual that respects adolescent life while maintaining family integrity. Can youth ministry leaders focus programming activities around adolescent rites of passage (e.g., graduation, first employment, driving, etc. as well as spiritual growth through retreat experience, service projects, and confirmation) that invite family participation or an extension of the celebration at home? Parents may be at a loss for how to ritualize with their teens, but will likely jump at the chance to participate at the teen's initiative. Can we give them ideas to take home?

These efforts can help teens and their families reflect on questions such as, "What is God trying to show us through this experience?" If families are explicit with some of their life changes, they will also be in closer touch with those rites of passage which occur implicitly. And they will be less likely to gloss over some important life-changes that family members experience.

A helpful example can be found in parallel prayers on the same topic. In his book, *Why Can't We Talk: Prayers for Parents and Teenagers*, Mobby Larson offers a collection of prayers written from a viewpoint of teenagers and their parents. Consider this example of "A Great Play."

From a teen:

> Hey God,
>
> Did you see what I did today? It was a fantastic play—the whole team was proud of me! I felt so good I could have burst! I knew it was going to be a good day...
>
> I came home full of excitement and tried to tell my folks about it, but they just told me to hurry up for dinner...

From a parent:

> Dear God,
>
> I blew it today... She came home all excited from a game and wanted to tell us all about it. But we were running late and had already held up dinner. By the time we had time to talk, she didn't want to any more... (Larson 24–25).

Significant faith encounters themselves sometimes provide a key moment of change, growth and passage. A year or so after obtaining my driver's license, I had a faith experience that was a beginning step toward shaping my adult life. Unfortunately, my family was not as receptive to my new found faith at 17 as they had been with my new found independence at 16. I grew up in a "good Catholic family," so they were a bit wary when I started talking about my "personal relationship with Jesus." Oh, they acted supportive and said nice things, but from the very beginning I was on my own for this life change. There was never a rite of passage celebrated around the dinner table. There were no well-meaning and "knowing" jokes. Perhaps they could not celebrate with me because I was moving into uncharted waters not yet experienced by anyone in the family. The result: even to this day, 15 years later, my parents are not comfortable conversing with me about my faith and ministry. The point is that families need and benefit from these rites of passage just as much as the individual.

SACRAMENTAL NATURE

The value of rites of passage goes beyond just facilitating change and transition. Rites of passage also provide sacramental moments for the family in their daily lives. These can be faith enriching, catechetical moments when teens and their families recognize God's activity in their lives, and respond to it.

John H. Westerhoff speaks of faith development in three phrases. *Affiliative faith* is "expressed as religion of the heart, more than of the head or will." Persons with affiliative faith are dependent on the community for the shape and expression of their faith. They are community dependent, and yearn for belonging and participation. Faith identity is rooted on the community rather than self, and spiritual life is enhanced through the work and ritual of the community.

Those teens who are ever-devoted to all activities of the youth program probably are persons of affiliative faith. Their need to belong drives them to participate in the welcoming environment of the parish youth program.

Searching Faith is marked by intellectual analyzing of beliefs and faith related practices. The mind dominates the heart, and questions arise much more frequently than answers.

For teens, this stage marks the search for religious and faith identity. They may "try on" several different belief systems for short periods of time, in the all consuming effort to answer who am I? where do I belong? what causes are worth living for? etc.

Amid this searching and intellectualizing, teens still carry the needs of affiliative faith: the need to belong and participate, even while they may struggle with the authority of the community. This is the time when they feel caught between the faith they were given as a child, and their own maturing faith. These are times of difficult and anxiety for both teen and community, but necessary nonetheless for faith to ripen into maturity.

Owned Faith, then, is the faith of adulthood; having gained a personal sense of identity and conviction. Westerhoff describes these individuals as "still in need of community and personally committed to a community's understandings and ways, persons with owned faith reveal themselves to be inner-directed, open to others, but clear and secure in the own faith identity." Even still the needs of earlier styles of faith continue.

Adolescent faith reflects that of both children and adults. Though it would seem adolescents would be primarily in the searching faith phase, this implies the broader community is helping them "search;" e.g., wrestle with their life-questions of self-esteem, personal strengths and weaknesses, loneliness, etc. Unfortunately, this support cannot be counted on, and so Westerhoff asserts that teens must have a community that deliberately nurtures and ritualizes affiliative faith.

Adolescent rites of passage mark times of change, transition, and maturity. Family rituals should not only address the teen's affective needs (feeling good and secure) but should also set a tone for healthy searching, intellectualizing, and questioning. Adolescent rites of passage can be brief windows of opportunity for God's grace to explode in the life of the teen and his or her family. If we are aware of the predominant style of faith (affiliative, searching, owned), the ritual will more likely hit the mark.

THE CHALLENGE OF RITUAL WITH ADOLESCENTS

Youth ministry of the past focused much attention solely on teens themselves to the point of segregation from adults and children. There are some advantages to this segregation; creating community of peers, providing activities that all can enjoy and relate to, speaking a common language, etc. Yet when it comes to key rites of passage for teens, segregation is neither helpful nor desirable for teens, their families, or the entire faith community.

Peer group isolation prevents growth. When teens are confronted with their adolescent challenges and transitions, they need to be grounded by their history (childhood) and uplifted by their hopes for the future (adulthood). They need to see folks who show them what has been, and what is to come. Rituals of separation cannot provide these broad range experiences. Also, too much segregation tends to put teens in a "fishbowl"-like situation for all around to see; which in turn serves to bring out their most bizarre and unpredictable behavior.

Separation hurts the family and community as well. It communicates that the generations have nothing in common and nothing of value to say to each other, which is simply not true. Adolescents need intergenerational experiences of community. Even while experiencing the highly volatile issues of adolescence, they are still human and still have many of the same needs as all persons. Their maturity depends on meeting these common human needs as much as meeting their specific developmental and social needs. Teens must be included in the normal life of the community and the family.

Full inclusion implies an understanding and acceptance of the particular adolescent needs as well. From an intergenerational viewpoint, how can we acknowledge and celebrate *adolescent* rites of passage? Just recognizing that most adolescent experiences are "normal," developmental, culturally universal, and foundational to maturity will allow the adult population to see that they are worth celebrating. These experiences need not be seen as abnormal, curious, or unique. Adults are challenged here to view adolescence through their own personal history and growth into adulthood. What was it like when you were a teen? Who were the folks who helped you ease into adulthood?

Experiences that trigger or complete adolescent rites of passage are not the same for all teens and their families. Yet some common experiences mark key points of transition and maturity. These may include such events as graduation, obtaining a driver's license, first date, first love lost, moving, new school, new car, first job, confirmation, etc. Parents and families should try to be aware of how these events impact the lives of their teens. It can be greatly beneficial for all to ritualize these times of change in the family. These are significant life events that need to be celebrated. These events open the door to new opportunities and new responsibilities. Celebrating and ritualizing them empowers all members to maintain their Christian purpose while adjusting to new status and roles. A few suggestions for family celebrations are appropriate here...

- Remember: the experiences of adolescence provide many opportunities to create and celebrate new ritual expressions and rites of passage as a family—if you are brave enough to seize them.

- If celebrating ritual moments is new to your family, start small. Choose an event or occasion that marks a real turning point in your life as a family (first job, getting a learner's permit, etc.) and mark it with a simple but festive meal that includes a prayer or reading, reflection or story telling, and a short blessing. If your family has made a habit or ritual sharing, know that some of your "traditional" family rites will fall to the wayside during adolescence as your family grows and changes.

- Involve all family members in planning and celebrating the ritual event. While the ritual may focus on an event of particular significance for a single family member, the *way* you celebrate should remind everyone of the interconnectedness of family life.

- Celebrate adolescent rites in adolescent ways. Incorporate music, food, readings, stories, etc., that speak to adolescent life.

- Involve family friends in your ritual sharing. Invite key members of your extended family and your adolescent's special friends to take part. Hospitality is a treasured trait in healthy families.

- Keep the sharing and ritual simple and straightforward. If the events you celebrate are central to your life as a family, God's presence should not be too hard to identify.

- Do not force participation. Schedule the celebration for a time that is convenient for all family members. Make the experience as attractive as possible. If a family member declines to take part, go ahead anyway.

The parish community can help a great deal in celebrating rites of life passage for adolescents. In a formal way, they can involve parents and family members in rites connected to graduation, confirmation, etc. Families then have a model which the can replicate informally. One Catholic high school involved parents in their commencement exercises by having them help distribute diplomas. This ritualistic involvement empowered many of those families to celebrate this key passage at home as well. It was already an event in which the whole family was participating.

The brief essays which follow offer different perspectives on how parishes and families can work in partnership to mark adolescence as a major time of passage for young people and for their families. More important than specific approaches offered is the challenge for families and parishes to work together to create new ways of celebrating adolescence and its meaning for the family and wider community.

WORKS CITED

Larson, Mobby. *Why Can't We Talk: Prayers for Parents and Teenagers*. Mystic, CT: Twenty-Third Publications, 1990.

Westerhoff, John H. "Rituals for Adolescence." *Access Guides to Youth Ministry: Liturgy & Worship*. Ed. John Roberto. New Rochelle: Don Bosco Multimedia, 1990.

CHAPTER 16:
RITUALS

Developing Alternative Rites of Passage for Adolescents

John H. Westerhoff, III

CONFIRMATION AND ADOLESCENT RITES OF PASSAGE

In most societies persons move from childhood to adulthood in a single move. Rites of passage or transition were established to aid that change in role and status. But in our society where adolescence lasts for more than a decade there is no single public rite that has meaning. Still the cultural need for passage from childhood to adulthood persists, and many have assumed or tried to make confirmation fill that important social role. But confirmation is not and never has been a rite of passage from one role and status to another. Confirmation is a rite of intensification, affirming role and status previously established at baptism. As such, it is conceivably a repeatable rite appropriate whenever one wishes to engage in it, aiding an individual to affirm and re-establish his or her role and status as a baptized person. Insofar as confirmation can never satisfy the needs of an adolescent, persons in our society during these years are left with a psycho-social void to be replaced by unhealthy rites of passage sometimes related to driving the car, engaging in intercourse, drinking alcoholic beverages or using drugs, and so forth.

A healthy rite of passage or transition has certain characteristics. The rite itself begins with a ritual/ceremonial separation from one's current status and role, followed by a period of transition characterized by the experience of liminality (being betwixt and between), ordeal (leading to an experience of "communitas"), and formation (preparation for one's new role and status). The rite ends with a second ritual/ceremonial which re-incorporates the person into the community in his or her new status and role.

In most simple societies there is a rite of passage for boys and girls which is intended to aid their movement from childhood to adulthood, a process which involves a liminal ordeal of separation from the community and a process of enculturation or formation so that they may be fashioned into persons able to function as adults in the community. A society which lacks such rites becomes dysfunctional, and persons who do not have the experiences of such rites tend to manifest unhealthy behavior.

Our society needs badly to create a true rite of passage *for* adolescence, which is very different from a rite of passage *from* childhood to adulthood. The Church in its history has developed rites to meet life cycle needs. Today we need to create a new one for adolescence and separate it from confirmation.

ALTERNATIVE RITES OF PASSAGE FOR ADOLESCENTS

Adolescents in our culture and society require a rite of responsibility. Somewhere around seventh or eighth grade or twelve years of age the Church needs to celebrate a ritual/ceremonial in which boys and girls are separated from childhood and officially inducted into the beginning of adolescence. It might best take place on their birthday and would be seen as an individual rite similar to the bar or bat mitzvah in the Jewish tradition. Parents would present their child to the community and pray a public prayer thanking God for taking away the full burden and responsibility of their child's faith and conduct, as well as asking for the graces needed to be present to and support their child as he or she moves through adolescence into adulthood. The child would make a statement before the community accepting the ordeal of learning to be responsible for her or his own faith and life. The community would give each child a gift, such as a Bible, to guide each one on the way. A sponsor, an adult other than the parents, chosen by the community and the child, would be presented and commissioned to be responsible for accompanying the child on his or her pilgrimage.

Somewhere around twelfth grade or eighteen years of age the church would celebrate a second ritual/ceremonial in which the adolescent would be separated from adolescence and inducted into the beginnings of adulthood. Again it would take place on his or her birthday and would be an event in which the sponsor presents the young man or woman to the community, summarizing his or her preparation, accomplishments, and promise. Such youths should make a statement on their readiness to assume responsibility for their faith and life and promise at an appropriate time in the future to renew their baptismal vows and covenant following significant preparation. During the service they would assume an adult role such as reading a lesson in the liturgy and perhaps would choose a saint they would like to emulate and be given a symbol of their life with a charge to assume responsibility for their faith and life and prayers for the graces needed to do. An appropriate party would follow.

During this eight-year period a program, part personal and part social, would be developed to aid adolescents to be able to assume responsibility for their own faith and life. If we can give birth to such a rite and its related catechetical process, I suspect we will experience few dropouts during adolescence.

CHAPTER 16:
RITUALS

Quince Años: Celebrating a Hispanic Rite of Passage for Youth

Angela Erevia, MCDP

BACKGROUND ON QUINCE AÑOS

The *Quince Años* (15 years) celebration marks the passage from childhood to adult life. It traces its roots to the native peoples of Latin America.

When Spanish missionaries arrived in Mexico in the 1500s, they found the Aztecs and the Maya practicing some rich religious traditions. Life for the natives was sacred; their whole lives revolved around their gods, temples, and religious events. In order to find favor with their gods, they ritualized every critical stage of life from birth to death. One such ceremony was the initiation rites at puberty, which consisted primarily of separating the child from his or her mother, introducing the child to the sacred, and initiating him or her into a life of service to the community. The elements of such ceremonies varied from group to group. The Maya ceremony was particularly interesting and very elaborate. Sylvanus G. Morley describes it in great detail in his book *The Ancient Maya* (Stanford University Press).

The Maya always designated a special day for the puberty rites, a day they believed to portend good fortune. A leader of the town was appointed to sponsor all the boys and girls participating in the rites. The sponsor's task was to assist the priest during the rites and to furnish the feast that followed. Four honorable old men called *chacs* assisted the sponsor and the priest.

On the day of the ceremony, all participants gathered in the courtyard of the sponsor's house which was purified by the priest to drive out evil spirits. Godparents were picked—an old man for the boys and an old woman for the girls.

The *chacs* then placed on the children's heads pieces of white cloth brought by the mothers. The older children were asked if they had committed any sin. If they said "yes," they were separated from the others. (We do not know whether they were excluded from further participation in the rites.) The priest ordered everyone to be seated and to preserve absolute silence. He then pronounced a benediction on the children.

Next the sponsor of the ceremony tapped each child nine times on the forehead with a bone given to him by the priest, moistening their foreheads, faces, and the spaces between their fingers and toes with water.

After this anointing, the priest removed the white cloths from the children's heads. The boys and girls then gave the *chacs* gifts of feathers and cacao beans. The priest cut the white beads which the boys wore on their heads. Pipe-smoking attendants gave the children a puff of smoke. The youth were then given food brought by their mothers, and a wine offering was made to the gods.

The mothers removed from their daughters the red shell each wore as a symbol of purity, indicating that they had reached the age for marriage. First the girls were dismissed, and then the boys. When the children had gone, the parents passed out presents to the officials and the spectators—pieces of cotton cloth. The ceremony then ended with much eating and drinking.

Clearly, these puberty rites situated young people within the adult life of their community, and had a profoundly religious character. A priest conducted the ceremony. The elderly took the important role of godparents. The parents provided gifts which were integral to the ceremony. A confession and benediction signified the reconciliation of the young with the people of their community. The period of silence indicated serious reflection on what was happening. A feast was given in the young people's honor. The whole ceremony was designed to recognize and affirm the young people.

CELEBRATING QUINCE AÑOS TODAY

Today, as in the days of the Maya, young people need the recognition and affirmation of adults as they search for their own personal identity. Adolescents, who are going through one of the most difficult periods of life, need significant people to surround them with love and care so that they may develop their self-esteem and believe in themselves.

One way that Hispanics do this is through the celebration of a young person's life at age 15, the age at which an intense push towards adulthood begins. A well-planned *quince años* enriches not only the 15-year-olds but their families and friends as well.

In preparation for the celebration—a Mass of Thanksgiving—the young people and all the persons involved take formal instruction. Lessons include a brief history of the *quince años* tradition and the reasons for celebrating it. Participants also explore the idea that God is calling the young people

to be prophets of their times, to articulate new ways of living the Christian values of the Gospel. The value of peer-to-peer ministry is also stressed. A study of the sacraments of Initiation is a key part of the program, focusing on new ways for the young people to celebrate their Christian commitment. Most of them were baptized as infants; therefore, a fresh look at Baptism, Confirmation, and Eucharist helps them to be more aware of their dignity and their place within the family and the Church community. Far in advance of the *quince años* celebration, there is a day of recollection that concludes with a celebration of the sacrament of Reconciliation.

Finally, the day for *quince años* comes. The Mass begins with a procession at which time the youth may present the following gifts:

Birth Certificate: a symbol of gratitude to God and to their parents for the gift of life.

Baptismal Robe: a symbol of their putting on the mind and the heart of Christ.

Baptismal Shoes: a symbol of their walking in the footsteps of Christ and their willingness to walk with others so that they too may discover Christ in their lives and follow after him.

Baptismal Candle: a symbol of Christ, the Light of the World, inviting them to be a light for one another and for us.

Confirmation Recuerdo (Memento): a symbol of the gifts of the Holy Spirit which made them holy people of God.

Crown: a symbol of their sharing in the mission of Christ as Priest, King, and Servant King.

The readings for a *quince años* Mass are carefully selected to emphasize the important role that the youth play in our family and in our Church community. At the appropriate times of the Mass, the young people are called by name. One such time is after the homily when they are called to stand before the Christian community to renew their baptismal promises. After

Communion, they make an act of consecration to Our Lady of Guadalupe and offer a rose to Our Lady as a sign of their fidelity to Jesus, her Son. Before the concluding prayers, the parents give a special blessing to their son or daughter who is participating in the *quince años* celebration.

The Mass concluded, a fiesta follows with gifts for the youths. Essential to the fiesta are song, dancing, and food as family and friends gather to celebrate and thank God for the gift of their 15-year-old's life!

Orita: A Rite of Passage for Youth of African-American Heritage

Nettie Cook-Dove

BACKGROUND ON ORITA

Orita (oh-ree-tah), an African word that comes from the Yoruba tribe native to Nigeria, Dahomey, and Togoland, means "crossroads," the point where two ways converge. This converging of two meaningful alternatives that cry out for one's loyalty is what choice is all about. The overall intention of the ritual is to help young people in the difficult passage to adult life and, particularly, to help them embrace the challenge of Gospel life in today's world.

Baptist minister Frank T. Fair developed the Orita ritual from African tradition for his son's sixteenth birthday. In Fair's vision, the recovery of individual moral discipline that is the focus of Orita can serve as a springboard to a concern for the future of the nation and the role the black community is to play. For blacks and other minorities in the U.S. it is "nation time," and there is a need to think in terms of a nation in which all men and women have a stake. The Orita process described here was developed by the community of Christ the King Parish in Miami, FL.

REQUIREMENTS

Requirements for the Orita ritual are meant to challenge the Orita pilgrim and ultimately to prepare him for adulthood.

The pilgrims and their mentors and parents collaborate on a schedule for completing the requirements. This planning will determine the length of time needed to enter into adulthood by means of this rite of passage, usually three months to one year. Requirements recommended by Fair are:

1. An understanding of the black experience in America
2. Managing the family budget
3. Community service
4. Exploration of career and educational opportunities
5. Citizenship
6. Bible study and reflection
7. Preparation for and execution of the Orita ceremony.

RECRUITING

Personal contact by parish leaders and young adults who have taken part in the Orita process in recent years is the most effective approach to recruitment. Personal letters and an open invitation published in the church bulletin can also be helpful.

Letters were sent to the parents of each prospective pilgrim with an application form to be returned, indicating whether the prospect would participate. If so, prospect and parents were invited to a welcome meeting. Young men who had participated in the previous year's ritual were also invited to this first meeting, along with their parents and their scrapbooks. Meeting participants were encouraged to take part in the Orita process and advised of the program schedule and requirements.

THE PROGRAM

During the second meeting, new pilgrims and their parents received program schedules and study guides to follow in meeting the reading requirements.

At the subsequent weekly meetings, the pilgrims became familiar with the Bible, and discussed selected parables from the Gospels. A member of the congregation gave uplifting spiritual lecture on following the teachings of Scripture to live as Christ wants us to live. Discussions also covered required readings from such books as *Up from Slavery* by Booker T. Washington and *The Souls of Block Folk* by William E. B. DuBois as well as progress reports about the pilgrims' individual preparations and communication with their parents and siblings.

Special topics and speakers at the weekly meetings included: the family budget; the rights and responsibilities of citizenship; career exploration with a placement specialist; community service with an experienced volunteer; and African traditional values with a graduate student from Kenya. In addition, the pilgrims were required to speak on assigned topics at Black Heritage Week celebrations and to prepare food for homeless people as part of the parish's ongoing program.

PREPARING FOR THE ORITA RITUAL

To prepare for the ceremony itself, pilgrims and parents were involved together in ordering invitations and medallions, printing programs, planning food for the reception, completing their scrapbooks and other exhibits for display at the reception, and preparing their addresses for the ceremony. A four-hour rehearsal covers all phases of the ceremony.

CELEBRATING THE ORITA RITE

Introductory Rites

1. Musical prelude: a) Organ prelude; b) Congregational singing ("Come By Here," "We Worship and Adore Thee," "Here I am Lord"); c) Solo ("Great Is Thy Faithfulness")

2. Opening procession

   a. Congregational singing

   b. Participants in procession: Parents and families of pilgrims; pilgrims; bishop, priests, deacons

3. Greeting and Welcome (pastor)

Presentation of the Candidates

Pastor: Who is it that comes to the Ritual of the Crossroads?

Pilgrims: It is, I, N. (Each pilgrim answers in turn.)

Pastor: Why do you come?

Pilgrims: We come because we are of the age of consciousness and have completed our assignments, and we desire God's blessing and the blessings of this religious community.

Pastor: Please stand. The Pilgrims come to the Ritual of the Crossroads because they are of the age of consciousness and have completed their requirements. Most importantly, they desire God's blessings and the blessings of this religious community. What do you say to this request?

All: Amen! Amen! Amen!

Liturgy of the Word

1. Old Testament Reading: Proverbs 4:20–25 (or Is 55:10–11)

2. Responsorial Psalm: Psalm 65:10, 11, 12–13, 14

3. Proclamation of the Gospel: Matthew 13:1–9

4. Homily

Celebration of Maturity

1. Invitation to Prayer (Pastor): Eternal God, in the process of becoming what we shall be, we pray that you will play an indispensable part in our lives, for you are, indeed, the source of all our life. We have come to celebrate the beautiful years that these pilgrims have been allowed to live. While they are still in adolescence, we pray that they may examine critically where they desire to be in the next ten years and afterwards. Grant that their hopes will be realized by helping others less fortunate and by giving their support to worthy causes. Let them always strive to know and to do your holy will. Amen!

2. Charge by the Congregation: Do your utmost to present yourself each day to God with a clean heart, as a workman and with nothing to be ashamed of. Be sure to tell the truth at all times when you speak. Be sure to shun empty speeches that violate what is holy, for they will advance to more and more ungodliness. Regardless of the advance in technology, the fear of God is the beginning of wisdom.

3. Litany of Desire

   Pilgrims: Lord, we pray for
      understanding.
   All: Lord, grand them understanding.

   Pilgrims: Lord, we pray for wisdom.
   All: Lord, grant them wisdom.

   Pilgrims: Lord, we pray to live
      righteously.
   All: Lord, grant them righteous lives.

   Pilgrims: Lord, we pray for strength.
   All: Lord, grant them spiritual strength.

   Pilgrims: Lord, we pray for courage.
   All: Lord grant them courage to live a
      godly life.

   Pilgrims: Lord, we pray for your sweet
      spirit.
   All: Lord, grant them your sweet spirit
      to live a godly life.

   Pilgrims: Amen!

4. Challenges

   Brief words of inspiration and challenge offered by 1) a young adult; 2) mothers' representative; 3) fathers' representative.

5. The Laying on of Hands

   The pilgrims kneel before the altar. They are blindfolded by their fathers to symbolize their unknown future. When the blindfolding has been completed, all family members, beginning with parents and grandparents, come forward and place their hands on the pilgrims' heads.

6. Prayer of Blessing (pastor, or deacon): Holy One, we give you thanks that you have led us by an inner light through the midst of darkness and on strange paths. We do not know what the future holds for these young men, but we know that you hold the future. Suffer no hurt, harm, or danger to overwhelm them. Let them make sensible choices so that they will not become slaves to foolishness or deny the best development of their character. May they let Jesus Christ so dominate their lives that they will not be selfish, afraid, or negligent in the service of others. May they have unfaltering trust in you as you guide them through the trackless paths of moral decisions and pluralistic beliefs. May the inner light guide them at midnight and through the swamps of conflicting ideologies.

7. Presentation of Medallion

   Fathers now place medallions around the necks of their sons who are still kneeling. Then pilgrims stand and blindfolds are removed. A representatives of the fathers addresses the pilgrims:

   Representative: This medallion symbolizes the crossroads, the history, and the middle passage our ancestors had to make in slave ships. Do you promise to war it well and make the best choices that you can make, never bringing shame on your head, on this religious community, or, above all, on your God?
   Pilgrims: We do.

Representative: Should you marry and have a child, will you consider passing this medallion on to them?
Pilgrims: We will.

8. Address by the Pilgrims

Each pilgrim gives a brief testimony concerning his experience of passage to maturity. The congregation will applaud each testimony, and sing "Amen!"

9. Pilgrims' Prayer: All-knowing God, be with us in our finite search for good ideas. Stir us from unchallenging mediocrity that demands nothing of us in return. Help us to fix our lives on a cause greater than ourselves, that we may save our souls. Let us delve into the past of our ancestry that we may feel a common cause with them in their strides toward freedom, justice, and human dignity. Father in heaven, grant us the intelligence to ask graciously the right questions so that we may divide truth from fiction. Help us through discipline to arrive at the right answers to questions. O God, grant that in you we may find the power of self-reliance and self-help. Let us encourage brotherly and sisterly socioeconomic enterprises among our people. And this day, as we look into the future, let our reach exceed our grasp that we may choose, at the Orita of life, what is noble and best. Through Jesus Christ our Lord. Amen!

Concluding Rites

1. Community challenge: Program chairperson offers brief words of challenge to all.
2. Blessing and dismissal (pastor)
3. Closing procession

BIBLIOGRAPHY

Fair, Frank T. *Orita for Black Youth: An Initiation into Christian Adulthood.* Valley Forge, PA: Judson Press, 1977.

Hare, Nathan and Julia. *Bringing the Black Boy to Manhood: The Passage.* San Francisco: The Black Think Tank, 1985.

Hill, Paul, Jr. *Passage to Manhood: Rearing the Male African-American Child.* Detroit: National Black Child Development Institute, 1989.

Karenga, Maulana. *Kwanzaa: Origin, Concepts, Practice.* Inglewood, CA: Kawaida Publications, 1977.

CHAPTER 16:
RITUALS

A Graduation Celebration

from Family Rituals and Celebrations

Because graduation is the culmination of so much that is intensely personal, one family invented a tradition that has become significant for them, the personal diploma.

The personal diploma began as something to complement the institutional diploma received by an 18-year-old son. In contrast to the somber black lettering on white parchment, this diploma is elaborately decorated with a colorful and intricate border that appeared at first to be a fruit-and-flower design but, on closer inspection, actually was interspersed with footballs, football helmets, and baseball mitts.

The text, done in calligraphy, was long and personal. It celebrated four years of high school, including adolescent compulsions, successes, and failures. It touched on such things as driving, dating, and working, as well as math, music, English literature, sports, and special family times.

Naturally, each graduate would deserve different commemorative details. This is how theirs began:

> *To our son _____ on his graduation on this, the 5th day of June, 19___, we present this diploma in honor of four rich, and sometimes arduous, years at _____ High School.*
>
> *As you collect this diploma and move on to the next stage of your development, we, your loving and proud parents, remember the vivid moments of these important years . . .*

The parents wrote the text themselves

and found a local artist to design their diploma. It is beautifully framed and now hangs in their son's room at college. This tradition is just the kind of personal and creative response that produces the warmth and satisfaction and pleasure we all want in our families.

Incorporate Scripture, prayer and story telling into your family graduation celebration.   Scripture: Ecclesiastes 3:1–8 reminds us there is a time for everything—and that God is with us in all seasons. It can serve as a reminder of God's ongoing presence in the midst of change.

Prayer: Develop a special family prayer that expresses your thanks and/or your hopes for your graduating son or daughter, or use the following:

Parent/Leader:

> (Name) you are a unique creation, a person blessed by God with life, a person called, in love, to grow and to share your gifts with others.
>
> We come together today to celebrate your accomplishments, to reflect on who you are for us, and to share our dreams for your future.
>
> May your graduation day be filled with happiness and joy.
>
> We rejoice in who you are for us as a family, calling to mind especially your gifts of _____ and _____.

(Family members can be invited to share comments and stories here that speak of the uniqueness and giftedness of the graduate)

> May God continue to bless you and challenge you.
> May you always be surrounded by people who support and love you.

May you grow more fully into the man/woman that God wants you to be, and that the world so desperately needs.

We ask this today, in hope and expectation that God will continue the great things already begun in you. Amen.

CHAPTER 17

Activities for Service and Justice Ideas

Thomas Bright

ACTION IDEAS INCORPORATING JUSTICE WITHIN THE HOME

Re-assessing Family Roles and Responsibilities

As a family, keep track of how family responsibilities are shared at home (who does what, how often, how long). After a month, evaluate what the list tells you about family roles and responsibilities. What criteria are used for deciding who does what—gender, talent, availability, desire, sharing the tough stuff evenly? Are family tasks shared justly? Why or why not? Try out a new configuration of sharing tasks round home for a month or two, then sit down again to evaluate how well the system is working. Young people's involvement in seasonal sports and extracurricular activities often means that some months are overcrowded while others are thin on outside commitments. Re-assessing family responsibilities on a regular basis can help see that tasks are shared equitably, keep everyone attuned to what is going on in family member's lives, and create a bit more openness to "going the extra mile" with household tasks when it is needed.

Family Finances

Talk through finances regularly so that all family members have a better idea about what is involved in budgeting and how much things really cost. Decide how and when major purchases will be made. Discuss together how the family shares its resources with others, how much of the family income goes to church, charitable and social change groups, and how the money is divided.

Youth, Families, and Peaceful Conflict Resolution

Sharing expectations and developing realistic guidelines for action and discipline before problems arise helps keep family tension under control when times get tough. Institute regular (biweekly, monthly, seasonal) family meetings to assess family needs, discuss family guidelines, ease tensions, and plan future family events. Develop an agenda together, keep track of what's been decided, and regularly rotate leadership.

Bring Justice into Your Family Celebrations

Add a new birthday celebration or holiday to those you presently celebrate, honoring a justice hero or heroine (local or global, unsung or universally recognized). Share and treasure their stories as part of your family's celebration of who it is.

Youth, Families, and Justice Spirituality

Incorporate justice in how you pray together as a family. Take turns offering grace before meals. Ask individuals to include three elements in their prayer: a general note of thanksgiving (Thank you God for food, and friends, and family), a specific personal insight or need prompted by the day's experience (thanks, too for the weather), and an element that incorporates a community or global perspective (may this meal strengthen us to continue your work of feeding the hungry or assisting those in _____ who are suffering from _____).

Youth, Families, and Ecology

Do an Ecology Home Inspection as a family. Pinpoint things that could be changed to make your home more ecologically sound. Determine ecology priorities, a schedule for improvements, and a responsibility list.

Eating for a Week on a Food Stamps Budget

Plan your meal menu a week or month in advance as a family, then shop together for the food you need. Keep your meal budget to $1.65 or less per person per day—the financial allotment provided to families that receive U.S. Government food stamps. As you eat your simple meals (and refrain from eating sneaky snacks on the side) think about and pray for those for whom this exercise is an ongoing necessity. Let the activity flow naturally into a discussion of the extent and causes of poverty locally and in the country.

DISCUSSION IDEAS FOR INCORPORATING JUSTICE WITHIN THE HOME

Discussing Justice Issues and Concerns

Families do not need to look far beyond the home to find justice issues that impact their lives and the lives of families like themselves throughout the world. Helping family members grow in their understanding of the justice issues they meet in day to day life can be an important first step to ongoing involvement in justice activities. Use any of the following approaches as a starting point with your family.

Justice Issues as Played Out in the News and Popular Media

Use the justice issues played out in daily newscasts or newspapers as a springboard for helping young people what they think about, or how they might react to similar situations in their own lives. A rash of stories or articles on environmental pollution, racism, homelessness, or world hunger offers parents an opportunity to share the stories or questions they have about the issue. It can serve, as well, as an opportunity for young people to look at how well they incorporate their own beliefs into their relationships with others at home, at school, and in the local community.

If you are watching the evening news together, ask what your son or daughter thinks about the situation being described. Raise questions about causes, consequences, and the options open to the people involved in the story reported. Move beyond the questions of who, what, and when, to the issues of why and how. Discuss, for example: Why did people respond as they did? What values are at stake in the story? How could things have been handled differently? How might you react in a similar situation?

Talk through an issue of local, national, or global injustice from your local newspaper or a news magazine, over a meal or at any other convenient time. Issues that impact "close to home," that is, that directly affect your child, the community she or he lives in, or people of his or her age, offer an easier starting place for family or one-on-one discussion. Let your child know what you think and why, without expecting him or her to mouth exactly the same sentiments. Talking the issues through together with respect for one another's thoughts and opinions is far more important than agreeing on all the details.

Popular media (music and movies, television programs and video games) provide abundant examples of justice issues that demand a considered response from Christians. Here too, the process of dialogue is far more important than the ultimate decision. Young adolescents can learn a lot about communication skills and interpersonal relationships from such discussions. They can also learn what Christians think about justice issues and begin to use these learnings in formulating their own views about issues of importance in their lives.

Justice Issues as Played Out in Life Experiences and Relationships

As older adolescents assume greater responsibility for their personal lives, expand their circle of friends and acquaintances, and take on part-time jobs in the "adult" world, issues of justice that once seemed abstract may become very real. Prejudice, or sexism, or unequal treatment in the work place may, for the first time, be personally experienced or experienced vicariously in the life of a friend. Having parents or other trusted adults around to share stories with, and to help differentiate the "crummy" from the criminal in personal experiences can be a great benefit.

Justice Issues in Popular Videos

View together a feature-length video which deals with issues of justice or human rights. Justice videos like the following can be rented through your local video store: *Cry Freedom, Mandela, Romero, Stand and Deliver, Gandhi, Dry White Season.* Consult *Media, Faith and Families* (Don Bosco Multimedia, 1992) for descriptions of each of these films and for activities to discuss feature films in the home.

If your parish has a library or resource center, check to see if there is a study guide for the video you are using. Prior to watching the video, see what family members know about the video and the issues with which it deals. Share any questions you may have about the issues and what you will be watching for during the movie. After viewing the film, discuss questions like the following:

- How did the film make you feel?
- What were the most memorable scenes or images?

- Which of the characters seems most interesting to you? Were there conflicts?
- What was this film all about? What did it say or teach? What did you learn that you did not already know? (could be one, two, or many things)
- Discuss which episodes, incidents, or images enabled you to understand better how people's human rights can be violated and/or protected.
- Have family members share any new insights or learnings they gained from the film.

ACTIVITIES FOR FAMILY INVOLVEMENT

Youth, Families, and Community Involvement

As a family keep track of how you share your time and energy with others through volunteer service commitments. After a month or two, evaluate what your service involvement says about you as a family. Discuss with one another what you're involved in and why. Do family members think they/you should be doing more or less? Why or why not? Are there ways to reshape present service commitments to allow greater family involvement? What about the balance of home and away-from-home activities? What can you do together to guarantee a better balance of the two?

Experiencing the Impact of Injustice on Peers

It is difficult for young people to understand the impact of injustice on people's lives until they experience injustice personally or see its effects on their peers. Investigate, as a family, the needs of youth living in residential treatment facilities in your community (drug and alcohol treatment facilities, detention and correctional institutions, residences for abused or abandoned children and youth, homes for pregnant teen mothers, etc.) Discuss together the problems and situations that forced young people into these settings and how these same problems are played out in your neighborhood or town. Talk with a social worker, chaplain, or minister at one of the facilities about how your family can support one of its young residents through letter writing and visits or by responding to regular or seasonal needs. Follow through on the contact.

A Hands-On Approach to Family Service

For many adolescents, "who I am" is defined largely in terms of "what I do." Involving them as family members in hands-on service to others helps them to understand that service is integral to who we are as Christian families and as church. Explore the possibilities for volunteer service with local soup kitchens and homeless shelters, hospitals and community service organizations. Choose, as a family, a service project and site that best fits your schedule and abilities. Prepare together for your service involvement, learning what you need to know to be comfortable at the work site. Do the project together, working as a family unit or in pairs, helping each other as needed. When the project is finished, debrief it together, sharing the highs and lows of the experience, your thoughts and feelings, and your suggestions for making the experience better next time around. Finally, bring your family experience to prayer, offering simple petitions of thanksgiving or need for what you learned about yourself and others through the experience and, especially for the gift you are to one another as a family.

When looking at service options, explore opportunities for both direct and indirect service.

Direct Service puts families in direct contact with those they are serving. Such projects may include: serving at a soup kitchen or homeless shelter, distributing items at a food bank, visiting a retirement or nursing home, working at a hospital or day care center, sandbagging with flood victims, helping Red Cross during local emergencies, responding to needs in your parish or neighborhood (chores for home bound, child care for single parents, visits to the sick, etc.), working with Special Olympics or L'arche communities for the developmentally challenged, participating in or initiating environmental programs.

Indirect Service puts families and young people in touch with the issues in a different way. It is not always possible to be in direct contact with those in need, and yet needs can still be met through indirect projects such as:

> *Collection campaigns.* Donation drives for food, clothing, money, and supplies are common and needed projects. Direct collection involves actively soliciting donations from family, friends, neighbors and bringing them to church. Indirect collection involves providing publicity and collection points at church or neighborhood stores. Families can take responsibility for emptying the collection containers when necessary, and arranging for distribution of items to agencies serving the needy.
>
> *Correspondence.* Pen pal programs can provide connections to people in need through written correspondence. Establishing pen pals with families in other countries can be a valuable tool for making global connections. Correspondence can be created with people in prison, care centers, military personnel, missionary workers, political leaders, and others not accessible by direct contact. Relationships developed through pen pals can be as life changing as those experienced face-to-face.

A Word of Family Concern

Write a joint letter to your state or congressional legislators about an issue of concern to your family. If the letter is about an issue currently on the agenda for legislative consideration, it will carry additional weight. By following the bill's progress through the legal process the entire family will get a better idea of how a bill becomes law and how people can let their voices be heard around on of equality and justice.

Acts of Boycott/Acts of Support

Issues of environmental concern or economic justice on a national or international level are sometimes hard to get a handle on. They often seem too big to get involved in, or too complicated to be able to do anything about. Boycotting offers one approach to cutting enormous problems down to individual or family size. If you are concerned about a company's environmental or employment practices, boycott their goods or services. Write a letter to the company as a family, detailing your concerns and the action you are taking. Boycotts in the past have proved very effective as a means of shifting company policies and practices—even with large national or international concerns like Gallo wines or the Nestle's Corporation.

ORGANIZING PARISH SERVICE PROJECTS FOR FAMILIES WITH YOUTH

People are too easily defined in our society according to economic categories. Direct service opportunities need to be designed in a way that allows people both to work *for* the poor and to work side by side *with* the poor. In this way we meet the poor as "people like us," people with talents and gifts to share, capable of impacting situations and structures that are harmful to the dignity of all. Parents play a crucial role in passing on values and modeling faith life. Parishes can assist parents in this task by organizing service project that help families work together around issues of justice and service. Organizing a service project for families with youth includes the following steps:

1. Explore the service opportunities already available through your parish, school, diocese, and local community organizations.

2. Select a service opportunity that meets the needs and resources of your group of families, *and* that allows them to work alongside those who are poor or otherwise disadvantaged.

3. Before moving to respond to the service need you've selected, learn a bit about why the service is needed. Use the resources of your own community or of the service site to help families explore: What are some of the problems and concerns faced by people in our community? What are the root causes of the problem? How long have these problems existed and how have they changed through the years? What signs of hope exist that the situation might someday change? Apart from involvement in direct service, what can be done to change structures that keep the problem in place? Understanding the history and causes helps us see the people hurt by injustice and inequity in a different light.

4. As you set up your service venture, make sure there's time allotted for people contact. In the case of youth, contact with peers is particularly important. Justice issues are seen much differently by youth when they're viewed through the eyes of their peers. Offer families options and opportunities for continuing their involvement in the project after the initial service event.

5. Evaluate the project as a group and bring your new experiences to prayer. Provide discussion questions, resource information, and prayer materials that can help families continue their involvement when they return home.

Further information on organizing service programming can be found in Chapter 13, "Service and Action for Justice" in *Access Guides to Youth Ministry: Justice*, Eds. by Thomas Bright and John Roberto, New Rochelle: Don Bosco Multimedia, 1990.

RESOURCES FOR ORGANIZING PARISH AND FAMILY INVOLVEMENT IN JUSTICE AND SERVICE

The following list of print and video materials provides a solid, basic collection of resources helpful in helping families with youth, and the broader parish community, to better understand issues of justice that touch the local and world community.

SELECTED RESOURCES ON JUSTICE AWARENESS AND ACTION

Acting for Justice

Baumgarten, Bruce, et al. *On The Move: Activities for a Year of Early Adolescent Ministry*. New Rochelle, NY: Don Bosco Multimedia, 1992.

Bright, Thomas, ed. *Poverty: Do It Justice!*. New Rochelle, NY: Don Bosco Multimedia, 1992.

Bright, Thomas and John Roberto. *Human Rights: Do It Justice!*. New Rochelle, NY: Don Bosco Multimedia, 1992.

Condon, Camy and James McGinnis. *Helping Kids Care: Harmony Building Activities for Home, Church and School*. Bloomington: Meyer-Stone Books, 1988.

The Earth Works Group. *50 Simple Things You Can Do to Save the Earth*. Berkeley, CA: Earthworks Press, 1989.

_____. *50 Simple Things Kids Can Do to Save the Earth*. Kansas City, MO: Andrews and McMeel, 1990.

_____. *The Next Step: 50 More Things You Can Do to Save the Earth*. Kansas City, MO: Andrews and McMeel, 1991.

Guy, Kathleen A. *Welcome the Child: A Child Advocacy Guide for Churches*. Washington DC: Children's Defense Fund, 1991.

Hollender, Jeffrey. *How to Make the World a Better Place*. New York: William Morrow and Co., Inc., 1990.

International Liaison of Lay Volunteers in Mission. *Let the Spirit Blow—The Response 1991*. Washington, DC: Published Annually.

Lewis, Barbara A. *The Kid's Guide to Social Action*. Minneapolis: Free Spirit Publishing Inc., 1991.

McGinnis, James. *Helping Families Care: Practical Ideas for Intergenerational Programs*. Bloomington: Meyer-Stone Books, 1989.

McGinnis, James, ed. *Helping Teens Care*. New York: Crossroad Publishing Co., 1991.

McGinnis, James and Kathleen. *Parenting for Peace and Justice*. Maryknoll, NY: Orbis Books, 1981.

McGinnis, Kathleen and Barbara Oehlberg. *Starting Out Right: Nurturing Young Children as Peacemakers*. Oak Park, IL: Meyer Stone Books, 1988.

NETWORK. *Parish Action Handbook: Legislative Advocacy*. Washington, DC: Network, 1987.

Office on Global Education, Church World Service. *Making a World of Difference*. New York: Friendship Press, 1989.

True, Michael. *Ordinary People: Family Life and Global Values*. Maryknoll, NY: Orbis Books, 1991.

Withers, Leslie and Tom Peterson, editors. *Hunger Action Handbook: What You Can Do and How to Do It*. Seeds Magazine, 1988.

Foundational Readings

Bright, Thomas and John Roberto, editors. *Access Guides to Youth Ministry: Justice*. New Rochelle, NY: Don Bosco Multimedia, 1990.

Children's Defense Fund. *The State of America's Children 1991*. Washington DC: Children's Defense Fund, 1991.

Guy, Kathleen A. *Welcome the Child: A Child Advocacy Guide for Churches*. Washington DC: Children's Defense Fund, 1991.

Morgan, Elizabeth with Van Weigel and Eric DeBaufre. *Global Poverty and Personal Responsibility*. New York: Paulist Press, 1989.

NCCB. *Economic Justice for All*. Washington, DC: USCC Publishing, 1986.

(*Catholic Update* condensed formats of NCCB pastoral letters are available from St. Anthony Messenger Press, 1615 Republic St., Cincinnati, OH 45210.)

The State of the World's Children 1991.
UNICEF. New York: Oxford University
Press, 1990.
(Available through: UNICEF, UNICEF
House, 3 U.N. Plaza, New York, NY 10017.)

Exploring Issues of Social Justice, Understanding Structures

The Big Picture. CRS. Baltimore: CRS, 1990.

Brown, Lester, et al. *State of the World
1990—A Worldwatch Institute Report on
Progress Toward a Sustainable Society.*
New York: Norton & Company.
Published Annually.

The Center for the Study of Social Policy.
*Kids Count Date Book 1991—State
Profiles of Child Well-Being.* Washington,
DC: The Center for the Study of Social
Policy, 1991.

Czerny SJ, Michael and Jamie Swift.
*Getting Started on Social Analysis in
Canada.* Ontario: Between the Lines
Publishing Inc., 1988.

Global Realities Fact Sheet. CRS. Baltimore:
CRS, 1990.

Holland, Joe and Peter Henriot. *Social
Analysis—Linking Faith and Justice.*
Maryknoll, NY: Orbis Books, 1983.

National Center for Children in Poverty.
*Five Million Children—A Statistical
Profile of Our Poorest Young Citizens.*
New York: NCCP, Columbia University,
1990.

Our Common Future. The World
Commission on Environment and
Development. New York: Oxford
University Press, 1987.

Roberto, John. *Caring for the Children and
Youth of Our World* (Network Paper No.
38). New Rochelle, NY: Don Bosco
Multimedia, 1990.

The World Bank Atlas. Washington, DC:
The World Bank. Published Annually.
(1818 H. Street, NW, Washington, DC
20433)

Reflecting as Christians on Justice Issues

Henriot, Peter, Edward DeBerri and
Michael Schultheis. *Catholic Social
Teaching: Our Best Kept Secret.*
Maryknoll, NY: Orbis, 1990.

Kavanaugh, John and Mev Puelo. *Faces of
Poverty, Faces of Christ.* Maryknoll, NY:
Orbis Books, 1991.

McGinnis, James. *Journey into
Compassion—A Spirituality for the Long
Haul.* Bloomington, IN: Meyer-Stone
Books, 1989.

NCCB. *A Century of Catholic Social
Teaching.* Washington, DC: USCC
Publishing, 1990.

Nelson-Pallmeyer, Jack. *The Politics of
Compassion.* Maryknoll, NY: Orbis
Books, 1986.

Pope John Paul II. *The Social Concern of the
Church.* Washington, DC: USCC
Publishing Office, 1989.

Sheridan SJ, E.F. *Do Justice!—The Social
Teaching of the Canadian Catholic
Bishops.* Toronto: Jesuit Centre for
Social Faith and Justice, 1987. (947
Queen St. East, Toronto, Ont. M4M 1J9)

*Shaping a New World: The Catholic Social
Justice Tradition 1981–1991.*
NETWORK. Washington, DC: Network,
1991.

Video Resources for Justice Awareness and Action

341. UNICEF. This World Summit for
Children video dramatizes the disaster of
the death of millions of children each
year and suggests attainable solutions to
protect children's lives. 13 minutes.
Purchase: $20 plus $2 postage and
handling.

40,000 a Day. UNICEF. A report by CBS's
"60 Minutes" with Mike Wallace
emphasizing the senseless deaths of
children from preventable diseases and
the limited role the media plays in
informing the American public about this
tragedy. 20 minutes. Purchase: $20 plus
$2 postage and handling.

*The Barrio Video Series: Charo of the
Barrio, Bread for the Barrio,* and
Messages from the Barrio. Columban
Mission Education, 1990. Each of the
three units contains a video program and
a leader's manual, lesson plans,
Scripture background,
activity/worksheets for duplication,
background information, suggested
resources, and prayer services.

Bento. Maryknoll Video. The story of a young African-Brazilian who is determined to make life better for himself and his neighbors in a poor neighborhood of Sao Paulo.

Between the Times: The Catholic Bishops and the U.S. Economy. Washington, DC: Campaign for Human Development. 45 minutes. Study guide included. Purchase: $49.95.

Bring Down the Walls: Reflections on a Century of Social Teaching. 12-minute presentation focusing on the heritage, principles, and practice of Catholic social teaching. Available from Lumen Catechetical Consultants, Inc., P.O. Box 1761, Silver Spring, MD 20915. Purchase: $19.91.

Central American Close-Up. Maryknoll Video. The stories of four Central American young people: Jeremias of Guatemala and Flor of El Salvador (Tape 1); and Carlos of Honduras and Balty of Nicaragua (Tape 2).

Down and Out in America. Explores the issues of poverty and homelessness in rural and urban USA. Available from MPI Home Video, Dept. 1500, 15825 Robroy Dr., Oak Forest, IL 65402.

Especially the Children. UNICEF. Filmed in Ethiopia, Egypt, India, Lebanon, Mali, Mexico, Nepal, Peru and the Phillipines, the video shows the desperate need for food and emergency services in the developing world and illustrates how UNICEF is working to meet these basic needs. 18 minutes. Purchase: $20 plus $2 postage and handling.

Heart of the Matter. Produced by the British Broadcasting System. Available through Bread for the World. Rental: $10. Using the Dominican Republic as a case study, this 35-minute video examines the causes and impact of debt on Third World countries and low income people.

Kenyan Youth: Preparing for the Future. Maryknoll Video. Three stories of determination, hard work, and dreams of a bright future from the youth of Kenya.

The Mouse's Tale. An animated cartoon from Australian Catholic Relief about a "fat" cat and a mouse (his conscience) exploring the issue of international food production and its relationship to hunger and famine around the world. Available from CRS. Purchase: $20; Rental $5.

An Overview of Economic Justice for All. Washington, DC: Campaign for Human Development. Purchase: $15.00

Refugees: A Call to Compassion and Solidarity. Baltimore: CRS, 1990.

Remember Me. UNICEF. Video portrait of what daily life is like for many of the world's hidden children--boys and girls with dreams they may never realize. Some of these children call their work their life. Filmed in the USA, Guatemala, Thailand, Nepal, Bangladesh, Egypt, and Tanzania. 15 minutes. Purchase: $20 plus $2 postage and handling.

The Richest Dog in the World. An creative, animated cartoon from Australian Catholic Relief which explores the plight of the world's poor and examines ways to effectively assist them to overcome their poverty and oppression. Available from CRS. Purchase $20; Rental $5.

The Rights of the Child. UNICEF. Focuses on the rights to which all children are entitled, including health care and education. Purchase: $20 plus $2 postage and handling.

The Silent Emergency. UNICEF. Shows diverse countries and circumstances in the developing world, where millions of young children still die every year from preventable illnesses. It illustrates how oral rehydration therapy, breast-feeding, and immunization lead the way to better health. 21 minutes. Purchase: $20 plus $2 postage and handling.

Voices for Development. An introduction to the concept of international development and the reasons why Americans, and Catholics in particular, should care about and become involved in supporting development efforts. The video provides perspectives from around the world and highlights the strong link between faith and justice. 20 minutes. Purchase: $20; Rental $5.

CHAPTER 18

Activities for Appreciating Ethnic Cultures

Thomas Bright

Men and women are not only themselves; they are also the region in which they were born, the city apartment or farm in which they learned to walk, the games they played as children, the old wives' tales they overheard, the food they ate, the schools they attended, the sports they followed, the poems they read, and the God they believed in.

—W. Somerset Maugham

RECLAIMING AND CELEBRATING FAMILY HISTORY AND ETHNICITY

One of every five families in the United States moves every year. The figure is a staggering one. Apart from the many new opportunities opened up by a move, relocation also involves many disruptions. Family members get separated from friends and from extended family. Often the separation from extended family means a loss of connectedness with family heritage and traditions. There are many approaches to reclaiming and sharing family history.

FAMILY IDEAS

Name Games

Talk as a family about where the names you carry came from. Why were parents and children given the first names they were? Were your names picked at random from a "baby names book" or were you named after a family friend or relative? If you were named after a relative or friend, who where they and why would you want to carry their name? What did they mean to the people who named you? Does the choice of names say anything about your ethnic or national background? What about your last name? What does it tell you about your ethnic or national heritage? What other last names are part of your family heritage? To what places and countries can you trace your family background?

Map Games

Trace the movements of your immediate and extended family across the surface of a U.S. or world map. Mark the travels of different generations or family members with different colors of yarn. Add snapshots, postcards, or momentos of their travels to the map.

Family Tree

Develop a family tree that goes back four or five generations. List people's names and birthdays, occupations and interests, places of birth and residence. Use visits to other family members to add to the roots and branches of your family tree. Interview older family members for stories about your extended family. Develop a photo/video album to accompany your family tree. Collect and share your favorite stories about family members and family history.

Gifts and Contributions

Discuss as a family what is unique or different about your family. What is different about the values you believe in, the customs you celebrate, or how you live as a family? What gift do you bring to the local community as a member of a single- or multi-ethnic family? What do you think is an important contribution that people of your ethnic background(s) bring to your community, country, world?

PARISH IDEAS

Peoples in the Parish

Use a youth group or intergenerational program to do an informal survey of the different ethnic and national groups that constitute your parish. What racial, ethnic, and national groups make up your parish congregation? How has the make up of the parish changed in recent years? Since its foundation? What are the major cultural values of the groups who constitute your parish? What values are shared across national or ethnic groups? What values are different? What difference do the values make in how people see themselves as church, in how they mix and celebrate together?

Move from your group learnings to a group project that involves young people and their families: create a family tree for your parish community or a parish map that traces the routes that eventually led people to your parish.

Discuss what it means to be a Catholic, or multi-cultured Church. Share ideas on what each ethnic or national group can reveal about who God is and what God wants for the people of this world.

GROWING IN APPRECIATION OF OTHER ETHNIC AND CULTURAL GROUPS

FAMILY IDEAS

Family Recreation

Find ways of spending recreational time together that opens your family up to different cultural and ethnic experiences. Take part in ethnic festivals and celebrations in your local community. Check out art shows, musical performances, etc. that expose your family to the perspectives and talents of different cultural groups.

Family Meals

Visit a restaurant that features ethnic cuisine, or have a regular *ethnic cuisine night* at home. Cook for yourself or invite friends from other ethnic groups to "swap" meals or dinner invitations.

Family Reading

Subscribe to periodicals or magazines that feature stories about people and places from different countries. When choosing gifts for birthday or Christmas presents, give a book that expands knowledge of other cultures and civilizations.

Family Vacations

Plan a family vacation that helps you learn as a family about other ethnic or cultural groups. The cultural diversity that exists in the U.S. usually means that there are opportunities for growth and enjoyment within driving distance of where you live.

PARISH IDEAS

Local Community Building Events

Build appreciation for cultural diversity into family and youth events. Plan and host an ethnic, pot-luck supper that features the cooking of the different ethnic groups in your parish. Incorporate a special holiday or holy day celebration that is special to each of the ethnic groups into your parish calendar. Involve the different ethnic or national groups in your parish in picking their date and determining how it will be celebrated. Invite families to share what their cultural heritage means to them and how they continue to live it out as a family.

Evaluate Parish Program Efforts

Evaluate your educational, worship and other programs and materials from a perspective of how well they incorporate an ethnic or multicultural perspective. How is an appreciation for cultural diversity woven into parish programs for families and youth?

Use the Resources of the Wider Community

Explore the opportunities for cultural and ethnic events with ethnic parishes and organizations in your area. Cosponsor events with ethnic parishes or diocesan ministries that allow youth and families from different cultures to learn about and grow in comfort with one another.

Extended Cross-cultural Events

Incorporate an extended, work camp or immersion experience into your youth or family ministry programs. Share information and resources for cultural exchange programs for youth, students, and families.

Encourage Story Telling and Learning About Cultural Diversity

1. Experiences of Cultural Diversity. As part of a youth or parent-teen event, encourage people to share their experiences of coming face-to-face with cultural diversity. Questions like the following can be incorporated into a reflection sheet or questionnaire:

   ■ How and when did you first become aware that your family had a specific ethnic/national/racial origin different from that of other people? How did you react to this new awareness?

   ■ When was the first time you met someone whose background was appreciably different that yours? What thoughts and feelings do you connect with that encounter?

   ■ From your personal experience, describe one way that you have grown due to your experiences with people of other cultures or traditions.

   ■ Describe an experience where you felt out of touch with, or unable to understand, the cultural values of other people.

   ■ How comfortable do you feel right now with people of other cultures or traditions? How comfortable would you like to be? What can you do to increase your comfort level with people of different traditions and values?

2. Identifying Ethnic Patterns: Mainstream U.S. and Other. People of different cultures and traditions develop distinct ethnic "patterns"—distinct ways of thinking, feeling, and acting. Differences between cultures are not described in terms of absolutes (either/or) but in relative terms (degrees of agreement or disagreement). Kathryn Choy-Wong offers the following values survey as a means of contrasting Western with Asian Pacific values. Though developed with an Asian Pacific American focus, the survey is useful with minor adaptations with young people from a variety of ethnic/cultural backgrounds. Adapt and duplicate the *Values Opinion Survey* and use it with your group as follows:

   a. Without identifying the extremes as Western/Asian Pacific, encourage a youth or parents' grouping to respond to the values survey from two different perspectives—first, as they hear mainstream U.S. culture speak to the issues presented; second, as they hear the voices of their personal ethnic or cultural background speak to the same issues.

   b. Discuss the different perceptions of mainstream culture in the United States. What were the major points of agreement or disagreement in the group's responses to the survey?

   c. Invite individuals to share any differences they discovered between the voices of mainstream U.S. culture and their own ethnic/national heritage. How strong are the differences? How do these differences in values or approach get played out in family life or in contact with the wider community? What can people do to keep the tensions to a minimum?

   d. Encourage the group to share their

learnings from the survey and discussion. Ask questions like: When is the tension between different sets of values healthy? When is it destructive? What does the activity have to do with communications between parents and youth or between people of different generations?

Values Opinion Survey

Values are not necessarily good or bad, right or wrong. They reflect your preferences, which are based on your personal history and background. The following is a list of contrasting values. Place an "X" on the line at the point between the two values that best represents your thinking. You may have varying degrees of preference. The "X" should be at or close to the number which corresponds to your degree of preference.

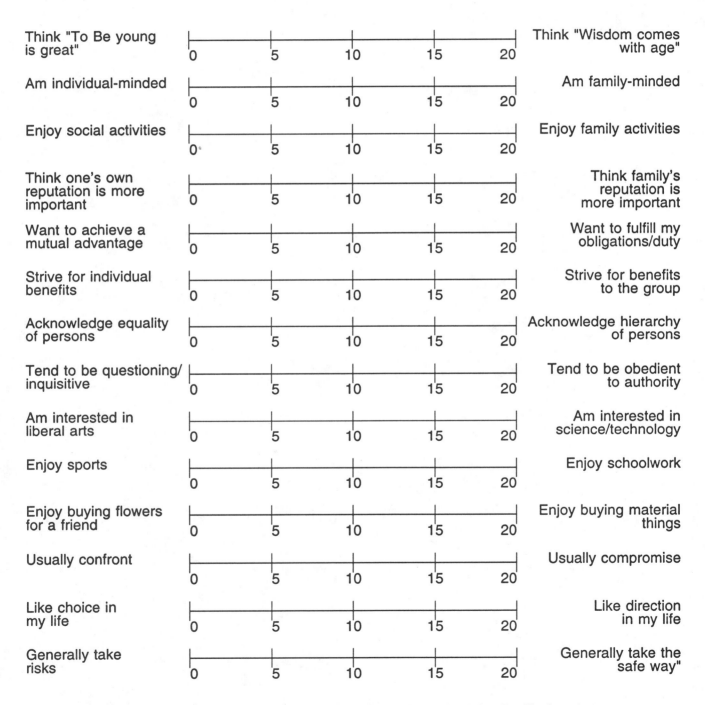

Think "To Be young is great"	0	5	10	15	20	Think "Wisdom comes with age"
Am individual-minded	0	5	10	15	20	Am family-minded
Enjoy social activities	0	5	10	15	20	Enjoy family activities
Think one's own reputation is more important	0	5	10	15	20	Think family's reputation is more important
Want to achieve a mutual advantage	0	5	10	15	20	Want to fulfill my obligations/duty
Strive for individual benefits	0	5	10	15	20	Strive for benefits to the group
Acknowledge equality of persons	0	5	10	15	20	Acknowledge hierarchy of persons
Tend to be questioning/inquisitive	0	5	10	15	20	Tend to be obedient to authority
Am interested in liberal arts	0	5	10	15	20	Am interested in science/technology
Enjoy sports	0	5	10	15	20	Enjoy schoolwork
Enjoy buying flowers for a friend	0	5	10	15	20	Enjoy buying material things
Usually confront	0	5	10	15	20	Usually compromise
Like choice in my life	0	5	10	15	20	Like direction in my life
Generally take risks	0	5	10	15	20	Generally take the safe way"

(Taken from: "Knowing Your Values" by Kathryn Choy-Wong, in *Asian Pacific American Youth Ministry*, David Ng, editor. Valley Forge, PA: Judson Press, 1988: 127.)